Evidence-Based
Policymaking

Evidence-Based Policymaking

Insights from Policy-Minded Researchers and Research-Minded Policymakers

Karen Bogenschneider

Rothermel Bascom Professor of Human Ecology, University of Wisconsin–Madison,
Family Policy Specialist, University of Wisconsin–Extension/Cooperative Extension

and

Thomas J. Corbett

Senior Scientist and Former (Retired) Associate Director,
Institute for Research on Poverty, University of Wisconsin–Madison

Written with financial support from the William T. Grant Foundation and The Spencer Foundation

Routledge
Taylor & Francis Group
New York   London

Routledge
Taylor & Francis Group
270 Madison Avenue
New York, NY 10016

Routledge
Taylor & Francis Group
27 Church Road
Hove, East Sussex BN3 2FA

Printed in the United States of America on acid-free paper
10 9 8 7 6 5 4 3 2 1

International Standard Book Number: 978-0-415-80583-4 (Hardback) 978-0-415-80584-1 (Paperback)

Library of Congress Cataloging-in-Publication Data

Bogenschneider, Karen.
    Evidence-based policymaking : insights from policy-minded researchers and research-minded policymakers / Karen Bogenschneider, Thomas J. Corbett.
        p. cm.
    Includes bibliographical references and index.
    ISBN 978-0-415-80583-4 (hardcover : alk. paper) -- ISBN 978-0-415-80584-1 (pbk. : alk. paper)
    1. Policy sciences. I. Corbett, Tom, 1944- II. Title.

    H97.B64 2010
    320.6--dc22

    2009052674

Visit the Taylor & Francis Web site at
http://www.taylorandfrancis.com

and the Psychology Press Web site at
http://www.psypress.com

Contents

Preface   ix
Foreword   xv

1   Exploring the Disconnect Between Research and Policy   1
     Reflections on What We Mean by Policy and Evidence-Based
     Policymaking   3
     A Promise Unfulfilled: A Historical Perspective   4
     What Went Wrong: Rounding Up the "Usual Suspects"   7
     What Makes Understanding the Science–Policy Connection So
     Challenging?   16
     Summary   22

2   Do Policymakers Want Evidence? Insights From Research-Minded
     Policymakers   25
     Why Are Policymakers Interested in Receiving Research From
     Professionals?   26
     What Kinds of Information Are Most Useful to Policymakers?   32
     Where Do Policymakers Go to Get Information?   41
     How Do Policymakers Like to Get Information?   44
     Summary   52

3   When Researchers Delivered Evidence to Policymakers   55
     The Wisconsin Idea   56
     Models for Bringing Research to the Policy Process   63
     Summary   74

4   Who Are These Knowledge Producers and Knowledge Consumers
     Anyway?   75
     Evolution of a Theoretical Perspective   76
     Stumbling on the Importance of "Culture" to Explain
     Communication Breakdowns   79
     Toward a Multicommunity Theory of Cultural Influences   91
     Summary   97

5   Why Research Is Underutilized in Policymaking: Community
     Dissonance Theory   99
     Exploring the Character of Community Dissonance   100
     Various Meanings of Research Use   104
     Some Elemental Concepts: Erecting the Building Blocks of a
     Theory of Community Dissonance   108
     Toward a Conceptual Framework for Thinking About Community
     Dissonance   114
     Summary   125

6   Breaking Through Stereotypes of Policymakers   129
     Researchers' Initial Impressions of Policymakers and How They
     Changed Over Time   130
     Unpacking How Policymakers Differ From Each Other and How
     Knowledge Brokers Can Leverage These Differences to Their
     Advantage   135
     Summary   146

7   What Knowledge Producers Should Know About the Policymaking
     Process   149
     Prominent Conceptualizations of the Policy Process   150
     When Research Meets the Policy Process: Welfare Reform and
     Science   151
     Nine Observations of the Policy Process: Obvious to Insiders,
     Surprising to Outsiders   153
     Summary   171

8   Barriers to and Rewards of Cross-Cultural Communication   175
     Milk for Poor Kids: An Improbable Policy Victory   176
     Researchers' Initial Impressions of Barriers to Working With
     Policymakers   181
     The Rewards of Relaying Research to Policymakers   188
     Summary   191
     Authors' Note   192

9   Communicating With Policymakers: Insights From Policy-Minded
     Researchers   193
     What Advice Can Researchers Offer About Communicating
     Research to Policymakers?   194
     Summary   222
     Authors' Note   226

10   Approaching Policymakers: Moving Beyond "What" to "How"   227
     Differentiating the Advocacy and Education Approaches for
     Working With Policymakers   228
     Advocacy and Education Across the Ages   229

Which Approach Is the Most Effective When Researchers Wade
Into the Policy Community?   233
Why Is the Education Approach Effective?   237
Some Prominent Objections to the Education Approach   247
How Can Educators Establish and Maintain a Nonpartisan
Reputation?   249
Summary   250
Endnote   252

11   Generating Evidence on Disseminating Evidence to Policymakers   253

        *Karen Bogenschneider, Heidi Normandin, Esther Onaga,
        Sally Bowman, and Shelley M. MacDermid*
      What Is Known and Unknown About Disseminating Research to
      Policymakers   254
      Baby Steps for Evaluating Efforts to Disseminate Evidence to
      Policymakers   266
      The Family Policy Education Theory of Change   268
      Summary   286

12   Where Do We Go From Here?   291
      This Book—A Small Step Forward in a Long Journey   292
      What Researchers Could Do and Why It Is So Hard   295
      Next Steps: Exploring an Action Agenda   298
      Summary   309

Appendix: Methodological Notes   313
      The Exploratory Researcher Study   316
      The Exploratory Policymaker and Policy Administrator Study   319

References   327

Author Index   339
Subject Index   343

Preface

The story of U.S. social policy reveals a disturbing disconnect between the research community, what we call *knowledge producers*, and the policymaking community, what we term *knowledge consumers*. Although the quantity of research has expanded dramatically in recent decades, its role in shaping policy decisions seldom matches the level warranted by the magnitude of the investment in science by government and the philanthropic communities, among others. This is a conundrum demanding thoughtful attention.

We believe that, despite much contrary evidence, there is a way of doing public policy in a more reflective manner. We believe, further, that a real hunger for evidence and objectivity does exist, that there are many policymakers out there who want research and analysis with which to inform their decisions. Policymakers are constantly exposed to those with fixed positions and prior agendas. They can get all kinds of information, much of it slanted or contradictory, as well as copious amounts of opinion, but little data that is reliable and helpful.

At the same time, there are many researchers who would like to apply their work to the so-called real world, to make a difference. However, turning quality research into sound policy requires more than a slick report dropped on a policymaker's desk. Reframing research in the accessible, nonpartisan, and timely manner that policymakers prefer is an important skill, yet one that few professionals learn in their academic training.

We believe this book makes several important contributions to this issue, among them, the exploration of (1) whether it is possible to do public policy in a more reflective manner, (2) why science has failed to inform social policy with any consistency, and (3) what pragmatic processes and procedures could be used to increase the utilization of research in policymaking. Let us briefly consider each of these in turn.

First, why has our ability to generate good research outpaced our ability to disseminate that evidence to policymakers? We examine the usual suspects for why knowledge producers and knowledge consumers do not easily interact and, when they do, why the quality of communication is often strained. Miscommunication and mistrust can occur even during interactions entered into with the best of intentions. It is as if each side marches to very different drummers, speaks distinctive languages, and sees the world through unique lenses.

Second, we believe that greater attention to theory will build a deeper understanding of why miscommunication and mistrust occur. Until we better appreciate the forces that separate and divide knowledge producers and knowledge consumers, we cannot effectively construct strategies for bringing them together. We expand on earlier theoretical frameworks in a number of ways. We dig deeply into the notion of *community* to unearth the more pervasive context of *professional culture*. We look at the related phenomenon of *institutional culture* to uncover clues as to the importance of this concept regarding how professionals think and behave. We argue that each member of the knowledge-producing and consuming communities brings a distinct cultural baggage to their professional roles. These cultural influences are drawn from some combination of institutional settings and disciplinary sources. That is, they are drawn from a specific organizational affiliation as well as from the more permanent norms and values inculcated during the socialization process associated with their academic preparation.

Third, we tackle the challenge of how to engage and educate policymakers so they can act on their interest in evidence-based policy, and take high-quality research and analysis into account in their decision making. We draw upon our conceptual framework to build a base of applied knowledge about how to better communicate across disparate professional communities. We attempt to link theory to practice by proposing a number of pragmatic processes and procedures that draw upon (a) advice from researchers who have been successful in bridging the research/policy divide, and (b) insights from policymakers about why they use research, what kind is most useful, where they seek it, and how they screen it for quality. We try to break through the stereotypes about what policymakers are like and provide an insider's view of how the policymaking process really works. Based on conversations with researchers and policymakers as well as a review of the literature, we identify several guidelines that emphasize how to build relationships with policymakers and what knowledge, skills, attitudes, and approaches are needed to take research findings from the laboratory to lawmaking bodies.

WHAT MAKES THE BOOK UNIQUE

Over the years, we have collected qualitative data from a number of informants. On the knowledge-consuming side, we interviewed policymakers, policy implementers, and policy managers representing different governmental jurisdictions at the state, local, federal, and international levels. On the knowledge-producing side of the equation, we interviewed basic researchers, applied researchers, and policy analysts. We also talked with knowledge brokers in foundations, government organizations, and research firms who serve as intermediaries between the two domains. We tapped some of the best and brightest from each of these communities so that we could elicit insights about how to advance the evidence-based policymaking agenda. Finally, we have reviewed the applicable literature and thought hard about how existing theory might help us understand what we have observed in our work with policymakers and researchers. Nothing, however, substitutes for our own work at the interface between research and policy, between the worlds of analysis and action.

This book includes a number of vignettes from the authors' experiences working with policymakers that builds upon the theoretical and empirical work of those who have thought about this topic over the years. Both authors have devoted good portions of their careers to bridging the gap between academia and public policy-making. In particular, we rely heavily on our work with two models for bringing research to policymakers that we helped formulate: the Family Impact Seminars or Seminars (a series of presentations, discussion sessions, and briefing reports for policymakers in 28 states) and the Welfare Peer Assistance Network or WELPAN (a group of senior welfare administrators from 7 Midwest states.) These initiatives give us a set of relationships and a wealth of experiences on which to guide our inquiry and exploration.

We wrote this book for anyone who wants to acquire the prerequisite knowledge, skills, and attitudes for effective policy work. We believe the book will be valuable to campus and off-campus instructors who want to excite their students about policy work with examples of how others got involved and with insights about why they were successful. This unusual juxtaposition of theory and practice will appeal to students in graduate and upper-level undergraduate courses in family studies, family policy, educational policy, law, political science, public administration, public health, social work, and sociology.

ORGANIZATION OF THE BOOK

In Chapter 1, we introduce the disconnect between research and policy as we see it. We take a historical look at the challenge of research utilization over time and suggest some reasons why research does not play a larger role in doing policy. We introduce the concepts used throughout the book and articulate a set of questions that guide our inquiry.

Because we think of research utilization as a two-pronged process, Chapters 2 and 3 examine the research/policy divide from two perspectives. Chapter 2 heavily relies on our interviews with research-minded policymakers. We use the voices of policymakers themselves to suggest that research is important to them in their jobs, but that the way research gets to them is critical. Chapter 3 turns to the researcher end of the equation to consider whether it is even possible to deliver research in ways that are useful in the policymaking process. We describe some specific venues for research dissemination, including our own work with policymakers, based on our belief that the vehicles through which most policymakers are exposed to research is integral to whether the information is heard and used.

Chapters 4 and 5 extend the theoretical work inherited from those who came before. Chapter 4 builds a more complex view of knowledge producers and knowledge consumers as well as the intermediaries that try to broker across these two communities. Building on earlier two communities theories, we construct an expanded conceptual model we term *community dissonance theory* in Chapter 5. This theoretical framework builds on the notion of *community* and introduces a more elaborate understanding of the institutional and professional cultures that guide how researchers and policymakers act toward and view one another.

Chapters 6 through 9 look at the use of research through the eyes and voices of policymakers and researchers who have been engaged in this venture. Chapter 6 examines what researchers should know about the inhabitants of the policy community and how accurate (and surprisingly inaccurate) their preconceived notions of policymakers may be. Chapter 7 looks at what researchers should know about how the policymaking process operates, offering a number of observations that will make it easier to interact in that world. Chapter 8 shifts our focus to policy-savvy researchers who explain why they do policy work, which barriers they encounter, and what rewards they experience. In Chapter 9, these experienced researchers describe the ingredients of their success, and offer insights and tactics for building relationships with policymakers and more effectively communicating research to them. Chapter 10 moves our attention from "what" to "how," with an examination of specific approaches that have proven useful in working with policymakers.

Finally, Chapters 11 and 12 shift our focus from analysis to action. Chapter 11 introduces some ideas for obtaining more rigorous evidence on evaluating programs for optimizing research use in the policy world. The concluding chapter offers a longer-range action agenda for altering the very culture of knowledge-producing and consuming communities, and improving cross-cultural communication for the purpose that we care about—enhancing evidence-based policymaking in the future.

A PERSONAL TOUCH

This is a personal work for both of us. It reflects both our passion for the way public policy is done and our vision for the way it might be done. Our purpose is simple: to enhance the use of evidence-based decision making in the public sector. Our motivation is straightforward: to improve the quality of government by bringing more rationality to the governance process. Our ambitions are modest: to stimulate a dialogue between those who spend most of their time producing knowledge (researchers, evaluators, and analysts), those who focus on the utilization of knowledge (legislators, agency executives, and program managers), and all those intermediaries who assist these officials.

Our own professional journeys led us to blend insights and evidence drawn from our professional histories as well as from the best theoretical and empirical work. Throughout this book, we tap many vignettes from our individual experiences along with examples from initiatives that we launched to bring research and analysis to the world of policymaking.

Relying upon our own stories is important, we believe, since many of our insights are drawn directly from our personal experiences. In our efforts to weave personal vignettes into the broader narrative in a seamless manner, we employ a somewhat nontraditional convention. Throughout the remainder of this book, Professor Bogenschneider will simply be referred to as *Karen* and Professor Corbett will be *Tom*. We hope that readers will excuse this bit of informality.

The reader also will note that we identify the source of some, but not all, the knowledge users, knowledge producers, and knowledge intermediaries that we interviewed. This is because some of these interviews were part of studies where we guaranteed anonymity. Other interviews were less formal and the subjects granted permission for us to use their names. Moreover, we only touch upon the methods we used to obtain input from our informants in the chapters of this book. Rather than repeating the methods every time that they are referred to, we provide in the

Appendix complete information on the methodology, along with the strong caveats and limitations associated with our evidence.

In the end, we are not naïve. We realize the limitations of this book. More interviews are needed of knowledge producers, knowledge consumers, and knowledge brokers. More evaluations of how to generate evidence on efforts to disseminate evidence are warranted. More analysis is necessary to assess whether our observations generalize to other settings and across policy issues. The need is there. The interest is there. We simply need a place to start.

ACKNOWLEDGMENTS

Many institutions and individuals were instrumental in bringing this project to fruition. First, we want to thank both the William T. Grant Foundation and the Spencer Foundation for their financial support. In particular, we wish to acknowledge Robert Granger, president, and Vivian Tseng, program officer, of the W.T. Grant Foundation, whose vision and enthusiasm is propelling research on research utilization to the forefront.

We also appreciate the many philanthropists who have encouraged our work, pushed our thinking, and provided the financial resources that policy work requires. The Policy Institute for Family Impact Seminars has been supported by the W. K. Kellogg Foundation (program officers Dr. Gail C. Christopher, Winnie Hernandez-Gallegos, Valorie Johnson, and Alice Warner-Melhorn), the David and Lucile Packard Foundation (program officers Lisa Deal, Mary Larner, and Kathy Reich), and the Annie E. Casey Foundation (program officers Don Crary and Michael Laracy). The Wisconsin Family Impact Seminars have been supported by Wisconsin Cooperative Extension Family Living Programs (particularly program leader Laurie Boyce); the Division of Continuing Studies at the University of Wisconsin-Madison (Dean Marvin Van Kekerix); the Helen Bader Foundation, Inc. (program officers Robin Bieger Mayrl, Kathryn Dunn, Bob Pietrykowski, and Helen Ramon); the Ira and Ineva Reilly Baldwin Wisconsin Idea Endowment at the University of Wisconsin-Madison (particularly Assistant Vice Chancellor and Coordinator of the Wisconsin Idea Project, Peyton Smith); the Lynde and Harry Bradley Foundation (program officer William Schambra); the A. L. Mailman Family Foundation (program officer Joelle Fontaine); the Robert G. F. and Hazel T. Spitze Land Grant Faculty Award; the Board on Human Sciences Engagement Award of the National Association of State Universities and Land Grant Colleges; and private gifts from Elizabeth C. Davies and Phyllis M. Northway. Several university and Cooperative Extension partners have supported this work through their generous co-sponsorship of seminars including the Early Childhood Excellence in Education Evaluation Project, the Institute for Research on Poverty, the Population Health Institute, the LaFollette Institute of Public Affairs, the School of Education, and the Sonderegger Research Center for Social and Administrative Pharmacy.

No single group of people has provided Karen with more innovative ideas and unwavering support than the board of directors of the Policy Institute for Family

Impact Seminars, who serve without reimbursement because of their commitment to the cause of evidence-based policymaking. Hearty thanks go to current and former board members Kristin Anderson Moore, Richard Barrows, Maria Cancian, Tom Corbett, Diane Cushman, Mary Fairchild, Jane Grinde, Mark Lederer, Ruth Massinga, Marygold Melli, Theodora Ooms, Robert Pietrykowski, William Schambra, Denise Skinner, Tim Smeeding, and Rebecca Young.

The Midwest Welfare Peer Assistance Network (WELPAN) received generous support from the Joyce Foundation for over a decade, especially the first project officer Unmi Song for recognizing the potential of peer assistance forums as well as the role played by Jennifer Phillips, who continued support for this vision.

We also want to thank Mick Coleman, University of Georgia, and Donald G. Unger, University of Delaware, along with other reviewers who prefer to remain anonymous. In addition, there are several people at the University of Wisconsin-Madison who made significant, if not crucial, contributions to this effort. Chief among them is Jennifer Seubert who cheerfully and meticulously labored to keep us organized, put the manuscript into final form, and resolved all the loose ends that turn book writing into a nightmare. We also want to sincerely thank Deborah Johnson for her editorial assistance and helpful suggestions on how to turn an unwieldy manuscript into a readable (we hope) final product. We also want to thank those at the Institute for Research on Poverty, the School of Human Ecology, and Cooperative Extension for all the kind and gracious help we received, especially the encouragement of IRP Director, Tim Smeeding, who has been especially interested in this topic. Karen also thanks those involved in the collection and analysis of data for our research projects: Stephanie Eddy, Bettina Friese, Elizabeth Gross, Carol Johnson, Kristen Johnson, Heidi Normandin, Jennifer Reiner, and Darci Trine.

Of course, this work would not have been possible without the contributions and input of a large number of policymakers over the years, too many to name individually. Unfortunately, those who make and execute public policies often are maligned and ridiculed. We have watched a number of policymakers at close quarters and generally find their efforts to be of the highest quality and their dedication to the public good to be unquestioned. The difficulty of doing public policy work should never be underestimated. Finally, we want to thank our spouses. They put up with much and get very little in return.

Karen Bogenschneider
Tom Corbett

Foreword

ROBERT C. GRANGER

Authors Karen Bogenschneider and Tom Corbett, using data from surveys, interviews, and their own rich experience, have written a book for researchers and policymakers who have been peering at each other from across the metaphoric divide. In doing so, they provide many fresh insights into how people in these roles tend to think about the other side, and the false assumptions each makes about the other.

In my work at the William T. Grant Foundation, where I have spent the past 10 years as head of grantmaking and then president, I have a view of both groups. The Foundation funds high-quality, empirical research in the social, behavioral, and medical sciences meant to improve the well-being of children and youth. Although we do not talk about it this way, many would characterize our approach with phrases such as "research to practice" or "bench to trench." This terminology presumes a system in which researchers craft interesting practices, strategies, or programs that practitioners should adopt and policymakers should encourage. I appreciated how the authors upend this formulation using examples from their own work, in which researchers had more to learn from policymakers and practitioners than the reverse. As the authors imply, to achieve robust theories and useful findings, research needs to begin with practice, rather than in the lab.

As the Foundation is interested in funding research that is useful to policymakers and practitioners, we have devoted considerable energy to trying to understand how to improve those connections. For many years, we approached this problem by focusing mainly on the quality of the research designs and methods we funded. Occasionally, we had a "hit," and work we supported was instrumental in moving a policy conversation or practice forward. For example, in the 1980s and 1990s, the Foundation funded several studies of innovations in welfare and anti-poverty policies that Tom Corbett discusses in this book. But too often, the research went into conference presentations, technical reports, and journal articles and then no further.

The Foundation was thinking in terms of "research to practice," and we knew we funded high-quality studies, so we initially approached the lack of uptake as a communication problem. We encouraged brevity, non-technical language, and a direct writing style so that persons without a research background could understand the studies. We also asked scholars to pursue communication through non-academic outlets such as the trade and daily press, in-person briefings, etc. To test this, we started to support such dissemination in a few areas, notably in improv-ing the quality of after-school programs, which was on the policy agenda and the focus of a cluster of our grantees. We quickly learned two things. First, policymak-ers, practitioners, and researchers have consuming jobs. If they are going to be connected, it is likely to be through intermediaries. In our world, such interme-diaries run the range from constituent group organizations such as the National Governors Association and the Council of Great City Schools, to advocates such as the Afterschool Alliance or Fight Crime, Invest in Kids. There are such groups in every domestic policy area and, as Karen and Tom describe, they understand the roles of both policymakers and scholars and can bridge the two.

Second, it became clear that while ongoing communication was necessary for connecting research and policymaking/practice, it was not sufficient. Scholars needed to provide evidence on questions that were useful to policymakers and practitioners. Too often, the research we supported was irrelevant to their work. In noting this, I am not suggesting that scholars should try to time policy debates and leap from one topic to another based upon an emerging policy agenda. My experience is that this type of intellectual ambulance-chasing is ill-advised. The strongest scholars stay focused throughout their careers on a finite set of questions that have enduring importance.

However, it is easy for scholars to insulate themselves from the daily phenom-ena that they are trying to understand through their empirical work. For example, if a researcher wants to understand how policies affect teaching, or how teach-ing affects student achievement, it benefits the scholar to spend time in schools and classrooms. If scholars want to understand how their work might be useful to policymakers, it makes sense for them to spend time with legislative staff who are working in a policy area, or executive branch staff trying to implement such policies.

At the Foundation, we support such experiences for early-career and more senior researchers, and we have created a mid-career program for influential schol-ars that funds fellowships in a policy or practice setting. However, such oppor-tunities are limited and demand more time than many can take, so researchers, policymakers, and practitioners need other ways to gain such insights. This book provides one such opportunity. The authors delve into the reasons for the discon-nections among policymakers, practitioners, and researchers and allow readers to walk in the shoes of their unfamiliar counterparts.

1

Exploring the Disconnect
Between Research and Policy

Success or failure in the application of social science [to the policy process]
depends on the mesh between scientific skills and political interests of the
social scientist on the one side, and the political skills and the scientific interests of the policy maker on the other.

—Suzanne Berger (1980, p. vii)

In the evaluation world, analysts start as agnostics. In the policymaking
world, legislators must advocate a position and defend it against all opposition. Program managers live in both worlds, but uneasily. They want to know
whether a program works and how to make it better.

—Joel Rabb and Don Winstead (2003, p. 21)

R on Haskins, formerly a respected Republican committee staffer and now a
Brookings Institution scholar, once was asked by several academics about
the role research played in what was, at the time, a contentious congressional debate about welfare reform. Without missing a beat, he responded that, based
on his personal experience, the best research might exert 5% of the total influence
on the policy debate, with an upside potential of 10%. Personal values and political
power, Haskins went on to say to his now silent and disappointed audience, were
what really mattered in Congress.

A distinguished state welfare official, who also has held a top research-oriented
position in the U.S. Department of Health and Human Services, told the following
story. Upon persuading a key Florida state legislator to support a reform initiative,
he asked for additional resources to evaluate whether the proposed changes might
be effective. The legislative leader paused and then commented with incredulity:
"If you don't know whether or not the program is going to work, why are you asking
me to sponsor it?"

1

Vignettes, of course, are not convincing evidence, at least as we employ the term in this book. Still—and to borrow a well-worn phrase from former vice president Al Gore—these stories touch upon *an inconvenient truth*. Those who believe that public policy and rigorous research ought to go hand in hand, that good government ought to be based on hard evidence drawn from rigorous and dispassionate analysis, confront a bitter reality. Too often, no such bond exists. Rather, we see a substantial gap, some may say chasm, between the production of knowledge and its utilization, between those we have labeled *knowledge producers* and those we call *knowledge consumers*.

Knowledge producers—academic researchers, program evaluators, and a variety of policy analysts who interpret data and research—continue to generate voluminous reports, papers, and research articles, sometimes for their own sake and sometimes with the explicit purpose of shaping public policy. At the same time, *knowledge consumers*—those who legislate policy, implement policy, and manage policy—continue to operate with scant, or at least very selective, attention to the vast stores of scientific knowledge available to them. The primary use of research is thought by some to be motivated by a desire to support prior positions rather than to inform decisions in the first instance (Shulock, 1999).

Why is this so? After all, we think of our nation as a politically advanced, rational society, with access to the best universities and scientists in the world. Moreover, we continue to produce ever-growing volumes of increasingly sophisticated research and policy-oriented analysis. "Contemporary poverty research is very much an American invention, with a degree of specialization and an institutional apparatus that is unmatched in other parts of the world" (O'Connor, 2002, p. 3).

Arguably, this U.S. comparative advantage in science all too often fails to inform our public decisions in any direct or substantive fashion, whereas some of our peer nations aggressively push evidence-based policy agendas even though their scientific capabilities fall short of ours. A U.K. white paper issued in 1999 committed that nation to using evidence and research so that policy could better deliver on its long-term goals (Cabinet Office, 1999). This initiative stipulates that evidence will henceforth play a critical role in policymaking. A recent Urban Institute publication affirmed that "in the United Kingdom and some other democracies facing challenges similar to ours, 'evidence-based policy' is gaining momentum" (Dunworth, Hannaway, Holahan, & Turner, 2008, p. 1).

This U.S. gap between knowledge production and its use to solve social problems is not a new challenge. Members of the policy elite have been trying to figure out how to bring research to bear on policymaking for well over a hundred years (Smith, 1991). Academics, in particular, traditionally have operated from the premise that good policymaking is an essentially rational process that functions best when driven by rigorous research and dispassionate analysis.

About a century ago, John Bascom and Charles Van Hise, while each served terms as president of the University of Wisconsin, nurtured an embryonic concept that Charles McCarthy, an early proponent, succinctly defined as "a willingness to experiment to meet the needs of a changing economic order" (as cited in Wisconsin Works Project Administration, 1941, p. 62). That is, the resources of science and the academy would be applied directly to the resolution of public challenges, a premise we return to in Chapter 3. Their passion for evidence-based policy development anticipated the sentiments of Nobel Prize–winning economist James Heckman, who asserted a century later that "social myths thrive in environments without data" (1990, p. 301). Many in the academy certainly recognize their responsibility to the policy world, yet that perspective is far from universal.

It is hard to shake the impression that we may be functioning in a policy environment that operates, ironically enough, according to an inverse relationship between science and politics—the more and better research we produce, the less effect it has on the policymaking process. With increasing amounts of data and analysis emerging from our universities and research/evaluation firms, the likelihood that even the most studious of public officials can sort through and make sense of the science available to them is not very high. And to make matters worse, the political payoff for using science often competes directly with input from constituents or interest groups. What exactly is meant, however, by this notion of making *evidence-based policy* or of using research to improve policymaking? Next, we take a moment to define terms.

REFLECTIONS ON WHAT WE MEAN BY POLICY AND EVIDENCE-BASED POLICYMAKING

Let's start with the concept of *policy*. We define *policy* as follows: "Policy is the development, enactment, and implementation of a plan or course of action carried out through a law, rule, code, or other mechanism in the public or private sector" (Bogenschneider, 2006). Sometimes policies are very specific and obvious. A law is passed governing who will get publicly funded health care coverage, under what circumstances, and at what price. But in a larger sense, policies can be less transparent and more diffuse. Think of the unwritten standards that govern behaviors in bureaucracies. Even though never formalized, they govern interactions between people and, thus, have the force of policy. How often have we heard the phrase "But we have always done it this way"?

For us, policy encompasses what a rule is, how it was developed, and how it is carried out. In that sense, our concept of *policy* is broad. We are concerned about any formulation that governs what is done, for whom, how, and under what circumstances. In another sense, our scope is much more limited. We focus primarily on social policies that directly attempt to improve the quality of life of individuals and families (Jacobs & Davies, 1994); in particular, our interests lie in how policies affect vulnerable families and children. Naturally, as we touch upon later, policies can be economic, environmental, legal, or international in character. Anything that regularizes relations and interactions between government and its citizens in the future is a policy. From our perspective, however, social policies involve a high degree of uncertainty about what is government's proper role and are associated with a universe of research and science that are subject to conflicting interpretation and application. The intersection of social science and social policy is fraught with a particularly high level of uncertainty.

Before we move on, let us consider for a moment the notion of *evidence*. We talk of evidence-based policy as if it were a tangible phenomenon, as if we possess a scholarly consensus on major issues that might be applied directly to difficult societal issues. The real world, however, is much more complex. Our science is not that definitive, nor is science the only legitimate and proper basis for making policy decisions. In fact, it may be far more accurate to label our vision as advancing evidence-informed policymaking or research-shaped decision making.

Clearly, we can tangle ourselves in very convoluted semantic labyrinths here. To simplify matters, we approach the topic with an initial premise that there is a set of scientific methods that serious scientists and scholars agree constitutes a proper way for helping us distinguish fact from belief. However daunting the challenge, the scientific community believes that a body of sound knowledge can be developed to help address even the most contentious of social policy issues. In short, this book focuses on the intersection between social policy and social research, and what can be done to improve the association between the two.

Davies and Nutley (2008) defined social research as "any systematic process of critical investigation and evaluation, theory building, data collection, analysis and codification aimed at understanding the social world, as well as the interactions between this world and public policy/public service" (p. 7). Social research encompasses the same rigorous methods, the same scientific protocols, as do all other research arenas. The practitioners of social research are bound by the same canons of behavior as their peers in the hard sciences and exhibit similar behavioral and attitudinal dispositions to their craft. Yet, efforts to bring the work of social researchers to the resolution of social problems have proved highly challenging, indeed. Few would assert that science alone can dictate how society governs itself, yet many have firmly believed for a long time that the role of rigorous analysis could, and should, be elevated over its existing role in doing public policy.

A PROMISE UNFULFILLED: A HISTORICAL PERSPECTIVE

Sheldon Danziger (2001) reviewed the history of welfare reform in the past half century and lamented that the Family Support Act of 1988 is the only time that policy reflected the findings of social science research. Alice O'Connor (2002) reached a similar conclusion regarding the seminal 1996 Personal Responsibility and Work Opportunity Reconciliation Act, widely considered the most significant welfare reform law since the Social Security Act of 1935. She characterized its passage as "a triumph of politics over scientific knowledge" and as "such a devastating blow to the poor" (p. 286). Despite huge investments in research and evaluation (e.g., the philanthropic community alone invested many millions in welfare-related research during this period), numerous informed insiders feel that the ultimate passage of welfare reform was driven mostly by personal perceptions, value preferences, and political calculus (Haskins, 2006).

Toward the close of the 20th century, social policy began to evolve from what had been a religious and ethical responsibility to a public challenge to be addressed in a more sober and dispassionate manner. What came to be known as the "scientific charity movement" emerged in the decades after the Civil War (Trattner, 1974). Help was to be provided to distressed families and communities through strategies based on careful data gathering and rigorous investigation. Simply doing good works was not enough to remedy society's obvious failings.

Within a few years, the academy began to reflect these changes. The discipline of sociology emerged as scientists sought to understand how people, as a collective, functioned. The American Psychological Association was formed at Clark University in the 1880s as academics sought to understand why individuals behaved as they did, particularly when they operated outside the norms of conventional society. In 1898, the first school of social work was established at Columbia University in an effort to systematically apply the slowly accumulating knowledge of social and individual functioning to solving public issues.

This trend toward investigation and science as a solution to social problems continued. Settlement houses, such as Hull House in Chicago, began to collect data on the communities they served and to use those data to push for policies that would address neighborhood issues in a systematic fashion. Help would no longer be provided to only one distressed family at a time. Rather, early social investigators such as Charles Booth and Beatrice Webb began to think about how information could be used to illuminate broader social challenges and to help shape their remediation through systemic policy and collective action (Nathan, 2000).

Politicians, too, demanded data to drive policy decisions. President Theodore Roosevelt was influenced to a large extent by census data that, he believed, spelled out a crisis in family life (Carlson, 2001). President Franklin Roosevelt attracted hordes of intellectuals to Washington by establishing various advisory and planning agencies, including his legendary Brain Trust that played an active role in the design of the New Deal. He also reorganized the Executive Office in the late 1930s in ways that ensured his successors would have access to intellectual resources. By 1939, 7,800 social scientists were working in the federal government (Carlson, 2002), and between 1940 and 1945, research expenditures increased by some 1,500% (Featherman & Vinovskis, 2001).

World War II served to stimulate an expansion in the use of science for public purposes, usually defense related. Curiously, the "historical apex in the public image of science" was the dropping of the atomic bomb (Bimber, 1996, p. 13). For many U.S. citizens, the bomb and many remarkable scientific advances during the wartime years, including penicillin and radar, were concrete examples of how technology could address some of society's most perplexing problems. Following the war, Roosevelt fully expected, as did the citizenry, that scientists would turn their expertise to peacetime pursuits including advances in health, jobs, and the standard of living. This confidence in science also was stated clearly by President Ronald Reagan (1983, para. 16): "I call upon the scientific community in our country, those who gave us nuclear weapons, to turn their great talents now to the cause of mankind and world peace, to give us the means of rendering these nuclear weapons impotent and obsolete."

By the 1960s, many assumed that, at long last, we had arrived at a new era of policymaking, one where reason and rationality were supplanting ideology and partisanship. Shortly before his assassination, President John Kennedy argued that the important national questions were complex but not driven by ideology. We could bring intellectual resources to bear on society's most vexing technical challenges, such as getting a man to the moon. Why not the same for social challenges? We seemed poised at the precipice of a new era in which a rational, dispassionate mode of decision making would prevail.

Economist Robert Haveman captured the optimism of the times when he noted, "Logic, data, and systematic thinking were to compete with, if not dominate, 'politics' in the making of public decisions" (Haveman, 1987, p. 33). After all, increasingly sophisticated computers permitted us to employ larger data sets and to subject our data to astonishingly impressive analytical techniques. The number of policy schools, think tanks, and evaluation firms exploded. Resources from the philanthropic community expanded dramatically. And governments at all levels invested increasing amounts in research focused on public policy issues. Federal support for research and related development grew dramatically, more than doubling from less than 1% of the gross domestic product in 1953 to almost 2% in 1965 (Congressional Budget Office, 2007).

One example of this growing confidence in the benefits of science was the creation of the Institute for Research on Poverty (IRP) at the University of Wisconsin–Madison in 1966. The Institute was the first federally sponsored academic think tank devoted to poverty-related investigations and was created during an era associated with a veritable explosion of policy-oriented studies. Whereas one would need less than two pages to complete an exhaustive bibliography of studies related to poverty in the early 1960s (Yarmolinsky, 1969), during the first 15 years of IRP's existence, the center "had published 35 books, 650 discussion papers, and 18 special reports, and had spent about $20 million" (about $100 million in today's dollars; Haveman, 1987, p. 5). The Office of the Assistant Secretary for Planning and Evaluation (ASPE), the primary research office of what is now known as the U.S. Department of Health and Human Services, grew dramatically through the 1970s, reaching some 300 staff at its peak. This represents a tenfold increase in a little more than a decade. In FY 1977, total federal expenditures on poverty research approached $90 million (National Research Council, 1979).

These halcyon days when science would shape policy, where ideology would no longer dictate public discourse, and where partisan identity would be muted were short-lived, indeed—if, in fact, they existed at all. As the 1980s progressed, faith in a proactive government buttressed by a sophisticated research and analytical apparatus increasingly was considered to be misplaced at best (Hayek, 1989) and perverse at worst (Murray, 1984). The abrasive influence of ideology and partisanship did not diminish. If anything, their roles increased, to the dismay of those seeking a reason-based policy process. Not surprisingly, federal support for research and development declined as a proportion of the gross domestic product until it leveled off at an investment rate similar to what existed in the early 1950s. This led Deichtman to conclude, "The impact of research on the most important affairs of state was, with few exceptions, nil" (1976, p. 390).

Similarly, the 1970s and early 1980s have been thought of as a golden age of study and thought on research use (Caplan, 1979; Lindblom & Cohen, 1979; Weiss, 1983). Scholars and policy wonks gave a great deal of thought to the way policymaking was done and how research and analysis fit into the doing and managing of public affairs. The conceptual framework of disconnected communities (i.e., researchers and policymakers) emerged and gained currency. But then interest began to wane, and a robust empirical research agenda on the topic soon became seen as arcane.

What remained was a continuing drift in the currency of policy discourse away from evidence and science. The political arena evolved in the direction of ideological purity and partisanship, and the academy increasingly moved from applied research toward more theoretical science. Not surprisingly, the ability to communicate across these two communities became increasingly problematic indeed.

WHAT WENT WRONG: ROUNDING UP THE "USUAL SUSPECTS"

What happened to the promise of science and dispassionate analysis? Without question, there are multiple explanations for the conundrum of why science fails to inform social policy with any consistency. To borrow Claude Rains's famous line from the movie *Casablanca*, let us round up some of the "usual suspects." These suspects, which have been identified in prominent theories of research underutilization in policymaking, tap into various quirks inherent in the character of the policymaking process itself, the structure of democratic institutions, and the limitations and complexities of scientific inquiry. Although the underutilization of theory is less prominently featured in scholarly theories, we also believe that it stems from the very nature of the social problems being addressed and the institutional environments in which knowledge producers and consumers operate. Each of these theoretical suspects undoubtedly contributes something to this gap between these two communities—knowledge producers and consumers. We review these categories of theories in the paragraphs that follow and Key Concepts 1.1.

Key Concepts 1.1 Science's Failure to Shape Policy: Rounding Up the "Usual Suspects"

Theoretical Approach 1: The Character of the Policymaking Process
- Expectations of what research can contribute are often unrealistic.
- Policy decisions are not driven solely by numbers.
- The real world changes faster than science can accommodate.
- Politics is becoming more polarized.

Theoretical Approach 2: The Structure of Democratic Institutions
- The complexity of democratic decision making played out in the public arena constrains the role of science.
- Power is intentionally fragmented, and the inevitable conflicts can paralyze decision making.
- America, among democracies, particularly prizes decentralized decision making.

Theoretical Approach 3: The Limitations and Complexities of Scientific Inquiry
- Science is better at dealing with technical issues than policy issues that encompass deeply held values and worldviews.
- The hard policy questions involve values, not the strength of science.
- The questions policymakers ask often elude the answers that science can provide.

Theoretical Approach 4: The Thorny Nature of Social Problems
- Science depends on known ends, good underlying theories, and plausible solutions. In contrast, the toughest social issues are "wicked" problems characterized by
  - no consensus on goals or ends,
  - no consensus on underlying theory, and
  - no consensus on strategy or solutions.

Theoretical Approach 5: The Institutional Environments in Which Knowledge Producers and Consumers Operate
- Researchers often respond to other researchers; policymakers respond to a host of different audiences.
- Policymakers work in an environment that responds to money and power; the research environment responds to evidence and reputation.
- Policymakers want definitive answers; researchers become accustomed to ambiguity.

Theoretical Approach 1: The Character of the Policymaking Process

There are several reasons why the very nature of the policymaking process may diminish the utility of science as a basis for making decisions. Our aim is not to be exhaustive here but rather to introduce a few factors for consideration.

First, expectations may simply have been unrealistic, premised as they were on a simple notion that social science research can be more or less injected directly into the policy process, what Pettigrew (1985) coined as the "hypodermic model" of research use. This model falls short because the policymaking process is far more complex than knowledge producers typically imagine. What's more, the social sciences seldom produce the kind of smoking-gun evidence that can settle disputes on social policies where contention exists. Results often vary and, indeed, sometimes contradict one another.

Second, policy decisions are not driven solely by numbers, nor should they be. Values and self-interest are inescapable inputs. In consequence, we can see why the metaphorical link between making sausage and making policy has survived so long. Given our diverse society, it strikes us as intuitively correct—you may or may not like the resulting policy product, but you certainly do not want to observe how the product was actually made. As Kingdon (2003) pointed out, the doing of policy involves a complicated, almost subjective, calculus that weighs a number of competing factors including values, career aspirations, media attention, and constituent views, among many others. Evidence can and does play a role, but it is often a subordinate one to other, more salient, factors.

Third, the real world sometimes changes faster than science can accommodate. Policymakers confront the world on a real-time basis. They often receive immediate feedback on emerging problems or promptly become aware of new policy and program responses. Academics, in particular, do not spend time in the so-called real world, so research and evaluations often are not timely, nor do they always address emerging problems and responses. Because academics tend to treat research questions as timeless, cutting-edge issues may not filter through the literature for some time.

For example, a nonpartisan legislative service agency in the state of Washington recently calculated the cost-effectiveness of 571 criminal justice prevention and intervention programs. This meta-analysis captured the attention of policymakers and practitioners across the country, who downloaded it from the Web 32,000 times (Aos, Miller, & Drake, 2006). Interestingly, this policy-relevant report emanated not from researchers at a university or policy think tank, but from nonpartisan staff who work for the legislature and respond in real time to the issues policymakers are facing. The pace of science is notably slower, leading Aaron to observe, "The findings of social science seemed to come after, rather than before, changes in policy, which suggests that political events may influence scholars more than research influences policy" (1978, p. 9).

Finally, politics is becoming more polarized. In point of fact, it is literally *politics* that is becoming more polarized, not the American electorate. In his penetrating analysis, Fiorina (2006) found that American citizens are not deeply divided, yet a small segment of the U.S. population has become more polarized—its political class composed of party and issue activists, interest group leaders, media commentators, and elected officials. Veteran political observers have noted that the level of partisanship has increased in the political class in recent decades (Fiorina, 2006; Rivlin & Klugman, 2006). Several suspects are blamed for this trend. Money has become a dominant factor in running for office, and the contributions flow to candidates who will deliver on the agendas of special-interest groups. The Internet, 24-hour instant news, and other recent communication innovations make the political process transparent—a good thing in many respects. But such ready access to information makes doing business across political aisles riskier because one's political base can easily become aware of and perhaps angered by any compromises or concessions that are made. The whole process of selecting candidates, with the growing importance of primaries, can weed out candidates representing the middle of the road. These early stages of campaigning bring out more extreme elements in each party.

Theoretical Approach 2: The Structure of Democratic Institutions

All rich democracies produce a cadre of academicians. Ironically, the very principle of democracy increases the complexity of using the academic data they produce in the decision-making process. A benign dictator, or small oligarchy, might well sit down and apply a rational process to policy decisions. This vision of wise and informed leadership comports well with the Platonic ideal of government as well as some precepts of Aristotelian thought. Wise leaders could survey the data to decide what problems were salient and which outcomes they want to achieve. They then could summon available research to determine what policies had evidentary support, and structure evaluations to assess whether policies were meeting expectations.

But the U.S. democracy does not work in such a linear fashion. We tend to fragment power in very deliberate ways. We celebrate the pull and tug of the democratic process, which serves to diminish the prospects of any policy actually seeing the light of day. In some important ways, our policy process presumes competition and contention, a kind of Darwinian process where only the sturdiest ideas survive. This, however, is hardly an atmosphere that embraces elegant reasoning and dispassionate dialogue. In the United States, the pathways for integrating the institutions of knowledge and power are, to borrow a phrase from Robert Frost, roads less often taken.

In other democracies, however, trails have been blazed between the state house and the ivory tower that allow for a more regular and rational interchange of ideas and insights. Traffic is heavier, according to Wilensky (1997), in democracies with a more centralized government, less fragmented policymaking, more dialogue among national labor and employer federations, and greater consensus about the role of government in addressing societal problems. Take, for example, the *disconnect* between research and policymaking in less centralized democracies such as the United States compared to the more deliberate and direct *connection* of knowledge producers and knowledge consumers in more centralized, corporatist systems such as Austria, Germany, Japan, Norway, and Sweden and, to a lesser extent, Belgium and the Netherlands (Wilensky, 1997). In these democracies, the argument goes, problems identified in the state house more readily bubble up to the ivory tower, and knowledge gained in the ivory tower more systematically percolates down to the state house.

Theoretical Approach 3: The Limitations and Complexities of Scientific Inquiry

The potential of science to bring reason and dispassionate analysis to policymaking is quickly tarnished by the limitations of social science inquiry and the disconnect between what policymakers want to know, which questions researchers ask, and what answers research could realistically provide.

The limitations of social science inquiry. For a number of policy questions, we have looked to research as some kind of final arbiter when science is ill suited to perform that role. Technical questions are one kind of challenge. They can be exceedingly complex (think of President Kennedy's charge to get a man to the moon). Given the willingness to spend enough money, science was able to provide the necessary input to realize that goal. The more problematic public issues, however, go well beyond technological questions. They encompass deeply held values and preconceived ideas about how the world should work.

Such issues are horses of a decidedly different color that may well exceed the authority of science.

For example, take the so-called *welfare magnet* issue—where differences in welfare payments were thought to induce poor families to migrate across state lines to take advantage of more generous cash benefits in neighboring states. When this became a highly contentious political issue in Wisconsin during the 1980s, many observers felt that what was really at stake was underlying fears that poor, Black families were being induced to relocate from inner-city Chicago, and elsewhere, bringing with them a host of social problems.

Researchers at the University of Wisconsin were commissioned by the state legislature to answer the question of whether the welfare magnet phenomenon existed. They gathered voluminous data and presented the results to a special committee formed to assess the results. The "evidence" convinced few, if any, of those with firm prior opinions on the matter, nor did it diminish the political controversy to any observable extent (Corbett, 1991). In fact, the major state newspapers were divided on whether the evidence proved or disproved the welfare magnet hypothesis. Not surprisingly, the policy debate raged on until welfare laws were reformed a decade later.

The Disconnect Between What Policymakers Want to Know, Which Questions Researchers Ask, and What Answers Research Could Realistically Provide Policymakers are taken with substantive meaning, whereas researchers are more taken with statistical significance. Finding statistically significant effects on outcomes of interest may prove convincing to scientists but unpersuasive to policymakers, who must weigh effect sizes with so many other factors of which scholars are only dimly aware. What would a new policy direction cost? How would key supporters view a new direction if it increased the role of government or challenged the prevailing political consensus? And worse, what if the new evidence endorsed policies and programs that upset key constituencies normally allied with the policymaker? Statistical significance merely confirms that an impact is not likely attributable to chance. Substantive significance means that the impacts are still worth pursuing after a whole range of other critical considerations are taken into account.

The utility of research for policy-development purposes is also limited by the ways in which researchers tend to frame research questions. Too often, the methodologies in which researchers are proficient drive the questions they ask. According to Weiss (1978), researchers "do not pick the research method to suit the problem but almost unwittingly see that aspect of the problem to which their methodology applies" (p. 45). Even when they get the policy question right, knowledge producers by the nature of their training tend to focus on narrow causal issues such as which specific program or policy or factor caused a certain outcome. They like to isolate the variable responsible for shifts in the outcomes of interest. Consequently, experiments often are structured to isolate the impacts of single interventions. Real-life and real-policy contexts, on the other hand, are complex and involve numerous interdependent influences. Both our analytic tools and our ways of framing research questions too often fail to incorporate that complexity.

Researchers also spend a lot of time worrying about internal validity. Do their methods permit them to isolate the explanatory variable(s) with scientific credibility? Or, might there remain alternative explanations for the variation observed in the outcome of interest? They define efficacy in "a special, narrow 'scientific' way" (Cartwright, 2007, p. 10) and spend less time and place less focus on external validity. Even the gold standard of evaluation, the randomized control trial, tells us that the treatment causes the relevant effect, but the results are valid only in the population involved in the trial. To what other populations can the results be applied? What kinds of demographic, social, economic, political, or contextual differences might make the application of a new research-driven insight risky or result in unanticipated side effects? What works in Situation A might not work in Situation B. A welfare reform initiative that works in a state with a booming economy might be doomed in an area with slack labor demand. Even slight differences in a successful program, evaluated in a hot-house environment where resources are not a question, can fail when introduced into the real world under ordinary circumstances. Even if the intervention works as intended, does the size of the benefits exceed the magnitude of the costs, and given the gravitational pull of the status quo, what are the chances that the intervention will continue after the demonstration ends?

Cartwright (2007) made this basic point. The blinding that is used in randomized control trials eliminates one source of confounding but ignores a whole host of others. "Nothing can count as evidence for anything except relative to a host of auxiliary assumptions; and the strength with which a body of evidence supports a hypothesis can never be higher than the credibility of these auxiliaries" (p. 14). Even with our most rigorous forms of scientific evidence, huge gaps in knowledge can remain. Often, practitioners have a better sense of crucial real-world differences that knowledge producers do not fully appreciate. Applying findings can be something of an art form.

Theoretical Approach 4: The Thorny Nature of Social Problems

Many of the most perplexing policy questions revolve around what we call *wicked problems*, where normative, theoretical, and partisan contention exists, and the problems themselves seem to exceed the authority of science. Technical questions are one kind of challenge. They can be exceedingly complex. But given a willingness to spend the money, science could provide answers to an array of what are essentially technical challenges.

For example, the prestigious National Academy of Sciences traces its origins back to the Civil War period. The emergence of ironclad warships played havoc with the operation of onboard compasses given that the new siding influenced the surrounding electromagnetic field. It proved embarrassing, not to say dangerous, when ship captains were ignorant of their direction during a naval battle. In response to this crisis, President Abraham Lincoln called upon the best scientists of the day to solve the problem, and they did. Buoyed by this early success, the federal government has been returning to the academy for help for almost a century and a half now, with admittedly uneven success. Lincoln could not turn to the academy to resolve the central crisis of the day—slavery and the distinct cultural and political divides that separated North and South.

For a long time, family policy has seldom resulted in any kind of rational discourse. The very concept of *family* intensified value conflicts about what was moral and good. Take the example of welfare reform, which has proved an intractable challenge because it touches on core societal issues—equality, fairness, family, personal responsibility, sex, and work, to name a few. Naive academics who entered the debate of welfare and other family policies thinking that evidence and statistical significance would rule the day soon encountered this sobering reality.

So-called wicked social problems typically involve emotional and normative questions where ends are in dispute, our theoretical understanding is uncertain, and no policy alternative enjoys widespread support. Commenting on a conference at the University of Wisconsin exploring ways to evaluate controversial welfare reform initiatives, Robert Lovell, a former evaluator of social programs in Michigan, highlighted

> the range of difficulties we face in applying the social science tools developed in the last 50 years to the problems faced by states in the next 5 years. This is not rocket science, it is much more difficult. The rocket engineer chooses among cost, weight, and reliability, has a very successful theory of physics to predict results, knows the goals exactly, and can test each component before assembling the product. Our tradeoffs among cost, reliability, timeliness, protection of subjects, and threats to validity are more complex, our theories have only weak, predictive power, we have as many goals as the number of programs we study, and we seldom have the luxury of studying each of our components separately. (as cited in Corbett, 1997, p. 9)

Theoretical Approach 5: The Institutional Environments in Which Knowledge Producers and Consumers Operate

The very institutions through which knowledge is generated and power is exercised often operate in ways that are counterproductive to evidence-based policymaking. What are we talking about here? Those who operate within the academic community clearly know what they have to do in order to thrive and advance. They must cater to their peers who more or less do basic research within narrow specializations. Working too closely with the real world bears considerable professional risk.

Nathan noted, "University-based social scientists interested in conducting applied research often have a hard time coexisting with their academic colleagues whose main interest is in theory building" (2000, p. 203). Anyone who has worked in a research university can attest to these tensions. All such institutions pay lip service to the three pillars of academic survival and advancement—research, teaching, and public service. Any junior faculty member who takes this trilogy seriously will experience a mercifully short career. Survival in top-ranked academic departments is based on research, research, and research. And not all research is equal; applied work counts less than basic work. Research published in outlets read by policy wonks and practitioners is not as valued within academic circles as research published in highly technical outlets. Even if an academic stumbles on a cure for poverty or teen drug use, public plaudits will not be matched by the admiration of peers. Instead, they want to see how many journal articles have been published, no matter how arcane and unread.

All of us in academia can cite numerous examples of this phenomenon, but we use one short vignette to reflect on this tension. Columbia University's Irv Garfinkel, while on the faculty of the University of Wisconsin–Madison, was very interested in some emerging ideas in the reform of the nation's child support system that he planned to pilot test in Wisconsin. Before proceeding, he asked his colleagues if pursuing such an applied research agenda would be wise professionally. The feedback was unambiguous; he would suffer as an academic, no matter the public good to be realized. Fortunately for child support policy in Wisconsin and beyond, he ignored his peers. Fortunately for him, the advice of his peers proved incorrect, and his academic career continued to thrive. He now holds a named professorship at Columbia University. Still, the tenor of the advice provided by his academic colleagues remains instructive.

Similarly, those operating in the real world encounter certain counterproductive institutional impediments to accessing and using good science. Policymakers function in an environment where money and power serve as dominant currencies of the land and often as keys to determining who has access to the policymaking process. There are unending demands upon the time of key decision makers. The number of decisions they must make is extraordinary. For example, the Montana legislature, which meets for 90 days every 2 years, is faced with 2,000 bill requests. Policymakers simply cannot study each issue before them or search for the best data and analysis to inform their decisions. Other institutional supports have emerged to fill this need.

Over the past several decades, whole industries have organized themselves around the task of ensuring that agenda-driven information gets to those who pull the levers of power. Both the quantity and effectiveness of lobbyists, advocacy groups, and agenda-driven think tanks have grown. In the early 1960s, the Brookings Institution was one of a handful of nongovernmental entities doing social policy analysis in Washington, D.C. Soon, however, a bewildering array of new venues emerged that regularly used research and analysis to weigh in on social policy issues, including the American Enterprise Institute, the Cato Institute, the Center on Budget and Policy Priorities, the Center for Law and Social Policy, the Hudson Institute, and the Urban Institute, to name just a few.

Although the quality and rigor of the analytical work varied across these new institutions, each organization's work was informed, at least in part, by a guiding ideological or normative perspective. For example, the Center on Budget and Policy Priorities generally saw government intervention to solve social problems as a good thing. The American Enterprise Institute remained skeptical of most such interventions, and the Cato Institute was decidedly libertarian in outlook. Many think tanks emerged, not to advance science in policymaking, but rather to reflect and support a given world view. Increasingly, the messenger was shaping the message.

Complicating matters, there is no shortage of "science" that could be brought to bear on any given side of a social issue. Political observers have witnessed what happens when a new policy direction emerges. An array of organizations immediately stake out opposing positions, each drawing on "evidence" to buttress their perspectives. For policymakers seeking truth, the situation must be hopelessly confusing. Often, it looks as if our entire policy apparatus is overcome with inertia with competing, policy-oriented organizations engaging in never-ending skirmishes in the marketplace of ideas. There simply are too many witch doctors with conflicting diagnoses of the problem and remedies to be tried. Not surprisingly, some members of the tribe, even when honestly seeking a policy solution to a social problem, turn away from science for answers.

Given all these shortcomings, the role of research may be perverse. Research and analysis can actually "corrode the kind of simple faiths on which political movements are based" (Aaron, 1978, p. 159). Lacking faith in the intrinsic neutrality of research can easily lead to a cynical view that research can be a weapon to buttress whatever position one favors and to beat down the positions staked out by opponents. With ever-expanding volumes of studies, the possibilities of finding supportive evidence increases dramatically. Policymakers can cynically cherry-pick studies and interpret data to fit their worldview, engaging in what Alice Rivlin once called "forensic social science" (1973). Stromsdorfer argued, "Policymakers, while not totally subjective and nonrational, will use whatever data are at hand to support their case, regardless of the methodological purity by which it has been developed" (1985, p. 258).

Focusing on a Primary Explanatory Suspect: The Notion of Community Disconnect

In the end we are left with a conundrum. As our capacity to increase the supply of research has increased exponentially, we seem less capable of bringing objective, dispassionate analysis to bear upon some of our most vexing and perplexing social challenges. Our operating premise, perhaps overly pessimistic, is that we can do little about many of the explanatory suspects that we have reviewed here, which suggests the futility of using social science research to impact the policymaking process. Indeed, it is unlikely that policymaking will develop into a rational or reflective process, that scientific knowledge will progress to fully understanding the complexity and variability of social problems, that researchers will develop methodologies that completely overcome the biases inherent in their studies, or that more centralized institutional and governmental structures will emerge.

Thus, we focus instead on the institutional environments in which knowledge producers and consumers operate. In this work, we introduce an extended model, which we call the *community dissonance theory*. This theoretical framework portrays knowledge producers and knowledge consumers as functioning within a discrete number of disparate communities that find it difficult to communicate with each other. This communication breakdown occurs because each community operates within distinct professional and institutional cultures with different goals, information needs, reward systems, and languages. Thus, the underutilization of research in policymaking is due to a communication gap that is attributable, at least in part, to behavioral factors. If the underlying forces are indeed behavioral, then they may well be less immutable and more malleable than many of the other factors at fault. If we acknowledge and pay careful attention to several pragmatic processes and procedures, we can increase communication across the two cultures and, in so doing, increase the utilization of research in policy decisions.

In keeping with this theoretical argument, we adhere to the more moderate view of many policymakers (Miller, 1996) and scholars (Mark & Shotland, 1985)—that research can have at least some incremental impact some of the time. However, we are fully aware of the complexities of using evidence to inform policy, the topic that we turn to next.

WHAT MAKES UNDERSTANDING THE SCIENCE– POLICY CONNECTION SO CHALLENGING?

Getting a handle on the relation between science and policy will require that we think about this question with depth and sophistication. In truth, there is no simple, linear relationship. Sometimes science is used, sometimes not. Sometimes it is used correctly, other times it is misused and misconstrued for political or partisan purposes. Sometimes researchers communicate well with policymakers, other times they appear to represent very different species. The relationship can be fruitful, frustrating, futile, and even fun.

To get us started down this road, let us capsulize on some of the challenges of getting knowledge producers and consumers on the same page (see Key Concepts 1.2). We delve into these in more depth as the book unfolds. Let us start with a few factors that may impede our understanding of the science–policy connection and that make quick fixes unlikely to be of much use.

Key Concepts 1.2   Major Reasons Why Understanding the Science–Policy Connection Is So Challenging

- Not all policy questions are alike.
- Not all knowledge consumers are alike.
- Not all knowledge producers are alike.
- Not all research strategies, results, and interpretations are alike.
- Not all interactions between knowledge producers and consumers are alike.
- The bottom line is that we live in a complex world. The challenge is to think through how to mitigate the impediments and difficulties that make communication between actors situated in these different communities so difficult.

Not All Policy Questions Are Alike

It is critical that both knowledge producers and consumers get the research questions right. Too often, researchers focus on questions of interest to them. That is, what will advance their scholarly careers or enhance their reputation? Worse, they investigate questions simply because they can—the data and methods are readily available or financial support can easily be obtained. Perhaps the most overlooked aspect associated with increasing the policy utility of research involves getting the question right. That involves ramping up the level of communication between knowledge producers and consumers before research initiatives are set in stone. It involves a whole new level of communication and cooperation between these two worlds. It involves new levels of communication to ensure that research taps the core issues of public interest in ways that can actually contribute to their resolution. Most important, this perspective suggests that the ideal points of interaction should begin not when the research is completed but rather when the questions of interest are initially formulated.

Not long after national welfare reform passed in 1996, Tom was asked to participate on an expert panel convened under the auspices of the National Academy of Sciences to address how best to evaluate the success of welfare reform. More to the point, the panel was to consider how science could help the reform movement advance in the right direction. As Tom listened to the top researchers who composed the panel, he began to wonder if the study group was headed in the wrong direction.

As technically sophisticated as the group was, being replete with members from academia and top-shelf research organizations, they were not particularly attuned to what was happening on the front lines of welfare reform. Welfare had become less and less about getting a check out the door and more and more about changing individual and family behaviors. Research questions and methods appropriate to understanding what had been an income-transfer program were less suited to assessing a set of complex initiatives focused on changing behaviors.

In short, the group of experts had to spend time and energy understanding what they were looking at in order to get the research questions right. If you don't do that well enough, everything else will fail. Feeling somewhat frustrated that the mostly academic-based committee members were disconnected from the rapid changes taking place in the culture of welfare offices across the country, Tom persuaded them to allow him to show a set of video clips he had taken at local sites in several states. Despite many good-humored jokes about who would bring the popcorn, the video, which had mostly local officials talking about how they were radically transforming welfare, was an eye-opener to the researchers. They realized that they risked developing recommendations for evaluation methods based on programmatic understandings that were quickly becoming outdated.

Not All Knowledge Consumers Are Alike

We must be far more appreciative of the complex character of the policymaking world. All policy is not made in the state house or the U.S. Congress. Too often, however, we approach the policy world as if this simple conceptualization were accurate. The world of knowledge consumers is as complex as the policy questions it considers.

On the knowledge-consumption side, we have those who make policy. Clearly, most legislators fall into this camp. But many higher-level officials in executive agencies also make policy as they interpret legislation, write regulations, and make the myriad implementation decisions that transform policy ideas into practice. At the same time, we have a host of public officials who manage policies and programs on a daily basis. Though tempting to dismiss this population as those who merely execute decisions made by others, this view would be naive indeed. As Lipsky pointed out in his book *Street-Level Bureaucracy* (1980), discretion at the operational level is a powerful tool for doing a lot more than merely carrying out what others have determined. Finally, there are all those who work the margins of the policy process in hopes of shaping policy decisions and how they are carried out. They also look to research to inform their particular craft. What each group needs from knowledge producers, however, may be quite different.

Karen and Tom have compared notes on the Welfare Peer Assistance Network (WELPAN) and Family Impact Seminars initiatives. WELPAN, as noted in the Preface, was a network of senior welfare officials who met to dialogue with their peers about cutting-edge ideas and directions. The Seminars are a model for bringing quality research to state legislators and other policy officials. Across these two initiatives, they have worked to bring research and sound analysis to a variety of policymakers. The Seminars focus on legislative branch officials but also include representatives from the governor's office and executive branch agencies. WELPAN focused on high-level civil servants from state welfare agencies but included, from time to time, top political appointees and bureaucrats with a more operational focus. Based on our combined experiences, two overriding lessons emerged. First, where you sit shapes where you stand. Legislators typically need general knowledge about what works and whether the policies being floated are good ideas. They need to be pointed in the right direction. Top political appointees in executive agencies need similar input, information on a more general level. As you move down the state agency bureaucracies, the information needs to change somewhat. Agency bureaucrats have specialized training and experience on a more narrow area of expertise. Information about why things work as they do, how to make things work better, and whether they apply to different populations emerges as salient pieces of the puzzle.

Despite these differences, there are many similarities. All policymakers are busy. They need input in a way that they can understand. They need a basis for trusting the messenger. Most important, they all make policy even though they are located in very different institutions. The policymaking process does not end with the passage of a law or the enactment of a regulation. There are many hands involved in determining what shapes the experience of the consumer of public goods and services. To exclude any of these actors is to fail to recognize the inherent complexity of the policymaking process.

Not All Knowledge Producers Are Alike

Similarly, we cannot assume that all knowledge producers are alike. They differ in so many ways. First, they differ by disciplinary preparation. Economists do not see the world in the same way that sociologists do, or political scientists, or those from any of the other disciplines that engage in social policy research.

Second, they differ in terms of methodological preferences. Some feel that social knowledge can be advanced only through formal experiments where partici-pants are randomly assigned to treatment and control groups. Others are very comfortable with observational studies using econometric and other advanced estimation techniques to deal, for example, with observed and unobserved het-erogeneity across key groups. Still others feel that contributions to the knowl-edge base can come from qualitative methods and case studies and that these less formal methods add richly textured information to the understanding of a complex world.

Finally, knowledge producers operate in very different institutional settings. There are academics doing basic research and academics doing applied work. Some are located in research-oriented universities, others in think tanks and policy firms, others in advocacy organizations, and still others within government itself. Each of these groups has its own operating climate and professional culture. Again, where one sits, as the old saying goes, shapes where one stands in critically impor-tant ways, such as how one thinks about research and what its contributions to the policymaking process might be.

The Institute for Research on Poverty (IRP) is a university-based interdisciplin-ary research organization. It is expected that cross-disciplinary communication and collaboration will occur focused on a common interest—the understanding of pov-erty and its amelioration. And some of the expected collaboration does take place. Over his 30-plus years at the Institute, Tom has noticed that challenges remain in achieving the ideal. The number of disciplines involved in poverty research has shrunk somewhat. Moreover, representatives from each discipline still struggle' with one another. When economists give a talk at a sponsored, brown-bag seminar, the audience often is dominated by economists. When a sociologist delivers the talk, the composition of the audience morphs in the expected direction—more sociologists. Tom occasionally noted that those in the audience from other dis-ciplines (than the presenter) could be seen glancing at their watches as if to say, "When will this drivel be at an end?" In short, each discipline tends to frame research questions in unique ways, bring different methods to the table, and look at data through distinct lenses. All academics are not the same. Rather, they live and operate within a unique culture that shapes how they see the world.

Not All Research Strategies, Results, and Interpretations Are Alike

We would live in a simple world if all researchers could mute their human frail-ties and biases, and if all agreed on which research strategies were appropriate. It is also true that things would be simpler if knowledge consumers could express what they needed to know to researchers. In the real world, however, it is clear that knowledge producers bring a set of preconceptions, or what economists would call *priors*, to their work—core beliefs, political dispositions, favored theories, and preferred values. Of course, some do better than others at managing or controlling their preferences and letting the data guide their work and its interpretation. No one, however, can completely escape the very personal and idiosyncratic frames through which they view the world. Similarly, methods often reflect the individual's training and sense of epistemological integrity.

How does each analyst conclude that something is true, particularly when it creates dissonance within his or her own value system or extant conceptual framework? Two researchers might choose different outcomes of interest to assess the success or failure of a policy. They might develop different econometric models and use different control variables or estimation assumptions when calculating how different policy regimes might affect the well-being of society. The end result can be extraordinary variation in results, or in interpretation, leaving policymakers both confused and sometimes cynical about what science can contribute to difficult social issues.

IRP convened a conference in June 2008 to vet draft chapters for the latest book, *Changing Poverty*, in a series examining progress in the fight against poverty. John Karl Scholz presented a graphic that essentially demonstrated that cash transfers for low-income families with virtually no earned income had fallen dramatically in recent years. On the other hand, cash assistance and other forms of public help grew dramatically for those low-income families who did have some earned income (Scholz, Moffitt, & Cowan, 2008).

For most of the academics in the audience, this was clearly a trend about which to be concerned. Their analysis showed that the poorest of the poor were getting less help. But is this the only reasonable reaction? A few in the audience, particularly those with more exposure to current policy debates, tended to respond differently, a fact they discussed informally among themselves. They interpreted the data as showing that the conscious policy shift launched in the late 1990s (i.e., to making assistance contingent on work) was, in fact, working as designed and that this was a good thing. According to this alternate line of thought, welfare had too long served to undermine basic societal values, including the value of work. It did so by giving adult caretakers cash support (or at least more support) when they chose not to work. Following this line of reasoning, these data indicated that we finally had the incentives right, that we were rewarding work rather than nonwork. Of course, whether this conclusion is supportable depends very much on the composition of this nonworking group and why they belong to this population. The real point is, however, that even the best analysis is subject to alternative responses. The path from evidence to conclusion is seldom a straight line.

Not All Interactions Between Knowledge Producers and Consumers Are Alike

Finally, not all settings and strategies where knowledge producers and consumers intersect are alike. How do you get information into the hands (and minds) of policymakers in ways that will be useful to them? Both worlds struggle with this issue. Think about it first from the policymakers' perspective. What if they confront what we call a *wicked social problem* where, as suggested earlier, desired outcomes are conflicted, where theory is unsettled, and where tactics for making progress are disputed? Where would the decision maker go for informative research? Would he or she read a lengthy report, seek out a technical briefing, or attend an academic conference? What about the researcher who might have an answer to the question or believes he or she has? What does he or she do with that knowledge—mail an article to a legislator or the governor, call and ask for a meeting, or work with some kind of intermediary organization or advocacy group?

The point is that producers and consumers come from different worlds. They operate differently and respond to very different cues. The primary objective of knowledge producers is the discovery of knowledge, whereas the primary objective of policymakers is the instrumental use of knowledge in the pursuit of specific goals, such as earning the respect of their constituents, ensuring reelection, gaining support for legislation, or influencing their colleagues (Bimber, 1996). Influence in the policy world is based on trust and common sense. Influence involves who is delivering the message, how information is communicated, and whether the message comports with underlying values. Influence in the research world is based largely on methods and procedure, convincing others that scientific protocols were followed in the pursuit of knowledge. Research is based on rigid adherence to scientific standards, whereas politics is based on compromise. Blending these worlds is not easy.

A number of years ago, the trade organization for welfare and related human service organizations held a meeting that brought together what it termed welfare CEOs and researchers from universities and top evaluation firms. The concept was to summit on how we should evaluate welfare reform as it unfolded. Over the first two days, a number of researchers lectured to the audience about what they were doing and why it was important to the audience. On day three, several CEOs were scheduled to talk about the management and policy issues about which they needed help. But only three researchers remained for the third day. Finding out what was on the mind of their purported audience apparently was not a big priority for many members of the knowledge-producing community.

However, this disconnect goes both ways. At a WELPAN meeting in March 2007, the members were asked a series of questions to help chart the future of the network. When asked in a forced-choice format whether future meetings should focus on innovative ideas drawn from research or from other states, all the states (save one) chose their peers as the preferred source of new ideas, a finding similar to that in a 2001 independent review of WELPAN (SAL Consulting, 2001, p. 14). Such experiences raised our curiosity as to why and how the currency of research has been so marginalized.

Taking on the Complexities of Building Science–Policy Connections

The hard truth is that we live in a very complex world. We touch on all of these complexities, some more than others, in the coming chapters. We do so with trepidation and hope. The trepidation emerges from our awareness of just how complex and demanding the task is of doing both good science and good public policy. For example, consider the fact that university-based academics alone are generating research and analysis at a rapidly increasing rate, far more than can be absorbed by even their academic peers, let alone busy decision makers. The political world, at the same time, is seen as drifting further and further into a partisan, ideological divide that appears to render science to a position of irrelevancy. In a recent discussion with Harry Holzer, professor of public policy at Georgetown University who frequently testifies before Congress, he noted how predictable congressional committees were in selecting experts to testify, with more care given to ideological balance than to the search for answers.

We are in an era where many argue that we must do more to promote marriage. In a sense, we argue moving in the direction of evidence-based policymaking as an effort to marry those who generate research, our knowledge producers, and those who use research as they go about society's business, our knowledge consumers. Like all marital efforts, it is easier said than done. These diverse communities must begin to talk with one another, often and openly. Self-imposed isolation, we argue, is counterproductive. The communication necessary to make any professional marriage work between producers and consumers *must* go both ways, advice not very different from what one would receive from a decent marital therapist. Ultimately, each will have to look honestly at the cultures within which it functions and be understanding of and sensitive to the culture of the other. Each may have to question basic assumptions and ways of doing business. Our challenge is to think through the ways in which we can mitigate the impediments and difficulties that make communication between actors situated in these different cultures so difficult.

SUMMARY

We tried to develop a book of broad applicability even though we focus largely on selected policy domains, namely, the social policy arenas of poverty and family policy. We also try to remain optimistic even though there is scant evidence that policymaking can be transformed magically into a rational, dispassionate undertaking. And we fully acknowledge that there is much to support a pessimistic perspective.

We know this gap between research and policy is quite unyielding despite the many initiatives that attempt to break down the barriers that exist. For example, the National Conference of State Legislatures and the Annie E. Casey Foundation have had a policy partnership designed to support legislative work on issues affecting family and neighborhood strengthening since 1992. This effort is designed, among other things, to increase the understanding and awareness of family economic success among state legislators and their staff in a bipartisan way so that they are better able to assess the promise and impact of policy proposals on low-income families (Noyes, 2007). And it is clear that some evaluation firms, policy think tanks, and representatives of the philanthropic community take great pains in preparing reports and documents that are written with a policy audience in mind. MDRC, perhaps the preeminent evaluation firm doing welfare and workforce development studies, takes great pains to do a good deal of testifying before public officials and to develop easy-to-read reports that summarize its research.

Furthermore, on the policy side of the great divide, we have seen politics become increasingly vitriolic and partisan in our nation's capital, particularly after 1994, when the presidency remained in Democratic hands and Congress turned

Republican after five decades of being in the minority. Almost everything became political, including how we measure the health and well-being of society.

But even in the midst of such partisan inertia, change did occur. A consortium of researchers, government officials, and representatives of the philanthropic community slowly pushed an agenda to develop child and family indicators of well-being. Through an improved set of social indicators, it was felt that both the detection of problems to be addressed and the effective employment of strategies to remediate these problems could be done. And progress was made when, in April 1997, President Clinton signed Executive Order No. 13045 formally establishing the Federal Interagency Forum and required an annual report to the nation on the status of the nation's children. This effort became part of a broader movement toward outcome-based governance, a way of doing public policy in a more reflective, objective manner that persists to this day.

We are heartened by the policymakers out there who seek information to use to make hard choices about what to do for whom. At the same time, there are many researchers who would like to apply their work in the real world. The average citizen wants good government, wants solutions over endless debate, and wants competence over scoring political points (Smith, 1991). Getting the knowledge producers and consumers together, however, has proved a lot more difficult than one might have imagined.

If we don't find ways to help researchers talk with policymakers, and vice versa, what might the future look like? Can we envision more partisanship and interest-group-driven policies? Can we envision even greater influence of money over science? And can we see further erosion of public support for social science research? When asked about what was important for academic researchers to know in working with policymakers, a state senator who held a leadership position replied as follows (response is paraphrased):

> The University seems to be isolated and does not encourage and initiate contact with policymakers. Academics need to be much better connected to politics; otherwise their budgets will get cut. In the face of significant cuts to the University and vindictive cuts to Extension, the University seems to think "this is not real." They seem to be living in a different world as their budgets get sliced and brutalized. The University doesn't seem to care, and academics don't want to get their hands dirty in the political process.

Improving communications between researchers and policymakers may be more than an academic exercise. For some in academia, it may be closer to a matter of survival.

In the end, we are not naïve. (Doing public policy will never become a fully rational process, nor should we expect it to be.) Any democracy must live with a give-and-take that is governed, in part, by values and positions that will never be fully informed by data or evidence. Differences of opinion will always be vetted in an environment where a marketplace of ideas plays out in the public arena. In an important way, this is a strength inherent in our democratic process. At the same time, there is much that evidence can do to reduce the level of conflict that tends to paralyze the policy process.

Science will never fully replace values and power in the development of policy or in the ways that public matters are managed. The role of research in shaping policy debates and informing public decisions seldom matches a level that its importance warrants and that is commensurate with the investment by government and the philanthropic community. Still, science can play a much bigger role than it does now.

In the end, we want no one to underestimate the difficulty of bringing evidence to the policymaking process. As hard as it is to do, we are hopeful. We believe that bringing empirical evidence to the policymaking process is doable despite all that it apparently takes to make it a reality. We look not to transform the character of doing policy or doing research. Rather, we look to better understand the unique cultures that frame how each group views the world. We look to those who have successfully traversed the terrains. We report here the tactics and strategies they have devised for building relationships and improving communication so that research and analysis can flow more readily, more freely, and more surely from knowledge producers to knowledge consumers and back again.

In this book, we share some thoughts about how to get started. Every arduous journey worth taking, as the old saying goes, starts with the first step. In the next two chapters, we begin by addressing two questions fundamental to an evidence-based policy agenda—first, whether policymakers are interested in receiving research and, second, whether researchers can be effective in delivering research to policymakers.

2

Do Policymakers Want Evidence?
Insights From Research-Minded Policymakers

The State Capitol is loaded with politics. It's not loaded with scientific research.

—**Senator Luther Olson**

Persist with well-researched and accredited information and keep at it. Politics belongs to the persistent.

—**Anonymous state legislator (as cited in State Legislative Leaders Foundation, 1995, p. 29)**

I n this chapter we alter our perspective. We turn to one of our primary communities of interest—knowledge consumers. We focus on their perspectives regarding research, its value to them and the work they do. Readers may be surprised by the views of our respondents who relay positive feelings toward the rigorous analysis that belies conventional wisdom. Their views also pose a challenge: Why don't we see more evidence of research use given respondents' apparently positive disposition?

Here we take an in-depth look at whether the main product (i.e., core technology) of one community—research—has relevance and usefulness in the other community—policymaking. At the risk of oversimplifying a complex phenomenon, we conceptualize the connection of research to policymaking as a bidirectional process—encouraging policymakers to become more research-minded and encouraging researchers to become more policy-minded. We will not be successful in bridging the two communities if policymakers are not interested in receiving information *from* researchers and if researchers are not effective in delivering information *to* policymakers. This is where we start. Without interest from both ends of the research–policy equation, even the slickest strategies implemented with the utmost precision will not work.

We begin by asking a fundamental question: Why might policymakers be interested in accessing rigorous analysis from the research community? We answer this question, in part, by drawing on the findings of the literature on research utilization that has been reviewed by others (Beyer & Trice, 1982; Feldman, Nadash, & Gursen, 2001; Greenberg, Linksz, & Mandell, 2003; Greenberg & Mandell, 1991; Innvaer, Vist, Trommald, & Oxman, 2002; Nelson, Roberts, Maederer, Wertheimer, & Johnson, 1987; Nutley, Walter, & Davies, 2007; Tseng, 2008; Weiss, Murphy-Graham, Petrosino, & Gandhi, 2008). The literature is dated and seldom based on observations of the phenomenon (Beyer & Trice, 1982). Largely absent are systematic studies of the users of research (Tseng, 2008) and the contexts in which research use occurs (Nutley et al., 2007). The limited studies that do exist suggest that research is most apt to be used when it has certain qualities and is delivered in specific ways. Yet from a pragmatic perspective, it is difficult to decipher how to operationalize these findings at the ground level (Nutley et al., 2007).

To fill this gap in the literature, this chapter goes straight to the horse's mouth—drawing on an exploratory study and in-depth interviews that we have conducted over the past 16 years with policymakers and policy administrators. As described in detail in the appendix, we interviewed 74 state legislators in Wisconsin (57% response rate) and conducted a Web survey of 56 high-ranking state agency officials from eight state agencies (61% response rate). Since 1997, we have conducted 94 face-to-face and phone interviews of state legislators and gubernatorial advisors of the Family Impact Seminars ranging in length from 15 to 75 minutes (response rate = 87%).

To provide a richer, more nuanced, and pragmatic understanding of the complex and circumstantial context in which research is used in policy decisions, we use the voice of policymakers themselves to describe why they are interested in research, specifically what kind is most useful, where they get it, and how they prefer to receive it.

WHY ARE POLICYMAKERS INTERESTED IN RECEIVING RESEARCH FROM PROFESSIONALS?

Cynics question the role science can play in a multifaceted process like policymaking in which policymakers are expected to respond to constituents, listen to the bids of special interests, and follow the ideological proclivities their supporters expect. Reflecting on research use in Congress, Farley wrote, "The words *research shows that* are the three most powerful words in our Capitol Hill vocabulary" (1996, p. 774). For state legislators, the impact of research on policy decisions is "huge," said Mary Fairchild of the National Conference of State Legislatures:

> Research is critical to the policy process, and I think legislators value research. They want information on what works and what doesn't work. They don't want to make investments in things that do not achieve the outcomes they are looking for. There are always, of course, unintended consequences, but when we have that information, to be able to use that information and translate it so legislators can use it in problem solving, it's huge.

Congressional committee staff persons are inundated with information from like-minded interest groups, yet they still welcome research to legitimate their bosses' policy positions. On the basis of the time that she spent on Capitol Hill, Carol Weiss (1989) characterized policymakers' need for information as "urgent" to see that the "right things are accomplished and the wrong things avoided" (p. 428).

One of the greatest of all ironies is that the evidence on the value of evidence in policymaking is actually quite "thin" (Nutley et al., 2007, p. 2). As a fledgling first step to examine the value of evidence from the perspective of the policy consumer, we turn to quantitative data from our exploratory study of 74 state legislators in a Midwestern state (see the methods and measures in the appendix). We asked these policymakers to rate five items regarding their attitudes about the usefulness of social science research, including *Social science research is useful for policymaking* and *Social science research can benefit policy decisions* (Cronbach's alpha = .89). On a scale of 1 (*strongly disagree*) to 6 (*strongly agree*), legislators agreed that research was useful in their work, with a mean of 4.40 and a standard deviation of 1.06. Second, in annual interviews with policymakers over a 15-year time span, policymakers told us that they use this information for a variety of purposes—to help make good decisions, to help avoid making bad decisions, to earn the respect of colleagues and constituents, and to build support for legislation they want to pass. Each of these purposes is described in policymakers' own words below.

To Help Make Good Decisions

Policymakers told us that they are "hungry" for good information. In the words of a legislator who first served in the Assembly and now serves in the Senate, "This is a job that you are hungry for information. I mean, you can't have enough information. Political or whatever … people in this job … are always striving to know stuff." This 14-year incumbent, who is known for his sense of humor, explained why he is "hungry" for information: "When we, as legislators, do research and want information when we pass a law, first of all, we want it to work, at least until we're out of office." What's more, research and analysis give him "confidence" in what he is doing as a lawmaker: "You do research and need information … to make you feel that you are doing the right thing."

Karen interviewed a Republican legislator who voted for rehabilitative services for juvenile offenders, based on evidence of their effectiveness. To Karen, this was a "statesmanlike" vote, given that it would be controversial in her conservative suburban district, which had low crime rates compared to neighboring Milwaukee. The legislator said she would have to educate her constituents about what is best for the entire state: "After all, we are a State." A Democratic legislator concurred that policymakers use research to help make good decisions:

> Well, anytime in the legislature that we were faced with a decision on a specific piece of legislation you always, at least I did, and I think most legislators do as well, want to make the best informed decision that you can. And granted …
> we all come with certain preconceptions as far as topics and issues that come

before the legislature. I always felt it incumbent on me to read everything I could get about a specific topic.

He quickly qualified his comments to avoid giving the false impression that lawmakers "just sit there and study and study and read things all the time, because that's not the nature of our jobs." He clarified that sometimes staff or other legislators do the reading, but irrespective of where the research comes from, having it available is "very useful."

Research is useful in the State Capitol, according to a conservative Republican senator first elected in 1990, to help ensure that policymakers get what they want and expect from their policy decisions. She went so far as to recommend that state government should rely more on technology transfer or even consider adopting a six-sigma, data-driven approach to help improve the quality of decisions, which in her opinion are too often based on personality and hearsay rather than on any evidence that policies are achieving their intended outcomes. What happens instead is that government "throws money at issues" and ends up adding more and more programs that, once enacted, develop a constituency and become exceedingly difficult to remove from the books even when a more effective alternative is available.

Another Republican senator gave examples of how research is useful in the political environment in which policy decisions are made. Without research, he has seen too many instances where decisions have been swayed by a "heart-wrenching story" or a single anecdote:

> It's sort of interesting because in the Capitol, we get removed, three or four steps, from the folks who actually have to deal with a lot of the laws that we pass. We don't have to meet them at the counter when they go to the family services department at the county or the city or the school … this gives us an opportunity to see, through studying, how this affects large groups of people, because if we do get involved, it's usually anecdotal information and so we deal with one or two people that talk to us about an issue. But we don't have the numbers and the research to say, "How does it affect folks in a large scale?" and that's very, very important.

Without knowing the scientific terminology of the academy, this legislator eloquently expressed the need for evidence that is generalizable to the population targeted by the legislation.

Finally, state senator Mark Miller explained to a gathering of knowledge brokers in the summer of 2008 that policymakers desperately need data from longitudinal studies even though he fully recognized how difficult and expensive they are to conduct:

> I think it's very important that the experts are presenting information that has had concrete results that can be demonstrated … it is important to see longitudinal studies that have gone on over 10, 20, 30 years because there aren't that many that are available to us. And, quite frankly, the decisions we make may have those kinds of impacts.

To Help Avoid Making Bad Decisions

Some social scientists argue that the primary use of research occurs at the back end of the policymaking process to justify policy decisions that have already been made (Shulock, 1999). Of course, legislators relayed instances where evidence was discounted when it did not support preexisting positions. Yet we were surprised by how many times policymakers told us that research is used at the front end of the policymaking process to help avoid making bad decisions (see Levin, 1952/2005). Republican senator Luther Olson said he always welcomes information that supports his view, but sometimes information contrary to his views is even more valuable:

> The most useful information I get is stuff that agrees with what my position is ... the best stuff is "Yep, Luther, you are right! This is the right thing to do, by God, and we got the information to prove it" ... and, once in a while, you find something on the other side that's so strong that you flip your position. And that is really useful because it's like, you know, I thought that I knew where I was going on this issue ... we're not talking those big issues, we're talking small things, and then you find out, you know I really didn't understand this whole thing or there's some new information that is very valuable ... "Boy it's a good thing I didn't go down that road because I would really look sort of foolish." So good information, no matter what side of the issue, is important, but the most invaluable is the kind that saves you from yourself.

Former Democratic assemblyman Peter Bock agreed that research can sometimes change the mind of a policymaker on the "smaller parts of the topics." For those unfamiliar with the culture of policymaking, he went on to clarify what "small things" means in "policy speak":

> People can change their minds on the smaller parts of the topic ... we're all self-made policy wonks in a way, and we come in with a perspective, whether it's liberal or progressive or conservative or whatever. So we come with our prejudices and our viewpoints on how things should be going, in general, on certain big topics. But I think we're all open-minded enough that if specific parts of those bills ... are presented in a very cogent and informative way that makes a strong argument that this is the best way of doing something, I think all of us are willing to say, "You know, I didn't think that it should be that way, but the argument is so strong, and the information and the analysis so clear, that perhaps we should be doing this part of it that way."

Familiarity with the premises of the policy culture breeds awareness of how research interacts with other forms of evidence. For example, in policymaking circles, the values of policymakers and the values of their constituents count. Ideology matters. Policymakers are not likely to compromise on the "big" things—the values and ideologies that they campaigned on and that brought them to office, such as whether policy issues can best be addressed with structural solutions that provide the conditions for change or cultural solutions that provide the motivation for change. Decisions on some issues such as same-sex marriage are driven by values or ideology, and evidence plays little role. However, policymakers are open to evidence on other issues that do not break cleanly along value and ideological lines (Matthews & Stimson, 1975).

Another way that evidence can influence the policymaking process, again which may be less obvious to outsiders or those on the sidelines of policymaking, is by countering the influence of ideology. A senator used his experience with the Family Impact Seminars to explain how research and analysis can dispel myth— an outcome political observers say is important in a culture where myth is often treated as fact (Heckman, 1990). We often receive unsolicited comments about the myth-busting potential of research and analysis on written evaluations of the seminars. For example, a Republican legislator commented after a seminar on parenting, "I wasn't sure that government had a role in parenting, but now I am sure we can no longer stick our head in the sand."

Finally, one veteran Republican explained how research can inform policy on the back end but not in the way that researchers usually construe it as justifying a decision that had already been made (Shulock, 1999). Quite to the contrary, she equated being a "good legislator" with being willing to rectify a decision if new evidence suggests the original vote or position was misguided or misinformed. She explained that if a bill or law initially supported was found to "hurt rather than help," good legislators will "boldly stand up in front of their district to say so."

To Earn the Respect of Colleagues and Constituents

In an institution where policymakers are called on to make countless decisions on matters big and small, they often turn to their colleagues for advice on how to vote. In lawmaking bodies, these advice-giving legislators are referred to as "go-to" legislators, and in scientific studies they are called "cue-givers" (Matthews & Stimson, 1975). These cue-giving legislators, who influence how policymakers vote, gain a reputation among their colleagues for having a high level of expertise on an issue and for being a legitimate information source. Relying on the expertise of their colleagues is a conscious attempt to build efficiency into a system that has become more complex in the second half of the 20th century (Matthews & Stimson, 1975). In the words of a 14-year veteran of the legislative process,

> Let me tell you how the legislature works. I mean, we have about an inch of knowledge. I always say we're an inch deep and about a mile wide: We know a little bit about a lot of things. And so what we really do, we research as much on a topic as we want to. If you're the chair of a committee, or a ranking member on a committee, but especially if you're the chair or it's your bill, you really research it a lot. You dig into things or try to, because that's your area of expertise. The way that the system works is really on a trust factor because we all can't know everything about everything. So we have people who chair committees or are ranking members or serve on committees that vote and send bills to the floor, and we trust our colleagues' judgment on these pieces of legislation. We trust that they did their homework.

This legislator also explained that one's reputation as the go-to person is not bestowed on someone because of such credentials as education, profession, or years of policy experience but earned based in part on one's level of expertise. One marker of expertise, according to this well-respected senator, is a legislator's grasp of relevant research:

> You don't want to propose something and, then, there's a question and you can't answer it because you didn't do your research. You want to know what the answer should be … so you have confidence in what you're doing. Really what this is, you do research and need information: It's to make you feel that you are doing the right thing. That this law is important, it moves things forward. Then you can take those convictions, that you did your research, that you're doing the right thing, and convince your colleagues that they need to vote for this bill because I have done the research … [and] … can answer the questions in front of committees or in front of the press or in front of my constituents.

To Build Support for Legislation They Want to Pass

Legislators are in the business of lawmaking, so their record of sponsoring and passing legislation helps earn the respect of their peers, the trust of their constituents, and the loyalty of their backers. A Democratic legislator pointed out that passing laws is necessary but not sufficient—it must be a law that is likely to achieve the goals that your party and your backers think will be best for the state. In a curious sort of way, research plays an important role in a political environment to help ensure that the laws they enact will achieve the goals they intend:

> We're partisan by nature, and we're on teams that play against one another. A lot of the important public policy decisions get tinged with that kind of undercurrent. You know, your team wanting to implement what they think is the best set of goals or directions for the state, and that's fine. There's nothing evil or bad about that. But in order to make those best decisions, it's good to have someone coming in and saying, "OK, we've looked at it. Here are two or three different studies. Here's what they do in eight different states, and here are the results."

So research can be useful in partisan politics not only to provide direction that will guide legislation toward its intended goals but also to provide ammunition that will enhance the prospects of its eventual passage. Some have dubbed this "forensic" use (Rivlin, 1973) and others "tactical" use (Tseng, 2008; Weiss, 1979). In an environment in which the specter of political advantage or disadvantage is ever present, it is paramount that the information on which a legislator bases his or her arguments and stakes his or her reputation is rigorous and reliable. According to a senator who has advised the Family Impact Seminars for 14 years,

> [When] you want to move something forward, there's always the other side … we live in a war zone to a point, where we want to push something through, and there's always the other side who doesn't want it to happen or wants to change it. So you have to find reliable information that reinforces your position but is also strong enough to withstand the attacks of the other side.

Weiss and Bucuvalas (1980, p. 90) put it more bluntly. If the research used by policymakers is unable to hold up under attack and ends up being "discredited by opponents on scientific grounds, they are left on a limb." In an oppositional environment, dangling on a precarious limb that could be subjected to a nefarious trim is an untenable position.

The reliability of information, according to a senator who operates a Midwest feed mill, is even more important in today's age of instant access to information, which academics refer to as the *democratization of science* (Henig, 2007). The senator gave the example of a school board that had made the case for passing a referendum to increase spending based on the argument that student test scores in the district were declining. Well, an enterprising taxpayer conducted a quick Internet search to learn that student scores had indeed gone down, but only in 5 of the 22 categories on which students were tested:

> With all this information out there, and all this research, you can't shoot from the hip anymore because people can do their research and find out information in a heart beat, and if you don't know what you're talking about, you lose all your credibility. And what happened to that community is that the board lost their credibility. They made statements. They were completely wrong, but it sounded good. In the olden days, "Heck, I'm an expert." But guess what? Everybody's an expert today with all the information that's out there, so you have the ability to do the research on any topic.

We have heard in the voices of policymakers themselves that they are interested in receiving research. Given this interest in becoming more research-sensitive, let us turn now to the real meat and potatoes of building stronger connections for information exchange between researchers and policymakers. In particular, we ask policymakers to tell us in their own words what kind of information is most useful, where they get it, and how they like to receive it.

WHAT KINDS OF INFORMATION ARE MOST USEFUL TO POLICYMAKERS?

To describe the use of research in policymaking, we rely on three main sources of data. We start with our exploratory studies and interviews of policymakers and agency officials as described in the appendix. We also draw from existing literature on research use among policy actors, including elected officials, executive agency officials, legislative service agency staff, and knowledge brokers who have tried to connect the two cultures. These studies were conducted in a number of settings (e.g., congressional committees, executive agency officials, local health and social service agencies, and work/welfare demonstrations) and drew from a range of disciplines (business, education, economics, health sciences, organizational sociology, political science, psychology, public administration, and public affairs; Jacobson, Butterill, & Goering, 2003).

What Does the Existing Literature Suggest?

The utilization literature that we summarize in Table 2.1 has identified a number of qualities that make research useful in policymaking. These findings paint research utilization with a broad brush by isolating variables that deserve the attention of those generating research on utilization and those disseminating it to policymakers. The ability of these studies to isolate variables is a strength of the literature, but in a perverse sort of way, it is also a weakness. The literature (Greenberg et al., 2003; Weiss & Bucuvalas, 1980) generally offers little guidance about which of these variables are more or less potent than others, in what ways might these variables interact with each other, and whether these variables apply only to particular policy actors in specific settings or have cross-cultural and cross-contextual validity.

TABLE 2.1   Characteristics That Make Research Useful to Policymakers

Characteristics	Description and Examples
Action orientation	Results have real-world applications (Nelson et al., 1987; Nutley et al., 2007; Weiss & Bucuvalas, 1980)
Challenge to the status quo	Results are new and exciting (Beyer & Trice, 1982; Weiss & Bucuvalas, 1980)
Conformity with user expectations	Results are consistent with user views of the world (Beyer & Trice, 1982; Innvaer et al., 2002; Nutley et al., 2007; Weiss & Bucuvalas, 1980)
Definitiveness	Results are clear (Greenberg et al., 2003; Greenberg & Mandell, 1991; Nutley et al., 2007)
Generalizability	Results are applicable to the jurisdictions or populations of interest to the policymaker (Greenberg et al., 2003; Greenberg & Mandell, 1991)
Manipulability of variables at a reasonable cost	Results are implementable, or brought to scale, without breaking the bank (Beyer & Trice, 1982; Nelson et al., 1987)
Objectivity	Results are not agenda driven, the research is done in a dispassionate manner (Beyer & Trice, 1982; Weiss & Bucuvalas, 1980)
Policy implications	The links between results and policy are clear (Feldman et al., 2001; Innvaer et al., 2002; Nelson et al., 1987; Weiss & Bucuvalas, 1980)
Presentation	Results are presented in a concise and understandable way (Beyer & Trice, 1982; Feldman et al., 2001; Greenberg et al., 2003; Innvaer et al., 2002; Nelson et al., 1987; Nutley et al., 2007; Weiss & Bucuvalas, 1980)
Quality	Research was conducted according to the protocols of science (Beyer & Trice, 1982; Dunn, 1980; Greenberg et al., 2003; Greenberg & Mandell, 1991; Innvaer et al., 2002; Nelson et al., 1987; Nutley et al., 2007; Weiss & Bucuvalas, 1980)
Relevance	Results pertain to issues policymakers care about (Beyer & Trice, 1982; Feldman et al., 2001; Greenberg et al., 2003; Greenberg & Mandell, 1991; Innvaer et al., 2002; Nutley et al., 2007; Weiss & Bucuvalas, 1980)
Timeliness	Results are available when policymakers need them (Beyer & Trice, 1982; Feldman et al., 2001; Greenberg et al., 2003; Greenberg & Mandell, 1991; Innvaer et al., 2002; Nelson et al., 1987; Nutley et al., 2007; Weiss & Bucuvalas, 1980)

Some studies hint at the possibility that certain variables will have a larger effect than others. For example, in a study of policymakers' use of data from randomized experiments, the timeliness of the research and political considerations were more important to its eventual use than the study's results (Greenberg et al., 2003). In another study (Weiss & Bucuvalas, 1980), researchers, grant reviewers, and agency officials rated the importance of research characteristics in their decision to use a study. Of 29 characteristics, the top 3 were "recommendations are supported by the data," "understandably written," and "objective/unbiased," all of which were rated higher than such characteristics as generalizability, technical quality, and action orientation. Some research characteristics appeared to operate, not in isolation, but in combination with each other. For example, when decision makers judged the technical quality of research to be higher, they were more likely to accept findings that did not conform to their initial expectations.

No known studies have examined cross-community differences in the ratings of these research characteristics, but the findings of some studies suggest that there may be important differences. For example, about half (54%) of agency officials reported that their best source of information is academic journals (Weiss & Bucuvalas, 1980), a response that we believe is highly unlikely from elected officials, given our extended interactions with this population.

What Do Our Policymaker Informants Suggest?

Because many questions remain unanswered, we took this body of knowledge and tried to get a street-level view of how these research characteristics resonate with the work culture of state policymakers. As described in the appendix, we asked 74 state legislators and 56 high-ranking state agency officials from eight state agencies to rate 19 characteristics of research that make it more and less useful to them in their job. These characteristics were drawn, in large part, from a landmark study by Weiss and Bucuvalas (1980) conducted with mental health researchers, grant review committee members, and executive agency officials at local, state, and federal levels. The mean ratings of all 19 research characteristics are displayed in Figure 2.1.

Extrapolating from these findings, it appears that research has to pass three tests to meet policymakers' standards for usefulness:

- The credibility test: Is the study of high scientific quality? Are the findings unbiased?
- The accessibility test: Does the report provide brief summaries of the key findings? Are the findings understandably written?
- The timeliness test: Are the findings available at the time the decisions are being made?

Although these findings are clearly exploratory in nature, research that passes these three tests appears more likely to be respected by policymakers for its usefulness in policy decisions, whereas research that fails these three tests is more likely to be rejected. Now let's dig deeper in our interviews for insight into why these tests are so important in the policy culture.

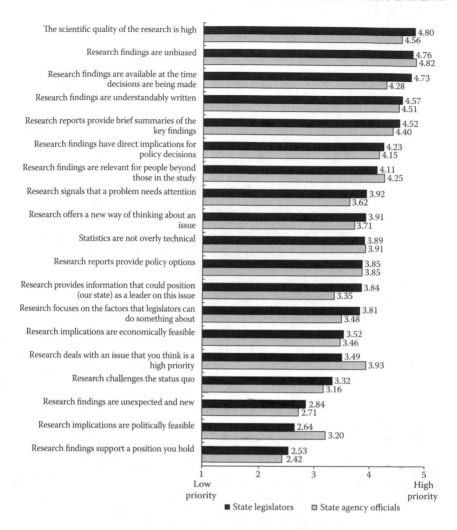

Figure 2.1   State legislators' and state agency officials' ratings of research characteristics. *Note.* State legislators' ratings are based on interviews of 74 legislators from a Midwestern state (response rate of 57% based on the entire 2003–2004 state legislature). State agency officials' ratings are based on 56 high-ranking agency officials from eight state agencies in that same state in 2003–2004 (61% response rate).

The credibility test. One Republican senator, in describing his job, explained that the need for credible information comes with the territory. Legislators don't sit and think up new ideas for legislation. What happens instead is that people present ideas to them and try to persuade them to see their point of view. His job as a legislator is not only to listen to their perspectives but also to listen to the perspectives advanced by others, which may conflict with each other. What he would like is a policy "God" who could sort out for him which information is credible:

> [As legislators] we say, "Do I have enough information to not embarrass myself by the decision I'm going to make?" … we all would like this God to be out there that says "[Legislator's name] here is the right answer. Here's some information that I have looked at both sides of the equation and this is where you should come down." Well, as you know, in life, there's nobody that does that for us.

A 25-year Republican senator concurred, explaining that the job of a policymaker is to continually search for the "truth" to help ensure that good decisions are made:

> How do I ever get information to make a good decision? How can I know what's fact, know what's fiction? Who do I believe? I think one of the toughest things when a legislator comes in to serve is, "Where's the truth?" And it's hard to know where the truth is. You get truth from this direction, truth from that direction, and truth from somewhere else. And then somebody in your district has an opinion. And that's the truth.

This search for credible information was a recurring theme in our interviews. A Democratic representative called it "objective information," which he found to be a scarce commodity in lawmaking settings. Perhaps objective information, like other commodities, follows the laws of supply and demand—its value to the consumer increases as a function of its scarcity in the marketplace of ideas. In policymaking institutions, most ideas come with a direction.

> But there was always a need for some sort of objective information. And it was very hard to find objective, nonpartisan forms of information to help you make a decision on the issue. And many times the decisions were based on things that you may have already decided one way or the other, but you want to implement an idea, and so you need some sort of analysis of how this has worked other places. Again, you don't want it to be slanted one way or the other. You want someone to have been able to study something and say, "OK, we've looked at it. We don't have a bias, and here are the results." And sometimes it's even better if there isn't a "Therefore, you should do this" at the end of it.

In the course of our conversations, policymakers claimed to have plenty of access to information. This is consistent with the findings of a study of policymakers in 17 states in which 6 of 10 legislators (61%) reported feeling overwhelmed by the volume of material that crosses their desk (Hird, 2005). The task at hand for our informants is assessing the credibility of information, which they do in a number of ways. A Republican senator explained that he learned about methodology to assess the quality of research. He criticized education research, claiming that it was "just terrible." He cited the conflicting research on school vouchers, concluding that both sides may be right depending on whether the control group is the general population or kids eligible for vouchers but who didn't enroll: "Because somebody comes up with a study and the other side who doesn't like it says, 'It wasn't done right. It was the wrong group … the constant was wrong.' So it's like, what good is this?"

A Democratic assemblyman explained that he assesses the credibility of the information he receives from sources that he knows are biased by playing off their advice against each other:

> And when I was lobbied by various groups, I always felt that it was a good thing in that they gave me information. When they came in, I knew who they represented and what side they were going to be on usually, but I would listen to the presentation and get the information from it. But it was a one-sided presentation usually, and you would ask them, "So, what's the other side going to tell me?" and get their reaction to that.

Weiss (1989) made a similar observation of the way congressional staff probe the competing claims and counterclaims that all offices deal with: "Their usual premise is that both sides are exaggerating and that the truth lies somewhere in between" (p. 421). This way of ferreting out the strengths and weakness of competing arguments is not too different from the process many of us use when we listen to sales pitches about whether tile or wood would be a better surface for the floor, or glass or steel would be a better material for the door. One other strategy for assessing the credibility of information was offered by a Democratic caucus chair: "Now, of course, sometimes you rely on someone to be your negative barometer, you know, because you always disagree with that person and so you rely on them that way."

The accessibility test. One aspect of accessibility that we heard over and over again from the legislators whom we interviewed is the importance of providing brief summaries of research and analysis that could easily be digested by busy policymakers. An assistant majority caucus chair on the Republican side of the aisle explained that it is important for academics to realize that legislators like to deal with the "facts," but they need the "CliffsNotes" version. Because of the many demands on her time, she asks her staff to summarize long reports for her. A Republican senator also relies on his staff to search for and summarize information for him:

> I'll tell my staff, "See what's on the Internet," and I don't say, "Copy all that stuff and give it to me." I want one page or a half page on what I really need to know, and if there's something on there that I really want to dig in deeper, then where do I find it.

A caucus chair on the Democratic side of the aisle recognized differences in the cultures of the institutions that policymakers and academics live in and cautioned about presenting information in a format that would work in an academic setting but not in the policy world:

> Because you live, many of you live, in the academic world, there is a tendency to provide a monograph to some legislator who's not really going to get into it, because it's not the meat and potatoes that they're normally used to.

He underscored the need to tailor information to the policymaker audience by describing to us what his colleagues in the legislature are like:

> Legislators are not, at least in my experience, terribly intellectual-type indi-
> viduals ... not academics. There's a few lawyers. So if someone gave us a report
> that was indexed and had 15 pages of endnotes at the end, that isn't going to
> get read. That's not going to get analyzed by me or many of my colleagues. We
> might give it to someone to say, "What does it say? Tell us what it says." So the
> important thing I think about getting information to the legislature is to make
> it approachable and readable, and if that means just having a two- or three-
> page synopsis or a condensed version. ... I think that will get read.

His comments about the need to craft information so that it is accessible to the
nonintellectual are particularly memorable because this advice came from a legislator who was probably one of the brightest, most thoughtful men that Karen has
ever met—inside or outside the legislature.

Nowhere is the culture clash more obvious than when knowledge producers
attempt to speak to knowledge consumers. The protocols for presenting data to
researchers differ dramatically from those for presenting to policymakers. A senator described a university-sponsored session that he attended on school funding,
an issue he cared deeply about:

> The charts they put up there were alright if you were a scientist ... they had all
> these little numbers ... to help us, some of them were black and some of them
> were red, but we didn't have a clue what this was about. This one is .567 and
> this one is .76. Well OK, fine, but that doesn't help us as legislators.

This description of the presentation is amusing, but underlying the humor is a
missed opportunity to provide information that the policymaker was seeking and
that the researcher probably could have provided, if only he had known better
what the policymaker needed.

The timeliness test. Another impediment to a smoother flow of information between the research and the policy cultures is timeliness. In our interviews, policymakers mentioned three aspects of timing that influence whether
research and analysis will be put to use—institutional timing, topic timing, and
issue timing. First, a Democratic representative explained that it is the responsibility of a would-be knowledge broker to learn how the policymaking institution operates so he or she would know when to make information available.
He illustrated the importance of institutional timing using the example of the
Wisconsin legislature:

> For instance, in Wisconsin, the legislature stops meeting in the even-num-
> bered years, this year, around April, and doesn't take up any new issues ... in
> the summer ... there's a lot of people running for reelection ... so, that's not
> a good time.

In addition to time constraints imposed by the legislative process, there are
also topic-related constraints. He recommended that research be made available
when the topic is relevant:

There are certain things as far as we're concerned occupying our time and interests that particular session or that year … if you're doing a study that the legislature isn't even considering at that time, that just might not be the right time to present that topic.

He also emphasized the importance of tracking the timing of a particular issue as it winds its way through the legislative process. Using the example of his state's major overhaul of its welfare program, he explained, "At times like that, it was good to have information available." When legislators find themselves muddling through a major policy issue, the need for information may be particularly time sensitive, as explained by a Republican senator: "Because a lot of the time we need the information within minutes. Finding it next week is too late for a lot of times." This same senator gave an example of how a Family Impact Seminar on prescription drugs had provided information that was useful, in large part, because of its timeliness:

We didn't have a prescription drug plan in the state, so this was a timely seminar because we were in the process of making decisions on what it should be. And I served in the Assembly on the Health Committee, and we were looking at one that was going to cost a million bucks. Well, I think it was like 20 bucks a person, that's nothing … you [Karen] had experts come in and talk to us and tell us what other states were doing, what it cost … so that helped me as a legislator sort of working on the fringes of that thing saying, "Well, if you're going to do it, you have to spend enough money to make it worthwhile. Otherwise, don't do it." And realizing if you start it … it's going to cost a heck of a lot more in a couple years than you ever dreamed. So don't go with the illusion that you spend $14 million today and in 3 years, it'll be $14 million. It will be a lot more. And guess what? They were right. Nobody was shocked. Well, some people were shocked, but not anybody that studied it.

The cross-community validity of the credibility, accessibility, and timeliness tests. We also found some evidence of the transcontextual validity of these findings regarding the credibility, accessibility, and timeliness of research findings. As described previously, we also gave this same list of criteria to a sample of high-ranking state agency officials in Wisconsin who worked in one of eight agencies that (a) would benefit from the use of social science research and (b) made decisions that affected children and families. Overall, 56 state agency officials responded to our Web-based survey (61% response rate). A full description of the methods can be found in the appendix.

The ratings of the agency officials were similar to those of the elected officials as shown in Figure 2.1. The same five characteristics topped the list (i.e., *the scientific quality of the research is high, research findings are unbiased, research findings are available at the time decisions are being made, research reports provide brief summaries of the key findings,* and *research findings are understandably written*). In MANOVAs that controlled for education and gender, only two differences were statistically significant. State legislators gave a significantly higher rating than agency officials on two items: *the scientific quality of the research is high* and *research findings are available at the time decisions are being made* ($t = 3.00$,

$p < .01$, and $t = 4.70$, $p < .01$, respectively). That is, the quality of research and its timing were more important characteristics of research from the vantage point of state legislators than state agency officials.

Surprisingly, when we ask researchers to rate the research characteristics as they think that policymakers would, what many researchers guess would be at the top of policymaker's list is often at the very bottom—*research findings support a position you hold*. Agency officials also gave this item the lowest rating, and it did not differ significantly from that of state legislators ($t = 0.40$, $p = .69$). When we asked policymakers to reflect on this finding, one legislator explained that this rating may not be entirely the way that legislators function but the "platonic way they would like to function." However, another explanation was more common.

Legislators explained that they like research that supports their positions, but even more important is being confident that they have correct and complete information before they present their ideas to colleagues and the media. Having the facts right means they are more apt to be trusted by their colleagues and reelected by their constituents. Of course, they admit to being quicker to embrace research that confirms their views and slower to accept research that contradicts them. Yet when asked to rate the importance of several criteria, the quality of research and its objectivity appeared to far outweigh the importance of whether the research supports their views.

Two other items received low ratings from agency officials among the 19 research characteristics that we presented to them. First, *research implications are politically feasible* received the second-lowest rating from the 74 state legislators that we interviewed and the third-lowest rating from the 56 state agency officials. Legislators rated political feasibility significantly lower than state agency officials ($t = -2.02$, $p < .05$), so political feasibility is less important to officials in legislatures than in state agencies. Perhaps this is because state legislators are more likely than state agency officials to perceive that they have the skills and opportunities to influence the political feasibility of issues or put proposals on the legislative agenda.

Finally, the item that was among the bottom three research characteristics for both legislative and agency officials was *research findings are unexpected and new*, a rating that did not differ significantly between the two groups ($t = 0.20$, $p = .84$). On the surface, it appears that whether research is unexpected or new is not very important to either elected or appointed officials.

Yet the story of research use may not be that simple. Based on additional analysis that we conducted with state legislators, when legislators are considered as a whole, *research offers a new way of thinking about an issue* is rated sixth lowest out of the seven research characteristics that we examined in the analysis. However, within-group analysis revealed that the rating of policymakers who were the most enthusiastic users of research was well above the sample mean, and the ratings of the other three types of research users were well below the sample mean. Thus, research that offers a new way to think about an issue is not highly rated by policymakers, on average, but it is of high priority to those legislators most likely to value, seek, and use research in their decisions.

In an attempt to disentangle different information needs in different cultures, we also asked policymakers and high-ranking state agency officials to rate the

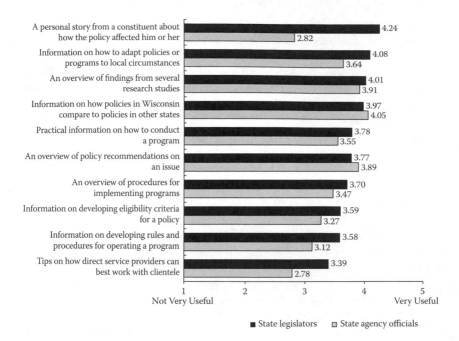

Figure 2.2　State legislators' and state agency officials' ratings of information types. *Note.* State agency officials' ratings are based on 56 high-ranking agency officials from eight state agencies in that same state (61% response rate).

usefulness of 10 different types of information in their policy work, all of which are listed in Figure 2.2. Of the top four information types, three were the same for legislators and high-ranking state agency officials. Both gave high ratings to *an overview of findings from several research studies* and *information on how policies in Wisconsin compare to policies in other states*—ratings that did not differ significantly from each other. The third common item was *information on how to adapt policies or programs to local circumstances.* State legislators tended to rate this item significantly higher than state agency officials ($t = 1.86$, $p = .07$).

However, one other difference emerged in these top ratings. The top information type for legislators was *a personal story from a constituent about how the policy affected him or her.* When asked about this finding, a senator, who is well respected for his command of the facts, explained, "If you give legislators the research and facts, and I tell a heart-wrenching story, I will win every time." Despite the esteem in which personal stories are held by elected officials, this same item was rated second to last, 9th out of 10, for state agency officials ($t = 7.29$, $p < .0001$).

WHERE DO POLICYMAKERS GO TO GET INFORMATION?

The literature suggests several sources of policy knowledge: books, conferences or seminars, cultural events, government reports, hearings, legislative service agencies, magazines, newspapers, peers, periodicals, personal networks, research organizations, scientific journals, staff, television/radio, think tanks, and universities

(Caplan, 1979; Hird, 2005; Nutley et al., 2007; Webber, 1992). What remains elusive is which of these information sources are used more extensively and by what types of knowledge consumers. Again, we interviewed a small group of research-oriented state legislators about their most common information sources. We interviewed 10 legislators who advise the Wisconsin Family Impact Seminars; of these, 7 legislators had time to answer the questions on where they go for information on children and families.

In response to an open-ended question on where they go for information on children and families, the 7 legislators who responded—4 of whom served in the Senate and 3 in the Assembly, 5 who were Democrats and 2 Republicans—mentioned 71 information sources. We tallied the results in two ways—the number of legislators who gave the response and the numbers in each category as a percentage of all responses (see Figure 2.3).

The results from these two approaches were remarkably similar. The top three information sources that policymakers turn to are nonpartisan legislative service agencies (staff that are hired by state government to provide research and analysis to legislators), their legislative colleagues, and state advocacy organizations (e.g., councils on aging, children, choice, and families). The nine sources mentioned the fewest times are the same irrespective of whether their responses were categorized by number of mentions (not shown) or by the percentage of total responses: internal experts,

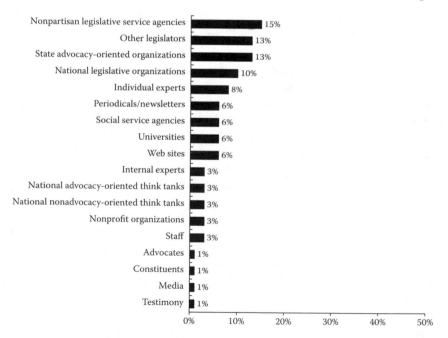

Figure 2.3   State legislators' preferences for sources of information on child and family issues presented as a percentage of information sources (N = 71). *Note.* A total of 71 information sources emerged from interviews of 10 legislators who advise the Family Impact Seminars in a Midwestern state (100% response rate), of which 7 had time to respond to a question on where they go for information on child and family issues.

national advocacy-oriented think tanks (e.g., Heritage Foundation), national nonadvocacy-oriented think tanks (e.g., the Urban Institute), nonprofit organizations, staff, advocates, constituents, media, and testimony. The sources that fall between these two extremes are the ones that are typically thought to be more prominent providers of information, including national legislative organizations (e.g., American Legislative Exchange Council, Council of State Governments, and National Conference of State Legislatures), individual experts, periodicals and newsletters, social service agencies, universities, and Web sites. For the top three choices, legislators explain in their own words why they turn most often to these information sources.

Nonpartisan Legislative Service Agencies

Consistent with previous research that knowledge consumers are more likely to rely on research from within their own organization (Beyer & Trice, 1982; Dunn, 1980; Hird, 2005; Nelson et al., 1987), one of the first places that state legislators turn to is legislative service agencies in the legislature itself. Republican senator Carol Roessler, recently appointed by a Democratic governor to be the Administrator of State and Local Finance in the Department of Revenue, explained that many legislators go directly to these nonpartisan agencies to have papers written on particular subjects. In her words, "They are great riches to us as legislators. We are very dependent upon them and the information they bring to us." Republican senator Luther Olsen explained why this nonpartisan and confidential information is so valuable:

> So we have impartial staff that … can do research for us. … But if I have a question on something that's financial or whatever, we have these folks who [can help us] that's their job. They write papers for us … if we have a question on something, we ask the Legislative Council, "Write me a paper and answer this question for me," and then they write a paper for us. So we have people that do the research for us. It's not academic, but it's sort of academic … they know how to talk to us, they know what we want.

Former Democratic representative Peter Bock explained why policymakers are comfortable turning to the agencies that they have at their disposal. Not surprisingly, this comfort level stems from the relationships that policymakers have developed with these nonpartisan staff, many of whom have served the legislature for decades: "We have relationships with them, they return our phone calls, and so they will do the hard work … of getting in touch with someone and … culling some of the information for us."

Legislative Colleagues

A number of legislators explained that their colleagues are a rich source of information. A 14-year Republican incumbent explained that legislators tend to "ID" other legislators who are "experts" in one area, and they rely on each other when they want to get more information. For example, a second-term legislator, who had become a well-regarded expert on human services, child welfare, and welfare reform, had introduced 12 amendments on behalf of her caucus.

State Advocacy-Oriented Councils and Organizations

Advocacy and lobbying organizations were a common source of information for state legislators. In our framework (see Chapter 4), we term these as *intermediary organizations*. When we asked a Republican legislator what sources of information he used, he looked us in the eye and immediately said, "You'd be surprised how much of it is political." Interestingly, state advocacy organizations were mentioned four to six times more often than national advocacy organizations, although sometimes they were freestanding state organizations and sometimes they were arms of or affiliates of national organizations.

Policymakers turn to lobbyists for several reasons, four of which we mention here. First, policymakers often know lobbyists and have long-standing relationships with them. Second, lobbyists are a ready source of research data, speech material, and partisan analysis, which can help policymakers analyze how policy proposals are similar to or different from their own attitudes and values as well as those of their constituents (Lindblom, 1968). Third, professional lobbyists, if they are good, can explain in 10 minutes what it would take a policymaker 2 hours to read about on their own (Lindblom, 1968). Finally, lobbyists capitalize on their capacity to provide policymakers with information to assist them in their decision making, compared to other organizations with a similar capacity but less commitment to communicating culturally relevant data and analysis.

Particularly telling was the comment of Senator Roessler, who has won countless awards such as the American Academy of Pediatrics Childhood Legislator Advocate of the Year, the Wisconsin Public Health Association Legislator of the Year, the Wisconsin Counties Association Outstanding Legislator Award, as well as awards from organizations representing the aged, builders, the cancer society, the Farm Bureau, and veterans. Despite this impressive 25-year record as a legislator interested in evidence-based information, she explained that she had virtually no contact with the university in her district:

> I have never called them for opinions or research to be done on particular issues. Every once in a while, it's very rare, that someone from a department would call me from there on a subject matter. It's extremely rare, maybe once or twice have I ever gotten a call like that. And I don't call the university here [University of Wisconsin–Madison] to get information.

HOW DO POLICYMAKERS LIKE TO GET INFORMATION?

In a recent review of the literature, Sandra Nutley and her colleagues (2007) concluded that studies have primarily evaluated strategies for disseminating research to the practice community rather than to the policy community. The data, albeit limited, suggest that one of the most effective strategies for a policymaking context is seminars or workshops that provide opportunities to discuss research with potential users or that adopt a more collaborative and interactive approach. We heard similar themes in our interviews with policymakers about the value of hearing from and interacting with experts on the issues they are debating and discussing.

Presentations or Seminars

The message that we hear over and over again is that policymakers prefer presentations over written material. In the words of longtime Republican legislator Carol Roessler,

> I also think that we listen much more closely as legislators in presentations and sessions where there are opportunities for give-and-take and asking questions, and having data and information presented to us in hand, and the opportunity for face-to-face discussion than we do with a pile of reference materials that we receive. Not everyone is going to read all that pile of stuff. ... It doesn't command the same type of attention that a presentation that you can go to at a certain time and have more time in that opportunity to explore the data that you're being given and ask questions of the people that are present with you.

Policymakers who served at the county level also underscored their preference for presentations. According to Mark Masters, chairman of the county board of supervisors in a rural county,

> You've got piles and piles and reams and reams of this information. The general county board supervisor will be most affected by the presentation first. Because you have his attention or her attention for a short period of time. You'll need the backup information because it will be used somewhere along the way. That early presentation is what's most effective in my opinion.

This stated preference for interacting with experts really should come as no surprise given that lawmakers are elected, in part, based on interpersonal skills that win over the trust of their constituents (Fenno, 1978). Moreover, lawmaking bodies are known to operate under a long-standing oral tradition (Jonas, 1999; McCall, Groark, & Nelkin, 2004; Weiss, 1987a). For example, policymakers gather information primarily through oral communication—hearing constituent concerns, listening to testimony, questioning lobbyists, and talking with legislative colleagues. Given this tradition, policymakers are said to "take pride in their ability to 'read people' rather than read reports" (Weiss, 1989, p. 414). Policymakers become so reliant on the give-and-take nature of their information gathering that a Minnesota legislator characterized what he sees on paper as "single dimensional," but what he hears from people as "multi-dimensional" (Jefferys, Troy, Slawik, & Lightfoot, 2007, p. 11).

A Wisconsin legislator explained how he uses personal contact as a form of quality control. He intentionally asks questions that allow him to size up the qualifications of experts and screen the credibility of their information—a strategy we now jokingly refer to as subjecting experts to the "smoke" test:

> If you just sent out an e-mail saying, "So there's this topic, and there's this report on this stuff," we wouldn't go too much farther because there's all kinds of those reports. … Because the original eyeball-to-eyeball questioning some-times, a lot of times, it gives us a feel, "Is this person credible?" … you just get that gut feeling that, "Yeah, I can trust what they're doing because we asked them questions, and they were able to answer them and make some sense, and they weren't blowing smoke."

A Democratic representative in the Assembly expressed similar sentiments about preferring to receive information through a presentation supplemented with written materials:

> Physical presentations by other human beings are what grab you. Otherwise there's the good likelihood, the strong likelihood, that one of the legislators will write "File" on the report that just came across their desk, as … I did and we all do. And it'll go in a file somewhere. But when there's a presentation, and … if it's a good speaker—entertaining, funny, or challenging or what have you … that's what gets us hooked. You know, we're human beings. We're "people-people." We like to interact with folks; that's one of the reasons we're in poli-tics. And so you have that dynamic of physically hearing and seeing someone which is very important, being able to listen to what they're saying.

Opportunities to Interact With Experts

One senator, who is a leader in the state and in the Republican Party on education issues, described a relationship that he had developed with a professor from the School of Education, whom he met while serving on an advisory committee for the school. The senator has been involved in discussions about revising the formula used to fund K-12 education, and the professor had developed an analysis of how a particular funding formula would affect each school district in the state; the profes-sor explained that in 335 of the districts, taxes would not increase, but they would in the remaining 91. The senator explained how valuable this kind of analysis is to him:

> [The researcher] took all his research and distilled it down to four or five points, the big picture points, that would be easy for me to sell somebody else. Well, maybe not easy, because it's a pretty tough thing we're doing here but … it would give people confidence to know that "No, this is not going to raise taxes and whatever."

After presenting these data, the researcher astutely asked the senator, "What do you think? Because here are some districts that would have to raise taxes." The senator looked at the data and asked the researcher to calculate what the achieve-ment levels were of the districts that would have to raise taxes. If these districts were achieving at an adequate level even though they were spending less per stu-dent, maybe the state should not ask them to spend more. The researcher offered to rerun his analysis to reflect the senator's suggestion. This kind of interaction between knowledge producers and consumers can help researchers become more policy sensitive and can help policymakers become more research sensitive. In the words of this Republican senator,

> That's the kind of thing that's really, really valuable because he's coming up with research ... saying, "I have a new way of doing something. And I am doing the research. It's research-based and I can justify it." And what really blows it over the top for me is that it's not just research in academia. He has gone out to school districts that have increased performance, and looked and said, "OK, you have increased performance out here. Are you doing those things that we're [recommending]?" ... and he's finding that they have. So it's not just research in the lab or in the classroom, it's practical application saying, "OK ... you can have confidence that if you do it as I say, it is improving education throughout the state of Wisconsin. You have to sell it." So it really helps us as legislators because it's sort of been field tested already, and we know it's not just something that's been done in the classroom.

From this example, it's obvious that these interactions between researchers and policymakers can be valuable to both parties, yet, based on our experience and that of others, they are rare (Jefferys et al., 2007; Levin, 1952/2005). One senator in a leadership position lamented that the university seems to be "isolated" and does not initiate contact with policymakers. To build more opportunities for such interactions between the inhabitants of the academy and the state house, several policymakers recommended that responsibility falls to academics to take the initiative to develop relationships with policymakers. According to a Republican legislator,

> I think if professionals are interested in giving us information, first of all, you've got to contact us and let us know what's going on, because we don't know who you are and we're not going to call you up. It doesn't happen too often I think, "Hey, is there anybody at the university doing research on this?"

A Democratic colleague concurred that these contacts were rare, even though the State Capitol was a short 20-minute walk and a local phone call from a major research university:

> I can think of a few times I went directly to the university, but a lot of times we use a screen ... someone to go for us or to interpret the information for us. ... I remember when AIDS was very big and there weren't a lot of people who knew things yet, I went directly to the university and got folks to give me some facts and information.

Some policymakers provided specific advice about ways in which professionals could initiate contact with them (see also Jefferys et al., 2007). Typically, policymakers advised us that developing relationships *with* policymakers should come before delivering recommendations *to* them. One legislator, who has risen to a leadership position in the Senate, explained that many of his colleagues view academics as "lefties that are not to be trusted," so it is important to first initiate contact in ways that can establish trust. Rather than starting out by saying, "Here's my research and here's what you should do," he recommended a more low-key approach of inviting policymakers to participate in a seminar, join a panel discussion, or speak in the classroom. Not only will these contacts enrich discussions and broaden exposure to politicians, he found that they sometimes lead to ongoing relationships. After establishing relationships with policymakers, he suggested asking them to introduce you to other elected officials. This senator said that he would be willing to make a phone call to recommend you to a colleague by saying, "He really knows his stuff and wants to share what he knows with you." If said in this way, the senator explained, it might have the potential to "create a more open mind" with his colleague.

Another senator, who had two preschoolers, recommended taking advantage of existing opportunities to get to know policymakers such as regularly scheduled listening sessions or office hours. She also advised establishing a relationship before making a request: "Don't load us up with information right away." Instead, just introduce yourself, explain your field of expertise, and make yourself available as a resource. Then later, you can explain that you have done some research and provide it to the policymakers with the "most important items highlighted."

A 25-year, award-winning legislator cautioned that persistence is very important. In her words, "If you care about an issue, you must follow up." She recommended working closely by the legislator's side through every meeting or hearing until the issue is resolved. On the basis of her experience working with academics, she warned against skipping events because you have a conflict, such as teaching a class. When the opposition is there, she emphasized how essential it is to be available to help respond to questions and explain the research findings in greater detail.

Concrete and Comprehensive Experiences

Clearly, the oral tradition is strong in legislative bodies, yet like other adult learners, legislators have different learning styles and prefer receiving information in different formats (Tough, 1971). For example, one 10-year veteran of the legislature, who was trained as a lawyer and is widely regarded for his intellect, recommended using a concrete, experiential approach. Using the example of the controversial issue of stem cell research, he recommended "taking legislators out to the lab because that's a hands-on, visual thing."

Senator Mark Miller, cochair of Wisconsin's powerful budget committee, underscored that the format he most prefers is contacting researchers directly. However, he used his experience with the Family Impact Seminars to emphasize the value of supplementing presentations by experts with information in a variety of formats:

> One of the things that the Family Impact Seminars does, is that it provides the information in a variety of formats. I know it's a lot of work doing the Family Impact Seminars, but it relates to the fact that we bring in information in different ways. And our staffs bring in information in different ways. Knowing that there is a booklet available online as well as a paper that has a summary of the presenters, oftentimes as an expansion of what the presenter presented, along with the bibliography. So there are additional resources that we can

access, or people who we can contact. We usually contact the researcher or the person directly as opposed to reading the research. It is available online. It is available as a paper document. I'm old enough where I'm reluctantly moving from paper to the electronic format. ... The seminars, not only the seminars, but also the breakout sessions or the brown-bag exchanges are very important. ... The newsletters, a multitude of ways of delivering information has proven useful. Just knowing that those Family Impact Seminar documents are out there is useful. I'll remember, "Didn't they do something about savings accounts a year and a half ago?" and I'll go and look it up. There's continuity with the organization, so I can go back and ask, "Who was that guy? Who was the one that talked about, such and such?" [The Seminars are] creating a very valuable resource for legislators.

Opportunities to Discuss Issues With Colleagues

Perhaps one of the most surprising findings in our work with state legislators is that they have few opportunities to become acquainted with each other, particularly their colleagues on the other side of the aisle. A Democratic senator in a leadership position lamented the lack of opportunity to engage in any serious discussion of issues: "When we discuss on the floor, it is just scoring points, not discussion." A Republican colleague concurred:

> In hearings, you may have a set limit of 5 minutes to testify and oftentimes a brief opportunity for questions. That doesn't lead to the kind of engagement that you want to have with legislators or with the experts that have been brought forward.

Policymakers explained the value of opportunities to discuss issues, citing their experience with the Family Impact Seminars, which provide an opportunity for some of the state's most liberal and conservative legislators, who often oppose each other on issues, to sit down and discuss policy alternatives. A Democratic senator explained that the seminar discussion sessions allow him to reliably assess what the "temperature is" for moving forward on an issue or whether his colleagues already have their minds made up and their words are no more than "conventional speak." Referring to the discussions with Seminar speakers and his colleagues, the senator underscored the value of being able to dialogue with his colleagues:

> I have learned more about the thought processes of my colleagues on that issue as a result of that kind of a conversation. And I found out that "Oh, here is a Republican that I had no idea was concerned and thoughtful about this particular issue," and that has created that spark for ongoing dialogue. That's a very important piece—to create that environment where we have the freedom to be able to discuss in an open and concrete way with people that can provide expertise and answer our questions.

However, state policymakers were not providing a carte blanche endorsement of all discussion opportunities but clarified that their value depends on the context in which they were held, what kind of information was made available, and who the participants were.

The context in which discussions occur. Some policymakers emphasized that it is important that discussions occur in a setting outside the typically contentious policymaking environment in which they usually operate. One senator explained that he is continually being bombarded by lobbyists who want to accomplish something, so he always has to have his defenses up. What is highly valued is having an opportunity to discuss issues outside the glare of the media and without the posturing of lobbyists. One legislator relayed that she asked a pointed question at a national meeting where lobbyists were present; as a result, the lobbying organization wrote a letter to the editor in a newspaper in her district criticizing the legislator's position. Policymakers pointed out that they have plenty of opportunities to talk with lobbyists, but few opportunities to discuss issues in a neutral, nonpartisan setting.

This same point was made by policy analyst Jere Bauer Jr., who has worked with policymakers for 22 years in a nonpartisan legislative service agency supporting the Wisconsin legislature. He characterized the discussion sessions sponsored by the Family Impact Seminars as an even playing field that is quite different from the environment of a committee hearing:

> It gives the legislators in the seminars a chance to interact with colleagues, which they get to do in a committee situation, but then there's always a hierarchy that's involved of the minority and majority party. They're meeting specifically to discuss a bill or a rule that needs to be addressed. Here you are meeting on a topic, but there's no one particular party or particular individual who is in charge of that. So everybody is an absolute equal. There's no majority or minority party there.

The kind of information made available. One legislator explained that he liked the Family Impact Seminar discussion sessions better than committee hearings because it allowed an opportunity to discuss any policy option, not just those included in the bills the committee is considering. A Republican senator explained that what he likes best about the research presented at the seminars is that it brings us "the facts." As explained by a Democratic legislator, factual data are particularly useful for forming partnerships with Republican colleagues because they provide a common frame of reference and carry no "partisan" baggage. Similarly, a member of Congress explained how research-based information can defuse divisiveness. In his words, "Rhetoric flows far more freely in the absence of factual information" (Miller, 1996, p. 339).

Who participates in the discussion. Seminar discussion sessions get rave reviews because they provide a venue for dialoguing about issues beyond one's own party and circle of contacts. Legislators explain that the discussions following the seminars allow them to identify other people who they did not know were interested in the issue and could become potential allies. This is particularly important for those in the minority party, who often must partner with someone in the majority party to have any chance of moving an issue forward. Daniel Vrakas, a former Republican

Assembly Caucus Chair, agreed that the discussion sessions have the potential to build consensus by bringing together legislators with vastly different viewpoints:

> They're valuable from the standpoint of the legislators getting to really have a one-on-one discussion with the presenters. But the other value that they bring I think is the legislators getting to familiarize themselves and become comfortable, in an informal setting, with themselves; because at the end of the day, it's not the experts that actually pass the legislation. At the end of the day, it's the legislators. And so this ability to bring legislators together that, frankly, have a very different viewpoint. ... And out of that discussion and out of the widely opposing viewpoints on how to solve a problem can come the middle area that we all know we try to achieve in government and move forward. So I think the dialogue that is created between legislators is very valuable.

Increasing importance of discussion opportunities. Opportunities to engage in informal interaction may be more important now than ever before for both state and national policymakers. Nationally, policy think tanks have become a growth industry, and the "marketplace of ideas" has become overly congested (Smith, 1991). In the 1990s, there were an estimated 100 policy research groups in Washington, DC, with nearly two thirds of them established after 1970. At the turn of the 20th century, these organizations published only 6,000 books annually, but today the number has reached 60,000. This monumental rise in both the production and the purveyors of policy ideas from both the right and the left has led political observers to conclude that the most valuable work may no longer be to generate new policy ideas but rather to "create a space for talk and discussion outside the contested turf of bureaucratic and partisan warfare" (p. 212). A member of a National Academy of Sciences panel made a similar observation:

> In the old days ... they used to have what they called *white papers* [italics added]. An issue would come up, the government would produce a white paper, and this would be the distillation of the best thought on this topic. There would be today a thousand white papers or their equivalent on any particular issue if it was controversial and meaningful. And each of those white papers would have its own outlets and ways of diffusing out into the public conscious and try to shape that policy discourse. So what decision makers really need now is a way to find safety in a place, kind of a private space in which they really can think about things and get good information that's given to them in a reasonable way because the rest of their world is just really crowded. It's overly crowded. So finding that place, that space, that venue in which you really can think about things and get information that's been kind of distilled without being agenda-driven, that's enormously valuable ... because it's a place where they can feel safe and talk about things with people that they trust.

At the state level, legislators also conclude that opportunities for dialogue may recently have ascended in importance, but for an additional reason. They report that the need for opportunities for informal interaction with their colleagues coincides with the advent of tougher ethics laws. Previously, lobbyists, political action committees, and special interest groups would sponsor receptions, picnics, and other informal gatherings that provided them opportunities to socialize with their colleagues, particularly members of the opposition party; however, as ethical restrictions have tightened, opportunities for discussion have declined precipitously even though the valuable role they play in policymaking has remained constant.

SUMMARY

The efforts of knowledge producers to build greater respect for and use of research in policymaking depends on several factors, one being whether policymakers are interested in research and whether they ever use it in their decisions. Based on our experience, efforts to increase the use of research in policymaking have been plagued by what we think of as the *Cinderella Complex*. Some researchers expect too much and become discouraged and drop out when research is not the final arbiter of policy decisions (Levin, 1952/2005). Some expect too little, what we think of as the *Scrooge Complex*. They drop out before they get started in the face of a "thin" body of evidence about the value of an evidence-based approach to public policymaking (Nutley et al., 2007, p. 2). We think the truth lies somewhere in between—research has the potential to influence some policy decisions some of the time, although most of the time that potential is unrealized.

The role of research in the policymaking culture formed the basis of the conversations with policymakers reported in this chapter. We heard "straight from the horse's mouth" that policymakers believe that research can be useful and the reasons they rely on it to guide policy decisions—sometimes for policy purposes (to help make good policy decisions and avoid making bad ones) and sometimes for political purposes (to earn the respect of colleagues and constituents, and to build support for legislation they want to pass). To determine whether research will be useful for these purposes, policymakers appear to process information through three filters: a credibility test, an accessibility test, and a timeliness test. Extrapolating from these findings, although cautiously, it appears that when research is able to meet all three tests—when high-quality and objective research is presented on a timely basis in a brief, understandable format—it is more likely that research will be perceived as useful in policy discourse and decisions.

The channels through which policymakers access research and analysis can be informative to would-be knowledge brokers in two major ways. First, the most time-efficient way to channel information to policymakers may be to work through the sources that they already turn to and rely on. Yet some knowledge producers have been effective in achieving access by taking the necessary steps to make contact, develop relationships, and present information in ways so useful that they become one of the resource people that policymakers use. For those interested in ratcheting up the use of research in policymaking, the take-home messages of this chapter are capsulized in Key Concepts 2.1. In Chapter 9, we discuss in more detail what steps knowledge producers have taken to build relationships and establish themselves as trustworthy sources of objective and nonpartisan information.

Key Concepts 2.1   Policymakers' Use of Evidence: Why, What, Where, and How

Why Are Policymakers Interested in Evidence?
- To help make good decisions
- To help avoid making bad decisions
- To earn the respect of colleagues and constituents
- To build support for legislation they want to pass

What Tests Must Evidence Pass to Be Useful to Policymakers?
- Credibility (high scientific quality, unbiased)
- Accessibility (brief summaries, understandably written)
- Timeliness (available when decisions are made)

What Kinds of Information Are Useful to Policymakers?
- A personal story from a constituent about how the policy affected him or her
- Information on how to adapt policies or programs to local circumstances
- An overview of findings from several research studies
- Information on how policies in the policymaker's jurisdiction compare to policies in other jurisdictions

Where Are the First Places That Policymakers Go to Get Information?
- Nonpartisan legislative service agencies
- Legislative colleagues
- State advocacy-oriented councils and organizations

How Do Policymakers Like to Get Information?
- Presentations or seminars
- Opportunities to interact with experts
- Concrete and comprehensive experiences
- Opportunities to discuss issues with colleagues (particularly discussions of factual information with policymakers beyond their own party in a setting outside the contentious political environment)

Second, one clear message emerging from these conversations is that policymakers are "people-people" who pride themselves on their ability to read people and who operate in an institution with a strong oral tradition (Bimber, 1996). It should come as no surprise that policymakers prefer to receive information in a seminar format that provides opportunities for interaction and discussion with colleagues in a neutral, nonpartisan setting that allows examination of a range of policy options. What's more, policymakers' "people" perspective also permeates their information preferences, as evidenced by the high priority that they place on personal stories from a constituent about how the policy affected him or her.

We make no claims that the policymakers whom we interviewed are a representative sample. Our respondents, in fact, are likely to reflect that segment of elected officials with a more active interest in research. Consequently, we supplement our interviews with studies from a number of disciplines in which research utilization is examined encompassing a wide range of settings where research has been used. The data derive primarily from state policymakers who may differ in unknown ways from policymakers in other jurisdictions. Yet others who reviewed the literature have suggested that the forces that shape research use at the local level are often similar to those among national policymakers (Nutley et al., 2007).

We began this chapter by portraying research utilization as a two-pronged process—encouraging policymakers to become more research-minded and researchers to become more policy-minded. Policymakers tell us that they are interested in receiving information if the right kind of information is provided at the right time in the right format. Now we turn to a discussion of whether researchers can provide the right kind of information at the right time in the right way.

3

When Researchers Delivered
Evidence to Policymakers

Scholarship for the sake of the scholar is refined selfishness. Scholarship for the sake of the state and the people is refined patriotism.

—**Thomas Chamberlin (1890, p. 9)**

But the Wisconsin tradition meant more than a simple belief in people. It also meant a faith in the application of intelligence and reason to the problems of society. It meant a deep conviction that the role of government was not to stumble along like a drunkard in the dark, but to light its way by the best torches of knowledge and understanding it could find.

—**Adlai Stevenson (as cited in Jack Stark, 1995, p. 101)**

This chapter touches upon what the past suggests for the future. As we begin to think about developing a strategic vision for the future of evidence-based policymaking, we turn our attention to earlier efforts to wed research and policy. What we think of as innovative is, in reality, seldom very original. In many cases, it builds upon what has gone before. The trick of contemporary innovative thought is to select the best threads of earlier work and to make sure that we do not lose any insights that might be gleaned from such efforts. Given this, we also look to the past for a foundation upon which to erect the architecture for the future.

We focus our historical exploration by discussing a concept known simply as the *Wisconsin Idea,* a principle that one anonymous writer in the 1930s summarized as "the boundaries of the university are the boundaries of the state." Theodore Roosevelt, as he accepted the presidential nomination in 1912, observed that "the University of Wisconsin has been more influential than any other agency in making Wisconsin what it has become, a laboratory for wise social and industrial experiments in the betterment of conditions" (Roosevelt, 1912, para. 41). A progressive Republican, Roosevelt embraced the notion of proactive government, of professional governance, as a way both to mute the excesses of what he saw as corporate greed and to ensure that all citizens could fully participate in the American dream.

This chapter ultimately is about relationships and the role they play in bringing research to public policy. If there is one insight that is repeated endlessly in this and subsequent chapters, it is that policymakers respond to people they know and trust. Those doing public policy are extraordinarily busy people. They might recognize the virtues of rigorous analysis, but they typically are balancing many sources of input as they make difficult choices replete with complex trade-offs. The vehicles through which most policymakers are exposed to research are critical to whether the information is heard and used. Therefore, we also examine two such vehicles, both administered through the University of Wisconsin and, thus, are expressions of the Wisconsin Idea. Both suggest lessons for the future. The first, the Family Impact Seminars, focuses primarily but not exclusively on state legislators, and the second, the Welfare Peer Assistance Network, focused on state executive agency officials.

THE WISCONSIN IDEA

In the late 19th and early 20th centuries, a set of working relationships developed between faculty at the University of Wisconsin and state policymakers. These relationships did not happen overnight. It is not even clear that the main actors were totally conscious that they were erecting a legacy. Still, by 1912, a vague concept known as the *Wisconsin Idea* had already taken shape. In the mid-1990s, Jack Stark (1995, p. 102) defined the Wisconsin Idea in this way:

> I propose to define the Wisconsin Idea as the University's direct contributions to the state: to the government in the forms of serving in office, offering advice about public policy, providing information and exercising technical skill, and to the citizens in the forms of doing research directed at solving problems that are important to the state and conducting outreach activities.

From its earliest inception, however, the vision behind the Wisconsin Idea was clear—that a public university had a responsibility to contribute to the public good. That basic concept remains alive today, a century later. A recent annual report of the University of Wisconsin Foundation bears the title *The Wisconsin Idea Thrives*. Among other things, the report provides a Web address where a number of state–university partnerships are outlined. Most of these contemporary partnerships focus on the hard sciences where, with some exceptions, value conflicts are few and the economic benefits to the state are likely to be significant.

What is most intriguing about the earlier evolution of the Wisconsin Idea is that the policy foci of the concept's pioneers were often on social and governance reforms, initiatives that typically were fraught with ideological and partisan significance. These early issues encompassed innovations in taxation, protections for vulnerable workers, professionalization of government, and how the legislative process actually functioned. The 1910 Wisconsin Republican platform noted, "We are proud of the high eminence attained by our state university ... we commend its research work. ... We regard the University as the people's servant, carrying knowledge and assistance to the homes and farms and workplaces" (Stark, 1995, p. 112). It is hard to imagine such language in a current political platform. Just how did this Wisconsin Idea emerge and evolve?

The inception of the Wisconsin Idea can be traced to the earliest years of the university. One year after the university's founding in 1849, the Board of Regents created a Department of Practical Application of Science, announcing the following in 1850:

> Recently, it has been the policy of the Board to give greater prominence to those departments of instruction which more particularly relate to the practical industries of our state. Reference is made especially to the departments of agriculture and practical mechanics.

Over the next several decades, periodic agricultural crises motivated farmers to turn to the university for help. In response, a series of Agricultural Short Courses were developed, and an Agricultural Institute emerged. Individual members of the faculty performed a great deal of what later would be called *extension work*. During Thomas Chamberlin's tenure as president (1887–1892), Hiram Smith, who considered himself a "scientific farmer," expanded the farmers' institutes, and their state support grew substantially. Based on the agricultural example, a Mechanical Institute was also developed to help the state's fledgling industrial and manufacturing sectors.

The groundwork for further collaboration was set. Some observers also feel that the strong Germanic and Scandinavian influences that shaped Wisconsin's early character also helped bring to the state a tradition of proactive government and egalitarian ideals. It has also been argued that the university emerged at the time when the modern model of a research university was taking shape, with generous imports of ideas from Germanic schools. Whatever the role of such contextual factors, it is very likely that personalities and relationships played a salient role, particularly in moving the university toward a strong reformist social agenda.

Two key figures, Robert M. La Follette and Charles Van Hise, were both members of the University of Wisconsin's class of 1879. La Follette went on to become a nationally known political figure and champion of progressive reforms; the Public Policy School at Wisconsin is named after him. Van Hise went on to a distinguished academic career and served as university president (1903–1918) during the crucial period in which the Wisconsin Idea fully developed. La Follette was the first state-born governor of Wisconsin, and Van Hise was the first state-born University of Wisconsin president. They collaborated often over the years, particularly as La Follette initiated a series of reform ideas seeking to diminish the disproportionate influence of special interests over state government. His basic instinct to enfranchise the powerless corroborated the interests of faculty to professionalize and rationalize the way government functioned.

Many assign credit for the Wisconsin Idea to Charles McCarthy, who served as a scholar and fellow in the UW history department from 1899 to 1901, when he received his doctorate. Upon graduation, he found a position in state government from which he established a library for the state legislature, which eventually evolved into the Legislative Reference Bureau. He reacted negatively to the prevailing practice of relying upon corporate lawyers and their lobbyists to draft legislation. Over time, he nudged lawmakers to use professionals attached to this legislative library for this bill-drafting function. His natural ties to the university also enabled him to tap the expertise available on the other end of State Street, which connects the capitol to the university campus. According to Robert Haveman (2008), McCarthy "developed an impressive information system about legislation and social issues and became known for his professionalism and integrity in drafting bills" (p. 3). The Wisconsin Idea was quickly maturing.

For most of the 20th century, the reformist spirit of the Wisconsin Idea was lodged in the economics department, which became a more or less autonomous academic unit in 1900. Over the next century, that department was to develop, retain, or recruit a remarkable number of scholars and reformers. Over the first half of the 20th century, the department tended to retain its own talent, hiring a number of its best PhD graduates, which provided continuity to the principle of public service embraced by institutional economics. One of the first of these reformers was John R. Commons, who joined the faculty in 1904. Far from a conventional scholar (he never completed his PhD at Johns Hopkins University), Commons was brimming with ideas, could inspire others, and was facile at what we would call today *lateral thinking* or seeing relationships across different social issues in creative ways.

A protégé of Commons, Edwin Witte (who, as discussed below, drafted the Social Security Act), praised his mentor as being an advocate of "institutional economics," that is, economics in action. This perspective, that scholarship in the service of real people and real problems was of the highest value, coincided perfectly with the emergence of the La Follette reform era in the state. Almost as soon as Commons had arrived on campus, La Follette recruited him to work on a civil service law and to help strengthen the Wisconsin Legislative Reference Library (later Bureau). The governor hoped to shift government positions from a patronage to a merit basis. He also wanted to eliminate a tradition whereby special interests drafted state laws because the technical capacity to draft complex laws did not exist within the legislature. Commons (1934) noted, "I now see that all of my devices and recommendations for legislation in the state or nation have turned on this assumption of a nonpartisan administration by specially qualified appointees" (p. 18).

A few years later, on the basis of work done for the City of Milwaukee, Commons and McCarthy turned their attention to the issue of employee safety. Out of this came one of the first industrial commissions in the country that focused on worker safety issues. This presaged the Occupational Safety and Health Administration (OSHA) by some seven decades and still exists today in the form of the Wisconsin Department of Workforce Development. The contributions of some of these key reformers are summarized in Key Concepts 3.1.

Key Concepts 3.1   Selected Contributors to the Wisconsin Idea

---

Charles Van Hise and Robert La Follette—UW classmates in 1879
- Van Hise was UW president during the development of the Wisconsin Idea.
- La Follette served as a progressive governor and U.S. senator during the developmental period.

Charles McCarthy—UW history scholar and key state innovator
- McCarthy created what became the Legislative Reference Bureau that weaned power away from special interests.

John R. Commons—UW economist during early decades of the 20th century
- Commons developed the concept of "institutional economics" or economics in action.
- He supervised many PhD students who contributed to the Wisconsin Idea.
- He suggested numerous reforms for Wisconsin across several decades.

Edwin Witte—Commons's protégé and economist at UW
- Witte supervised the drafting of the Social Security Act for President Franklin Delano Roosevelt.

Arthur Altmeyer, Robert Groves, and Wilbur Cohen—Protégés of Commons and Witte
- Altmeyer and Groves helped design the Social Security Act and other parts of the U.S. social safety net.
- Cohen was a major Washington figure on human service programs through the 1970s.

Robert Lampman—UW economist and member of President Kennedy's Council of Economic Advisors and protégé of Witte
- Lampman drafted a chapter of the report to the president largely thought of as a blueprint for President Johnson's "War on Poverty."
- He served as the first director of the Institute for Research on Poverty.

Robert Haveman, Irwin Garfinkel, Barbara Wolfe, and Sheldon Danziger—recent UW faculty, inspired by Lampman
- They contributed to social policy innovations in Wisconsin.
- Each served as the director of the Institute for Research on Poverty.
- Each was recognized as a major force in poverty research and policy development.

The first generation of reforms peaked in 1911–1912. With considerable input from university scholars, that session blazed the trail with a number of reforms, including the following: the first workers' compensation program in the nation, the first workable progressive income tax in the country, the Industrial Commission noted previously, a limitation on the working hours of women and children, a state life insurance program, and statewide coordination across agencies to enhance their efficiency through a Board of Public Affairs. A number of faculty members periodically moved back and forth from the campus to state government, helping to strengthen the Legislative Reference Bureau, among other things. For a time, evidence and analysis replaced power and self-interest in the making of public policy in Wisconsin.

In 1913, a law, based on Commons's analysis of wage boards in Australia and England, was passed creating a minimum wage concept for women and children. Though narrower than Commons had suggested, it became the first model for the minimum wage that was to become national law a few decades later. In 1930, working with Robert La Follette's son, Governor Phillip La Follette, Paul Rauschenbush and Commons worked on what would become another first in the progressive social agenda. Wisconsin enacted the first Unemployment Compensation Act in the nation.

At the onset of the Great Depression in the 1930s, the federal government had a minimalist role in managing the economy or mitigating the adverse effects of unfettered free markets. That salubrious role was left to states like Wisconsin, which employed the creativity and scholarship of its state university to develop models for a proactive government. The Wisconsin Idea in action was to blossom further as the federal government responded to the extreme economic distress of the 1930s and as that federal role evolved in subsequent decades. Moreover, the principles and values of institutional economics were passed down to succeeding generations of Wisconsin scholars. Let us briefly trace that narrative.

During his academic career at Wisconsin, Commons supervised 40% of the students awarded degrees in economics. One of his students was Edwin Witte. When Franklin Delano Roosevelt put together a Committee on Economic Security to respond to the challenges posed by the worldwide depression of the 1930s, he tapped Witte to come from his University of Wisconsin faculty position to chair the commission. Witte, drawing upon his experience with the Wisconsin Idea, was able to hit the ground running. Bringing in the expertise of Wisconsin colleagues such as Arthur Altmeyer and Harold Groves, he was able to develop the most ambitious set of social reforms in the history of the nation. Those reforms, encompassed in the Social Security Act that became law in the summer of 1935, forever transformed the federal government's relation to the economy.

Witte brought more than ideas to Washington; he also brought human capital. During his tenure as head of the Committee on Economic Security, he had one of his students, Wilbur Cohen, as an assistant. Cohen went on to a long, respected career as a policy analyst and leader in Washington, DC. Among his other positions, he served as head of the Social Security Administration and as secretary of what is now known as the Department of Health and Human Services under President Lyndon Johnson.

A generation later, Robert Lampman, also a student of Witte, was to make yet another salient contribution to the federal government's response to economic challenges. Lampman was a member of the Council of Economic Advisors under President John F. Kennedy in the early 1960s. He coauthored in 1963, along with

Burt Weisbrod, another UW economist, what became one of the most famous chapters ever prepared for the council's annual report to the president. Essentially, Lampman documented that although poverty was falling as the economy improved in the post–World War II era, this expanding economy would not "lift all boats" or guarantee the elimination of poverty. Rather, he argued that the "lifting all boats" metaphor had its limits—there would be pockets of structural poverty, groups that would remain poor even in the best of times by virtue of geographic isolation or very low human capital. For these target populations, direct interventions that focused on specific challenges would be necessary.

Not long after Lampman's chapter caught the attention of President Kennedy, the young president was assassinated. Johnson assumed office with a vague idea of picking up themes that had been circulating in Kennedy's inner circles, one of which was to do something about poverty. Lampman's analysis and research presented a rationale and template for federal action. In 1965, the "War on Poverty" was launched, and the Office of Economic Opportunity (OEO) was created to direct that war from the White House. The OEO staff quickly recognized that they were charged with an enormously ambitious agenda for which they had few intellectual resources at their command. Poverty had not been a seminal concern within the academic community, which meant there was precious little research to inform their plan. Lampman's chapter was a rare exception, but still a rather thin foundation on which to guide future strategies for such an ambitious national agenda.

In response, the OEO approached Lampman, who had returned to his University of Wisconsin faculty position, to see if Wisconsin would host a research institute that would focus on poverty. Lampman himself recalled that the university's reception to the idea of a poverty research think tank was less than enthusiastic. Barbara Newell, assistant to then-chancellor Robert Fleming, remembers that the pause in Wisconsin's response to the federal solicitation emerged from a need to reflect on how best to organize such a research entity. Newell recalled Fleming giving her the following challenge:

> Barbara, Wisconsin has a great tradition of policy analysis and government service. The Madison campus has an outstanding cadre of researchers dealing with welfare issues, each working in his/her own sphere. Yet, social problems do not fall neatly along disciplinary lines. Policy development and evaluation can only be effective if it is approached in a multidisciplined way. Let us see if we can bring faculty efforts together in a synergistic way. (Newall, 1990, p. 37)

After some further negotiation over academic freedom issues, the Institute for Research on Poverty (IRP) was launched in 1966 with Lampman serving as its first interim director. For over four decades, the IRP has continued to produce high-quality research.

The Wisconsin Idea story continues. For a period of time, the Institute was *the* place to be if you wanted to do poverty-related research. Moreover, poverty was a hot topic that was now attractive to a number of young academics. For a whole new generation of scholars—including Robert Haveman, Sheldon Danziger, Irwin Garfinkel, Robert Gottschalk, Robert Moffitt, Barbara Wolfe, and so many more—Robert Lampman was a father figure. He identified research questions, gently motivated researchers to pursue poverty-related work, and critiqued their work in his gentle and encouraging fashion. Tom recalls a memorial held at IRP to honor Lampman's legacy. On the elevator on the way to the event, he realized that he was riding with two Nobel Prize–winning economists—James Tobin and Robert Solow. Attending the memorial was a large portion of the national academic community then involved in poverty-related research. This was the Wisconsin Idea in action.

At the end of the 1970s, the Wisconsin State Legislature established a committee to look at the question of welfare reform. Once again, the state turned to the university for help. Tom, by then a PhD student in the School of Social Work, was drafted as a key staff member for the study. Robert Haveman, an economist and former IRP director, was tapped as the study director. Irwin Garfinkel, John Bishop, and several other IRP researchers also played salient roles in the committee's work. In January 1979, the final report of the Welfare Reform Study Committee was published (Wisconsin Department of Health and Social Services, 1979). Partly because the committee had access to some of the best researchers in the country, the report laid out a broad and ambitious reform agenda, calling for dramatic changes in the tax system, child support, workforce development, and the welfare system. Over time, several recommendations became state law, including a trailblazing, state-level, refundable, Earned Income Tax Credit and dramatic changes in the child support system (discussed in greater depth below). John Commons would have been proud.

Of course, not all narratives are linear. First, fewer and fewer academics attached to traditional disciplines are interested in doing applied work. The economics department at the University of Wisconsin–Madison, for example, no longer recruits faculty who might be interested in working on poverty-related issues. Like other top academic departments, it concentrates on theoretical work as opposed to real-world problems. Moreover, the Institute for Research on Poverty (IRP) has far less federal support for poverty research, an agenda that is no longer a public priority. Still, the work done at IRP remains first-rate and highly regarded on the national stage.

Second, the State of Wisconsin does not automatically turn to the university when confronting difficult policy challenges. This was never as true as when the State of Wisconsin embarked on a dramatic reform of welfare in the 1980s and early 1990s. The focus of reform shifted from simplifying administrative systems and developing reforms outside of traditional welfare to controlling the costs and perverse incentives of the welfare system itself.

After a number of incremental reforms in the late 1980s, Wisconsin was ready for dramatic change. Republican governor Tommy Thompson tapped a wellspring of popular support for transforming the very culture of welfare. Democrats, growing increasingly aware of how unpopular the cash welfare system had become, joined Republicans in calling for the elimination of the Aid to Families With Dependent Children (AFDC) program in 1993 and replacing it with some form of work-based alternative. Arguably, that kind of radical reform would demand innovative thinking and quality research, the kind of challenge that fit perfectly within the vision of the Wisconsin Idea.

Despite several overtures by IRP researchers to help the state in this endeavor, the Thompson administration went elsewhere for assistance. Lawrence Mead, in his book *Government Matters*, described this failure of the Wisconsin Idea at this critical juncture in the following way:

> The "Wisconsin Idea"—a close collaboration with the state university—had earlier been crucial to the state's leadership of national social policy. ... In the 1980s, experts from the university's Institute for Research on Poverty had conceived the state's pioneering child support reforms. On welfare reform, however, such a partnership was impossible ... most university academics opposed Tommy Thompson's conservative brand of reform. They shared his desire to raise work levels on welfare, but they opposed enforcing work as a condition of aid. This reflected not only their greater liberalism but their belief that barriers in society, such as lack of jobs or child care, largely accounted for low work levels and other difficulties among the poor. To the governor's team, however, mere conditions never could explain social problems. Such associations were "totally useless" for policymaking, said Jason Turner, a senior welfare official, because IRP would "infer causality where there was none." Rather, the administration blamed past failures on the permissive character of traditional welfare. So, the "Wisconsin Idea" was maintained, but the administration turned for advice to outside sources. (Mead, 2004, pp. 107–108)

Relationships between university academics and Wisconsin officials around social policy issues have improved in recent years. Still, a powerful lesson can be drawn from this brief, truncated history of the Wisconsin Idea. Academics and government officials can work together for the betterment of society. Such a collaborative arrangement does not necessarily come easily. As with any marriage, there can be periods of misunderstanding and mutual suspicion. This is a relationship that demands constant attention and care. Arguably, though, the effort is worth it. Looking carefully, one can trace the outlines of our contemporary social safety net (e.g., Social Security, workers' compensation, unemployment compensation, child support, etc.), along with other aspects of contemporary governance (the professional legislative support staff, the progressive income tax, the state Earned Income Tax Credit, etc.), in one way or another to the Wisconsin Idea.

MODELS FOR BRINGING RESEARCH TO THE POLICY PROCESS

We next turn to two initiatives that reflect the Wisconsin Idea. The first is the Family Impact Seminars series, and the second is the Welfare Peer Assistance Network (WELPAN). Both initiatives are liberally referenced throughout this work. Both were explicitly designed to bring quality input into the policymaking process. Both assumed that existing venues for bringing rational analysis to the policy process were inadequate. Both were based on developing relationships of trust as the necessary foundation for creating an environment where good research and analysis might matter. Both were clear expressions of the central tenet of the Wisconsin Idea—that research and policy were natural partners—though each model sought to cement that relationship in different ways.

Each model, in its own way, challenged a core assumption about how political and bureaucratic figures relate to data and knowledge. Bimber (1996) captured the conventional wisdom as follows:

> What is the nature of a politician's need for information? A simple assumption about the nature of politics itself is in order as a starting point. It should be assumed that politics is not a search for knowledge but a search for power. That is, the primary objective of politics is not the discovery of knowledge, but the instrumental use of knowledge, along with other resources, in the pursuit of various goals. (p. 21)

Each model contradicts this accepted wisdom by bringing high-quality research to policymakers and administrators. If you bring the information in the right way, they will listen, and they will listen with care and with considerable interest.

The two models differed in important respects as well. The seminars focused on state legislators, though other policymakers could participate. WELPAN focused on higher-level state welfare officials, or what we call executive agency staff. The Seminars focused on a broad range of substantive topics that affected family well-being, whereas WELPAN was narrower, focusing on welfare and related work-force development issues. The Seminars focused on bringing high-quality research to its target audience, whereas WELPAN balanced that objective with the goal of providing a venue for welfare officials to interact with their peers. The Seminar series, though each individual program is state specific, is becoming a national initiative through the Policy Institute for Family Impact Seminars. WELPAN was always conceived as a regional model. Let us look at each model individually and then seek to enumerate the common lessons, insights, and challenges:

The Family Impact Seminar Concept

The Seminar concept was the brainchild of Theodora Ooms. Working in Washington, DC, in the 1970s, she was concerned that the impacts of policies and programs on families did not receive the same attention as impacts on the environment, the economy, or poverty. She also thought that ideas could be powerful political tools and that research could produce policy-relevant ideas. In 1976, Ooms developed the Family Impact Seminar concept to strengthen the connection between research and policymaking in Washington, DC. For about two decades, she organized Seminars in the nation's capitol to bring the best available research to bear on current policy questions in ways that illuminated their relevance and effects on families. The core elements of the model were short, punchy presentations by researchers; very careful vetting of presenters for quality and objectivity; time for interaction between the audience and the researchers; and a succinct and comprehensible briefing report that audience members could take with them. Most of all, Ooms worked hard to be as nonpartisan and objective as possible.

By the early 1990s, it was clear that devolution was pushing more and more policymaking to the states. In response, Ooms reached out to replicate the Seminar model in several states. She and Susan Golonka, now at the National Governors Association, tapped Karen to organize the Seminars in Wisconsin. The rest, as they say, is history. Since 1993, Karen has organized some 28 seminars on a variety of family-focused topics. Of the 132 legislators currently in office, 74 have attended at least one seminar, and another 27 have sent an aide, so the Family Impact Seminars have reached over three quarters of those in the 2009–2010 legislative session. All of the seminars have received very high ratings for objectivity and balance. As one state legislator noted, "The ability to present and prepare unbiased research based on objective analysis and without political taint is truly refreshing." They remain as popular as ever.

When Ooms moved on to other challenges in 1999, she selected Karen to continue the mission of promoting a family impact perspective in policies and programs. Karen organized the national Policy Institute for Family Impact Seminars in 1999 and focused more explicitly on spreading the Seminar model among the states. Currently, the Institute provides technical assistance and training to some 28 states that are conducting, or planning to conduct, Family Impact Seminars. The Institute has organized its work around the following purposes:

- To assist policymakers, the Institute disseminates research and policy reports that provide a family impact perspective on current policy issues.
- To assist professionals who want to create a better dialogue between researchers and policymakers, the Institute provides technical assistance on what it takes to connect with policymakers and how to establish Family Impact Seminars in their own state.
- To assist those who enact and implement policies and programs, the Institute provides procedures for conducting a family impact analysis and a number of checklists for examining how responsive policies, programs, and institutions are to family well-being.
- To assist those who work with policymakers, the Institute conducts original research with policymakers on how they use research in their decisions and with professionals on what knowledge, skills, and attitudes are needed to communicate timely, high-quality information to policymakers in an accessible format.

Today, the Seminars target a variety of state-level policymakers including legislators, legislative aides, governor's office staff, legislative service agency staff, and agency representatives. The traditional seminar process begins with a 2-hour event that consists of two or three presentations given by a panel of premier researchers, program directors, and policy analysts. Each seminar is accompanied by a briefing report that summarizes high-quality research on the topic and draws implications for families and for state policy.

The discussion sessions that follow provide a neutral, nonpartisan setting outside the political environment for policymakers to discuss issues and seek common ground. A working lunch is scheduled where only legislators meet with the panelists and engage in a deeper dialogue in a comfortable environment. An invitation-only discussion session for the heads and top administrators of the relevant state agencies allows an examination of how the research presented at the seminar applies to Wisconsin and what the next steps might be. In addition, one-on-one sessions are scheduled with key legislators, top agency officials, or even the governor. Policymakers are also encouraged to directly contact researchers for additional input. CDs of each seminar are made available so that legislators can listen as they drive back and forth from their districts to the state capitol. Finally, a high-quality Web site makes available audio of the speaker presentations, over 130 briefing reports written specifically for state policymakers, family data, family impact checklists, and additional sources of policy-relevant research and analysis (see www.familyimpactseminars.org).

Of course, there are critical attributes of the Seminar concept that are not as visible. Looking closer at the Wisconsin Seminars as an example, we see the following: Karen works closely with legislative leadership on both sides of the aisle. She selects only those seminar topics that her legislative advisors want and believe will benefit from research-based information. She works tirelessly to find respected researchers or analysts who use rigorous methods, are objective, and communicate well. Finding someone who meets these criteria is not always easy. She works with speakers to make their presentations succinct and comprehensible with less focus on methods and more focus on policy relevance. Finally, she works with the experts to write briefing reports that policymakers (or at least their aides) might actually be tempted to read.

Amazingly, the model works. It brings research to a target audience we ordinarily dismiss as being driven disproportionately by power and vested interests. Take, for example, one seminar planned at a time when legislators were hearing a ground swell of concern from families about how rising health care costs were affecting access to and affordability of health care. In particular, small employers were facing sticker shock at the cost of providing health care for their employees. One policy option that was under consideration, employer purchasing pools, was identified by Family Impact Seminars advisors (i.e., 10 legislators and 1 governor's office staffer) as the issue most likely to be debated and acted on in that session. Wisconsin already had legislation on the books (although it had never been implemented) to establish employer purchasing pools for small businesses (i.e., grouping small employers into a larger group to spread risk and offer a larger choice of benefits with more stable rates). At a seminar planning meeting, which included several experts on the issue, one state agency staffer revealed that they had commissioned a study on the feasibility of setting up employer purchasing pools in the state. They agreed to release their findings through the seminar and an accompanying briefing report.

The seminar attracted 110 participants, including 28 legislators and 35 legislative aides. An additional 5 legislators attended a luncheon discussion with the speakers, bringing the total to 33. During the day's activities, 59 legislative offices were represented. Another 15 ordered copies of the briefing report or an audiotape of the seminar, which meant this seminar reached 74 legislators and their staff— over half of the offices in the Wisconsin legislature.

As part of the day's activities, the governor's top health care advisor asked for a special 1-hour meeting with two seminar speakers and two high-ranking state agency officials. In this meeting, he relayed that he needed four pieces of information in 5 days to put before the governor for possible inclusion in his state budget proposal. After an hour, he asked that the meeting be extended, but 15 legislators were waiting to meet with the speakers. After the 75 minutes allotted for the legislative discussion, the chair of the Assembly Health Committee asked if the discussion could continue, because state legislators so seldom have the opportunity to talk with experts, especially those from out-of-state who have no vested interest in what happens in Wisconsin. However, 20 high-ranking state agency officials were waiting to meet with the speakers. The state agency discussion session was organized around the four questions that the governor's advisor had raised earlier. After the scheduled 90 minutes, the state secretary in attendance asked what time the speakers were flying out and whether the meeting could be extended another 30 minutes.

Seminar speakers reviewed research that voluntary, unsubsidized insurance pools have little or no effect on health insurance costs or coverage rates. Consistent with this research, no further legislation was passed, and the legislation on the books was not implemented.

The shocking conclusion is simple. Legislators will pay attention to research if it hits the right topic in the right way at the right time (see more Seminar evaluation data in Chapter 11).

The Welfare Peer Assistance Network (WELPAN) Concept

As noted earlier, the WELPAN model differs in several important ways—target audience, subject matter, protocols, and even purpose. Still, the model proved to be an effective strategy for bringing research and analysis to its target population of interest, career state welfare officials. Let us start with the origins of WELPAN.

The WELPAN model, like the Family Impact Seminars, also can be traced back to Washington, DC, though in a very indirect way. The first inkling of the power of peer interaction occurred when Tom was at the Department of Health and Human Services in 1993–1994 working on President Bill Clinton's first welfare reform bill. A few weeks after arriving in Washington from his academic post at Wisconsin, he came to a not-so-original conclusion—Washington was rather isolated from the real world. To create a countermeasure to this isolation, he conceived of a series of seminars where representatives from some of the best local welfare reform initiatives around the country would be brought in to interact with federal staff laboring away to put a national reform plan together. With just a touch of humor, he called the seminar series "bringing the real world to Washington."

The first seminar brought officials from highly successful work-oriented welfare reform initiatives in Kenosha, Wisconsin, and Riverside, California, along with a teen pregnancy program operating in Pennsylvania suggested by Rebecca Maynard, another academic on loan to the Department of Health and Human

Services to work on the bill. On the day of the seminar, at the last moment and almost on a whim, Tom decided on a different format than just having the local officials present their models to a federal audience that was used to show-and-tell presentations. Instead, he put the local program officials around a table and situated the federal officials around the periphery of the room. The "panelists" would talk to one another, prompted by a series of questions. The federal "audience" would then have a chance to interact after the initial, within-panel dialogue.

As the morning unfolded, a funny thing happened. The so-called panelists seemed to forget about the audience of federal officials. They fed off one another, becoming more insightful and honest than ever would have been the case in a direct presentation of their model. They really talked with one another, seemingly forgetting about the audience. In doing so, they became more open, touching on failures and challenges rather than merely glorifying successes. What emerged was a dialogue that went to a deeper understanding of what they were doing and why. It is not totally clear whether the federal audience was better informed at the end of the session, yet what did become clear is that the panelists began to bond with one another in a visible way generated, in part, by a set of understandings that only those who share in a common challenge can appreciate.

Tom tried the same format in a couple of other venues and experienced similar outcomes. One was a meeting in December 1995 on state-level indicators of children's well-being held at the National Academy of Sciences. A number of state officials from the Midwest attended. Toward the end of the session, the discussion turned to creating a regional network for following up on this discussion. Unmi Song from the Joyce Foundation attended this session. She raised the possibility with Tom that a similar network might be useful for welfare officials, given that welfare reform and employment issues were closer to the foundation's substantive focus.

Contextual forces also played a part in WELPAN's creation. It was increasingly apparent that devolution was driving the locus of policymaking in the welfare arena to the state level. Drawing on his experiences with peer panels, Tom wondered what would happen if he brought together senior welfare officials in a format that replicated the "bringing the real world to Washington" experience. With modest support from the Joyce Foundation, he brought in Theodora Ooms to help him organize the first meeting of welfare officials from seven Midwest states in October 1996. National welfare reform had just passed. As Theodora and Tom called around, there was little enthusiasm and a lot more of "Well, we are really busy but maybe a 1-day meeting." One state official responded by asserting that she was not interested in attending any meeting "where Wisconsin told everyone else how great they were." The Wisconsin invitee, in turn, was very cool to the idea, worrying that any event facilitated by IRP would have some kind of hidden liberal agenda. It was not an auspicious beginning (see Boehnen, Corbett, & Ooms, 1997, for further detail on the origins of and early thinking on WELPAN).

By the end of that 1-day meeting at the Joyce Foundation in Chicago, another strange occurrence took place. The attendees from the seven states (Illinois, Indiana, Iowa, Ohio, Michigan, Minnesota, and Wisconsin) had their appointment books out. As they struggled to find a date when they could meet again (they were in the midst of implementing national reform and were, in truth, very busy), one of them suggested that maybe they could all get together on a Saturday. Tom recalls sitting back in wonder—the magic had struck again.

What exactly is this peer experience? The premise of WELPAN is that horizontal communications, sharing among peers, is an invaluable source of innovation and improvement in social policy. This horizontal pattern of interaction arguably will replace top-down or vertical communication patterns where both policies and programs are essentially dictated from Washington. The traditional strength of WELPAN is that it provides a safe forum for public officials to dialogue about the programs and people for whom they bear some responsibility. Repeatedly, members stressed that WELPAN is one of the few opportunities they have to think strategically about the challenges they face, to vet research and analysis in productive ways, and to try new ideas and concepts out on their peers who face the same pressures and challenges. As Ann Sessoms, member from Minnesota, once asserted, "I never get a chance to really think about what we are doing until I get on the plane to come to these meetings."

In short, WELPAN is a member-driven network of senior welfare officials seeking better strategies for serving low-income families through

- *exchanging* creative ideas and effective strategies for designing, administering, and evaluating social welfare programs;
- *exploring* topics of common concern;
- *assessing* and *interpreting* high-quality research, analysis, and their collective experiences;
- *sharing* collective knowledge with policymakers and the general public; and
- *anticipating* emerging issues and *articulating* future directions of social welfare systems.

Over the years, the network members identified issues in need of in-depth discussion, analysis, and information gathering. They identified resources from the states, universities and evaluation firms, policy organizations and think tanks, national trade organizations, and other experts. They brought these resources in to examine their ideas and to vet the input through their collective expertise and experiences. Furthermore, the network synthesized these inputs, as filtered through the members' own experiences as senior welfare officials, into discussion papers, reports, and videos for use by member states, other public officials, or broader audiences. Finally, the network has used its internal learning opportunities and the products that have emerged to inform and influence debates on major policy decisions affecting low-income families.

Unlike the Seminar model, there was no one set of meeting protocols, though there were some predictable activities. A typical meeting was 2 days in length and held in the board room of the Joyce Foundation's Chicago-based offices. It starts with a "state roundup," where representatives from each state take about 20 minutes to share issues and activities in their states. This part of the session is for members only (other than IRP staff). Often, during the afternoon of the first day, outside experts have been invited to attend. These might include university researchers, program evaluators, policy and program experts, representatives from other jurisdictions and other branches of government, and so on. Adequate time is allowed to interact with the resource person and to vet their input among themselves.

The morning of the second day typically starts with a review and discussion of topics of interest to the network. Additional resource people might be invited, but often this day is reserved for members only. The members might dialogue further about the input from the first day, discuss research and analysis passed out in advance by IRP staff, or focus on issues that arose during the preceding day's discussion. The second day would also focus on consensus products being developed by the network (see www.irp.wisc.edu/initiatives/outreach/welpan.htm for a list of consensus products). Toward the end of the second day, the dialogue would transition toward planning for the future. WELPAN is a member-driven organization.

There were departures from this standard model. Some meetings were held in state capitals and typically involved field trips to examine state and local innovations. Some involved meetings in Washington, DC, and would focus on attempts to shape the national debate on selected topics. And some meetings were explicitly research-oriented or involved inviting numerous outsiders (e.g., local officials doing service integration).

No matter the variations in individual sessions, some principles were inviolate and core to WELPAN's success:

- First, the network was essentially owned by the members, who chose topics, approved all products issued in the name of WELPAN, and exercised control over which outsiders should attend meetings and when or how they can participate.
- Second, the network was structured to provide a safe place for members. What was said in WELPAN meetings stayed in the meetings, unless it was clearly for public consumption or corresponded to public positions taken by the group as a whole. Nothing was produced or disseminated unless all agreed. Even minutes, which were not publicly disseminated, were edited to omit sensitive statements.
- Third, the network provided a forum for thinking outside the box. It gave members an opportunity to actually reflect on what they were doing, really digest cutting-edge research and analysis, and think in a future-oriented way. As Sally Titus Cunningham, an early member of the network from Iowa, observed, WELPAN gave you "a chance to brainstorm, to be reflective, to problem solve ... that's the great practical use, to hear about particular strategies, operational issues that you can leverage into your thinking as you are developing your program."
- Fourth, the network provided a chance to bond. An electronic mailing list, maintained by IRP, enabled members to interact with each other outside of the meetings. The Joyce Foundation often noted that it was the most active Listserv in any of its projects. Members would often call one another for advice or to seek solace. Sometimes, most remarkably, some members asked if they could attend meetings after they had left their positions. This was true of Jean Rogers, the first Wisconsin representative,

who initially was antagonistic to WELPAN because she so distrusted IRP at that point.

- Fifth, the network was kept small, so everyone could sit around the table. This encouraged intimacy and sharing. On average, there were two representatives from each participating state.
- Finally, the network provided visibility to the participating states. The name WELPAN earned a certain cachet over time and was recognized by federal officials and others as an entity with something important to contribute.

Like the Family Impact Seminars, the WELPAN experiment was based on trust, on relationships. The members came to trust one another and to trust the facilitators. One of the members said at a meeting that Tom was a perfect facilitator, because he did not know anything. After the laughter died down, she clarified what she meant to say, which is that he had no observable agenda, that he was not pushing his own ideas or pet reforms (see Chapter 10 for a discussion of education versus advocacy approaches). The states represented very different values and approaches to their responsibilities, so common ground was not ensured. But the environment provided a place where real dialogue was possible, and members found that the common challenges were greater than their differences. And although bringing research to the members was not the priority of WELPAN, it proved to be a wonderful venue for doing just that. The members could interact fully with the researchers, play out the policy relevance of the research with their peers, and assess whether and how they might actually use the information. The reticence policymakers might have in interacting with knowledge producers lessened when they could vet research within a group process they had come to trust.

An independent review of WELPAN was conducted in 2001 about 5 years after the network had been launched. The positives, as gleaned from in-depth interviews with the members at that time, were described as follows (SAL, 2001, p. 13):

WELPAN provides an opportunity to share and gain practical knowledge regarding reform that can be transferred to other states. "Our welfare reform programs have been directly influenced by WELPAN meetings and discussions with other WELPAN members."

WELPAN facilitates strong relationships between state administrators, which allows for a higher level of access and information exchange between states than was possible before WELPAN. Many note that prior to WELPAN, it was very difficult to obtain information from other states, and therefore sharing from state to state was very modest. "The level of trust that leads to candid one-on-one discussions is invaluable."

WELPAN creates opportunities to step back from the details of day-to-day work and look at the big picture. WELPAN meetings allow members to regain perspective. "You get so caught up in dealing with the mechanics of welfare reform that you forget about the overall purpose of your work."

WELPAN facilitates access to very useful information and welfare reform professionals. "I truly believe that WELPAN gives us access to information that would be difficult, if not impossible, to access by ourselves."

WELPAN joins multiple voices into a single powerful voice. "There is strength in numbers, and so to the degree that WELPAN can have an impact on future policy and success for welfare reform, it is a good investment of time."

One would think that WELPAN would continue to be a success. At one time, three separate models were in operation. Besides the Midwest group, Barry Van Lare, with support from the Packard Foundation, organized a West Coast version called WestPAN. Richard Nathan and Tom Gais, operating out of the prestigious Rockefeller Institute of Government at SUNY–Albany, briefly organized a similar group of southern states. It was clear that the states participating in each of these networks saw the value of the network and wanted to continue. In response, Barry Van Lare, Tom Gais, and Tom Corbett banded together in an effort to secure broader foundation support for a set of regional networks. But the philanthropic community is too narrow and categorical in its approach to social issues. The typical response was as follows: We will fund a meeting on topic X or a glossy report on topic Y but not underwrite the processes through which to transform the way we normally do business.

It may well be that welfare was no longer a good organizing principle for the WELPAN network. Jennifer Noyes, who later cofacilitated WELPAN with Tom (and who was the final W-2 administrator under Governor Thompson), argues that the original WELPAN should have been transformed into a more vital network that focused on the integration of welfare, workforce development, and related human service systems. It is the peer assistance process that works, that kept officials coming back year after year when they had little time or energy for other meetings.

Common Issues, Insights, and Challenges

In summary, the utility of the Family Impact Seminars is without question. Repeatedly, legislative attendees remark that they find the seminars one of the only places to get good information and to talk to their colleagues from the other side of the aisle. Similarly, peer networks are attractive to executive agency officials. Otherwise, the Midwest network would not have sustained itself for a decade.

Though the Seminars and WELPAN are quite different in many key respects, they have some similarities that are quite striking:

- The target audience must run the show. They must select topics of interest and not merely be the audience for whatever is on the researcher's mind (or plate).
- Any research content brought to the table must be relevant and timely. These folks generally do not have the time to peruse research for the sake

of knowledge, but rather they use research for purposes instrumental to their professional roles.

- The venue through which research is brought to their attention must be seen as neutral, nonpartisan, and nonagenda driven. You will lose these audiences as soon as they smell a preconceived agenda, at least one that does not comport with their own.
- Research content must be delivered in a succinct, clear fashion. The language must be relatively free of jargon. The focus must be on policy relevance and not methodological sophistication, though methods are not irrelevant.
- There must be ample time for interaction with those presenting the materials. The policy audience must have a chance to explore the research in a nonthreatening manner with research purveyors who fully appreciate the difficulties of making and administering policy and the limitations their culture imposes on research use.
- The venue must be seen as a safe and nurturing place. Policymakers must feel they can speak out without fear that their comments will show up in the media or that they will be ridiculed for their lack of research sophistication. They must also feel they can stray from ideological or partisan orthodoxy in order to pursue new ideas or consider original ways for using the information.

Our overview of the Family Impact Seminars and WELPAN, two expressions of the Wisconsin Idea, also give us pause for reflection. Why has it been so difficult to secure financial support for these venues? Despite the track records of both endeavors, foundations and other funding sources are generally unresponsive to overtures to support mechanisms for bringing research to the policy table, particularly on issues that are not predetermined but rather bubble up from the policy audience and require response on a real-time basis. They would prefer to fund proposals that map neatly onto their application deadlines to prepare yet another glossy report telling officials what to do, which often goes unread, or another conference where experts "talk to" an audience in ways that are not very likely to elicit a response. If there is one thing the Wisconsin Idea, writ large, tells us, it is that we have to think hard and work hard on the human dimension of bridging the gap between those who produce knowledge and those who consume it. Productive relationships and deeply collaborative models are very possible; they are just not easy.

We do not argue that the Wisconsin Idea is the only model for a working relationship between the academy and the state. We do not argue that the Family Impact Seminars and WELPAN are the only, or even the best, venues for bringing research to the policy community. What we do argue is that all of us must spend as much time, energy, and resources in thinking about how we bring our research to the policy table as we do about creating that knowledge in the first instance. There is the old philosophical conundrum: Does the falling tree in the forest really create any sound if there is no one around to hear it crash? Well, has any knowledge really been created through policy-focused research that remains unknown within the policy community?

SUMMARY

The story of the Wisconsin Idea in the social policy arena is one that gives us a good deal to think about. There were periods of intense collaboration followed by periods of minimal interaction. At the same time, true collaborations have occurred periodically, with such intimacy between knowledge producers and knowledge consumers changing the world.

This brief historical tour suggests a challenge. Then–UW chancellor Fleming, at the very inception of the IRP in 1966, recognized that the relation between many social problems and the culture of a discipline-focused academy is problematic. Issues such as poverty or family policy clearly span several disciplines. At the same time, the institutional culture of research universities continues to encourage individual research (so that credit can be clearly attributed) and within-discipline scholarship. Wisconsin has tried to buck this trend in a number of ways, including the use of what are called cluster hires, or giving disciplinary departments hiring authority if the new hires are brought on board in a way that facilitates cross-disciplinary work. Confronting deeply entrenched cultural foundations, however, remains difficult.

In the next two chapters, we begin to erect a conceptual framework in which trust and relationships play an instrumental role. This theory is rooted in the concepts of *community* and *culture*. It stresses some simple propositions—that where we are located institutionally and how we are prepared professionally shape how we see the world and act in that world. If we understand these influences more deeply, we can begin the process of enhancing understanding and communication.

4

Who Are These Knowledge Producers and Knowledge Consumers Anyway?

Where shall wisdom be found?

—Job 12:28

Facts are stubborn things and whatever may be our wishes, our inclinations, or the dictates of our passion, they cannot alter the facts and evidence.

—John Adams (1735–1826)

*T*hroughout this book, we return to a single question: Why do knowledge producers and knowledge consumers have so much trouble communicating with one another? Presumably, each side has a stake in what the other does. Those doing public policy need research to ensure that their decisions are based, at least in part, on some kind of empirical foundation. At the same time, researchers can profit from knowing the kinds of management and theoretical uncertainties that confound policymakers. In theory at least, such feedback ought to serve as critical input as analysts refine existing research and as they formulate future agendas.

These mutually reinforcing needs seem to support a natural reciprocity between what Caplan (1979) termed "two communities theory" or what Shonkoff (2000) described as a "three-cultures" network. Reality, however, paints a very different picture. Researchers and policymakers do not easily interact. When they do, the quality of communication is often strained. Miscommunication and mistrust occur even during interactions entered into with the best of intentions. The parties appear to march to different drummers, speak distinct languages, and see the world through unique lenses.

In this chapter, we explore the institutional and professional foundations for why these two communities find it so difficult to relate to one another. We propose a conceptual framework in Chapter 5—the community dissonance theory—for thinking about how distinct subgroups in each community might view the world. Although any framework is simplistic, we hope our effort offers a starting point toward better understanding. Until we better appreciate the forces that separate and divide researchers and policymakers, we cannot effectively construct strategies for bringing them together.

EVOLUTION OF A THEORETICAL PERSPECTIVE

The theoretical roots for community dissonance theory and its various manifestations are drawn from C. P. Snow, who thought hard about the connection between science and government a half century ago. He captured the cultural differences between those who seek knowledge and those who use knowledge as follows:

> To be good, in his youth at least, a scientist has to think of one thing, deeply and obsessively, for a long time. An administrator has to think of a great many things, widely, in their interconnections, for a short time. There is a sharp difference in the intellectual and moral temperaments. (Snow, 1961, p. 72)

For Snow, this disconnect across communities was both palpable and substantive. As we look about the policy and research worlds, we come to a similar conclusion.

Bogenschneider and colleagues (Bogenschneider, Olson, Mills, & Linney, 2006) reviewed several theories proposed to explain the lack of communication between those who produce scientific knowledge and those using that knowledge for public policy purposes. One theory focuses on the nature of policymaking, contending that it is a fast-breaking, self-serving, influence-driven process incompatible with the methods of social science, which, in general, are more time intensive and reflective in character. Conversely, a second theory focuses on a perceived limitation of social science research. Many social scientists are quite conservative in disposition and, thus, often are unwilling to share their work given the reservations they harbor about the finality of their work and fears about using incomplete and imperfect information to guide policy decisions. A third theory contends that the underutilization of social science knowledge is an artifact of a democratic, free-market system that lacks formal institutional structures for facilitating the integration of knowledge and power.

Whereas each of these theories may have some validity, we are particularly struck by the possibilities inherent in a fourth theory, one that is anchored in the concept of *distinct communities* that too often reflect incompatible cultures. That is, in the theory's simplest form, the worlds of those who produce knowledge and who use knowledge are quite different. Members of those worlds see things differently and, therefore, act differently. And much like a fish that does not comprehend the water in which it exists (Doherty, 1999), members operating in each world may appreciate neither their own context nor the context of others with whom they are interacting. A synopsis of these major theoretical orientations can be found in Key Concepts 4.1

Key Concepts 4.1   Major Theoretical Explanations for the Underutilization of Research in Policymaking

---

- The Two Communities Theory (Caplan, 1979): The underutilization of science is attributed to limited understanding and communication between social scientists and policymakers. Each side is divided into its own "community."
- The Three Cultures Theory (Shonkoff, 2000): This theory focuses more on culture as opposed to Caplan's community, but it emphasizes similar factors that divide knowledge producers and consumers. The concept of knowledge consumers is expanded by distinguishing between policymakers and policy administrators.
- Elaborated Multi-Cultural Theory (Bogenschneider et al., 2006): This contribution expands our understanding of the dimensions along which members of each community or culture differ. Nine such dimensions are proposed in three categories—information needs, work culture, and writing preferences.
- Community Dissonance Theory: The theory proposed in the current book expands the notion of two communities to a number of community groupings where each is formed around a core technology that defines the tasks professionals perform as well as the institution's purpose, culture, and structure. Each of these communities, whether they be basic researchers, applied researchers, intermediaries, policy doers, or policymakers, is shaped by professional and institutional cultures in ways that differentially affect how their inhabitants think, act, and behave.

Caplan (1979) suggested that underutilization of social science research results from limited understanding and communication between social scientists and policymakers, each representing a distinct community. Each has different goals, information needs, values, reward systems, and languages. Social scientists generally conduct research for the sake of discovery, whereas policymakers utilize research for the purpose of developing pragmatic means of solving problems (Booth, 1988; Linquist, 1990; McCall, 1996).

Shonkoff (2000) proposed three distinct cultures, as opposed to communities, but his meaning is similar. On the knowledge-using side of the divide, he divided people into two subgroups—those who make policy and those who implement policies and programs. Bogenschneider and colleagues (2006) used group distinctions similar to those of Shonkoff—researchers, policymakers, and policy administrators. However, she did a more systematic job of laying out the behavioral and attitudinal consequences of belonging to one community as opposed to another. She organized nine consequences associated with community affiliation into three primary categories—information needs, work culture, and writing preferences—and then described how each group differs along three dimensions within each major category.

In some important ways, these community- and culture-based concepts are not distinct explanatory theories. Rather, they are an encompassing concept that blends a set of narrower explanations. Proponents of a community theory typically enumerate several obstacles to communication between researchers and policymakers. For example, social scientists employ increasingly complex methodological and statistical procedures, which are difficult to explain to lay audiences (Booth, 1988). Many researchers do not know how to present their findings in ways that might influence policy decisions (DeLeon, 1996; Scott, Mason, & Chapman, 1999). Instead, they generate lengthy research reports that contain discipline-specific language aimed at other scientists that is not readily understood by those outside of academia (Nelson, Roberts, Maederer, Wertheimer, & Johnson, 1987; Patton, 1997; Weiss, 1990; Weiss & Bucuvalas, 1980). This pattern of communication (or lack thereof) becomes self-perpetuating because translating research findings into accessible formats provides small payoffs and few short-term benefits in academic circles (Boyer, 1990; DeLeon, O'Keefe, VandenBos, & Kraut, 1996; Lynton & Elman, 1987; McCall, 1996).

The *two-communities* and *three-cultures* concepts hold promise, yet they still fall short in at least three ways. First, they divide the world into two or three groups—researchers and policymakers, or researchers, policy types, and practitioners. That categorization comports rather closely with our bisected world of knowledge producers and consumers. However, as we will elaborate, the real world is far more complicated. There are important subgroups in both the world that produces knowledge and the world that uses knowledge. We miss much by obscuring these very real distinctions.

Second, we must develop a richer understanding of such concepts as *community* and *culture*. We know from earlier studies that belonging to an institutional community shapes attitudes, behaviors, perceptions, and sense of self. For example, in policy settings (Caplan, Morrison, & Stambaugh, 1975; Mooney, 1992), the underutilization of research has been attributed to institutional obstacles such as political considerations, established patterns of information gathering (Webber, 1986), and the increased partisanship of state legislatures (Hird, 2005). Are these organizational influences the only forces at work? Just how strong are these influences, and how aware are members of each group of the forces that shape their world? In fact, where one works does not tell the whole story. The intellectual and social preparation that one absorbs through one's educational training also exerts a theoretically profound influence. In his examination of researchers and practitioners, Small (2005) ignored institutional culture and attributed miscommunication to professional socialization that dictates what ends social scientists seek, to whom they respond, how they work to achieve those ends, and what behaviors are considered appropriate. In this chapter, we propose focusing on both *institutional culture* and *professional culture*, because both are pervasive forces in shaping behaviors in the work world.

Third, recognizing the existence of distinct communities tells us little about how any adverse effects associated with these concepts of *professional* or *institutional culture* might be ameliorated. Although the culture in which one is immersed can be enriching, it also contains a downside. It can narrow the way in which individuals see the world and their professional role in that world. Possibilities are missed. Miscommunication and misunderstandings can arise. And such failures go unaddressed because those involved fail to see any other way of doing business.

In this chapter, we propose a theoretical construct labeled *community dissonance theory*, which expands on the conceptual frameworks of Caplan (1979), Shonkoff (2000), and the earlier work of Bogenschneider and colleagues (2006) in a number of ways. First, we start with clear definitions of several related, but distinct, constructs. Community dissonance theory attributes underutilization of research to a communication gap between knowledge producers and knowledge consumers who engage in different core technologies and function within a discrete number of disparate communities that make it difficult to communicate with each other. This communication breakdown occurs because each community operates within distinct professional and institutional cultures with different communication styles, decision-making criteria, questions of interest, reward systems, salient constituencies, and time frames. By community, we mean the group within which a professional most closely associates, which for our purposes includes an undifferentiated grouping of knowledge producers (i.e., researchers) and an undifferentiated grouping of knowledge users (e.g., policymakers). By culture, we mean a whole set of norms, values, reward systems, and operating protocols and premises that shape how people view their role in the world and inform how they act on a day-to-day basis.

Second, we briefly examine the related phenomenon of *institutional culture* to look for clues as to the importance of this concept in affecting how professionals think and behave. Then we introduce the notion of *professional culture* and suggest ways in which it might function differently from institutional culture. Third, we attempt to push thinking forward by addressing the theoretical shortcomings just noted.

STUMBLING ON THE IMPORTANCE OF "CULTURE" TO EXPLAIN COMMUNICATION BREAKDOWNS

Some two decades ago, Tom worked with a small team of academics consulting with officials from Kenosha County, Wisconsin, as they put together an innovative, integrated, human-service model. This effort first blended the then-cash-assistance program for poor families with children (Aid to Families With Dependent Children) with various programs drawn from the workforce development systems. As such, it represented one of the earliest attempts at systems integration by signaling that work was to be a truly integral part of any welfare reform strategy.

Despite the best efforts of the consulting academic team, which included well-known poverty scholars such as Lawrence Mead and Michael Wiseman, early efforts to blend agencies from the work and welfare worlds did not go well. Communications across these two systems (welfare and workforce development) largely failed, misunderstandings and mutual suspicions emerged, and collaborative activities sputtered amidst accusations of incompetence, if not willful sabotage. At one point, the local welfare officials simply stopped working with the local Private Industry Council (PIC), the entity having overall responsibility for overseeing work programs in the county. This rupture occurred despite apparent agreement on the intent and direction of the proposed reforms and despite requirements in the state laws that the PIC be a formal partner in pilot programs.

The local welfare officials persisted, however, and eventually did assemble a one-stop agency that fully blended the welfare and workforce development functions, an innovation that gained international fame and served as a model for many other sites in both the United States and abroad. But the consulting academics remained fascinated with the level of cross-system contention and conflict evidenced in the early going. The reality of doing systems integration appeared to be a lot more difficult than merely proposing it.

Upon reflection, they concluded that the interinstitutional friction observed might be attributable to what they termed, at the time, conflicted *institutional philosophies*. Briefly put, the welfare and workforce systems organized the world in different ways. They responded to different constituencies and stakeholders. They organized their tasks and activities around distinct missions. They defined success in separate ways. In short, each system's *raison d'être*, or reason for existence, made collaboration challenging. At the risk of oversimplification, the welfare system focused on the poor family and whether the family had sufficient economic resources. The workforce system typically concentrated on employers and on meeting their labor needs. The institutional antennae of these respective systems were simply not oriented on the same things. As a result, they viewed their professional worlds, and their place in those worlds, quite differently.

But the real problem back in the early days of the Kenosha experiment was not the differences between the two systems that were being nudged toward a form of institutional marriage. The real issue was that the planners and managers proposing the match were largely unaware of the depth, character, and intractability of conflicts that threatened this arranged programmatic marriage. Managers and workers from each system blamed their peers in the other system of duplicity, ignorance, or even worse sins. We had a ways to go before fully understanding that even well-intentioned policy entrepreneurs function within institutional cultures that shape how they view the world and their professional role in that world.

In the mid-1990s, we stumbled across another example of how powerful and pervasive these professional cultures are. We learned through trial and error that culture, much like an invasive species, infiltrates the kind of information each culture needs and the format it prefers. Karen was riding the wave of having planned six successful Family Impact Seminars for state policymakers on topics ranging from child support to welfare reform. When state legislators identified interest in a seminar on teenage pregnancy prevention, she turned to a recent meta-analysis of teenage pregnancy prevention programs that used rigorous program evaluation standards to identify five programs that were successful in delaying sexual involvement, increasing contraceptive use, or preventing teenage pregnancy. She persuaded the directors of two of these evidence-based programs to speak with state policymakers in the Family Impact Seminars venue. Given the stellar program and evaluation credentials of these speakers, she decided to expand the invitation list to include members of a state board that focused on the prevention of adolescent pregnancy. Many of these members were program directors and program managers that delivered prevention and intervention services to adolescents across the state.

In response to our coaching on how to tailor their message to a policymaking audience, the seminar speakers used clear and accessible language to describe their programs, weaving in an appropriate mix of program detail and policy implications. When the seminar evaluations were tallied, we were surprised to find the ratings were lower than usual. An enterprising graduate assistant reanalyzed the evaluations and noticed a bimodal pattern of results—some participants gave the seminar high marks and enthusiastic endorsements, but a sizeable number expressed disappointment and dissatisfaction. The evaluations divided along community lines. A state legislator offered the accolades we had come to expect: "Your format was excellent. I have very little free time to attend briefings, but can always work around an hour and a half briefing scheduled in advance."

In stark contrast, the program staff reported that the information was too superficial for their taste. They criticized the short length of the seminar and suggested that we plan conferences up to two days in length. In particular, they complained that we had attempted to do something that seemed impossible—bridging two disparate communities in the same setting. In the words of a program administrator, "Don't invite politicians and people who deal with the real world to the same seminar; they [politicians] deal more with unreal issues and are not reality-based."

The choice of words like "unreal" and "not reality-based" reveal the depth of the cultural divide. From the policymakers' perspective, the speakers had met their expectations for a brief overview of the field that provided state-of-the art evidence on whether a public investment was likely to pay off. However, from the vantage point of the program staff, the speakers had missed the mark by failing to detail what the program protocols were and which best practices the program needed to succeed—details essential for program replication and effective adaptation to local circumstances.

Our well-intentioned efforts to bring together two communities that share an interest in preventing teen pregnancy had backfired because of our misunderstanding of how the information needs of one community differed from those of the other. In hindsight, if we had been more culturally competent, we would have parlayed these differences in culture into differences in information packaging and delivery. This humbling experience taught us that there may be no such thing as a competent knowledge broker, broadly defined. Effective knowledge brokering is context specific, requiring an understanding of the culture out of which knowledge emerges and the culture toward which it is directed.

Examples abound of the disconnect between researchers and policymakers in our work at the intersection of the two cultures. For example, some researchers never even attempt to cross the divide, as exemplified by the Harvard-educated educational policy professor who worked at a major research university. He asked for advice on a presentation, confiding that over the past 20 years, he had frequently lectured to students on educational policy but had never addressed a group of policymakers. Others cross the great divide but fail to understand the culture on the other side. We think of the distinguished professor whose record of raising $40 million of research funding and earning several lifetime achievement awards made him a household name to anyone in his field. Following a seminar presentation interspersed with relevant research, appropriate humor, and concrete examples, he offered to give his opinion on the subject at hand in the Q & A portion of the program. To his dismay, not one policymaker asked what he thought they should do. What he failed to understand is that evidence would play a role in the policy decision (several policymakers noted in their evaluations that they would factor the evidence into their decision), but so would values. His values were no more important than those of policymakers and may have been less so; policymakers had been elected, in part, based on the values that they hold in common with their constituents—and he had not.

These vignettes exemplify what we learned back in the early days of the Kenosha effort to create the welfare-workforce development, one-stop agency outlined above. We stumbled on the concept of *institutional philosophy*, as we called it then. Later, we often referred to it as *institutional culture*. In 2004, Sandfort used the term "deep structure" of an organization to denote similar concepts. And by 2005, in a paper coauthored with James Dimas, James Fong, and Jennifer Noyes, Tom employed the term "institutional milieu."

By 2005, we had become convinced that this concept of *philosophy, culture*, or *milieu*—whatever it was to be called—was indeed a critical factor in doing service integration (delivering social services to families in a holistic, coordinated manner as opposed to distinct program silos). At the same time, this important notion of *institutional culture* remained poorly understood either by those doing integration or by those studying it. Still, it was clear that we had tapped into something fundamental. This became increasingly evident as we interacted with officials doing service integration in a variety of venues. Time and again, as we introduced the topic of institutional culture, they would affirm (typically with gusto) that this concept appeared to touch on the most problematic barrier to progress that they faced.

Exactly what does this concept of *culture* have to do with how we bring research to policymaking? It has quite a bit, actually. The role of institutional culture has become better understood over the past several decades. Based on our experience, it dramatically shapes the way public (and private) officials think and act. It shapes their worldview, their perception of self, how they relate to peers, and how they interact with customers and stakeholders.

At the same time, we introduced earlier another cultural influence over how individuals view themselves and others in the work world. We call this *professional culture*. For some, this concept of culture can precede the influence of institutional culture and can magnify, or confound, its effects. We flesh out both concepts below, starting with the institutional variant.

Exploring the Concept of Institutional Culture

We view institutional culture as located within a specific agency, program, or organization. Exactly what is institutional culture? Basically, the *culture* of an organization is a fancy term for the underlying values that inform the way it does business. These values, in turn, shape the way the agency functions and makes decisions.

What shapes an institution's culture? One major determinant is an organization's "core technology"—the core activities or functions performed by an agency or program. This notion first introduced by James Thompson (1967) over four decades ago is still useful today. For example, for policymakers, their core technology is to make laws, often using a sifting and winnowing process that tries to make sense of the multitude of ideas that are floated in the policymaking process. Policymakers seldom sit down and think up ideas themselves; instead, they find themselves in the position of evaluating the ideas that come to them from lobbyists, special interests, advocacy organizations, and constituents as well as from policy analysts, researchers, and think tanks who are all willing to tell them what needs to be done and how it could best be accomplished. Policymakers sort through these ideas, screen them for consistency with their constituency and ideology, and decide which of them are meritorious. Decisions on the merit of an idea are seldom static, however. Ideas are tugged at in the policy process, with policymakers forced to continually reassess when to compromise their initial position and when to hold firm.

Let us concretize this discussion with some examples. In the world of publicly provided human services, each program has a more or less distinctive core technology. Some programs essentially issue benefits (food stamps or child care subsidies). Such programs typically are highly routinized and associated with formal bureaucracies. Other programs deliver a routinized service (job club or job search assistance), but also contain service dimensions that require professional judgment and frontline discretion. We think of these as semiroutinized and their institutional environments as being less formal. Finally, we have programs that, for example, intervene in the lives of dysfunctional or challenged families to remedy problems or transform behaviors (e.g., family violence and child welfare issues). Such programs are fully nonroutinized. Here, typical institutional environments are open and characterized by a strong sense of professionalism, much discretion, and a bottoms-up management style. These style differences tell us a lot about what knowledge is sought, how aggressive the seeking is, and who does the searching.

Academic researchers, by definition, locate themselves in universities. As institutions, universities are slow to change. Edward Zigler (1998) noted the response of an acting president of Yale University when asked how Yale would fare during a period of rapid change in leadership. The president replied, "Yale had remained great for nearly 300 years not because it was resistant to change, but because it changed only one brick at a time" (p. 532). Ironically, academia is filled with structural and cultural rigidities, yet the day-to-day working environment is one of flexibility and creativity. Researchers essentially operate as academic entrepreneurs in environments of relatively little bureaucracy. They are rewarded for creative, independent thinking. Much of what shapes their behavior is drawn from the professional norms they bring to their positions.

Most of those administering public policy, those charged with turning policy concepts into actual programs, function in bureaucracies. They operate in institutional environments structured around rules and regulations. Public agencies tend to be hierarchical and rule-driven, conforming to the Weberian vision of bureau-cracies. The first inclination of bureaucratic officials is not a creative or indepen-dent response, as with academics, but rather a response that would be consistent with and acceptable to their superiors (Holzer, 2009). They are attentive more to treating clients uniformly and fairly than to being creative. As we suggest else-where, there are exceptions to the rule, depending on the core mission and tasks of each agency. Still, the general rule prevails; those administering policy enjoy less flexibility in the exercise of their professional roles. Karen has found that any report that a state bureaucrat wrote for policymakers had to be approved by those higher on the administrative food chain.

Policymakers fall somewhere between the institutional culture of the academy and that of bureaucracies. Using Congress as an example, Bimber (1996) explained that over the past 100 years, the institution has evolved from more centralization to less. Prior to 1910, power was consolidated in the speaker, but after the "Revolution of 1910," power flowed downward to the committee. In the 1970s, power devolved further from committees to subcommittees. However, the power hierarchy in legislative bodies is not static, as exemplified by the case of the 104th Congress when power reverted to Speaker Newt Gingrich. The committee structure of most legislative bodies is hierarchical in nature, with the leadership appointed by the majority party. However, the number of committees and the rules that guide their operation serve to decentralize the concentration of power.

The bottom line is that the influence of institutional culture can be pervasive and encompassing. Organizations embody and express values, some explicit and some not. These values are reflected in the nuanced signals transmitted through-out the organization in so many ways, in the rewards that are allocated for appro-priate behavior, and in the leadership style that develops. When cultures change or clash, as suggested above, incumbents either respond or exit. This happened in many instances as agencies underwent dramatic transformation as part of a wel-fare reform dynamic in the 1990s. Some saw wholesale staff turnover as programs migrated from a benefits-issuing focus to a behavior-changing focus. Institutional culture clearly is a powerful and undeniable force.

Exploring the Concept of Professional Culture

We now shift our attention from the concept of *institutional culture* to the con-cept of *professional culture*, which grows out of the training and education that one receives in preparation for a career. Although academic research tends to be discipline-oriented, it embodies a number of inherent signals and rewards that are associated with a certain regimen undertaken to prepare for selected types of career trajectories. Think back, for a moment, to the Middle Ages when guilds were prominent. Youths apprenticed to a certain guild would learn the specific technical skills necessary to a certain trade. But they would also incorporate a form of socialization that developed the values, attitudes, social skills, networks, and etiquette appropriate for a member of that particular society.

Contemporary examples abound. We are all familiar with the training regi-mens for military personnel. There is a boot camp experience or the plebe year for service academies. The operating concept is to break down the way candidates think about the world when they enter military service in order to build up a new way of thinking about things. Some academic professions simulate, at least in part, the military experience.

Law school devotes the first year of study to getting future members of the bar to think like lawyers. This is, in part, a pedagogical process that goes well beyond the mere acquisition of substantive knowledge about the law or how to function in various legal situations. The first year is also dedicated to framing how prospective lawyers organize facts, think through questions of law, and express themselves in the unique vocabulary of attorneys. That first year of law school is as much about *how* to think as it is about *what* to know.

Business schools devote much time to grounding aspiring members of that club in the principles of the market. This goes well beyond accounting or marketing protocols. It encompasses a way of looking at society and inculcating a due respect for the hidden hand of the market. No one really knows how this hidden hand works or how billions of transactions actually result in optimal market performance. Yet many business precepts become articles of faith to be internalized by those seeking membership into that world.

Similarly, students of social work spend time absorbing the core values of their profession in addition to the theories and practice skills necessary to their avocation. They also balance an immersion in various theories explaining human behaviors with training in ethics and interpersonal skills. In many programs, the first year of graduate work is oriented toward grounding students in a core understanding of what it means to be a social worker, whereas the second year permits students to explore their individual career path as well as to absorb a more advanced theoretical basis for pursuing their profession.

Finally, let us consider public policy schools, which have grown in number and importance over the past several decades. The curricula of these schools are often dichotomized into technical and professional foci. The technical preparation concentrates on things like microeconomics, planning models, program evaluation, and statistics. At the same time, these schools often employ lecturers with real-life experience in legislatures and bureaucracies, and they require students to gain applied experiences through internships or class assignments situated in actual policy settings. These schools recognize that technical virtuosity is only part of the skill set needed to perform in the policy world. Doing policy is part craft, but it is also part art. Knowing the culture of the policy world may be as important as knowing the substance of the issues or the latest analytic techniques.

The point of these examples is that the concept of *professional culture* is powerful indeed. Preparing someone to function in an academic discipline is not just about intellectual substance; it is also about socialization into a whole set of cultural norms and mores that shape attitudes about what is valued and what behaviors are considered appropriate. It is about setting a relational context that governs interactions between members of a kind of guild (the academic world) and the real world outside the ivory tower. Recruits learn a language associated with the discipline and a set of signals about how to govern oneself in ways that comport with professional standards.

The real emphasis of most doctoral-level study in the social sciences, however, is on becoming a researcher, on learning the canons of research. This is more than just learning methods and statistics, though that is critical. It is about thinking like a researcher. This is very close to thinking like a lawyer or a social worker in that the socialization process shapes one's approach to the world, tapping into views such as how we know truth, how we assess competing claims of what is to be believed, and how we distinguish good input from bad. Consider, for a moment, the whole notion of a null hypothesis. A properly socialized researcher does not accept plausible propositions at face value. He or she is trained to hypothesize that any proposed relationship in the real world is false until this so-called null hypothesis is rejected by rigorous evidence obtained according to the canons of science.

For those grounded in the culture of science, there was a rather clear demarcation between thinking like a civilian and thinking like a scientist (or an academic). A so-called civilian might well give play to the values and passions that policy issues bring into play, whereas an academic researcher would (or at least should) give greater weight to scientific evidence to support conclusions. When scientific thinking trespasses into civilian territory, the clash of the cultures can be amusing. Take, for example, a wine-tasting exercise among friends. Although most of the party guests enjoyed tasting the wines, rating each one, and quickly honing in on their personal favorites, the scientist among them took the scoring sheets, criticized the rating scale, and then proceeded to calculate the standard deviations of each wine's ratings along with how the preferences differed by age and gender.

A scientist can entertain any number of hypotheses about what causes a certain outcome of interest. When arriving at a conclusion, however, he or she should be guided by the evidence. There is a wonderful example from the work of Sara McLanahan, now professor of sociology at Princeton University. Early in her career, she embarked on a course of research into what accounted for differences in children's well-being and their later success in life. Her prior position was that single mothers, when given proper income and other supports, could raise children as well as mothers from two-parent households. She herself had been a single mom for a number of years. No matter how she ran the numbers, however, the evidence did not support her assumptions, and she accepted what the evidence told her. Her intellectual journey was eventually captured in the popular press in an article titled "The Education of Sara McLanahan" (Whitehead, 1993).

Or take the case of Marion Howard of Emory University. As an assistant professor, she pulled together an interdisciplinary team of scholars who used the latest theories of adolescent decision making and studies of adolescent health to develop a teenage pregnancy prevention program that she was confident would be so groundbreaking that it would guarantee her tenure. The program taught decision-making skills so that when teens were propositioned, they could carefully weigh the pros and cons of engaging in sexual activity. To the team's surprise, this well-designed and carefully conceptualized program produced null results. It appeared that the teens used the decision-making skills but came to the unexpected conclusion that sex was right for them now. The (lack of expected) results sent the researchers back to the drawing board to design a program that taught young teens how to "say no" to sex. This time the training was conducted by peers a couple years older than the target teens. These mentors taught eighth graders the skills for diverting social and peer pressure to become sexually active. Evaluations of this reincarnated program showed that it worked as expected—low-income youth who did not participate in the program were four to five times more likely to become sexually active than those who participated in the program (Howard, 1988).

As these examples illustrate, researchers as a group tend to be cautious. They look to carefully and systematically build on existing theory and entertain new interpretations only when the preponderance of evidence brings conventional wisdom into doubt. Great pains are taken to identify spurious relationships and proper causal directions. We recall a humorous graph on the door of some PhD students. On the vertical axis was listed the estimated aggregate mean temperature going back some 300 years. On the horizontal axis were estimates of the number of pirates over this same period. As the estimated global mean temperature rose, the number of pirates dropped (at least until the recent increase in piracy off the coast of Somalia). The policy conclusion was obvious: To reverse the oncoming catastrophe associated with global warming, we should all become pirates.

Those grounded in the culture of research, however, are steeped in the mindset that the world out there beyond the borders of the academy is replete with casual causality. To researchers, too many people look at temporal associations and assume causation. But scientists know full well that correlation is not causation. We need theory, and we need empirical support derived from rigorous experiments and analyses before drawing summative conclusions about how the world operates. Breakthrough studies must be replicated, hopefully numerous times, before new ways of looking at things become part of the intellectual landscape.

By the time scientists earn their doctorate, they generally have fully embraced the canons of their discipline and the culture associated with being a researcher. Methods may vary, but the procedures of scientific inquiry are well understood. The importance accorded to publishing in peer-reviewed journals goes unexamined. The views of peers also situated in academia remain of compelling importance. When scientists speak as a researcher, their opinions become more guarded, and their conclusions are drawn less quickly. There is a sense of responsibility that we bring to our public voices, or at least there should be.

By the time newly minted doctorates enter the work world, they bring with them a whole array of internalized norms. These should, if they are to remain faithful to their avocation, shape the way they view the world no matter where they happen to be employed.

The Intersection of Institutional and Professional Cultures

All of us, then, bring two sets of cultural influences to the table. One set is framed by our professional or academic training; the other is framed by the institutional setting in which we work. These influences constitute the contextual framework through which we function. They provide us with signals about the most critical dimensions of our lives as professionals. To whom should we pay attention? What rewards will mean the most to us? How shall we react in given situations? What type of vocabulary will we use both in speaking and in writing? How will we view the importance of others? The list goes on.

We argue that all members of the knowledge-producing and knowledge-consuming communities bring a distinct set of cultural baggage with them to their professional roles. As we have argued, the influences are drawn from some combination of institutional sources and disciplinary sources. That is, they are drawn from a specific institutional affiliation as well as from the more permanent norms and values inculcated during the disciplinary socialization process associated with one's academic preparation.

What exactly do we mean by this? How do these sources of influence interact? Take the example of Professor X, who is a tenured professor at a top research university. He or she would bring the academic norms absorbed as part of his or her academic training, shaded somewhat by the specific disciplinary preparation. For example, in making causal inferences, most economists feel comfortable using econometric modeling that statistically accounts for intergroup heterogeneity, whereas other social scientists feel comfortable only with experimental designs that employ random assignment techniques.

In addition to the cultural influences drawn from their academic training, they would also respond to the culture of the specific academic institution in which they were located. Being in a top research university would only amplify the signals and reward structures associated with being an academic researcher. Their professional antennae would be sensitively attuned to their research peers—behaviors and investments that resulted in peer-reviewed journal publications would trump activities directed at public service and teaching. Some of this would simply be "in the atmosphere" of a research university. But in other ways, Professor X would know full well that his or her prospects for advancement, honors, and the coveted corner office would rely heavily on publications, no matter what the institution might say about the relative importance of teaching and public service.

For Professor X, professional training and institutional affiliation complement one another. But what happens when that interaction is less complementary? Professor Y may also have a doctorate in the same discipline as Professor X. He or she, however, does research in a university that highly values teaching and public service. Surely, Professor Y does not jettison the norms and values that were ingrained during the socialization process. However, the institutional signals and rewards arguably are less complementary and, we would hypothesize, less powerful. Not surprisingly, colleges and universities espousing a teaching mission value teaching. They recruit, retain, and promote based upon excellence in teaching. They highly value students' evaluations of faculty performance in the classroom.

Now, take a third researcher who has similar academic credentials. Professor Z is on a different career trajectory. He or she is located in a public policy evaluation firm. The institutional culture here is quite distinct from what one would find in a university setting. Here, the core technology of the organization is oriented toward the public policy world and not toward fellow academics. The product is not knowledge generation per se but the evaluation of public policies and programs and, in some cases, the promotion of specific policies or programs. Clearly,

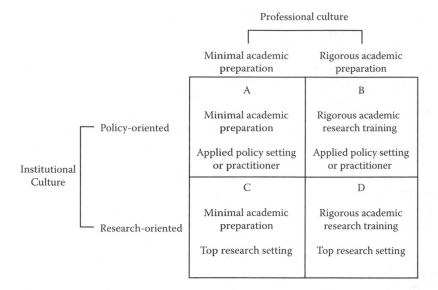

Figure 4.1   The intersection of professional and institutional cultures: A macro look.

the stakeholders differ, and as a consequence, the criterion for determining both professional and organizational success will differ.

In Figure 4.1, we lay out a stylized depiction of the intersection between professional and institutional cultures on a more or less macro level. In this simplified 2 × 2 figure, we lay out the extremes. Along the horizontal axis, we have two professional cultures. One requires a researcher with minimal preparation, perhaps a couple of courses on the way to a professional degree. The other requires a PhD who has been rigorously trained in research methods. Along the vertical axis, we posit two institutional cultures. The first is policy-oriented organizations or ones that implement and manage programs. The other is top research universities or research-oriented organizations that employ rigorous research and evaluation methods.

We argue that cells A and D involve the least potential conflict between professional and institutional norms. That is, minimal research preparation would meld more seamlessly with the institutional culture in a policy-oriented organization, just as rigorous research preparation would mesh more systematically with the institutional norms in a research-oriented organization. Similarly, we argue that cells B and C do offer possibilities for conflict where rigorous research training may clash with the dominant institutional culture. Whether such conflict arises depends on the circumstances, but the adverse consequences for optimal communications are very real. Two PhDs, one doing analytic work in a government office and the other doing research in a predominantly teaching university, probably have more in common than two researchers in a top-level university, one doing theoretical work and the other policy-oriented work. Of course, not all evaluation firms are alike. Some are serious about applying the most rigorous scientific methods possible. MDRC was created in the 1970s with help from the Ford Foundation to facilitate the conduct of large federally supported experimental evaluations of controversial welfare reform strategies of that era. Over time, MDRC became a proselytizer of rigorous experimental evaluation methods as the gold standard for accumulating knowledge about what works in the social policy arena. The RAND Corporation, created largely to do defense-related analyses, conducts social science analyses on par with top research universities. Similarly, Abt Associates, the Brookings Institution, Mathematica Policy Research, the Urban Institute, and a handful of others are known for bringing the highest research standards to assessing policy innovations in the social welfare arena.

Other organizations also purport to do policy research and evaluation though they are driven by a specific ideological or agenda perspective. Organizations such as the Center for Law and Social Policy and the Center on Budget and Policy Priorities have reputations for doing sound work. But they organize their work around specific motivating agendas. Each sees a strong public role in assisting vulnerable populations. Still others take a conservative view of the world. The American Enterprise Institute generally does research that supports a response to public issues that is based on free-market principles. The Cato Institute analyzes social problems from a libertarian perspective. We could go on.

The work done in these policy-oriented organizations may be sound, but the underlying differences in perspectives cannot be discounted. Therefore, they sometimes drift in the direction of ideological or partisan advocacy at the expense of methodological or analytic rigor. As such, science may not be the governing value, and truth may be balanced against other competing purposes. The institutional environments may trump academic norms. It is not always that science is jettisoned in the pursuit of political truth, though that can happen. Rather, evidence tends to be selected, interpreted, and organized in ways shaped by ideological and partisan priors.

Finally, many researchers operate within government. Legislatures have staff dedicated to analyzing topics before them. Executive agencies have research, evaluation, and/or statistical units to help guide policy and assess results. Such within-government research functions have increased, at least in visibility, as the push toward performance-based and outcome-based management principles has gained momentum.

At the federal level, research capacity has waxed and waned but at times has been very sophisticated. In the social policy arena, Vee Burke exercised sophisticated scholarship in her long years of service for the Congressional Research Service. Legislators on both sides of the aisle sought out her work. Howard Rolston headed the research shop in the Administration for Children and Families, the Department of Health and Human Services, for many years. He was a champion of doing rigorous experiments as a way to enhance our knowledge base in social policymaking. Many other examples can be drawn from the Bureau of Labor Statistics, the Census Bureau in the Department of Commerce, the Government Accountability Agency, the research arm of the Department of Agriculture, and so forth. Henry Aaron mentioned once that the professional staff of the Office of the Assistant Secretary for Planning and Evaluation in the Department of Health and Human Services in the late 1970s was on par with the top academic economics departments of that era. Just before Donna Shalala left her position as chancellor of the University of Wisconsin–Madison to become Secretary of Health and Human Services in the Clinton administration, she met with researchers at the Institute for Research on Poverty for a briefing on poverty and welfare issues. She remarked during that session that strengthening the department's analytic capacity would be a top priority for her because she could not imagine running the department absent access to top-quality research.

The point is that the production of knowledge is not the exclusive province of the academy. Knowledge production exists within government as well. Think of the roles played by the National Institutes of Health and the National Institute of Mental Health. Often, knowledge production involves seeking out information developed elsewhere and translating it for policymakers and practitioners. In this sense, government-based researchers, evaluators, and analysts typically serve as intermediaries. They scan for new knowledge, compile and interpret it for the program units and strategic decision makers, respond to inquiries for relevant research on current issues, and/or develop or manage research, evaluation, and analysis agendas where the actual work is outsourced to others. These intermediaries increasingly play an irreplaceable role in the production, management, and use of knowledge.

So far, we have been simplistic in our exploration of the general effect of culture on the use of research in policymaking and management. Let us next turn our attention to the reality of the institutional contexts in which research is both done and used. The world is much more complex than it has been treated to date.

TOWARD A MULTICOMMUNITY THEORY OF CULTURAL INFLUENCES

There is an old saying that where you sit determines where you stand. Organizational position influences preferences and behaviors. At the same time, one's professional preparation also plays a critical role. The next step is to extend our understanding of the complex array of institutional settings in which knowledge production and use take place.

As a point of departure, we attempt to create a much broader understanding of the institutional settings in which knowledge is generated and used. Prior conceptualizations were fairly simple. We had researchers and policymakers, or sometimes theorists added policy managers, policy administrators, or practitioners. The real world, however, is much more complicated than that. In Table 4.1 we lay out a more nuanced depiction of institutional settings in which knowledge is created, transmitted, vetted, and used. In effect, this is a look at the intersection of institutional and professional cultures on a more micro, or detailed, level.

Along the horizontal axis, we keep our framework relatively simple. We suggest three distinctions. First, we have knowledge producers, the people who do research, evaluate programs and policies, and plumb secondary data sets in order to glean new ideas or confirm hypotheses about what is happening in the world. But the world of knowledge producers is far more complex than most have treated it. We are not just talking about researchers in academia. We are talking about a

TABLE 4.1   The Intersection of Institutional and Professional Cultures:
A More Micro Look

Institutional Culture	Professional Culture		
	Knowledge Producers	Knowledge Intermediaries	Knowledge Consumers
University-Based Settings			
Research-oriented universities	X		
Policy and professional schools	X	X	
Teaching-focused colleges	X	X	
Intermediary Organizations			
Think tanks	X	X	
Evaluation firms	X	X	
Policy organization		X	
Philanthropic organization		X	X
Government trade organization		X	X
Government Settings			
Government-based research/analysts	X	X	X
Frontline service provision			X
Executive agency management/support		X	X
Executive agency/cabinet leadership			X
Legislative/judicial			X

variety of individuals working in a range of settings from top research universities
to government agencies.

Second, we have intermediaries. These folks are less involved in the creation of
knowledge than in its translation for the end user. They perform a range of useful
functions or tasks. They review and summarize research for consumption by busy
policymakers and managers. They intuit emerging research questions and initiate
analyses to address those issues. They respond to specific questions from those in the
policy realm. They serve as emissaries from the policy community to the research
community, particularly when policymakers find it difficult to cross the cultural
divide. In general, intermediaries do just that—work across the cultural divide.

Finally, we have knowledge consumers. Traditionally, some have thought of
knowledge consumers as those who create laws—legislators or top appointed political officers. But that view is too narrow. Making policy is only one dimension of
doing policy work. There are those who implement policies, develop programs,
manage agencies, evaluate and monitor performance, determine legal questions,
and actually interact with customers, among other functions. All need knowledge,
though the type of knowledge they need and the way they use that knowledge may
differ dramatically.

This matrix is a crude and shorthand way of capturing the professional preparation discussed above as it interacts with the professional roles one adopts. Though
the correlation is far from unified, we believe there is a correspondence between
the kind of academic preparation received and the professional orientation assumed

throughout one's career. That is, knowledge producers tend to be products of academic preparations that ground them in both the methods and the culture of science. They tend to accord greater weight to hard evidence collected through rigorous analysis than through direct experience and subjective interpretation.

At the other extreme, knowledge consumers often were exposed to academic regimens that focused on the substantive and technical issues that they would deal with in their future professional lives. Namely, what do they have to know about the technologies, politics, target populations, and trade-offs inherent in the content area they will manage or develop rules about? A variety of professional schools prepare individuals for careers in the human services arena. Most require that their students be exposed to research methods or learn how to use research for policy and practice. Still, these schools do not thoroughly ground their students in what the culture of science is, how to think like a researcher, and how to conduct cutting-edge research.

Of course, this is a gross generalization. Many who wind up as knowledge consumers have very general liberal arts training or academic preparation in a particular aspect of the policy process—the law, accounting, political science, and so forth. Take legislators, for example, whose particular skill may be that they have no distinct grounding in a particular discipline. This frees them to listen to constituents and to move easily across topical areas and content with ease and fluidity. Our columns, then, provide us with an easy, though admittedly crude, first cut at determining the orientation a person brings to the table. Next we turn to the specific institutional setting in which they are positioned.

Along the vertical axis, we lay out a range of institutional positions arrayed along a conceptual continuum loosely corresponding to a theoretical production-consumption scale. At the top of the scale, we enumerate the usual actors associated with what we have termed knowledge producers. Through this depiction we attempt to provide greater clarity on the variety of institutional settings in which those involved in shaping and doing policy find themselves. Let us start at the top and move to the bottom.

University-Based Settings

Many knowledge producers involved in the policy process often are located in top research universities or other institutions where cutting-edge work is done. We tend to think of these top researchers as being embedded in tenure-track, discipline-focused, academic departments—economics, family studies, political science, sociology, and so forth. But that stereotype is inaccurate on three counts.

First, not all policy-oriented researchers are in "traditional academic settings." Some are in policy or professional schools. Others may be located in the academy but not hold tenure-track, faculty appointments. Second, being located in the academy does not preclude you from being a knowledge consumer in our sense of the term. Obviously, the very process of doing science demands that you regularly consume the output of your peers. Most academics scan the real world for ideas about what to look at and how to formulate research questions. Thus, many academics find themselves doing policy in one way or another. They consult with government, serve on commissions, and accept public positions (at least temporarily and without forfeiting their academic ties). For example, Tom served as a senior policy advisor in the U.S. Department of Health and Human Services working on welfare reform during the early Clinton administration. In effect, he was outsourced to the federal government for a proscribed time period.

Intermediary Organizations

As mentioned earlier, policy-relevant research is no longer confined to universities. In the early days of the War on Poverty launched by President Johnson in the 1960s, the Office of Economic Opportunity (OEO) was created to coordinate a broad-based attack on economic destitution in the United States. When the OEO decided it needed to know more about the phenomenon under the policy microscope, where could it turn? It turned to Robert Lampman, an economist at the University of Wisconsin, who had served on President Kennedy's Council of Economic Advisors (see Chapter 3). Subsequently, the Institute for Research on Poverty was created in the mid-1960s. At the time, there were not that many institutional alternatives for the OEO to consider as it pondered strategies for generating poverty-focused research.

Today, the landscape is much different. When the Clinton team was putting together its welfare reform proposal in 1993–1994, where did it most often turn for research, analysis, and evidence to help with its planning? It was seldom academia. Granted, two of the principals, David Ellwood and Mary Jo Bane, were recruited from Harvard to serve in key positions in the U.S. Department of Health and Human Services. Still, the Clinton administration turned to the think tanks and evaluation firms that had sprouted up in the prior three decades.

Academia was no longer the primary source of knowledge because the competition had grown in number, sophistication, and availability. Tom recalls working for Ellwood at the Office of the Assistant Secretary for Planning and Evaluation in 1993–1994. When an analytical issue needed to be addressed, seldom did anyone suggest calling an academic source, though it did happen on occasion. The perception was that academics were too slow and their first allegiance was to their academic peers and whatever research they were doing. Moreover, their understanding of the policy issues was likely to be dated and their appreciation of critical political realities misinformed or outright naive. No, the planners turned to places such as the Center for Law and Social Policy, Center on Budget and Policy Priorities, MDRC, Urban Institute, and similar organizations.

We think of these as primarily *intermediary organizations*. They do research and evaluation, but they also have one foot in the policy world. They see policymakers as their primary clients. In addition to producing knowledge, they also see their role as translating extant research and analysis in ways that enhance their utility for those doing public policy. Still, some of these organizations, or the incumbents populating these firms, do high-quality research and publish in respectable academic outlets. To greater and lesser degrees, these firms bridge the knowledge-producing and knowledge-consuming worlds.

Of course, these organizations vary dramatically along a number of dimensions. Some orient themselves more around ideas than policy, some are driven more by ideology than data, some do original research and analysis, and others work closely with government officials. Nonetheless, each contains a common element—serving as a bridge between rigorous research and those seeking answers for policy purposes.

Because these intermediary organizations play such an important role in bridging producers and consumers, we look closely at them. Admittedly, our categorization is subjective and open to debate. Moreover, our examples are players at the federal level even though comparable examples do exist at the state level, though to a lesser extent. Furthermore, our illustrative players are limited to those that focus largely on social policy issues. Our purpose here is not to cover the waterfront but rather to capture seminal insights about the nature and role of these intermediaries. Despite these caveats, the exercise is important because not all intermediaries are equal, and the differences are critical to facilitating communication across the knowledge production–consumption divide.

Think tanks (e.g., Brookings Institution, RAND Corporation, Urban Institute). We define these entities as institutions dedicated to the creation of new ideas, insights, and innovative analyses using high standards and sophisticated methods. Moreover, they tend toward agenda-free work, at least relatively speaking, with fewer political litmus tests for the selection of staff, topics, and internal review processes. In many cases, senior staff are competitive with faculty at top research universities and do work on par with these institutions. At the same time, their target audience does not focus primarily on the community of scholars. Their raison d'être is to shape the larger set of ideas that inform public discourse.

Evaluation firms (e.g., Abt Associates, MDRC, Mathematica Policy Research, Inc.). These kinds of firms focus on evaluations of existing and proposed policies and programs and, in some instances, conduct higher-level analyses of secondary data to inform public policy. They compile existing research and program evaluations for policymakers and do briefings at the state and national levels for key policy types. They operate comfortably in the academic world, but they clearly see their target population as the policy community. They keep their scientific standards high, sometimes influence those standards by insisting on the use of rigorous experimental methods, and even influence the research agendas of the academy.

Policy-oriented organizations (e.g., American Enterprise Institute, Cato Institute, Center on Budget and Policy Priorities, Center for Law and Social Policy, Children's Defense Fund, and Child Trends). These are institutions that, in general, are organized around the policymaking process. Some are organized around specific target populations, others around driving political concepts such as *free markets* or *libertarian principles*, and others around topical or substantive areas such as poverty or workforce issues. In general, however, they all are driven by a desire to influence policy. They prize access to policymakers. They select both topics and personnel based on their ability to work in that so-called real world. They spend a lot of time thinking about how to communicate with the real world. However, as we discuss in the next chapter, their eagerness to influence policy raises flags, at least for some, among the very people they want to influence.

Philanthropic organizations (e.g., Annie E. Casey Foundation, Joyce Foundation, Kellogg Foundation, Lynde and Harry Bradley Foundation, Mott Foundation, Packard Foundation, Pew Charitable Trusts, and Robert Wood Johnson Foundation). Some foundations explicitly work in the policy arena. Why include them because they mostly fund programs and policy development where the work is done by others? In our experience, foundations spend a lot of time and energy thinking about what policy movers and shakers need to know and how to convey that knowledge in effective ways. Thus, they serve as conduits between the production and consumption universes. Think of the Annie E. Casey Foundation Kids Count initiative, a project that assembles social indicators on children in every state, and nationally, to keep child well-being on the public agenda. This project also has generated a great deal of academic attention to the topic of social indicators (Hauser, Brown, & Prosser, 1997).

Government trade organizations (e.g., American Public Human Services Association, National Association of Counties, National Association for Welfare Research and Statistics, National Conference of State Legislatures, and National Governors Association). This set of institutions, located close to the public sector, represents either levels of government (e.g., counties or governors) or selected governmental functions (e.g., welfare). They are separate from government but often exist through public fees and dues. They do play a role in bridging the production–consumption gap. Their Web sites and conferences expose members to the latest research and analyses. They seek out emerging questions and span the landscape for relevant work and, just sometimes, help shape emerging research agendas.

Government Settings

We now turn to those entities typically referred to as knowledge users—policymakers. We constrain this grouping to those located in government itself. But again, this is not a homogenous group. Most observers clearly see the legislative branch as the makers of public policy. Researchers interested in shaping policy would love access to this group. Yet legislators are merely one aspect of the policymaking world. Let us now take a look at several diverse and distinctive populations or entities that make up the world of public policy.

Government-based researchers/analysts (e.g., the Congressional Research Organization, the General Accountability Organization, National Institutes of Health, nonpartisan legislative service agencies in state legislatures, and the Office of the Assistant Secretary for Planning and Evaluation in the U.S. Department of Health and Human Services). There are a host of government, or quasi-public, officials whose very job is to generate and utilize research and analysis. Their functions vary. In some instances, they identify and fund sound research irrespective of its immediate utility. But in most cases, they identify emerging management and theoretical issues of interest to their bosses or stakeholders and outsource the research work or do environmental scans to assemble available work. Because a great deal of their work is focused on answering questions of interest to their larger organizations, they often use the work of others. By virtue of their positions, they also spend a lot of time thinking through the institutional and political contexts that might mediate what the research means. They are often very attuned to the real-world caveats that might limit the application of pure science or rigorous analysis to a social challenge.

Frontline service provision. This group comprises those who actually deliver (or manage those who deliver) public goods and services. Normally, we do not think of these as policymakers, but any honest appraisal of how the real world works disabuses us of this simplistic view. Even in the most routinized benefits-issuing system (where computers determine eligibility and benefits), there exists a lot of frontline flexibility in the way people are treated and information is collected. In more complex systems, discretion and professional judgment are unavoidable. Lipsky (1980) wrote about *street-level bureaucrats*, where policy is made at the place where customers and systems interact. These practitioners should be a huge audience for research and analysis.

Executive agency management/support. This group of government users encompasses a broad set of public officials who constitute the core civil service at the management and support levels. They are often thought of as implementers or managers but not makers of policy. However, this view is strikingly naive. The core civil service types are the repositories of institutional knowledge and typically know a great amount about policy and program content. Given these comparative advantages, they can do much to steer policies and programs in directions of their own choosing. Besides, they know that they will be around for a long time and political appointees will not. Therefore, they have a vested interest in keeping themselves informed.

Executive agency/cabinet leadership. These are the agency heads and their closest deputies and advisors, all typically political appointees. They have close access to governors or the White House. They interact with legislative bodies. They often have the trust that comes from shared values and common political allegiances. They are well positioned to do *boundary spanning*—looking outside their own institutional domains for new ideas and directions. They are a prime target for those seeking to influence policy.

Legislative/judicial. There is little dispute about the role of the legislative branch in the doing of public policy. There is less agreement on who the target population really is. Is it the legislators themselves, their staffs, or the interest groups and lobbyists that have real and substantive access to legislators? The legislative branch has grown into a complex, multiheaded phenomenon (witness the growth of K Street in Washington, DC, where lobbyists and lawyers tend to congregate). We also include the judicial branch here because it interprets the constitutional legality of policies and programs, often taking a real role in overseeing controversial policies or intruding into the management of programs where legal wrongs occur. Lawyers typically draw on research to prepare briefs and legal arguments on constitutional issues.

SUMMARY

Those discussing the underutilization of research in policymaking started out with a simple dichotomy. There were those that did research and those that used research. This framework—knowledge producers and knowledge consumers—was founded on a distinction that easily conformed to the straightforward way that two communities of theory thought about this challenge. But that bifurcated view of the world is much too simplistic, as recent theorists have recognized and we discuss above. We have different kinds of producers, different kinds of users, and many individuals and institutions devoted to bridging the patterns and content of communications across these two universes. Understanding these complexities is critical to advancing any agenda for understanding why research may be underutilized and for optimizing the use of research in the real world.

We also started out with a simple notion of *culture*. Researchers and policymakers thought about things differently, and those differences confounded communication and cooperation. Fair enough, but we are suggesting that culture is a more complex, contextually specific phenomenon than we realized initially. At a minimum, the way we organize our professional worlds emerges from the institutions where we are located and from the way we were professionally trained and socialized.

Do we have these worlds laid out correctly? We do not know for sure. Other conceptual arrangements are both possible and plausible. But we think our framework advances and illuminates the theoretical discussion. The real question is how our more complex model plays out in the ways that real people think and act and communicate. We move to that question in the next chapter.

5

Why Research Is Underutilized in Policymaking
Community Dissonance Theory

In public policy making, many suppliers and users of social science research are dissatisfied, the former because they are not listened to, the latter because they do not hear much they want to listen to.

—Charles Lindblom and David Cohen (1979, p. 1)

Enabling cultural change may be as important a focus as enabling change in practice.

—Isabel Walter, Sandra Nutley, and Huw Davies (2005, p. 348)

For a number of years, almost like a rite of spring, the Wisconsin legislature squared off with the administration of the University of Wisconsin–Madison over the amount of time faculty actually spent in the classroom. This is an inevitable flash point between politicians grudgingly allocating scarce tax dollars largely for the purpose of educating the future labor force, and university officials trying desperately to maintain the school's status as a world-class research institution.

The clash between cultures is never unexpected, but it is sometimes amusing. There is an apocryphal story about a legislative hearing on university teaching loads at the University of Wisconsin system's flagship campus where a conservative rural legislator suspiciously asked a professor just how many hours he spent in the classroom. "Nine" was the response (this occurred some time ago, before a full-time teaching load was reduced to six credit hours per semester). Satisfied, the legislator eased back in his chair. Almost immediately, struck by a thought, he straightened up again and fixed the professor with a questioning stare: "You DO mean nine hours a day, don't you?" Slack-jawed, the professor could only return his hostile gaze with stunned silence. Sometimes, professional worlds are so different that communication borders on the improbable.

In Chapter 4, we developed an organizational landscape, what we might think of as the conceptual architecture, within which knowledge producers and consumers function. We laid out a complicated world where two forces that shape professional environments interact and, thus, help frame the worldviews professionals, whether researchers or policymakers, bring to their job.

This chapter picks up where we left off in the previous chapter. Here, we address two key subsequent questions—how should we think about the cultural influences associated with community identity, and how do these influences play out in the real world? These are questions we find littered throughout the policy world. Laying out a theoretical framework for describing the world is a stimulating intellectual exercise. But any such framework is consequential primarily to the extent that it informs the way we see the world and, as such, leads to a better appreciation of how the world operates. That is, any theoretical framework worth its salt helps us understand how the world functions and even why it functions so.

In this chapter, we examine prior thinking on the meaning of research utilization in the policy world and previous theories on this disconnect between the research and policy communities before introducing a new conceptual framework that we call *community dissonance theory*. We slowly and surely erect each elemental concept and then carefully build them into the foundations of this new theory. We conclude the chapter by defining community dissonance theory and summarizing the insights that we believe it brings to understanding the underutilization of research in policymaking. We begin with three vignettes that illustrate how the character of community dissonance plays out in the policy world.

EXPLORING THE CHARACTER OF COMMUNITY DISSONANCE

An earlier version of the title to this chapter referred to a condition we termed *community confusion*. We realized, however, that we are talking about something just a bit more intractable. *Confusion* implies disorientation, lack of clarity, or direction. Our experience suggests that the failure of groups on either side of what we call *the great divide* between those who produce knowledge and those who consume it are more than a little out of sorts with one another. In fact, they approach one another warily at best and too often with hostility. We think the word *dissonance* conveys a more accurate measure of what we see, a disconnect that renders good communication difficult at best. To begin to understand the meaning of community dissonance, we start with a few vignettes.

Vignette 1

In the latter half of the 1970s, Tom was tapped by former colleagues in state government to help out with a legislatively mandated study of Wisconsin's welfare system. Reflecting growing dissatisfaction with cash welfare as the primary strategy for assisting poor families, the charge from the legislature was to do a comprehensive review of existing programs and to develop creative policies to address recipients' needs while enhancing their attachment to the labor market.

The mid-level state bureaucrats charged with managing the study and staffing a blue ribbon committee created to oversee the effort were interested in reaching out to the university. This was a perfect expression of the long-touted Wisconsin Idea (see Chapter 3), where the boundaries of the university were the boundaries of the state. The resources of the academy were to be applied to solving real-life, public policy issues. Tom, working both ends of State Street (the capitol on one end and the university on the other), helped recruit a former director of the Institute for Research on Poverty (IRP), economist Robert Haveman, to chair the blue ribbon committee. Tom also recruited other IRP affiliates to volunteer their time to work on issues such as reform of child support, ideas for a state Earned Income Tax Credit, and changes in the state's manpower and economic development programs.

The resulting report was generally well received. Some members of the university community, particularly then-IRP director Irwin Garfinkel, continued to work with state officials on ideas generated by the study group. Over time, some elements of the proposed set of reforms were enacted, particularly in the child support and tax arenas.

At the end of what had been a stimulating dialogue about reform possibilities, one based on a collaborative interchange between the academy and the state, Professor Haveman expressed concerns to Tom about his own involvement. His colleagues in the economics department, he argued, would not understand his investment of time and energy in this effort. The issues under discussion were visible and pressing, and the policy solutions were seen as creative, yet no published articles in refereed journals were forthcoming. Haveman stressed that he now would have to work that much harder to make up for "lost" time. Whether correct or not, he felt his academic colleagues would discount his public service at best or question his commitment to scholarship at worst.

Vignette 2

Fast-forward another decade to the late 1980s. Welfare reform is now a full-time preoccupation at the state and national levels. Washington is passing the Family Assistance Plan, a set of reforms that the late senator Daniel Patrick Moynihan believed would be—erroneously as it turned out—the final reform thrust of the 20th century. But the real impetus for reform was being played out at the state level. Under the guise of what came to be known as the New Federalism, states were increasingly undertaking aggressive reforms of the Aid to Families With Dependent Children program. The federal government encouraged these local reforms by permitting states to waive selected federal rules under the condition that such initiatives be rigorously evaluated.

Wisconsin, under Governor Tommy Thompson, was particularly aggressive and achieved a national reputation as a welfare reformer with a series of hard-line reforms. One early initiative was the Learnfare program, a policy that linked cash welfare benefit levels to school attendance by the children in families receiving aid. This controversial idea presaged a spate of subsequent reforms that conditioned benefit levels on client behavior, what became known as the *new paternalism*. Federal officials approved the program on the condition that it be evaluated using an experimental design. Given its controversial nature, Learnfare would appear to be a strong candidate for dispassionate, rigorous analysis by neutral members of the academic research community.

The state dutifully issued a request for proposals (RFP) to do the required evaluation. A research team from IRP responded to the RFP led by then-director Charles Manski, now a highly regarded econometrician at Northwestern University, and Gary Sandefur, a respected sociologist and now a dean at the University of Wisconsin–Madison. Both were eminent scholars with a strong intellectual interest in the links among education, welfare, and poverty. Eminence and expertise, however, played a minor role in the highly charged political atmosphere of welfare reform circa the late 1980s.

Even before the review process had begun, a former state colleague informed Tom that IRP would not be awarded the contract. At least one member of the review board had been told to make sure the award went elsewhere. Sure enough, four of the five members gave the IRP proposal the highest marks, whereas one member rated the proposal low enough to place the IRP team second overall. It seemed that the governor had decided that IRP was too liberal to be trusted with a proposal in which he had invested so much politically. Clearly, the governor would not trust the messengers of science, even if the best of analytical methods were employed. Trust, after all, is a paramount virtue in politics.

In retrospect, the IRP team proved lucky. The evaluation contract went to a team from the University of Wisconsin–Milwaukee. When their results failed to demonstrate Learnfare's effectiveness in improving school attendance, state officials negotiated with the UW–Milwaukee team to rework the evaluation's conclusions. Failing that, and after mutual recriminations played out in the press, the evaluation contract was cancelled.

Vignette 3

Tom also recalls a time when he was asked by the majority leader in the Wisconsin State Assembly to participate as a nonvoting member on a special legislative committee on welfare reform. Through his work with the committee, he became friends with the chair, John Antaramian, a Democrat representing a blue-collar, working-class district in the southeastern part of the state.

Over the course of the committee's work, Tom and John developed a comfortable working relationship. Even after the committee finalized its work, John would call on Tom for advice on welfare issues. Eventually, they initiated a working relationship that expanded to a small group of legislators from both sides of the aisle. It was clear, however, that this working relationship was an outlier case. Whenever the conversation drifted to the university, deeply held prejudices emerged. The dominant political perception was that academics were arrogant, distant, elitist, greedy, naive, self-absorbed, and totally clueless about political realities. And these were the good points mentioned. More than once John claimed to really like Tom, but he had little use for the rest of those eggheads.

When John was leaving the legislature to assume the post of mayor of a medium-size city, a good-bye party was held for him and others who were leaving. The festivities were attended by the usual set of colleagues, staff, lobbyists, and reporters. That very morning, yet another headline newspaper article "exposed" how little time university professors spent in the classroom. As Tom was exchanging warm wishes and reminiscences of the welfare wars they had been through together, he reminded John of the morning's headlines. Suddenly, the politician became animated, pointed his finger at Tom, and began yelling in a loud voice, "University professor, university professor," as if all the politicians in the room would turn and descend upon the hapless academic.

It was all in affectionate jest, of course, but the underlying sentiments were clear. From a legislative perspective, the academy looks like a distant land populated by strange and equally distant people. The cultural divide not only impedes communication but also fosters negative stereotypes. Misunderstandings quickly can escalate to outright hostility.

Anyone who has attempted to bridge the gap between government and the academy will recognize these stories. They are legion. Knowledge producers and consumers do not mix easily.

In the first vignette, a top researcher with an interest in applied policy questions faced a common dilemma. How can he maintain his academic credibility while investing time and energy in matters unlikely to generate scholarly output? This strikes at the very core of both the professional and the institutional cultures. What are the dominant rewards attached to the environment in which one operates, and how do one's peers view the work being done?

The second vignette digs even more deeply into the cultures that divide the two worlds. Here we tap into the core of how each culture views itself and each other. The IRP academics proposing an evaluation plan saw themselves as third parties who were genuinely interested in understanding the effects of a dramatic policy initiative. The governor saw academics as hostile to his plans to radically transform welfare. From his point of view, an evaluation was of little value. The Learnfare initiative was a political winner, yet the evaluation numbers had mostly a downside bias because virtually all social reform evaluations show modest gains, typically less than the political rhetoric promised. Any knowledge gains must be balanced against potential political losses.

The final vignette illustrates the character of the divide separating knowledge producers and consumers. In this instance, they were thrown together in a way in which prior feelings and stereotypes could be addressed and mitigated. The story hints at a powerful lesson—that personal relationships can be a powerful antidote to established prejudices, but also that those negative priors are not easily dispelled.

VARIOUS MEANINGS OF RESEARCH USE

Prior Thinking on Meanings of Research Use

We begin building a theoretical foundation by first reexamining what it is we are talking about. What do we mean by *research use*? Could it be that the definition plays a role in how we think about the degree to which research is used in the doing of policy or in the impediments to its use? How we think about this core concept may well shape how we think about everything else. Let us take a moment to reflect on this issue.

A number of observers (Nutley et al., 2007; Tsengi, 2008; Weiss, 1979) touch upon various meanings of research use. Prior thinking offers several kinds of use.

Instrumental. The results of research or other rigorous analysis are used directly to make identifiable policy decisions. This is close to what has been called the hypodermic metaphor for research use (Pettigrew, 1985). There is a direct and rational application of knowledge, collected according to prevailing canons of science and dispassionately applied to the policy questions at hand.

Conceptual. Research results are utilized to alter or transform the way selected issues are perceived or to modify the character of a dialogue about those issues. This is close to Weiss's (1987a) enlightenment model and Bulmer's (1987) "limestone" metaphor (Bulmer, 1987), which describe research use as the slow accretion of evidence that, not always consciously, transforms the way social issues are framed.

Tactical. Research results are employed to support decisions that have already been made or to justify positions arrived at for ideological or partisan reasons. This could imply that research use is not dispassionate, but may be skewed in its selection or interpretation based on prior positions. Another implication of using research—not before the fact to reach decisions but after the fact to justify them— is that this contributes to citizen perceptions that policymakers make rational decisions, which reflects favorably on the political process and a democratic system of government (Shulock, 1999).

Imposed. Imposed use could be mandated by someone else, such as the recent frenzy with requiring that practitioners use only evidence-based programs. Such mandates raise questions about how the strength of program evidence is determined, whether the same results will be achieved under different local conditions, and whether program planners learn habits of making decisions based on the quality of the science or merely acquiesce to "toeing the line" to satisfy regulatory or financing requirements (Weiss, Murphy-Graham, Petrosino, & Gandhi, 2008, p. 41). The inference to be drawn here is that this type of use may be more political and less substantive in nature.

Process. Finally, there is a use that emanates from mere participation in a scientific initiative. The act of doing research, of thinking through the research challenge, has value-added input into policymaking and administrative processes. Even if no such use exists in reality, it is one that we pressed upon our students over the years. An overview of these traditional meanings of research use and the new thinking that follows can be found in Key Concepts 5.1.

**Key Concepts 5.1   Traditional and Updated Thinking
on Uses of Research for Policy Purposes**

Traditional (Nutley, Walter, & Davies, 2007; Tseng, 2008; Weiss, 1979)

- Instrumental: The direct use of research informs specific policy decisions.
- Conceptual: The use of research helps shape the way issues are perceived or discussed.
- Tactical: The use of research supports decisions already made, usually for other reasons.
- Imposed: The use of research that is mandated by someone else that satisfies regulatory or funding requirements.
- Process: The use of research alters decisions or management practices that stem from the very act of doing research.

Updated (the current book)

- Allocation shifting: Research is used to decide how to distribute scarce resources.
- Tactics shifting: Research is used to shape and inform detailed design, implementation, or management decisions within given policy responses.
- Solutions shifting: Research helps make decisions on basic policy choices given agreed-upon outcomes and preferences.
- Framework shifting: Research is used to alter or transform how we think about certain policy issues or choices.
- Salience shifting: Research is used to put new issues on the agenda or to alter the queue of issues already on the public agenda.
- Awareness shifting: Research is used to bring new issues to light that previously had not been part of the public dialogue.

New Thinking on Various Meanings of Research Use

Granted, this is a good start at thinking through the various kinds of uses out there. Still, terms such as *instrumental* and *conceptual* are vague and will fail to resonate in the worlds of policy and practice. In this section, we introduce a framework that we believe enhances the coherence, consistency, and comprehensiveness of earlier thinking. The new framework starts with narrow uses of research in policymaking and then moves to increasingly broader levels of thought. In all instances, we frame each use in terms of a shift from a prior understanding of how the world works or should work to a different understanding. Of course, in the real world, knowledge sometimes confirms prior thinking, but of most relevance for our interests is thinking of research use within the framework of changing extant understandings or *shifting* mind-sets as a basis for making public decisions.

Allocation shifting. Scientific knowledge can be used to determine the best allocation of resources and effort. This gets at the very heart of who wins and who loses, but is based upon evidence of where relative need is distributed or where relative effects have been measured (Aos, Miller, & Drake, 2006).

Tactics shifting. Scientific knowledge can shape and inform detailed design and implementation decisions within chosen policy solutions. For example, home visitation, partly based on experimental evidence, has gained currency as a policy intervention to mitigate certain family dysfunctions. The research also appears to inform us that not all ways of doing home visits work equally well and that the qualifications of the visitors can be critical to observed positive outcomes.

Solutions shifting. Scientific knowledge can identify preferred policy responses based upon evidence that sheds light on their relative performance against agreed-upon criteria. Years ago, the minimum wage, though controversial, was widely viewed as the preferred policy solution for helping working-poor families. Research showed that this approach was not target efficient, and the preferred solution shifted to work supplements such as the Earned Income Tax Credit.

Framework shifting. Scientific knowledge can be used to slowly, or abruptly, transform how we think about issues. Surely, the Copernican revolution several centuries ago radically altered how we looked at our immediate universe. Suddenly, we were no longer the center of the universe. In family policy, the importance of the father's involvement and the measurement of positive youth outcomes have gradually become accepted. How we look at social and economic issues goes a long way toward determining the range of possibilities that come into serious play.

Salience shifting. Scientific knowledge can be used to identify new issues to be placed on the public agenda or to alter the salience of a topic in public or political discourse. Consider the issue of global warming for a moment. Over the past several decades, science has pushed the issue at first into the public arena and then to a position of salience where its critical importance is widely debated.

Awareness shifting. We do believe that a benefit of "doing" research or of exposing knowledge users to the discipline and perspectives of knowledge producers is to affect what we call *awareness shifting.* What do we mean by this shift in awareness or in how a doer of public policy looks at his or her craft in a different way?

When you put on the hat of a researcher, you think differently about policy. You become more careful about defining what outcomes might be of interest to policymakers. You think hard about how you will know if something is working or not. You think through what kind of comparative data you need and how much of a difference is required to decide whether a solution is worth pursuing. You think hard about what evidence you will need to show that A is better than B. A research paradigm typically demands creating a plausible narrative or theory of change that systematically links inputs and protocols to proximate and more distal outcomes.

When policymakers are exposed to research, Karen has been surprised at the shifts that she has observed in how they think about research and researchers. First, Karen has found that with increasing exposure to the Family Impact Seminars, researchers have slowly and surely come to value the perspective that research can bring to the policy process. We like to say that policymakers "vote" with their feet, as evidenced by the number of legislators from widely ranging political perspectives who attend the seminars. Of Wisconsin's 132 legislators currently holding office, 74 have attended at least one seminar and another 27 offices have sent an aide, so the Family Impact Seminars have reached over three quarters of the 2009–2010 Wisconsin legislature. We have been struck by the anecdotal comments written on seminar evaluations. Policymakers frequently comment on their surprise at how practical research is and how down-to-earth researchers are. In fact, we received so many such comments that we began to systematically use what we call *attribution questions* to inquire about the ways in which the Seminars have changed attitudes about research and researchers. In follow-up phone interviews, 73% of legislators report that because of the Seminars, they are "quite a bit" more likely to see the practical value of research, and 47% say they are "quite a bit" more likely to view researchers as approachable (see Chapter 11 for details).

Why are these definitional distinctions important? Different uses raise distinct trade-offs and costs. Think about this for a moment. If you have a narrow technical policy problem to solve (a simple tactics-shifting use), relying on research to make a decision may prove an easy and cost-free approach. Some of the other uses, however, are more problematic. Putting a new issue on the policy agenda (salience shifting) or adding new policy and programmatic responses to a problem (solutions shifting) can be controversial. Resources are scarce, so new issues are likely to threaten existing allocation patterns.

Moreover, framework-shifting research is likely to upset the existing political and partisan consensus about how the world works and what the public responsibility is for any problems in that world. Any changes are likely to exacerbate long-held ideological and partisan tensions. There is an old saying that the only people who like change are babies with wet diapers. A simple example may illuminate this reality.

For about two decades now, most scholars have argued that the existing measure of poverty is outdated and misleading. As examples, some scholars have argued that many sources of income are not counted, whereas others feel that wage and consumption trends would result in raising the threshold. Many have called for a retooling including an expert panel convened by the National Academy of Sciences. No change has been forthcoming, though. Some in the policy community worry it would raise poverty rates or lower them, one outcome threatening the right and the other the left (awareness-shifting concerns). Others worry that how poverty is distributed across jurisdictions may change, thus impacting the allocation of resources based on local poverty rates. Any zero-sum game (allocation shifting) is always a dramatic political drama. As a result, we remain stuck with a key "official" measure of poverty that all thinking folk know is seriously flawed.

This leads to one final wrinkle in the meaning of research use. Early on we mentioned the specter of "wicked" social problems where there is strong contention around several dimensions of a policy question. At the extreme, there is disagreement about the nature of the problem, the magnitude, its causes, or what the most effective solutions might be. In addition, there is likely to be little consensus on the efficacy of proposed responses and the cost of each. In fact, there may be little agreement on what success would be like and what kind of opportunity costs and externalities would be faced. That is, policymakers would debate the trade-offs of responding at all.

Clearly, awareness-shifting and salience-shifting research can easily raise wicked social problems. Controversy, however, can arise in any of the research use types that we propose. For example, solutions-shifting research can evoke contentious political debate if the evidence appears to favor new policy responses that contradict existing approaches supported by strongly entrenched constituencies or if it favors particular political partisans in predictable ways. Allocation-shifting evidence is almost always a zero-sum game. When distributional analyses are done to decide how to reallocate school funding or close down military bases, evidence often takes a backseat to politics and power.

In the final analysis, how we think about the potential contribution of rigorous knowledge to any policy question depends on several factors. What is the potential use of the research? Is the issue a wicked problem or a more technical one? And finally, just how high and impenetrable are the cultural barriers that separate producers from users?

SOME ELEMENTAL CONCEPTS: ERECTING THE BUILDING BLOCKS OF A THEORY OF COMMUNITY DISSONANCE

Clearly, the research and policymaking worlds experience difficulties communicating with one another. In the previous chapter, we laid out the foundations for the kinds of cultural conflicts that separate these worlds. Below, we build upon earlier work that explores how the cultural lenses through which we interpret the world play out in the real world. Before we get too deeply involved in that discussion, however, we touch upon three building blocks essential to understanding how the culture of a community shapes the consequences associated with membership in that community. These three building blocks are an organization's "core technology," a discussion of what we mean by the ambiguous term *community,* and a brief discourse on how previous scholars have conceptualized these communities and the various ways that they use research.

First, the Notions of Functional Category and Core Technology

A number of observers have commented on the differences in the ways in which knowledge producers and consumers function (Bogenschneider, Olson, Mills, & Linney, 2006; Bulmer, 1987; Maynard, 2006; Myers-Walls, 2000; Shonkoff, 2000; Small, 2005). All of these commentators start from a single perspective, that "research use does not take place in a vacuum. It is always embedded in particular institutional contexts whose idiosyncratic cultures, structures, and politics temper the ways in which research gets taken up by policymakers and practitioners" (Nutley et al., 2007, p. 303).

The existing conceptual frameworks differ in various ways, yet attempt to convey similar content. There are natural groupings or functional categories into which professionals self-identify. As noted previously, some commentators have employed frameworks based on two functional categories; others have employed three categories. By *functional category*, various authors intend to convey a basic self-identity that grows out of the core technology inherent in the professional niche that they occupy. Some employ two-category frameworks, and others employ tripartite distinctions, the latter distinguishing between policymakers and those that administer, implement, manage, or carry out those policies.

Let us examine the construct of the functional category more closely. The notion of the functional category is closely aligned with our notion of an organization's core technology. What does an organization produce? What are the essential tasks required to generate those products? Products, in this sense, do not necessarily mean physical outputs. They might just as well be ideas or advice. The critical notion is that product shapes purpose, which, in turn, shapes essential tasks, which, in turn, influences the operating culture and structural architecture of an organization. What an institution looks like and how it really operates, as opposed to what it looks like on the formal organizational chart, emanates from this general sense of core technology.

Let us make this more concrete. Between the early 1990s and the early 2000s, welfare in some U.S. jurisdictions evolved from a routinized to a relatively non-routinized program. Welfare for several decades had been a benefits-oriented system. The underlying worldview was uncomplicated—the compelling misfortune of disadvantaged families was a shortfall of resources, and the public obligation was to make good that deficit. Program purposes were fairly limited—accurately and efficiently get the checks out the door to eligible families. The time horizon was short. Each month was a new accounting period where assets and income were, in theory at least, recalculated to determine if a shortage of resources existed and the magnitude of that shortfall.

In such a system, horizontal equity was paramount; each family was to be treated in the same way. The worker–client interaction tended to be uniform, episodic, and regularized. Typically, no one asked applicant families what their problems were, where their strengths lay, or how to best move them into society's mainstream. The gatekeeping function was to separate the eligible from the non-eligible; the ongoing case management function was to calibrate monthly income need (according to complex rules) for eligible families.

In such a system, bureaucratic norms emerged as an institutional virtue that, in turn, encouraged vertical, or top-down, command-and-control authority patterns. At the extreme, local agency and worker discretion was further constrained by the introduction of computerized decision-making systems. In effect, welfare rules were programmed into a centrally controlled computer, and existing manuals were rewritten to translate all discretion into clear-cut, binary choices: If the situation is A, you must do X; if the situation is B, then you must do Y. Such a paradigm had the virtue of clarity. Program and organizational boundaries were clear; professional roles were fixed. Frontline workers carried out a narrow range of responsibilities for their own caseloads.

What members of the WELPAN network called the *new face of welfare* focused much more on behavioral change in clients rather than on addressing immediate income shortfalls. The program challenge was to encourage positive behaviors and discourage those perceived as counterproductive. Such behavior-modifying programs tend to be dynamic and based on client change over time, not static systems in which each month is an independent accounting period. They tend to be so multidimensional and individualized that workers must accommodate professional norms that rise above bureaucratic rules.

In turn, organizational forms in which workers function are transformed, becoming flatter and less hierarchical. Horizontal communications, increasing information transfers across peers and peer institutions, replace vertical patterns. Agency boundaries become more porous as service integration and one-stop program models emerge. Entrepreneurship and outcome-oriented institutional philosophies begin to supplant risk-aversive public monopolies. Operational discretion replaces traditional command-and-control management strategies. Malleable organizational forms that can respond quickly to new situations supplant traditional rigid bureaucratic forms.

This new culture demanded a new worker. In the past, welfare managers wanted "left-brain dominant" workers, those who excelled at routinized detail and worked well at linear, unvarying tasks. Suddenly, the need is for "right-brain" workers, who can see the big picture and are creative problem solvers. The new management challenge evolved to where management focused on motivating staff to forget the rules (within reason) and focus on finding creative solutions to complex family challenges.

This example, drawn from welfare reform, brings home the crucial lesson of core technology: Our professional lives are shaped by what we are expected to do and by what our institutions are designed to produce.

Second, Revisiting the Concept of Community

The question then becomes how this essential insight plays out in the professional and institutional worlds in which the producers and consumers of knowledge operate. The extant literature talks a lot about how researchers and policymakers come from different worlds. As we have emphasized, this theoretical foundation can be traced back to Caplan (1979), who attributed the underutilization of research in policymaking to a lack of communication between researchers and policymakers who have different goals, information needs, languages, and values. He identified these two worlds as distinct communities and argued that their effective integration "involves value and ideological dimensions as well as technical ones" (p. 461). That is, enhancing cross-community communication involves dealing with each community's underlying cultures.

In Small's (2005) examination of the two communities of researchers and practitioners, he attributed this cultural divide to professional socialization that dictates what ends social scientists seek, who they respond to, how they work to achieve those ends, and what behaviors are considered appropriate. However, as detailed in earlier chapters, we believe these differences stem not only from professional culture but also from the culture of the institutions in which professionals operate. For example, institutions such as a legislature, lab, or family service agency each have different work environments, ways of knowing, and reward structures (Myers-Walls, 2000).

TABLE 5.1   Dunn's (1980) Five Domains of Culture

Domains	Definitions
Products	The separate communities focus on producing distinct outputs.
Inquiry	They employ separate modes of inquiry and different methods for arriving at conclusions about what is true or not.
Problems	They tend to look at different issues and challenges as being worthy of their time and energy.
Structure	They operate within different environments that function according to distinguishable authority patterns, senses of responsibility, power and incentive systems, and so forth.
Process	Their day-to-day lives differ in terms of pace and other factors.

Subsequent observers focused even more on the cultures that dominated each community. As early as 1980, Dunn began to think harder about the dimensions across which essential points of friction might arise. He viewed them as contingencies across five domains labeled products, inquiry, problems, structure, and process (see Table 5.1).

The terms *community* and *culture* are somewhat fungible, but a distinction can be drawn. A community defines the group within which a professional best fits. Here is where I belong. This is what I am. For example, Bogenschneider and colleagues (Bogenschneider et al., 2006) used three community groups—researchers, policymakers, and policy administrators. Shonkoff (2000) also used three community groups, which he labeled as *science, policy*, and *practice*. Our way of talking about these issues is framed by distinguishing knowledge producers from users as if there are two distinct communities. It is a convenient way of organizing our thoughts, though it is highly simplistic, as we discussed in the previous chapter.

As we introduced in Chapter 4, a culture captures a whole set of dimensions along which beliefs, values, dispositions, and perceptions are shaped by the community with which one identifies. Culture, in effect, is the expression of community. As noted earlier, the most common sense of community in the literature is an undifferentiated grouping of knowledge producers (i.e., researchers) and one or two groupings of knowledge users.

Previous Conceptualizations of Community and Dimensions of Research Use

As with most theoretical frameworks offered to explain a complex issue, the details have evolved over time with individual observers highlighting different communities and suggesting nuances that they believe capture critical dimensions of their research use. For example, Small (2005) discussed bridging research and practice in the family and human sciences and focused primarily on incongruities in cultural practices and situational demands, methodological and statistical limitations of family science, and epistemological differences in knowledge and theory across the two realms. Myers-Walls (2000) framed evaluators and program staff (her variation of the two-communities concept) as being an "odd couple." She then went on to identify differences in six domains: temporal, cognitive, definition of excellence, patterns of communication, daily lifestyle, and how each used the tools of their trade. Others picked up on these dimensions to fill in how the cultures embedded in these distinct communities might play out in the real world.

Shonkoff (2000), as noted, took a slightly more nuanced version of knowledge users, distinguishing between those who make policy and those who carry out policies. But his way of thinking about each group did not differ all that much from that of prior authors. The community (and culture) of science primarily pursued a professional goal of constructing theory and creating knowledge. This culture was obsessed with methods or how knowledge was created and tended to be cautious about specifying causal links between predictor variables and measured outcomes. These stylistic factors lead to distinct differences in how members of the scientific community approach their work and govern their professional lives. Although they can be very busy, their focus is longer-range, more discipline-driven, and organized around understanding as opposed to doing.

Shonkoff (2000) feels that members of the policymaking community are focused more on doing than on understanding. They approach the products of quality research and analysis as only one input into their job. Their lives are hectic and crisis-driven. They must balance numerous stakeholders and interest groups that may lay claim to their professional lives and fortunes. Knowledge can come from many sources; often vignettes or interpretations of truth from salient stakeholders in their environment prove to be the most compelling. In the end, knowledge for its own sake may prove a lot less important than information that supports their ideology or can advance their own political agenda.

Finally, Shonkoff sees practitioners as needing a different kind of knowledge that will help them design and implement policy decisions well and efficiently. They may also face intense political dynamics and interest group pressures. At the same time, they are closer to the consumers of programs and policies and, thus, are more constrained by expectations that what they do actually works. They also engage in the delicate task of implementing ideas in ways that balance idealism with exigencies that exist in the real world, including scarce resources. In the end, how to do something may be as important as what to do.

Bogenschneider and colleagues (2006) took these basic themes and laid them out more systematically. They developed a table with three communities, three broad cultural domains, and three behavioral elements within each domain (see Table 5.2). In short, they identified nine ways in which researchers, policymakers, and policy administrators saw the world or responded to the world differently. Let us review the salient distinctions across the three overarching domains—information needs, work culture, and writing preferences.

This kind of typology is rather typical of recent thinking on community and cultural differences across community groups. Other theorists might be cited, but their offerings would not differ substantially from what is provided above. One glaring deficiency with existing thought, it might be added, is that the integration of the concepts of *community* and *culture* is broad, overly general, and even somewhat superficial. Perhaps a brief discourse on how to better integrate these

TABLE 5.2   Differences in the Information Needs, Work Culture, and Writing Preferences Among the Three Communities of Researchers, Policymakers, and Policy Administrators

Characteristics	Researchers	Policymakers	Policy Administrators
Information needs	They focus on what they do not know and prefer questions as opposed to answers. They continuously seek more detailed information on increasingly narrow topics, though they occasionally reflect back on larger theoretical paradigms. They also prefer representative data, ideally random samples, but generally data on which generalizations can be made with few caveats.	They prefer answers, not questions. They gravitate toward comprehensive overviews that emphasize malleable factors that policy can influence. They particularly like comparative data across political jurisdictions (the scorecard phenomenon).	They focus on what they need to know to implement and manage polices and programs. They prefer more detail than policymakers, but detail that is focused on solving operational concerns. They prefer data sources that shed light on their target populations and program needs of concern to them.
Work culture	They are cautious, skeptical, tentative, and reflective, at least as a general rule. They have an epistemological preference for evidence based on statistical probability, rigorous methods, and peer-reviewed journal articles. Many are stimulated by ambiguity and complexity.	They are required to respond quickly to fast-paced changes in a fluid environment that evolves in light of events and pressures they cannot easily control. They make decisions based upon what is feasible and consistent with political calculation and ideological values. Complexity is not valued.	They are action oriented and pragmatic, and they must often act with incomplete information and insufficient resources. They typically balance knowledge with professional judgment and direct experience. They can be energized by complexity but must simplify enough to make hard decisions.
Writing preferences	They focus more on how they arrived at conclusions rather than on what they were or how they might be used. They organize products logically and build slowly. They engage in in-depth discussions, often replete with disciplinary-focused technical jargon, and use many sophisticated graphics.	They don't pay as much attention to methods unless they are threatened by the results. They want results first, and they focus on the practicality of results. They want concise, easy-to-read presentations that touch upon current issues.	They do pay attention to things such as samples, typically because they want to make sure that information is on target and relevant to their programs and populations. They also want practical information up front, not buried. They will tolerate reports of moderate length because they need more detail.

Source: Adapted from "How Can We Connect Research With State Policymaking? Lessons From the Wisconsin Family Impact Seminars," by K. Bogenschneider, J. R. Olson, J. Mills, and K. D. Linney, in *Family Policy Matters: How Policymaking Affects Families and What Professionals Can Do*, 2nd ed., pp. 245–276, by K. Bogenschneider, 2006, Mahwah, NJ: Lawrence Erlbaum.

concepts might help us push thinking on community and cultural differences further along.

TOWARD A CONCEPTUAL FRAMEWORK FOR THINKING ABOUT COMMUNITY DISSONANCE

Up to this point, we have been erecting the conceptual architecture upon which to erect a fuller understanding of how membership in a community shapes the way its members see and behave in the world. In the previous chapter, we laid out a fairly complex view of what we termed *professional culture* and *institutional culture*. We loosely defined *culture* as the stew of beliefs, values, dispositions, and perceptions that helped shape one's worldview. That is, the concept of culture is the milieu that surrounds us and influences our behavioral patterns in ways that may escape conscious awareness.

We also argued that there are two sources of culture. One source is derived from professional training. These are rules and values repeatedly drummed into us by virtue of sitting in classes, working with mentors, and associating with peers. Second, there is an institutional source of culture. These are the signals, rewards, incentives, or outright rules one is exposed to by virtue of one's job or institutional location. We incorporate both professional and institutional culture into community dissonance theory. Moreover, one of the tenets of the theory is that consistency across professional training and institutional location can serve to heighten the influences of cultural identification; dissonance can create confusion or ambiguity.

The real question is the following: What do we mean by the concept of *culture*? What values are we talking about, what perceptions, what behavioral patterns? How would we distinguish one milieu from another, and what difference does it make? As a starting point, recall Table 4.1 in Chapter 4. There we laid out a nuanced list of knowledge producers and users. That detailed enumeration of distinct groups, or communities, is unwieldy when we shift to an exploratory dialogue about the consequences of institutional and professional identity. To make our discussion workable, let's collapse this longer list into the following five distinct categories of target communities: basic researchers, applied researchers, intermediaries, policy doers, and policymakers (see the aggregated target communities in Table 5.3).

In effect, we offer a truncated set of institutional actors that range from those who build intellectual theory to those who bridge the knowledge producer–user worlds to those who shape the overall course of public policy. Each community is situated in its own unique organizational setting with a particular core technology. Each community views the world through a set of lenses that shapes what it sees and how it behaves.

Just what are these perceptual and behavioral dispositions? Building on prior work, we posit 12 dimensions organized into six domains where distinctions can be detected, which we lay out in Table 5.4. We term these categories the *dimensions of culture*. We believe each dimension is important to a full understanding of the consequences of institutional and professional cultural influences on how incumbents think and act. As above, however, the longer list can prove unwieldy.

TABLE 5.3   Aggregated Target Communities

Target Communities	Role
Basic researchers	They are focused on developing new knowledge irrespective of whether or how that knowledge is applied in the real world.
Applied researchers	They are focused on issues and questions with real-world applications.
Intermediaries	As a group, they try to bring research and analysis to policymakers and/or those who try to stimulate appropriate research and analysis on current management or policy questions.
Policy doers	They are responsible for designing, managing, or applying the intent of policies.
Policymakers	They are responsible for making basic decisions about the direction of policies.

TABLE 5.4   Domains and Dimensions of Culture

Domains	Dimensions
I–Focal interests	1. Salient domains of interest—What substantive topics are likely to attract these individuals' attention?
	2. Salient questions of interest—What kinds of intellectual, theoretical, policy, or management issues will make these individuals sit up and take notice?
II–Targets of interest	3. Salient constituencies—What is the audience of prime interest for these individuals? To whom do they direct their information and attention?
	4. Salient stakeholders—Whom do they pay the most attention to? What are the most relevant interest groups or individuals in their respective professional world?
III–Cognitive frameworks	5. Epistemological issues—What processes do these individuals use to make decisions about what they know, and to whom do they pay attention?
	6. Decision-making criterion—How do these individuals make decisions about research and policy matters?
IV–Interactional preferences	7. Preferred presentational style—How do these people like to present information to others? What style or distribution tactics do they prefer, and how do they prefer to receive information from others?
	8. Preferred communication style—How do these people like to interact with others? How do they relate to constituencies and stakeholders?
V–Feedback loops	9. Organizational signals/rewards—What kinds of institutional signals are important to these individuals? What kinds of things constitute critical professional or organizational rewards?
	10. Concept of success—How do these individuals define "success" in their professional world? To what uses do they put knowledge?
VI–Contextual preferences	11. Relevant time frames—What is the dominant pace in these people's professional world? To what kind of time pressures are they exposed?
	12. Comfort zone—Where do these individuals find comfort in their professional life? Conversely, what is likely to make them tense or uncertain?

Because distinctions across some dimensions may not be transparent, let us walk through in more detail what we mean by each dimension. At the same time, to make our task more manageable, let us pare down our list to a more discrete number of dimensions.

Dimensions 1 and 2 tap the issues, topics, and questions upon which incumbents in each of our basic communities tend to focus. Domains of interest are the general areas of knowledge such as theoretical development, specific hypothesis testing, evaluation information, tactical details on implementation, or basic descriptive information about the world. Questions of interest take us to a more discrete level of concern within each of these broader categories. For example, is a person likely to ask whether economic incentives can affect broad changes in how people function (e.g., broad categories of policy interventions), or is the individual more likely to focus on how individual rehabilitative (i.e., specific and targeted) interventions work? We are essentially tapping the level of abstraction here. Although the distinction between Dimensions 1 and 2 is valid, we combine them into a single category termed *focal interests* or *Domain I*.

Dimensions 3 and 4 tap the critical question of which targets (natural groupings of people) in a person's environment disproportionately grab the individual's attention. The first dimension focuses on what we normally think about as the target audience. The knowledge producer is developing new knowledge for whom? The policymaker is making new laws for whom? This is a question of intended audience. On the other hand, whom do individuals worry about as they go about their work? Which groups represent salient threats or opportunities? The first dimension identifies the target of the work; the second identifies those stakeholders that disproportionately influence how the work is done. We collapse these two dimensions into the category *targets of interest* or *Domain II*.

Dimensions 5 and 6 tap ways in which members of distinct communities think differently. Dimension 5 taps the essential epistemological question: How do we know what we know? What information is accepted as valid, usable, and worthy of including in one's work? Dimension 6 zeros in on a specific calculus that one goes through in arriving at what is knowable. What is the basis for making a decision about how one should act based upon knowledge? In short, Dimension 5 looks at what inputs have credibility, whereas Dimension 6 asks about the basis for acting on what is considered credible knowledge. We label these two dimensions the *cognitive frameworks* or *Domain III*.

Dimensions 7 and 8 tap two related dimensions that represent styles of relating to others. How do they differ from one another? Dimension 7 is narrower. Essentially, it looks at preferred ways of communicating specific knowledge or professional input to a peer or target audience. Conversely, how do the audience members prefer to receive such input? In effect, what is the preferred presentational style irrespective of whether the audience members are senders or receivers? Dimension 8 takes a broader look at interpersonal interactions. How do members of the group generally relate to others? What relationship styles and strategies generally work, or don't work, for them? We label these two dimensions *interactional preferences* or *Domain IV*.

Dimensions 9 and 10 give us some concept of what aspects of the person's organizational context serve to shape his or her cultural perspective. Dimension 9 examines the set of feedback mechanisms that individuals face and to which they must pay attention. That is, what kinds of things do they look for in their professional and institutional cultures to determine if they are playing by the formal or informal rules and whether they will be rewarded for their efforts? Dimension 10 leads us to a narrower issue of what constitutes success for members of various communities. What do they look for in determining if they are on the right track? Is the ultimate goal to discover knowledge for knowledge's sake, or is the goal to use knowledge for instrumental purposes to help further specific goals (Bimber, 1996)? We label these two related dimensions *feedback loops* or *Domain V*.

Finally, Dimensions 11 and 12 summarize larger ways in which the community groups differ. Dimension 11 looks at the issue of time, or the pace at which the different cultures operate. This does not mean day-to-day activity levels necessarily but rather the relative time frames over which the major aspects of one's professional life are measured. Dimension 12 captures a host of remaining differences that are associated with preferred ways in which incumbents in various groups function. Under what circumstances are they likely to feel in their element, and in what circumstances are they likely to feel out of their element? We label these two related dimensions as *contextual preferences* or *Domain VI*.

Now we attempt to put our building blocks together. We cross our sense of distinct communities with the dimensions across which they might differ in terms of perceptual and behavioral dispositions. Slowly, we have created the architecture for understanding the pervasive and nuanced influences that professional and institutional culture have in shaping the disconnect among the various communities that sustain the gap between the production and utilization of scientific knowledge.

Finally, we introduced an expanded set of dimensions for thinking about how culture plays out with respect to perceptions and behaviors that tend to separate communities. Then, as a final step, we reworked the complexity we consciously erected in developing our concepts of community and culture into a more manageable, yet still complicated, framework of domains and groups. In short, we erected a complex conceptual architecture to demonstrate just how complex the real world is before simplifying things in order to talk about how the world works, according to our vision.

The balance we seek is between acknowledging the complexity of the real world while describing it in ways that are comprehensible. To do so, we offer Table 5.5 and develop a narrative that builds upon the 30 cells that represent interactions between discrete communities and distinguishable cultural outcomes. We do not attempt to describe each cell in detail. Such minutiae would surely constitute a narcotic that would numb the most studious of readers. Rather, we push the envelope in ways that build upon earlier work, make it more systematic, and formalize our thinking about community and culture in ways that might permit more systematic empirical work in the future.

We erect our building blocks into a narrative that we hope contributes to understanding why various communities have so much trouble getting along. We started this chapter with three vignettes designed to bring home with some

TABLE 5.5   The Intersection of Community Affiliation and Cultural Dispositions

Cultural Domains	Producers (Research Types)			Users	
	A Basic	B Applied	C Intermediaries	D Policy Doers	E Policymakers
I–Focal interests	I-A	I-B	I-C	I-D	I-E
II–Targets of interest	II-A	II-B	II-C	II-D	II-E
III–Cognitive frameworks	III-A	III-B	III-C	III-D	III-E
IV–Interactional preferences	IV-A	IV-B	IV-C	IV-D	IV-E
V–Feedback loops	V-A	V-B	V-C	V-D	V-E
VI–Contextual preferences	VI-A	VI-B	VI-C	VI-D	VI-E

force the extent to which knowledge consumers and producers can fail in their efforts to communicate and cooperate. With our theoretical building blocks in place, perhaps the extent of the cultural divide is a bit less puzzling. Below, we explore each cultural domain in turn. As we do so, we must recall that we have simplified the world considerably both by combining individual subcommunities into larger aggregations (e.g., combining several distinct groupings of organizations that serve to bridge the producer–consumer divide into a single category termed *intermediaries*) and by collapsing individual cultural dispositions into broader domains (see Table 5.3). We organize the resulting narrative around six cultural domains.

Focal Interests

Basic and applied researchers generally gravitate toward different substantive and topical interests than do intermediaries or certainly policy doers and policymakers. Basic researchers, themselves, can be distinguished from their applied brethren. In particular, they look to advance our theoretical understandings of the world irrespective of whether there are immediate or pragmatic impacts. They seek abstract knowledge about how the world works that is applicable in very general ways and will have predictive power over time. Researchers, both basic and applied, are much more interested in methodological questions. For the basic researcher, however, the issue of how a conclusion was arrived at often will generate far more attention than what the conclusion is.

If you read academic journals, you will quickly see a ritualistic rhythm to how articles are constructed. They start with extensive literature reviews and a rationale for why this work will advance our theoretical knowledge base. Great attention is paid to describing the data used and methods applied. Because the best work makes causal claims, one must carefully establish the credibility of those claims. At the end, often in a perfunctory way, assertions about policy relevance might be made. These are often an afterthought and rendered with little appreciation of logistical, fiscal, or political realities.

Various communities think about the utility of knowledge production in different ways. Using our research use schema, basic researchers drift toward uses of their work that might be described as framework shifting. Applied researchers drift in the direction of solutions shifting. Intermediaries often look to research from a salience-shifting or allocation-shifting purpose. Policymakers look at research in the same way, though they often view the utility of research and analysis products through the filter of partisan values or political calculus. Policy doers, managers, and practitioners tend to be more practical, seeking input that is characterized as tactics shifting and allocation shifting, with occasional interest in solutions-shifting knowledge.

At the other end of the community spectrum, policymakers and policy doers generally want applicable input. Academic literature strikes them as disproportionately weighted toward methods and seriously wanting in usable information. Naturally, they gravitate toward trusted intermediaries in search of usable research. They want someone to vet the credibility of available knowledge, recognizing full well that many intermediaries are located in agenda-driven institutions. And they want translators who are cognizant of real-life realities that must be considered before pursuing any course of action.

Cultural confusion is inevitable. Researchers in academia seek narrow issues that can be addressed in peer-reviewed journal articles. Policymakers want solutions-shifting knowledge (what works), and policy doers want tactics-shifting insights (how to make it work). Researchers focus on statistical significance (a true effect). Policymakers and policy doers want practical input that is applicable to their particular context. The list of potential conflict points is lengthy.

Targets of Interest

Here we shift our attention to those groups that attract the attention of our various communities. Whom do they think about as they do their work, and who has the relatively stronger claims on their attention as they scan their respective environments?

Researchers are most concerned with other researchers. (Would we expect anything else?) They organize their work and expend their energies with an eye on their peers. The more ensconced a researcher is in the academy, the more likely he or she will focus on a small set of peers who operate in a very narrow sphere of expertise. That is how academic careers are sustained and advanced.

As we move toward applied researchers and intermediaries, the target audience expands and the range of significant groups broadens. They must balance reference groups that focus on theory and methods with groups that focus on results and application. The relative attention paid to these competing types of reference groups shifts as one moves from researchers to those identified as intermediaries.

Often, there is a balancing act, a sense of trade-offs. If you are concerned about academic prestige or scholarly advancement, the mere association with policymakers or policy doers can be detrimental. You can lose points by attending policy-oriented conferences or producing research reports that are "dumbed down" for popular consumption. At the annual IRP summer conference oriented toward serious researchers in economics and sociology, presenters typically use very complex slides with lots of numbers and equations on each one. They emphasize methods and data and seldom comment on policy implications. The policy-oriented session is reserved for a lunch or dinner slot, so as not to be confused with the "serious sessions."

Obviously, policymakers and policy doers respond to a different set of professional or institutional actors. Depending on their specific organizational location, they continuously scan their environment to keep track of several sources of potential influence—clients, funders, political friends and enemies, the press, and the public. Their lives are extraordinarily complicated. They may well be concerned with the credibility of research results, but their litmus test is seldom confined to methodological purity.

Cognitive Frameworks

This domain focuses on how various communities think about their work. How do they conceptualize their world? How do they make decisions about what is right and wrong? What is worthy of their attention? Here again, there are substantial differences across our communities of interest. In short, how do people know what they know, and how do they conceptualize success in their professional spheres?

Researchers typically are cautious in approaching the concept of "truth." Great stock is placed in relying on the canons of science and in carefully testing causal hypotheses. Basic researchers, in particular, approach knowledge building from a skeptical perspective. The starting point is the null hypothesis—the premise that a hypothesized truth is "not" really true until alternative explanations for the observed reality have been ruled out as false. "Real" researchers always look for reasons to discount purported findings.

Tom recalls his early undergraduate training in psychology at Clark University, the university where Freud delivered his U.S. lectures and where the American Psychological Association was founded. He did a psychology research project one summer with support from the National Science Foundation. Two professors were discussing a series of experiments involving how variable reinforcement schedules impacted the learning curve of rats negotiating complex mazes. The research results were leading to a specific conclusion about which reinforcement schedules were more efficacious.

As Tom observed their dialogue, he was taken by the fact that these professors refused to accept their findings at face value. They continued to search for other, spurious reasons unconnected to their own theoretical understanding of the world to explain away the statistically significant results. Perhaps there were visual cues the rats were using that could be controlled in future experiments by randomly rotating the position of the maze. Or perhaps the maze should be cleansed after each trial so that olfactory cues were not present. The list went on. The lesson he absorbed early on was that a "real" scientist never relaxed in the pursuit of truth but kept looking for reasons to discount even positive empirical results that supported their theoretical priors.

In the same scientific tradition, David Olds and his colleagues modeled this patient pursuit of the truth in their development and evaluation of the Nurse-Family

Partnership program. Over the past 30 years, this program has been evaluated with the sine qua non of evaluation methods—the randomized control trial. When contrasted with comparison groups, nurse home visiting has been shown to prevent child abuse and neglect among high-risk, low-income families who are visited prenatally and during the first 2 years of a child's life. These evaluations have been published in the top medical journals, and the program was recently endorsed in a review that appeared in the highly respected journal *The Lancet*. In April 2009, the nonpartisan Coalition for Evidence-Based Policy issued a statement supporting the effectiveness of Olds's program and suggesting that there are few validated effects for six other home visiting models. Despite these authoritative endorsements, Olds was cautious in his assessment of the program's effectiveness in his comments at a recent policy training Karen helped organize at the 2009 biennial conference of the Society for Research in Child Development:

> There is a Web-based information system in which family nurses—program sites—enter data on every visit that allows us to monitor the ongoing performance of the program, to use that information for continuous quality improvement, and for research on improving the basic model because the basic model is not good enough. We are pleased with it, but … it will always be a work in progress. … There are a number of things that we think that we can do better as we roll this program out.

Success for researchers often lies in disproving the null hypothesis. It lies in finding statistical significance and in having those findings scrutinized by one's peers. Ultimate vindication is found when one's work is replicated. When a finding is repeatedly found, one's confidence in its validity grows, and one can assume with confidence that results generated from random samples, in fact, represent population parameters.

Statistical significance, however, might not be critical to a policymaker or policy doer. For one thing, large samples can produce statistically significant differences where the gap between a treatment group and a control group is actually very modest. Researchers define success when they look across the study sample and observe an average change that is statistically significant in the desired direction. However, intermediaries may define success as a large effect in only one individual, even if the average effect remains unchanged. For example, if a Family Impact Seminar contributes to even one legislator introducing legislation that is evidence based, that would be defined as substantively significant, irrespective of whether it was statistically significant (see Chapter 11). For policymakers and policy doers, lack of enthusiasm also can flow from other sources. An experimental finding can be arrived at in a hothouse experiment, a focused program that targets a population of interest with a high level of resources. The savvy policymaker or policy doer might immediately recognize that going to scale would be fiscally or logistically infeasible. They might recognize that an intervention, or policy, might contradict public sentiment or go against the prevailing political wind.

Those of us who have observed cultural conflicts between producers and consumers have witnessed variants of a sad drama. The researcher cannot understand the lack of interest in the empirical findings that have stood up to rigorous scrutiny by peers. The policymaker is astounded at the naïveté of the researcher. Why can't this egghead see what is so obvious—that the larger cost of doing what the data suggest will incur unacceptable political costs or generate intractable management challenges? A researcher might feel he or she has achieved a breakthrough when he or she develops a new estimating technique that results in a more accurate estimate of a population parameter that differs from the old estimate by a percentage point or two. The policymaker or policy doer is likely to respond to such a breakthrough with a resounding, "So what?"

Interactional Preferences

Members of these communities differ dramatically in how each operates as social beings and in terms of learning styles. These differences are not trivial when assessing how cultural conflict might play out. For researchers, the human element, although not irrelevant, is viewed with suspicion. Truth is located in the data and their careful use. Danger is found when humans, driven by passion and prejudice, interpret and manipulate numbers according to subjective whims. This is the reason for statistical tests, replication of results, and continuous vetting of findings by one's peers. The prevailing modus operandi in the research world is "trust but verify."

Those on the knowledge-consuming side of things operate very differently. Values and preferences are important. The quality and character of subjective inputs into a policy or programmatic discussion are to be valued. Numbers are certainly important but so are expertise, testimonial evidence, and other sources of input. What is most critical is trust: Do you trust the messenger? Is the message credible? What is second in importance is accessibility: Can you understand the message? What is third in importance is timeliness: Does the message have anything to do with what is on the political table at the moment? In other words, is the message relevant?

Those operating in the nebulous world of intermediaries once again balance multiple factors, depending on where they are institutionally located. Agenda-driven organizations act more like policymakers. Perceptions and positions are more likely driven by factors other than empirical evidence. Values and political preferences hold considerable weight. Those who see themselves as honest brokers pay more attention to methods and the canons of science in pursuing truth. Yet they still expend a great deal of energy in cultivating relationships with policymakers. They realize that long reports on what works may satisfy funders but may go unread by busy policymakers; they must have access to deliver their message and the credibility to be taken seriously.

Feedback Loops

We all live in organizational settings that are replete with signals and rewards. We all live in interpersonal contexts where behavior is bounded and subtle messages about what is acceptable are ever present. We term this cultural domain as *feedback loops* because it essentially captures how we relate to one another. How do we convey information? How do we "talk," verbally and otherwise? These communication strategies, whether conscious strategies or inbred patterns, are ways in which we convey signals to our professional and institutional peers.

Let us think about this for a moment. Watch top researchers in a session with their peers, an academic conference, or what is called a "job talk" in academia, where scholars display their comparative advantages to advance their careers. Granted, there are exceptions to the rule, but typically they talk fast, lapse into jargon, and emphasize technical virtuosity. The purpose may be less to communicate than to obscure substance in an impressive array of dazzling methods. The Chicago School (University of Chicago) was renowned for the savagery of the intellectual arguments as research was vetted among colleagues. Truth was not to be pursued in a collegial and civil exchange of ideas. Rather, truth was the residue of ideas and arguments that still stood at the end of a bitter vetting struggle analogous to a form of Darwinian intellectual survival of the fittest.

That may well be the extreme case, but the point being made is simple. Academics and top researchers operate in a highly competitive environment. People get to the top of this world after years of competing with others to graduate to the next academic level, to obtain advanced degrees, to land jobs in top universities, to get tenure, to secure research support, to publish in the best journals, to win prestigious named positions, and so forth. Surviving in this world is a continuous zero-sum game. Competitors are continuously fearful of slipping behind in the ongoing race. Paranoia and insecurity are rampant. In such a world, communicating clearly is not necessarily prized. Sophistication of ideas, innovativeness, nuance, and complexity are what counts.

Many years ago, a fellow graduate student told a wonderful story. She was trying to explain to a grandparent the topic that was the subject of her master's thesis. In doing so, she fell into the jargon of her academic discipline. Her aged relative murmured something about being both impressed and totally lost. So, the student rephrased the description of her research question of interest, communicating the same information but now using simple words and declarative sentences. Now, however, her grandparent looked a bit surprised, saying with just a touch of incredulity, "But, my dear, everyone knows that!" For too many academics, maintaining the mystery of their expertise is very important; too much clarity might take away a bit of the mystery associated with their craft.

Policymakers also operate in highly competitive environments. Politicians, in particular, must win elections and compete in the political marketplace of ideas and values. The medium of exchange, though, is qualitatively different. Great value is placed on simplifying complex matters so they can be communicated effectively. Although politicians surely dissemble their positions, often to appeal to all sides in controversial issues, communicating well is a valued commodity. Say it in a sound bite. Besides, policymakers typically are beset with innumerable issues and overwhelming demands on their time. They must cut to the chase quickly; nuanced debate is an unaffordable luxury.

In this setting, intermediaries, as in so many other areas, are torn. On the one hand, they are drawn to sophisticated methods. After all, many were professionally socialized in similar ways to researchers in top universities or think tanks. They want any original work they do to stand up to serious scrutiny. At the same time, they see policymakers as a legitimate, if not primary, target audience. Therefore, they want to reduce complexity to declarative statements that might actually be heard and to state those assertions with some boldness. This is quite a balancing act—to be correct, comprehensive, concise, and confident all at the same time.

Contextual Preferences

Finally, we touch upon what we call the contextual factor. Members of each community feel more or less comfortable in certain environments. Let's start with the dimension of time frames. Researchers think of their work, or at least the questions they pursue, as timeless. Building theory is a long-term process. Care must be taken at each stage: theories tested carefully, experiments replicated, results vetted, and all steps subject to endless scrutiny and debate. It is not often that social science gets tested against real-world expectations as were the theoretical and experimental physicists working on the Manhattan Project during World War II. The atom bomb would either work or not, and hopefully not work so well that the whole world would evaporate in a mushroom cloud.

At the same time, researchers are often rewarded for attending to very specific research questions. The definition of an expert, after all, is someone who knows more and more about less and less until he or she knows everything about nothing. And so, the best researchers often can achieve brilliant breakthroughs but in content areas that seem overly narrow to policy types. Trained to focus on detail, they can get so involved in the twigs that they cannot see the branches, never mind the forest.

Policymakers and doers, on the other hand, often see their world as operating at hyperspeed. A kaleidoscope of issues and crises can pass before their eyes on a continuous basis. When Tom worked in Washington on welfare reform in 1993–1994, helping to craft the first Clinton welfare bill, the pace of work and the complexity of the work were daunting. When analyses were needed, seldom did anyone say, "Let's get an academic involved in this issue." What would happen if they did? Most academics would say something like, "Well, I could develop a research proposal next summer. Or, my research does not quite fit into your questions, sorry." If you're lucky, you might get the following: "I'll see if any of my graduate students are interested." Or, you might get a response along the lines of, "Well, I do have some thoughts on that topic, but I would like to replicate that work before making any recommendations." The policy folks in Health and Human Services wanted feedback in a couple of days, not next semester.

Of course, the contexts people feel comfortable in touch on many dimensions of life, some of which are covered in other parts of this book. For example, most researchers are numbers oriented, not people oriented. They like to work alone or maybe in small teams. They like narrow topics, not issues that cross substantive areas or disciplines. They are comfortable with ambiguity and complexity. They seek uncertainty and mystery. They feed on analysis and numbers, complexity, and intellectual challenge. Many prefer to communicate in the arcane language of mathematical expression.

Now, think about your typical policymaker and policy doer. They are people oriented. They prize certainty and simplicity. Trust and a personal relationship are highly valued. They must work with many others. They must shift attention from topic to topic. They have little tolerance for pondering perplexing questions when they need plausible solutions.

Because the worlds of knowledge consumers and producers are so different and so complex, we ultimately need theories that incorporate a number of different communities rather than the simplistic worldviews based on two or three communities (e.g., researchers, policymakers, and policy administrators). In reality, each community, even when defined in greater detail, remains sufficiently idiosyncratic that members of one community are not sure how to relate to members of another. Members know the ground rules of their own community—the language, nuanced cues, and behavioral patterns. Venturing into another community is a risky undertaking. The higher they are in their own community's hierarchy, the greater the risk of a potential loss of face and professional embarrassment. It is easier to stay put, to fight the inevitable professional struggles that arise in a playing field that is known.

SUMMARY

In their recent book, Nutley and colleagues (Nutley et al., 2007) argued that theoretical development to explain research utilization has been limited. The two communities theory resonates with us as a starting point because of its insights into the critical disconnect between the communities of research and policy. Yet its construction strikes us as too limited and its conceptualizations too constrained. In this chapter, we attempted to address theoretical shortcomings by delving more deeply into the complexity of this disconnect among relevant communities and by describing the sources of miscommunication and misunderstanding with greater clarity.

We began by going back to the basics—exploring what research utilization means. We proposed new theoretical constructs that maintain the coherence of prior concepts that have emerged from the research world, but we expanded upon them by incorporating the important perspective of what research utilization means to the policy world. We think that policymakers are less likely to think in terms of whether their research use is *conceptual, instrumental,* or *tactical.* Instead, policymakers are more likely to think in terms of why they seek out information and for what purposes they put it to use in the policy world. Does research shift awareness of issues, alter their salience, or offer new frameworks for thinking about them? Does research shift policy solutions, administrative tactics, or resource allocation? Defining research utilization by these policy purposes may make it more likely that we can predict if and when research utilization will occur and to identify the forces that may magnify or mitigate its use.

We then moved beyond the two communities theory (Caplan, 1979) by proposing a new conceptual framework that we call *community dissonance theory.* We believe this theory expands our thinking from the notion of two communities to a number of community groupings where each is formed around a core technology that defines the tasks professionals perform as well as the institution's purpose, culture, and structure. Each of these communities, whether it be basic researchers, applied researchers, intermediaries, policy doers, or policymakers, is shaped by professional and institutional culture in ways that differentially affect how their inhabitants think, act, and behave.

We enriched this notion of community by situating it within the concept of *culture*. We all live in some type of cultural stew—a professional and institutional mix of beliefs, values, dispositions, and perceptions. These cultural environs are the waters in which we swim on a daily basis. Those waters are so encompassing that we can barely appreciate the real nature of that supportive fluid and what it does to shape our world. In particular, we detail six dimensions of culture that include focal interests, targets of interest, cognitive frameworks, interactional preferences, feedback loops, and contextual preferences.

We also put these elemental concepts together by crossing our sense of distinct communities with the cultural dimension across which they might differ in terms of perceptual and behavioral dispositions. Taking these together, we erected a rather complex conceptual foundation on which to base our theoretical perspective but one that we think comes closer to explaining just how complex the disconnect between research and policy is in the real world.

In the end, we arrived at a new conceptual framework that we call *community dissonance theory*, which we define in the following way. Community dissonance theory attributes the underutilization of research in policymaking to a lack of communication between knowledge producers and knowledge consumers from a number of disparate communities who engage in different core technologies and operate in distinct professional and institutional cultures. These cultures, in turn, shape the communication styles, decision-making criteria, questions of interest, reward systems, salient constituencies, and time frames of the members of each community.

We realize that we have simplified a very complex topic. Without question, we have obscured the rich, within-group variation that we know, in reality, exists. Not all knowledge producers, even those focusing on basic research, are alike. Similarly, some lawmakers in the same settings could care less about research, and others aggressively seek it out to help them make the best decisions possible.

Clearly, we have simplified our descriptions of *community culture*. Just as clearly, we have only touched upon the attributes and characteristics that would be encompassed by a more comprehensive treatment. These shortcomings do not detract from our central message, however. Culture shapes how we think, act, and perceive our world in ways that we never fully appreciate. It can facilitate or impede communication across communities and worlds. Unless we have some sense of the professional and institutional cultures in which we operate, we may never really grasp why we struggle with those of others. Languages collide, nonverbal gestures fail to communicate, and expectations go unfulfilled.

As we worked to explore these concepts, we struggled with the words that best captured what we were talking about. Was it cultural confusion? Perhaps we are talking about conflict? In the end, we concluded that *community dissonance* best taps what we are struggling to define. The term *dissonance* implies a level of disconnect that is not always conscious or intended. It is more of a lack of align-ment where the diverse communities do not mesh well despite mutual needs and interests. Our sense of *dissonance* suggests that a better understanding of the cul-tural dynamics that foster this failure to connect can lead to assertive strategies to improve the situation. The implications of community dissonance theory for research utilization are summarized in Key Concepts 5.2.

Key Concepts 5.2   Selected Implications of Community Dissonance Theory for the Use of Evidence

- Work hard to understand how your professional education and train-ing may have influenced how you look at the world.
- Reflect on how your current professional position shapes the way you deal with other people and your view of evidence.
- Try to sense how others look at the world. If you are a knowledge producer, envision how knowledge consumers might think and act and respond. What might be their preferred communication styles, decision-making criteria, questions of interest, reward systems, salient constituencies, and time frames?
- Think comprehensively about why policymakers seek out informa-tion and for what purposes. Does research shift awareness of issues, alter their salience, or offer new frameworks for thinking about them? Does research shift policy solutions, administrative tactics, or resource allocation?
- Take risks and spend time getting to know the institutional and pro-fessional cultures of knowledge-producing and knowledge-consuming communities other than your own. There are some things you cannot know from books or the literature that are best learned firsthand.
- Put your ego to the side. It is easy to become arrogant if you are trapped within the confines of your own culture, but it is far more honest and edifying to recognize that your worldview has limitations and biases. No one has a corner on understanding. We can all learn from one another.

We supplement this theoretical discussion of culture with a more pragmatic and perhaps more optimistic perspective in Chapter 8. Researchers, who are bicul-turally competent, describe the cultural barriers they encountered on their forays into the policy world and how they have learned to overcome them.

But first, we consider in some depth what we think of as fundamental under-standings that researchers and intermediaries must familiarize themselves with if they are going to communicate across rigid and resistant cultural barriers. Once again, we find ourselves forced to simplify the complex world of knowledge pro-ducers and consumers that we propose in community dissonance theory. We could easily devote a chapter to each of the target communities that we laid out above—basic researchers, applied researchers, intermediaries, policy doers, and policymakers—and quite honestly also to every one of the subcommunities within each of these broad categories. However, in the next two chapters, we limit our scope and examine in some depth only one knowledge consumer, policymakers, and within that broad category, the elected official. Then we turn our attention to the core technology of elected officials—lawmaking and the processes through which it occurs, observations that we have found to be obvious to insiders but often quite surprising to outsiders.

6

Breaking Through Stereotypes of Policymakers

A politician thinks of the next election; a statesman of the next generation.

— **James Clarke (1810–1886)**

A statesman is a politician who places himself at the service of the nation. A politician is a statesman who places the nation at his service.

— **Georges Pompidou (1911–1974)**

One dimension of our research and policy cultures is similar—inhabitants of each community often stereotype whatever they do not understand about the other community. For example, who hasn't heard policymakers stereotyped as egotistical, opportunistic, and self-serving? Who among us is not aware of instances where researchers are referred to as eggheads, nerds, and absent-minded professors? What academic wouldn't bristle at being referred to in the way that Karen's young son used to introduce her to his friends: "My mom's a doctor, but not the kind that does you any good at all!" Policymakers and researchers are easy for naysayers to stereotype. If these stereotypes remain unchallenged, they can result in entrenched misperceptions that can strain communication and sabotage efforts to collaborate across these conflicting cultures.

In previous chapters, we argued that members of the research and policy communities, as well as those who serve as intermediaries between the two, are conditioned to see the world in different ways and to behave in accord with those disparate worldviews. Often, they are not fully aware of how deep and pervasive are the cultural differences that separate them. In this, and succeeding chapters, we tap into the words of our informants to give texture to our conceptual framework.

Our earlier study of researchers who are considered exemplary policy communicators suggests that stereotypical thinking about policymakers, specifically the elected officials whom we focus on in this chapter, is very widespread. The initial contacts researchers made with policymakers often highlighted the cultural barriers that divided them. However, none of these stereotypes persisted as researchers gained more awareness of, exposure to, and experience with policymakers. This finding should not be surprising given its consistency with the tenets of community dissonance theory—that the underutilization of research is due to a communication gap between knowledge producers and knowledge consumers who engage in different core technologies and operate in distinct professional and institutional cultures that affect how they think, act, and communicate. A corollary of the theory is that research utilization could be increased with greater familiarity with alien policy cultures and better understanding of its inhabitants, at least when that exposure occurs under the right conditions.

To provide a more in-depth and nuanced understanding of what policymakers are like, we rely on a two-pronged approach. We draw on the insights from policymakers themselves, who provide an insider's perspective of their experiences around the core technology of making laws. We also draw upon the observations of researchers and professionals who are one step removed from the policy process, but who have observed it up close and personal. This chapter begins by discussing researchers' initial impressions of policymakers and how they changed in several respects after they had logged in more time in the policy community. We also review two studies, one qualitative and one quantitative, that push the envelope by looking beyond the generic label of policymakers to examine within-group differences in those who ply the policy trade. Each study is followed up with a discussion of why it is important to dissect the ways that policymakers differ from each other, and how this knowledge can inform our efforts to be better brokers of research-based information and analysis.

RESEARCHERS' INITIAL IMPRESSIONS OF POLICYMAKERS AND HOW THEY CHANGED OVER TIME

In interviews of researchers who eventually became successful in bridging the gulf between the research and policy cultures, 11 of 14 reported that they initially held negative stereotypes about policymakers. Consistent with community dissonance theory, it appears that researchers view policymaking through the lens of their own culture, which seems to taint their first impressions. Researchers reported that they initially thought that policymakers had "short attention spans," "were driven by money," and were "looking for easy solutions to complex problems, unwilling to take risks, and arrogant." One researcher said his initial thought was that policymakers "just want a sound bite."

In keeping with the tenets of community dissonance theory, we found that open communication and prolonged contact with policymakers helped dispel these stereotypes and break down cultural barriers. Perhaps most important for the purposes of this chapter is that none of their negative stereotypes were confirmed. Perceptions of policymakers changed in several respects, including comprehending what this species called *policymakers* is really like, understanding what motivates them to seek public office, and appreciating the skills it takes for policymakers to succeed in their world. Each is discussed in turn below.

What the Policymaker Species Is Like

Mary Fairchild, a senior fellow at the National Conference of State Legislatures, provided an interesting window into what policymakers are like based on her experience working with them for over 20 years. She expressed her surprise that the media and people she meets at family reunions and social gatherings are so "cynical" about policymakers, which flies in the face of her assessment that legislators are "top quality" and "ethical." She explained that there is a "huge premium on honesty" in the policy process. Policymakers might be able to achieve some short-term goals by being "Machiavellian" in their approach, but these are not the sorts of public officials who continue to contribute to the policy process in the long run. In her words,

> I don't want to pretend like it's, you know, just this wonderful, beautiful group of people that get along. I mean, there is supposed to be controversy. But … I think we can be really proud of our elected officials as human beings and they represent all the different aspects of society, I think, pretty realistically … I'm always disappointed when most of the attention focuses on the scandal, the negative.

These perceptions of policymakers seemed to be independent of the work setting of the professionals that we interviewed. Fairchild's perceptions of policymakers, from her vantage point at a government trade association, were similar to the comments of a researcher at a land-grant university that is renowned as one of the top research institutions in the country and that was recently recognized for its commitment to science in the public interest. When this researcher initially started working with policymakers, he relayed that he had no preconceptions of what they would be like. Over time, he grew to have a lot of respect for the commitment that he observed in policymakers:

> They are for the most part young, very idealistic, got involved in politics because they want to make a difference. They work very long hours, [and] spend an enormous amount of time working.

In fact, he said that he could recall working this long and hard only when he was working on his PhD and trying to get tenure. A positive perception of policymakers also emerged from a researcher housed at the policy-oriented research organization Child Trends. In the words of Kristin Anderson Moore, former president and now senior scholar,

> People in the policy community are really pretty committed, very hardworking, smart. They are trying to do a good job. If you understand their starting point and their assumptions, then what they are doing really makes much more sense. So I have, you know, maybe a more nuanced understanding of them.

Similarly, Edward Zigler, a developmental psychologist who worked with policymakers at the federal level for 44 years, found them to be "dedicated public workers who really wanted to hear what research could tell them, and to use this information to form better policies" (Zigler & Styfco, 2002, p. 13).

Looking across these interviews of exemplary communicators, one recurring theme is how these stereotypes of policymakers break down when you come to know them as individuals. One researcher found that her stereotypes changed when she was able to "put a human face on policymakers." A researcher at one of the nation's leading evaluation firms explained that the more he worked with policymakers, the more he "demystified" them in his thinking: "You learn that they put their pants on one leg at a time."

According to University of Wisconsin Cooperative Extension specialist Dave Riley, these perceptual shifts were predictable because it is always the case that as you get to know people, they become more like themselves and less like your preconceptions of them. Alternatively, it could also be true that rather than the professional's preconceptions changing, policymakers themselves could change over time, as all of us do. In fact, policymakers' attitudes about research and researchers could evolve as more communication flows between the two cultures. Riley then relayed a compelling example of how a policymaker whom he worked with for several years changed over the course of his political career:

> Do legislators change over time? Do they grow? And I think, "Yes, they do." Part of it has to do with whether they have power or not. The best example of that was our former governor here who when he was a legislator was a real ideologue. He was in the minority party for most of his term and so his job was to point his finger at the problems in the other party, and he's saying "No" all the time, kind of a negative campaigner. Once he had real political power as the governor, he pinned his hopes on welfare reform and all of a sudden he became very practical. He was no longer ideological. Because he wanted this thing to work … you'll do what it takes to make it work. So he used to be opposed to child care. Suddenly, he realized child care is necessary if welfare reform is going to work. And so he wanted to know how do we create child care? And then he kind of discovered that if the child care is high-enough quality, you not only get the parents in the workplace, but you help the kids avoid welfare when they grow up. So he wanted to know, how do we make child care better? And I see him as growing from an ideologue, who wasn't very practical, into a very practical guy who could talk with anybody and who respected expertise way more.

What Motivates Policymakers to Seek Public Office

Another perceptual shift among the researchers we interviewed was their coming to better understand what motivates policymakers to run for office. A sociologist, now a dean at a major research university, gradually developed a lot of respect for policymakers as he came to realize that their decision to get involved in public life was often motivated by their idealism and desire to make a difference. A similar observation was made by another academic researcher, who previously had served as the deputy assistant secretary of the U.S. Treasury Department: "Policymakers are largely people who want to do a good job under constraints of time. They try to do the best they can under these constraints."

At the state legislative level, Mary Fairchild of the National Conference of State Legislatures observed that people do not run for office for monetary gain, especially at the state level. In her words, "I really do think that people run for office because they want to make a change, a positive change." One prescription drug researcher with 25 years of experience concurred that he encountered more politics than one would expect, but also observed more successes than he anticipated: "Parties working together, coming together for the common good." After working with policymakers for 10 years, one academic said that his initial negative impressions were not substantiated:

> I see them in more complex ways now. I have more of an appreciation of the contributions some of these folks make. They don't make a lot of money, they get a lot of grief, they get called at home, [they] have a few areas in which they want to make a difference, on which they have to work year after year, before they make a difference.

Appreciating the Skills Policymakers Need to Succeed

Researchers came to appreciate the skills it takes to succeed in policymaking. One health researcher, who has worked with policymakers since the 1970s, said that he was taken by the level of knowledge that policymakers possess and their ability to focus on the really important questions. Others were impressed with policymakers' interest in listening to information "even if it goes against their personal ideology." One researcher, who spent the early part of his career safely ensconced in the ivory tower, said his stereotypes changed as he became more involved in the policy arena:

> I came to appreciate the best part of a politician and public official ... the pragmatics, the way they have to make alliances, the way they have to be swayed by public opinion, have to take the pulse of their constituents ... they remember people's names, they are gracious, they thank people, they build relationships.

In addition to applauding the skills that policymakers possess, another researcher went one step further and compared the skills of policymakers to those of researchers. The researchers fared less favorably: "They [policymakers] are obviously premier communicators, they know how to talk. ... We are nerdy researchers. They are high-level speakers." One researcher, who is a member of an international team analyzing family policy in the United States, the United Kingdom, Canada, and Australia, also contrasted the policy community with the research community, reaching the conclusion that the job of a policymaker is harder than his job as a researcher because policymakers have to make decisions: "A researcher can say 'on one hand and on the other hand,' [but] a policymaker has to decide." One fellow at a nonpartisan policy research firm also compared the constraints that policymakers face to the ones that she encounters: "Policymakers have constituents that they have to answer to, have constraints around them—what they focus on and what their option set is. As a researcher, I don't face those constraints." Chief among these constraints were the budgetary and political considerations that "academics can largely ignore."

Summary of Changes in Researchers' Perceptions of Policymakers

The researchers' initial forays into policymaking were met with surprise at how little they knew about the policymakers' world. At the same time, the researchers came face-to-face with how little policymakers knew about what researchers could bring to the table. One researcher said, "Policymakers were somewhat unrealistic about what you could and couldn't get out of research." This mutual misunderstanding on both sides of the research–policy divide led to mutual disappointment—policymakers trying to fit research into the realities of the political world, and researchers worrying about what adjustments it would take to see their programs become a political reality. In response to this clash of cultures, one respondent worried that her research was being "pushed in a direction I wouldn't have taken it."

Similarly, another researcher, invited to talk with the surgeon general about using his program model for a national initiative, experienced firsthand the tensions that occur when the two cultures try to work together in a way that remains true to the core operating principles of each:

> I felt that the policymakers were interested in watering the program down and altering the program that we were testing. This has made me more sensitive to the challenges that policymakers have—to conduct work with limited dollars to cover a lot of people. And my concern is that you end up watering down programs and compromising their effectiveness.

Despite these challenges, researchers' perceptions improved as the researchers became more successful in building relationships with policymakers. Several researchers said they had grown to deeply respect policymakers for their commitment and intelligence. For example, one explained that he has come to appreciate that policymakers have "wisdom, knowledge, and experience to bring to the table, and that is no less than my knowledge and experience." Other researchers came to see policymakers as collaborators and were "able to establish a common mission in many respects" with them.

In sum, a critical insight from these exemplary policy communicators was how easy it is for researchers to stereotype policymakers, who, at first blush, appear to work in a strange and foreign land. A surprising two thirds of researchers, who eventually ended up comfortably navigating between the two cultures of research and policy, held a number of negative stereotypes about policymakers when they first ventured into the policy arena. As researchers worked more closely with policymakers, they were less apt to engage in stereotyping and they were more apt to understand how these working relationships could result in promoting a common agenda, that of improving the quality of policy decisions.

The discerning reader will no doubt question the generalizability of these findings. How much confidence can we have that policymakers in general are committed, honest, and hardworking? What portion of the policymaker population is motivated by idealism and the desire to make a difference? How common is it for policymakers to be premier communicators who can take the pulse of their constituents and listen respectfully to views different from their own? This chapter would be misleading if it conceptualized policymakers as a homogenous group just because policymakers are elected to the same job and work in the same setting (Levin, 1952/2005). This tendency to study policymakers in the aggregate, rather than examining disaggregated subgroups of policymakers, has contributed to a scientific understanding of policymakers and their research use that is "unduly simplistic" (Weiss & Bucuvalas, 1980, p. 248).

UNPACKING HOW POLICYMAKERS DIFFER FROM EACH OTHER AND HOW KNOWLEDGE BROKERS CAN LEVERAGE THESE DIFFERENCES TO THEIR ADVANTAGE

Studies of research utilization in policymaking have been approached much like the proverbial black box. The adult education literature is replete with evidence that adults have different learning styles and prefer information in different formats (Tough, 1971), yet this knowledge has not been seriously and sufficiently extrapolated to the policy world. Studies typically examine differences across groups of decision makers such as the Weiss and Bucuvalas (1980) study of researchers; grant-review-committee members; and executive agency officials at the local, state, and federal levels. Few studies tackle the important challenges of disentangling the differences within these groups in regard to their legislative behavior and whether they respect or reject the use of research in policy decisions.

We begin by describing differences in policymakers' backgrounds and behavior based on observations from both policymakers and professionals. Then we turn to two studies that flesh out some of these differences, followed by a discussion of what we see as the import these differences may have for would-be knowledge brokers. By no means do we claim that this listing is exhaustive, but nonetheless we present it in the spirit of stimulating discussion about differences in how policymakers think about and make decisions.

Differences in Policymakers' Backgrounds and Behavior

Those who may know policymakers best, policymakers themselves, described several ways that their colleagues differ from each other in background, interest in policy, motivation, and preparation. First, a state Assembly caucus chair, who interacted with colleagues on a daily basis, described his colleagues as not "terribly intellectual-type individuals," who came to the legislature from all walks of life—farmers, insurance salesman, a couple of lawyers. These varying backgrounds shaped the ways that they approached and thought about issues and how they functioned as a policymaker.

Second, a 25-year veteran of the state Senate made the surprising observation that policymakers' interest in policy varies: "Not every legislator works on legislation. Some do nothing to work on legislation." A county board chair recommended identifying those members who will listen to and sort through research rather than those who "have their minds made up 10 years ago … and are not going to change their minds." In the study described below, it appears that some legislators see their job as less about making policy and more about serving their district by greasing the skids for government grants and contracts or by helping their constituents navigate the government bureaucracy.

A 25-year veteran of Wisconsin politics also relayed a third difference she had observed in her colleagues—their motivation for working on issues. On the basis of her experience, she thought some policymakers were "looking for the headlines" and others were really committed to moving issues forward. A Democratic assemblyman made a similar point:

> There are workhorses. [Senator's name] is a great example of those who really gets in there and does his work and is really respected. And then there are those people who don't spend a whole lot of time here and so might not be as worth your while to contact them or to push your research on those kinds of folks.

To identify those worth your while, one professor recommended some obvious ways to assess interest, such as a policymaker's position and seniority on a related committee, but also some less obvious indicators, such as personal interest in your issue and a general commitment to the public good. Ben Levin (1952/2005), a professor who served a stint as deputy minister of education in Ontario, explained that policymakers run for and remain in office for the most varied of reasons, some obvious and some less so:

> Some politicians are truly ambitious for themselves. Some have deep commitments to particular public issues or a rather general wish to do some good. Some are drawn to politics by personal connections—a friend or family member, for example. Some love the excitement that politics can offer. Still others end up in the race almost by accident, because somebody thought they might be a good candidate and talked them into running. Once elected, people may stay because they like it, they get used to it, or because they do not have other options. (p. 14)

Finally, in his work with policymakers, Dave Riley, a researcher and endowed chair at the University of Wisconsin–Madison, observed differences in how informed policymakers are on the issues of the day. He explained that he may have had fewer stereotypes of policymakers than other people, given his experience being elected to a political office a quarter century earlier. Nevertheless, he was "always resurprised by how normal they [policymakers] are … a true representation of democracy":

I still am constantly surprised at times at how normal and everyday policy-makers are. They play on hockey teams and … they're just the regular normal sort of people in many ways, and you don't expect that somehow when you see them in the paper or on the press. But there's another way in which the Wisconsin legislators did surprise me as compared to policymakers I've met in the past. Some of them are remarkably well-read. It has surprised me when I'm waiting in their offices and I look at the books on their shelves and then they pull them off and start talking about stuff they've read. Some of them really do their homework and really know things well and, of course, some of them are exactly the opposite too. They are an incredibly varied bunch.

To expand on these observed differences in background, interest in policy, motivation, and preparation, we turn next to two studies—one that is a qualitative examination of federal policymakers and one that is a quantitative examination of state policymakers. Both attempt to unpack other dimensions of how policymakers differ from each other. The first study examines differences in policymakers' views of constituents and how these differences affect their electoral behavior. The second examines within-group differences in how policymakers' value research, seek it out, and use it in their jobs. Following each study, we give implications for delivering research to policymakers.

Differences in Policymakers' Home Style in Their District

This qualitative study focused on 15 sitting members of the U.S. House of Representatives, 2 representatives-to-be, and 1 representative-elect (10 Democrats and 8 Republicans). We focus on this particular study because it provides a deeper assessment of salient cultures, or ways that policymakers view their worlds. This analysis gives us a good assessment of the idiosyncratic manner in which they organize their professional worlds and thereby establish what is critical to their professional fortunes.

Over an 8-year period in the early to mid-1970s, Richard F. Fenno Jr. of the University of Rochester traveled with elected representatives to their respective districts located across the country. His resulting book, *Home Style: House Members in Their Districts*, was published in 1978 and aims to understand what representatives' views are of their constituency and how these perceptions affect their behavior. Among other findings, Fenno described four *home styles*, that is, the ways that policymakers present themselves in their districts. He placed policymakers along a spectrum that ranges from developing personal relationships to discussing policy issues: person to person, the popular local boy, issue independence plus one-on-one, and articulating the issues.

Each style also includes a third element—service to the district—which will not be covered here. Policymakers whose primary style is servicing the district—interceding for constituents with federal bureaucracies or bringing federal funding into the district—seem less relevant to our interest in increasing research utilization in lawmaking. Fenno's four styles will be briefly described followed by a summary of how understanding these differences can enhance the delivery of research to policymakers.

The person-to-person style. Congressman A views his district as homogenous. This southern, rural, and conservative district is primarily composed of one-party conservatives whose livelihood depends, in large part, on one industry. Congressman A is the third generation of his family who has lived and held office in the district, so he feels a deep sense of identification with his constituents. In fact, he thinks of his district not in geographic terms but rather in terms of personal contacts: "I represent a district in which my constituents and I have total mutual confidence, respect, and trust—95 percent, nearly 100 percent" (Fenno, 1978, p. 62). He presents his connections to his constituents in almost every conversation that he has, drawing on an encyclopedic memory of names and faces; family events including births, marriages, illnesses, and deaths; and his deep knowledge of the district's agriculture and architecture, its flora and fauna, its industry and history. "He continually files, sorts, arranges, and rearranges his catalogue of linkages—person to person, place to place, event to event, time to time" (Fenno, 1978, p. 63). Following a Rotary Club speech, he named all 40 people present and what they did for a living along with other assorted information about each of them.

Congressman A's style of campaigning is based on cultivating personal, face-to-face relationships with people, a task that is difficult to delegate to others. In fact, he is so committed to his style that he seldom campaigns or makes public appearances in one growing part of his district because it is not rural; it is populated heavily by people from outside the state, so campaigning would require a style based less on interpersonal relationships. His style involves little attention to or articulation of issues, and he was least comfortable in a format that included a lecture followed by questions and answers. Fenno (1978) observed that Congressman A's issueless style may depend, in a curious way, on an underlying consensus on issues such as race, foreign aid, government spending, and social conservatism. His style is one of being a stabilizer and maintainer. Thus, there are stylistic and strategic reasons for avoiding a focus on issues because they could be controversial and end up alienating some supporters. Even when faced with an electoral challenge, he speaks not about issues but instead about an American heritage built on family and community connections; this theme reinforces and legitimizes his legislative style of maintaining personal relationships with people in his district.

The popular local boy style. Congressman B represents a heterogeneous district with rural, suburban, and urban constituents who work in a highly diversified economy. He describes his district as ideologically conservative, although it is not a one-party district like that of Congressman A; about 21% are Democratic and 21% Republican, with the rest being politically independent. Congressman B talks more about public policy than Congressman A but primarily on the single issue of a strong national defense, which he believes has support from the vast majority of his constituents. However, when asked about his political success, he attributes it not to his national defense posture, even though it is an important issue in his district, but rather to being popular:

> Contrary to what people say—they say voters are issue-oriented and all that …
> for most of the people I know it's more a matter of personality. They pick out a

personality whom they like, who they think is like them, whom they have confidence in, and they trust him to do what's best for them. (Fenno, 1978, p. 73)

In a district that is suspicious of outsiders and fearful of the unknown, Congressman B's local credentials are golden. He was born and raised in the district and spent his whole life there. In high school and college, he was a local hero—a team captain, star athlete, and president of his high school class. He views an election campaign much like a popularity contest. In Fenno's (1978, p. 74) words, "He is unfailingly nice to everyone, is invariably good-humored, and gives off an immense liability as a person." Because of his animus for popularity and aversion to controversy, he avoids taking positions on contentious issues. Unlike Congressman A, when he comes home to his district, he has fewer face-to-face encounters and accepts as many speaking engagements as possible. His presentation style is more impersonal and distant than that of Congressman A, making it appear that his remarks are directed more to demographic groupings than to individuals. For example, Congressman B works to court the women's vote with his characteristic friendliness, masculine charm, and good humor, yet he maintains the same distance that he does in his relationships with other constituents.

The issue independence plus one-on-one style. Congressman C represents a typical suburban district bordering one of America's largest cities. He describes his district as mature first-, second-, or third-ring suburbs populated by well-educated, affluent, White residents. Congressman C thinks of his district as having two characteristics that define his presentation style: a high degree of interest in issues and a tradition of independence in politics. As a Republican in a district that typically votes 25% Republican and 35% Democratic, Congressman C presents himself as an issue-oriented independent to court the 40% in his district who are independent or of no known political affiliation.

Unlike Congressmen A or B, Congressman C thinks of his strongest supporters, not in terms of community ties or family and personal reputation, but rather as people interested in specific issues. He is not a single-issue candidate like Congressman B, although he does not believe that campaigns are won or lost on issues alone:

> The best way to win a vote is to shake hands with someone. You don't win votes by the thousands with a speech. You win votes by looking individuals in the eye, one at a time, and asking them. Very rarely will anyone ask you about how you stand on something.

To be elected in his district, Congressman C believes that you must be thoughtful and informed on the issues, but there still is an element of the personal relationships that Congressmen A and B have with their constituents.

For Congressman C, the clincher is not how to present himself but rather how to find constituents to present himself to in a mobile district (30% of the population turns over every 2 years) with an active, frenzied lifestyle (i.e., long work hours in one or more jobs, business trips, active involvement in civic and recreational activities). Meeting people at their workplace or organizational settings are his favorite ways to make contacts, especially if they allow one-on-one time so he can present himself as concerned about their interests. Media is one way of gaining visibility, but its costs end up preoccupying Congressman C (and others like him in heavily urban–suburban districts) with the problem of raising enough money to purchase airtime.

The articulating-the-issues style. Congressman D's district was so heterogeneous that it could best be described as three different worlds—a city, its suburbs, and the rural countryside. The three worlds each seemed unaware that the other two worlds were even a part of the district. The fastest-growing portion of the district, the suburbs, included some areas whose population was primarily White, Anglo-Saxon, and Protestant and others that had primarily blue-collar or ethnic residents. Thus, the district was not only socially and psychologically diverse, but segmented as well.

Congressman D's ties to the district were not deep or strong; in fact, he lost the suburb in which he grew up by 1,000 votes in the last election. He was propelled into politics by his strong opposition to the Vietnam War, which forged a political style that has been issue-based ever since. Thus, those who are his strongest supporters back him, not because they know him or have a personal relationship with him, but because they agree on the issues and on the importance of emphasizing the issues. He developed a home style that relied on his own personal verbal agility in debating, discussing, and explaining issues. In each campaign, he pressed for debates with his opponents because this played into his personal strength of being able to articulate and respond to questions on the issues. In his first two campaigns, he presented himself mainly through coffees in constituents' homes, often as many as 8 or 10 a day. Once in office, he scheduled open meetings, a setting in which he excels, in every city and town in his district. During each session of Congress, he held nearly 200 such meetings, during which he reminded constituents of the importance of his personal strength—being able to discuss any issue, explain his votes, and debate differences of opinion: "No congressman can represent his people unless he's quick on his feet, because you have to deal with 434 other people—each of whom got there by being quick on his feet" (Fenno, 1978, p. 95).

Yet he was keenly aware that his style at these town meetings involved more than his openness to discussing the issues and his agile and articulate presentation of self:

> People don't make up their minds on the basis of reading all our position papers. We have twenty-six of them, because some people are interested. But most people get a gut feeling about the kind of human being they want to represent them. (Fenno, 1978, p. 95)

Even though Congressman D evidenced the most issue-oriented style of the four policymaker types, he still recognized that his constituents desired access, communication, and relationships with their elected officials—qualities that he believed were important to reelection and also contributed to good representation. In the open meetings, he reached out for constituent trust by relaying the sense that this kind of give-and-take format required a special kind of congressman, a special kind of constituent, and, therefore, a special kind of relationship: "He massages the egos of his constituents by indicating how intelligent, aware, and concerned they are to engage with him in this new, open, rational style of politics" (Fenno, 1978, p. 96). Yet his attempt to connect with his constituents did not include connecting with their personal problems, which were delegated to his staff who accompanied him to the open meetings.

A related theme in his bid for reelection was that he was a new kind of politician. He worked hard to disavow himself from the old-style politician that inhabited an "outrageous and outmoded" Congress. Thus, for a person who was not comfortable in person-to-person campaigning, presenting himself as an accessible, issue-oriented nonpolitician was a style that could win support in each of the distinct worlds of his district without alienating any of them.

How understanding differences in legislators' home style can inform research delivery. Fenno (1978) took a giant step forward in building understanding of within-group differences in policymakers in his study of 18 members of the House of Representatives. Fenno provided a conceptual framework for thinking about policymakers based on what they perceived their constituents to be like and what home style they developed to respond to that constituency. On the basis of 36 separate visits and 110 days spent observing representatives in their districts, Fenno categorized policymakers' home styles on a continuum ranging from the least to the most person-oriented home style and from the least to the most issue-oriented home style. Situated at one end of the continuum is Congressman A, with his style of cultivating personal, face-to-face relationships; at the other end of the continuum is Congressman D, with his accessible, issue-oriented, and participatory style. Falling in between are Congressman B, with his friendly, charming, single-issue style, and Congressman C, with his independent, issue-oriented, personally attentive style.

For those interested in connecting research to policy, the obvious lesson is that there is no "one-size-fits-all" delivery mechanism. Not every policymaker is interested in policy, so an issue-focused approach will work with some policymakers but not all. Policymakers may be more likely to respond to familiar approaches, particularly those that they personally use with their constituents. Making connections with policymakers like Congressman A may require focusing on relationship building, whereas reaching policymakers like Congressman D may require focusing on issues. Those in the middle like Congressmen B and C may respond to both relationship- and issue-oriented approaches, although Congressman B will likely focus on a narrower set of issues.

In a curious sort of way, it is entirely possible that policymakers who are less issue oriented may be more receptive to research and analysis because they are unlikely to have taken a previous position or campaigned on the issue. However, if issue-oriented policymakers are reached before they take positions, they may be open to research that provides new ways of thinking about issues that, if adopted, could be incorporated into their campaign materials, discussed at open meetings, and broadcast over the airwaves. Of course, these speculations are testable hypotheses rather than assertions of fact and warrant further investigation.

Delivering research effectively does not require knowing the home style of every policymaker. However, it does require using different delivery mechanisms and providing policymakers with a diversity of options so they can self-select into those most consistent with their personal style. Fenno's study suggests that adapting to policymakers' style requires both a relationship-oriented and an issue-oriented approach. To alert policymakers to relevant research, those with a relationship-oriented style are likely to resonate more with personal appointments, discussion sessions, and presentations from a trusted information source, whereas policymakers with an issue-oriented style may prefer policy briefs, newsletters, and presentations from any subject-matter expert.

Next, we turn to another study that examines within-group differences in how policymakers utilize research in their decisions. This is a study that Karen and her colleagues with the Family Impact Seminars conducted in Wisconsin and New York.

Differences in Policymakers' Use of Research in Policy Decisions

In one of our studies, we examined how the core technology of one culture—research—is valued, sought out, and utilized in the core technology of the other—lawmaking. This study was driven by questions such as the following: Are there policymakers who see no value in seeking out or using research in their decision making? Do some policymakers believe research is so valuable that they seek it out themselves? Are there others who fall somewhere between the two extremes, believing that research can be useful but still not useful enough to devote time and energy to search for it? Do all policymakers rely on the same characteristics to assess the utility of research in policy decisions?

The sampling frame consisted of (a) the entire state legislature ($N = 129$) in Wisconsin, subtracting two seats pending elections and one vacant seat, and (b) a randomly selected subsample ($N = 67$) of the larger New York legislature, which totals 212 members. These two states are similar in that neither has term limits and both are full-time legislatures with a high number of professional staff. They are different, however, in terms of geographic and political character. Wisconsin is a small Midwestern, moralistic state with a substantial rural population, whereas New York is a large, eastern, individualistic state with a large urban metropolis (Elazar, 1984). We interviewed 109 state legislators, of which 74 were in Wisconsin (57% response rate) and 35 in New York (52% response rate). (Full details on the sample and methodology can be found in the appendix.)

We used cluster analysis to classify policymakers into groups using three variables—their attitudes toward, knowledge of, and use of research in policy decisions. For this study, we defined *research* as information based on scientific studies. Attitudes toward the usefulness of social science research in policy decisions were measured using a five-item scale, *Valuing of Research* (Cronbach's alpha = .80; Caplan, Morrison, & Stambaugh, 1975). *Research Access* included six behavioral items that assessed the extent to which policymakers sought out research on issues important to them through means such as looking at program/policy evaluations, reading research reports, asking the nonpartisan service agencies of the legislature for research on an issue, attending seminars or presentations where research is discussed, and calling researchers or experts for advice (Cronbach's alpha = .65). *Research Use* included three items that assessed the use of research on issues important to them, including taking the results of research into account in their decisions, talking with colleagues about research on issues important to them, or using research to justify decisions they had made (Cronbach's alpha = .74).

Using these three measures in a cluster analysis, the resulting policymaker clusters were almost identical among the Wisconsin and New York legislators, so the states were combined for the remaining analysis. Four policymaker clusters emerged to which we assigned the following descriptors: *Cluster 1, Enthusiastic Users*; *Cluster 2, Skeptical Users*; *Cluster 3, Enthusiastic Nonusers*; and *Cluster 4, Skeptical Nonusers*. These labels provide a convenient way to discuss the clusters but with the caveat that policymakers labeled *nonusers* do access and use research to some extent, although not nearly as extensively as those labeled *users*. The scores of each cluster on the valuing of research, research access, and research use can be found in Figure 6.1.

Cluster 1—Enthusiastic Users. In statistical tests, Enthusiastic Users of research had significantly higher scores than any other cluster on valuing research and research use, and significantly higher scores than Clusters 3 and 4 on research access (see Figure 6.1). Policymakers in this group were enthusiastic about the value of social science research in policymaking and reported actively seeking out research about policy/program evaluations and what other states were doing by reading reports, asking legislative service agency staff, attending seminars/presentations, and calling researchers/experts for advice. They also reported significantly higher levels of use than any other group, as indexed by talking with their colleagues about research and taking the results into account when making decisions

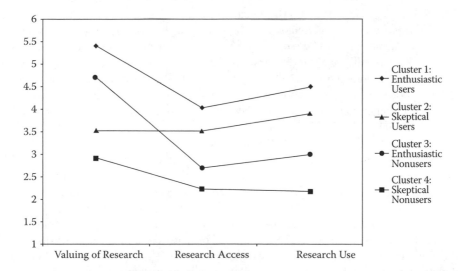

Figure 6.1   Policymaker cluster means in the combined sample. *Note.* Cluster analysis was based on 109 state legislators, 74 from Wisconsin and 35 from New York.

or justifying decisions they had made. Overall, 25 cases or about 1 in 4 legislators (23%) were classified as *Enthusiastic Users.*

Cluster 2—Skeptical Users. Skeptical Users placed significantly lower value on research than policymakers in Clusters 1 (Enthusiastic Users) or 3 (Enthusiastic Nonusers) and significantly higher than policymakers in Cluster 4 (Skeptical Nonusers). That is, they were more skeptical when asked about the value of social science research as a basis for making policy decisions or providing legitimacy to decisions already made. Yet they reported significantly higher levels of research access and use than Clusters 3 and 4. Thus, despite their skepticism about the value of research, these policymakers still were relatively active in seeking out research and using it in policy decisions. About 1 in 4 legislators in the sample (24%) fell into this cluster.

Cluster 3—Enthusiastic Nonusers. Enthusiastic Nonusers had relatively high scores on valuing research, significantly higher than the skeptics (Cluster 2 and Cluster 4) but significantly lower than the Enthusiastic Users (Cluster 1). Even though Cluster 3 rated the usefulness of research in policy decisions significantly higher than Cluster 2 (Skeptical Users), they still reported lower levels of both research access and use than their legislative counterparts in Cluster 2. Enthusiastic Nonusers also accessed and used significantly less research than Cluster 1 (Enthusiastic Users), but reported more use and similar levels of access compared to Cluster 4 (Skeptical Nonusers). This cluster was the largest of the four with over one third (36%) of legislators so classified.

Cluster 4—Skeptical Nonusers. Skeptical Nonusers had low scores on all three variables. In statistical tests, these policymakers were the least enthusiastic about the value of research in policymaking. This group included those significantly less likely to use research. Like Cluster 3, the Skeptical Nonusers were less apt to access research than Clusters 1 and 2, differences that were statistically significant. About 1 in 6 (16%) legislators fell into this cluster.

Differences among policymakers in demographic variables and preferred research characteristics. Few demographic differences emerged across the clusters. When we collapsed the clusters into users and nonusers, users of social science research were significantly more likely to be female than male. Moreover, the users of research were more likely to seek out research themselves as well as access it through staff, whereas nonusers were more likely to access it predominantly through staff (for details on the methods and measures, see the appendix and Bogenschneider, Johnson, & Normandin, 2009).

We also examined whether different types of policymakers placed a higher priority on certain characteristics of research than others. As described in the appendix, we examined research characteristics that emerged in earlier studies (Caplan et al., 1975; Kingdon, 2003; Shulock, 1999; Weiss & Bucuvalas, 1980) using a multinomial analysis that compared the clusters to the reference group of Enthusiastic Users. The priority that policymakers placed on several characteristics of research did not vary significantly across clusters. Specifically the quality of the research, its apparent objectivity, its action orientation, and its presentation (i.e., brief summaries of policy options that are understandably written) were critical factors in determining likely use across the board.

However, cluster membership was associated with policymakers' ratings of three characteristics of research. First, the research characteristic *new ways of thinking about an issue* differentiated Cluster 1, the Enthusiastic Users, from the other three clusters. That is, those policymakers who saw the most value in social science research, who sought it out and used it in their decisions, were not cautious or self-serving but instead were looking for unexpected or new findings that challenged the status quo and could position their state as a leader on an issue. The most enthusiastic users of research also placed a higher priority on political feasibility, such as whether the research is framed in a way that makes it useful in the policymaking process. Finally, policymakers who assigned a lower priority to research findings being available when decisions are being made had greater odds of being in Cluster 4. Not surprisingly, those least likely to use research—Skeptical Nonusers—placed less importance on its timing.

How understanding differences in research utilization can inform research delivery. The results provide several lessons for advancing evidence-based policymaking. First, the findings confirm that some, but not all, policymakers are interested in using research to guide policy decisions. Expecting that all or most policymakers will be interested in research and analysis is clearly unrealistic. This study sheds some light on the equivocal findings that have become the hallmark of the literature on research utilization in policymaking. For example, those who reject the argument that research is used in policymaking likely focus on the segment of the sample that reports infrequent use of research. In this study, just over half of the sample (53%) was composed of Enthusiastic and Skeptical Nonusers who were well below the sample mean (0.50 *SD* to 1.25 *SD*) for research use.

To the contrary, those who claim that policymakers respect the role of research in policymaking probably narrow in on those who report that they value, seek out, and use research in policy decisions. In this study, almost half the sample (47%) was composed of Enthusiastic and Skeptical Users who were well above the mean for research use (0.5 *SD* to 1.5 *SD*) of their legislative peers. The conceptual error of zeroing in on one segment of the population and assuming that it represents the whole provides false guidance to those who would translate research for political consumption.

Second, these findings shed light on who should be the target of policy dissemination. Although far from conclusive, the results raise the interesting prospect that research should be disseminated to both policymakers and their staff. Consistent with one earlier study (Weiss & Bucuvalas, 1980), policymakers who are the most frequent users of research not only have staff who seek information but also ferret it out themselves.

Third, these findings, although informative, do not suggest that knowledge brokers need to place policymakers into research utilization clusters, because many characteristics of research that policymakers find useful do not differ among those who use more or less research in their decisions. For example, almost all of the policymakers assigned a high priority to the quality of research and its presentation, action orientation, lack of bias, and timeliness (with only one exception). However, knowledge brokers may be able to elevate research use by targeting the characteristics of research that are highly valued by those policymakers who are the most enthusiastic seekers and users of research. Capturing the attention of Enthusiastic Users requires a dual focus on providing research that presents a new way of thinking about issues and framing it in ways that recognize the importance of political considerations in the policy culture.

Finally, a provocative cluster that warrants investigation is what we call the *Enthusiastic Nonusers*, who are enthusiastic about the value of research but seldom use it in their decisions. Are these policymakers low-hanging fruit ripe for picking by knowledge producers and brokers? Given their low ratings on access, are they unfamiliar with research and, therefore, unaware of its potential value? Does the research that comes to their attention deal with the important questions that policymakers are debating, or is it outmoded or so futuristic that its relevance is unclear? Does the research that reaches their desk fail to pass muster in terms of being action oriented, accessible, high quality, and unbiased? An intriguing question that remains unanswered is whether Enthusiastic Nonusers could be converted into Enthusiastic Users by providing the kinds of information policymakers seek at the time it is needed and in the formats they prefer.

SUMMARY

We believe that this chapter addresses an issue that is fundamental to any effort to advance evidence-based policymaking—understanding the nature of the policymaker audience. This idea seems quite novel in attempts to generate and disseminate research to policymakers. Yet it builds on a long-standing scholarly tradition that demands a clear articulation of the attitudes, behaviors, and motivations of the client or learner. Social workers claim ownership of this insight based on their old adage to "begin where the client is," just as educational psychologists take credit for long ago establishing the principle of understanding the learner as a core component of effective teaching.

Karen often jokes with state legislators that her long-standing quest is to learn to think like a policymaker. Legislators find this quite amusing and warn her that it may be an impossible, perhaps futile, endeavor. In reality, though, her quest forms the foundation of any effort to bring research to the attention of policymakers in ways that are likely to influence the decisions they make. The first lesson that Karen teaches any new staff member or graduate student is to fix in their mind an image of a policymaker—what they do, which types of information they need, how they are likely to use it, and the ways in which they prefer to receive it. She tells them to imagine the kinds of information that policymakers need when they give a stump speech on the Fourth of July, make brief comments at a Kiwanis meeting, or write a newsletter to constituents. Fixing on this image of a policymaker is vital irrespective of whether the task at hand is planning a seminar, organizing a discussion session, or writing a briefing report (unless one cares little whether the product will be delightful for one's colleagues but dreadful for policymakers).

Of course, this advice has the intended benefit only if the image of the policymaker is an accurate one. Accuracy depends on fixing on more than one image—policymakers whose home styles are based primarily on relationships exist alongside those whose styles are based mostly on policy issues. We also have policymakers who are enthusiastic about seeking and using research in their decisions alongside those who are enthusiastic but have not yet translated this enthusiasm into concrete action. You get the point. Several points about applying this understanding of policymakers in the real world are detailed in Key Concepts 6.1.

Key Concepts 6.1   Understanding the Policymaker Species: Moving Beyond the Stereotypes

- Open your mind to overcoming stereotypes of policymakers. Contact and communication with policymakers help dispel negative stereotypes and break down cultural barriers.
- Learn about the nature of the policymaker audience and how policymakers are both similar to and different from one another. They differ in background, interest in policy, motivations, and preparation for the job. Policymakers develop different "home styles"—campaigning and legislative behaviors that respond to the perceived needs and expectation of their constituents. Policymakers also vary in their attitudes toward, knowledge of, and use of research in policy decisions.
- Use different delivery styles to adapt to the different learning styles of policymakers. Relationship-oriented policymakers will resonate with personal appointments, discussion sessions, and presentations from trusted sources. Issue-oriented policymakers may prefer policy briefs, newsletters, and presentations from subject-matter experts.
- Make contact with policymakers and also their staff. In some, but not all offices, staff assume the responsibility for collecting research-based evidence.

This quest to better understand the policymaker audience is made even more urgent by one of the most important takeaway messages from our interviews of exemplary policy communicators—how easy it is to stereotype policymakers and how wrong these initial impressions often are. Four of five researchers, who later became exceptionally skilled at navigating the research–policy divide, admitted to us that their initial impressions were dead wrong. These wrongheaded stereotypes can sabotage any efforts at bicultural boundary spanning. The good news is that these stereotypes were not immutable but proved malleable as researchers gained more exposure to policymakers and experience interacting with them.

We are reminded of the advice of one researcher who recommended approaching policymakers as an anthropologist and a change agent: "Work on understanding the policymaking process, become fascinated by it, become a student of it, learn from these folks. Many will be happy to teach you." We couldn't agree more.

In the next chapter, we turn to observations of the policymaking process, many of which are obvious to insiders but often surprising to outsiders.

7

What Knowledge Producers Should Know About the Policymaking Process

Laws are like sausage. It is better not to see them being made.

—Otto von Bismarck (1815–1898)

It seems important to me that men of good will should make an effort to understand how the world ticks; it is the only way to make it tick better.

—Charles Percy Snow (1961, p. 66)

*T*he metaphorical link between making policy and making sausage endures because it taps into an elemental truth. When faced with the roles that money, ideology, and influence play, knowledge producers often react with dismay and shy away from the political fray. Naively, they assume that if the research product is good, no special knowledge of policymaking, no Herculean effort is needed, because research will automatically be incorporated into the mix of ingredients that produce policy decisions. This line of reasoning goes something like this: For an input as sacred as research, surely its influence will rise above politics and partisanship and be espoused with the same reverence in the state house as in the ivory tower.

This naïveté has persisted because cultural blinders obscure the fundamental differences in how the worlds of research and policy function. The modus operandi used to guide decisions in the traditions of science could not be more different from the practices, protocols, and processes through which the wheels of government grind out policy decisions. Given these differences in products and processes, knowledge producers find themselves frustrated and disappointed that the policy process pays so little regard to research. Too often, this disappointment morphs into disdain for the political process itself and disparagement of those involved in it.

In our experience, and in that of our informants, many knowledge producers shy away from engaging in policymaking simply because they find the process byzantine and inscrutable. If they want to influence public policy, where in the process do they intervene, with whom do they make contact, which kinds of information should they bring to the table, and what kinds of reception should they expect? Should they focus on legislators, their staff, executive agency staff who design and manage policies, or practitioners who actually interact with clients? Each group plays a part, yet no one fully controls the policymaking process.

As newly elected president Dwight Eisenhower was preparing to ascend to the ultimate position of power, his predecessor, Harry Truman, purportedly observed that he felt sorry for Ike. The former general, he noted, was used to giving orders and being obeyed. Ike would now find that, as president, he would give orders and absolutely nothing would happen. In this chapter, we delve in some depth into institutional culture, in particular into the setting where laws are made. We begin by reviewing some prominent albeit contradictory conceptualizations of the policy process itself. We illustrate the process with a story of how welfare reform was enacted that exemplifies how diffuse, incoherent, and highly complex policymaking can be. We follow this vignette with nine observations of the policy process that we have pulled together from the empirical literature, the reflections of our informants, and our own experience.

PROMINENT CONCEPTUALIZATIONS OF THE POLICY PROCESS

Disagreements abound about whether policymaking is a rational process. At one end of the spectrum, some subscribe to the classical, technical-rational view that policymakers systematically utilize data and analysis to arrive at decisions aimed at optimizing benefits for the greatest number. At the opposite end of the spectrum, others perceive policymaking as a confused, erratic process under no one's rational control. Other views fall somewhere between these two extremes. To some, policymaking is a top-down process. Decisions are dominated by an elite group of political leaders, special interest groups, and influential citizens (Lindblom, 1968) who engage in "wheeling and dealing" in a smoke-filled room to outmaneuver an adversary. To others, policymaking is a circular process. Citizens relay their opinions and preferences to policymakers, political parties, and interest groups who reciprocate with information, analysis, and political advice that, in turn, helps citizens better express their own needs (Lindblom, 2005).

These conceptualizations are not without consequence because they shape public perceptions about policymaking, leading some to be increasingly pessimistic about politics as "more polarized, short-sighted, fragmented—and often less intelligent—than it should be" (Smith, 1991, p. xxi). Others are cautiously optimistic about the contributions policy has made and can continue to make to the collective good (Levin, 1952/2005). These perceptions matter because they affect views about how much government should be doing. Some denounce government as so untrustworthy and unreliable that it should be limited to only essential functions, whereas others denigrate government for not doing more to address serious problems such as global warming, human rights violations, and growing income inequality (Levin, 1952/2005).

These conceptualizations also matter to knowledge brokers interested in making their way into the policy world, a decision-making arena with enormous powers to affect large numbers of citizens through decisions such as declaring war, imprisoning people, levying taxes, protecting the vulnerable, stimulating the economy, and so forth (Levin, 1952/2005). Infusing research into policy decisions like these requires knowing why and how government acts as it does. By no means are we suggesting the need to act in a partisan way, but rather we are suggesting the need to understand in some depth how the policymaking system works (Levin, 1952/2005). In our view, knowledge producers have turned a blind eye to doing what knowledge producers do best—becoming a student of what they do not understand. This ethnocentrism about the policymaking process diminishes chances of building better, stronger connections between the institutions of knowledge and power.

Granted, countless books and monographs have been written that describe the processes and players through which a bill becomes a law (Levin, 1952/2005; Lindblom, 1968; Ross & Staines, 1972) and the administrative and political constraints imposed on policymakers by the institutions in which they operate (Caplan, Morrison, & Stambaugh, 1975; Mooney, 1992; Webber, 1986). We will not attempt to replicate these treatises here. Instead, we will describe the policy process for the express benefit of those who want to better broker the use of research in policy decisions. Sometimes real-life experience can be instructive.

WHEN RESEARCH MEETS THE POLICY PROCESS: WELFARE REFORM AND SCIENCE

Tom observed firsthand the process whereby welfare reform legislation was enacted during his stay at the U.S. Department of Health and Human Services. On loan from the University of Wisconsin, he served as senior policy analyst in the Office of the Assistant Secretary for Planning and Evaluation (ASPE). ASPE was the organizational locus around which planning for President Bill Clinton's welfare reform bill, the 1994 Personal Responsibility and Work Opportunity Reconciliation Act (PRWORA), took place.

In many respects, this was an ideal laboratory for doing evidence-based policy development. Harvard professor David Ellwood had assumed the assistant secretary position at ASPE, and Mary Jo Bane, his colleague at Harvard, assumed leadership of the Health and Human Services Unit with programmatic responsibility for the Aid to Families With Dependent Children (AFDC) program. AFDC was an object of considerable popular revulsion and, thus, a particular target of reform. At the same time, changing welfare invoked mind-numbing technical and political challenges, and raised concerns that the most vulnerable members of society (poor children) would be further disadvantaged. Both David and Mary Jo were dedicated to the principle of bringing the best research to bear on the contentious questions at hand.

How well did this idyllic marriage of knowledge producers and knowledge consumers work? For the record, the PRWORA was published on June 21, 1994, too late to receive serious political discussion before the fall congressional elections that turned the House of Representatives over to the Republicans, who were then led by Newt Gingrich. They quite naturally had their own ideas about the role of government, as embodied in the *Contract With America*. Clinton's plan, as originally devised, was essentially dead, but that says more about politics than either its merits or the character of the policymaking process through which it was developed.

In fact, the very attempt to advance an evidence-based strategy for reforming welfare proved somewhat problematic and may have inadvertently contributed to the quick demise of Clinton's proposal. In the welfare arena, there is a mountain of research and analysis on most of the critical issues. Take the labor supply question: Do welfare payments reduce work effort? It is a simple enough question. Yet the research offers a range of estimates depending on what methods are used, how the question is framed, which data sets are employed, how the modeling is done, and so on and so forth. It is feasible to arrive at a consensus, but the process is long and can be painful. Multiply the transaction cost (time and effort needed to arrive at a conclusion about the research) by the sheer number of issues on the table, and the complexity becomes daunting.

Complexity, however, was not the only challenge. Scores of studies had been done on specific interventions designed to reduce welfare use and increase labor market participation. Some focused on the job search process, others on enhancing human capital, still others on remediating various work impediments. Researchers naturally wanted to isolate the contribution that individual interventions might have on any observed outcomes. However, program evaluation expert Peter Rossi has often noted that the expected value of any one social experiment is zero; some work a little, some not at all, and some go in the wrong direction. In the aggregate, nothing changes very much.

The welfare literature was less discouraging than other program evaluations. In fact, there was rigorous evidence that a number of things did work. But if you took the typical (successful) evaluation back in the early 1990s, you would find something like the following in terms of net effects: Examining the difference between those in the experimental and control groups, welfare use might fall a handful of percentage points, labor supply might inch up by 5 percentage points at most, and earnings might jump as much as 30 percentage points but from a very low base and certainly not enough to lift a struggling family out of poverty. In short, many things worked, but no single approach worked very well. Many plausible ideas did not work at all well in practice.

This was not great news for the research-driven welfare gurus. Under political pressure to end welfare as we knew it and impose time limits on welfare receipt, they faced tough choices. The evidence said we could at best reduce welfare modestly. To do so, we needed lots of public service jobs, child care, and other supports for those people who had reached their time limits. But reform was not supposed to cost money, or not much anyway. The available research led to very tough choices and no easy answers. So, the internal debate dragged on month after month. When Tom first arrived in Washington in late spring of 1993, the administration thought a bill would be done in mere months. By fall, we were no closer to a proposal. At the beginning of 1994, welfare reform was almost scuttled by the administration in favor of health care reform. In the end, a complex bill was produced that could not match the expectations that had been climbing with each passing month.

In the end, the key to successful reform was found outside of the strategies that were amenable to rigorous experimental evaluation. No single intervention or small set of interventions was the key. Rather, real reform meant changing the very culture of welfare and the institutions through which it had been delivered. But broad cultural change was pretty much beyond what our evaluation methodologies of that era were capable of capturing. How do you randomize broad systemic change across treatment and control groups where the very intent of reform is to transform how clients and system workers think about welfare? The cost, political impediments, and logistical challenges were daunting, and, thus, rigorous investigation essentially eluded our best minds.

Others were not put off by the lack of scientific evidence. A number of policy entrepreneurs plunged ahead, pushing broad-based change absent evidence-based support on likely outcomes. What happened? Welfare rolls plummeted well beyond anything anticipated by the research literature, and money was thus available (for a time at least) to invest in child care along with training and other work supports. In fact, Mary Jo Bane (2001) conceded in her presidential address to the prestigious Association for Public Policy Analysis and Management that the aftermath of the welfare law had been different from what she had expected: "much larger caseload declines, significant increases in employment, fewer demonstrably adverse effects on children, and declines, though small ones, rather than increases in poverty rates for single mother families" (p. 191). However, she was quick to point out that certainly the law had not "caused" these gains that emanated, in part, from a good economy and an increase in Earned Income Tax Credit (EITC) and child support payments. Nevertheless, the law had not resulted in the dangerous consequences she had initially predicted.

Does this little story suggest that the role, or potential role, of research is overstated or, worse, perverse? Not in the least. The real lesson is that research is not an easy panacea. Often, the findings are not easily transferable, the results may be mixed, the long-term impacts unclear, and the costs prohibitive. What's more, the inputs are made into a policy process that is not easily amenable to acting on research findings.

NINE OBSERVATIONS OF THE POLICY PROCESS: OBVIOUS TO INSIDERS, SURPRISING TO OUTSIDERS

We present below nine observations of the policymaking process that have emerged from our interviews of lawmakers and effective knowledge brokers as well as the observations of other policy analysts, pundits, and scholars, particularly those of

TABLE 7.1   Nine Observations of the Policy Process:
Obvious to Insiders, Surprising to Outsiders

1.	Policymaking is, in fact, a rational process.
2.	Taking the politics out of policymaking is not possible, nor should it be.
3.	Policymaking is fluid and unpredictable.
4.	A full-time opposition shapes policy dynamics.
5.	Error-free decisions are expected to be made with haste.
6.	Policymakers wrestle with problems ranging from the wee to the wicked.
7.	Policymaking is one of the most complex undertakings known to humankind.
8.	The values of policymakers and their constituents are potent policy levers.
9.	Policymaking favors the status quo.

Ben Levin (2003, 1952/2005). As shown in Table 7.1, these observations encompass the forces and values that guide how policymakers act, the way the institution operates, the nature and complexity of the issues that compete for attention, and the criteria and incentives that drive policy decisions.

Observation 1: Policymaking Is, in Fact, a Rational Process

One disconnect between the cultures of research and policy is a competing perception of what constitutes rational behavior. Rationality in the research world usually entails conforming to the classical definition of decision making—defining a problem, clarifying goals and objectives, listing alternative ways of achieving them, investigating the consequences of each alternative, comparing potential consequences, and choosing the option with the purported outcomes that most closely match one's goals and objectives. Relying on these premises, we found it hard to find examples where major policy decisions have been made in this prescribed manner (Nutley, Walter, & Davies, 2007). Yet it clearly would be a mistake to conclude that policymaking is not rational (Lindblom, 1968) just because it is guided by different premises, responds to dissimilar signals, and operates in a nonlinear fashion.

Like any complex process, policy decisions have multiple points of participation that make it difficult to identify who initiated them, what the drivers were, and how decisions ultimately were consummated. This difficulty in mapping out the intricate ebb and flow of policy production, however, should not be confused with irrationality. For example, in a pluralistic society, there are a number of competing interest groups, each with different goals, values, and desired ends. Policy ends that are ideal for one group may be an anathema for another. This is not unexpected in a democratic political system that encourages the pursuit of sometimes competing ends by such stakeholders as citizens, interest groups, political parties, and policymakers themselves and that resolves any resulting differences through a back-and-forth process of negotiation and compromise. The result is unlikely to be a proposal advanced by any single group. Instead, it is likely to be a conclusion that suits some stakeholders more than others, advantages one interest group at the expense of another, and maximizes some political ends while minimizing others.

So in a roundabout manner, if all the participants and points of participation are taken into account, policymaking is a rational process but not necessarily in a straightforward way that conforms to the tenets of the classic decision-making model. Policymakers are interested, not only in applying research evidence to their decisions, but also in representing the views and values of their constituents in a political system designed to reconcile the inevitable differences through civilized debate in a public setting. Put simply, "Theirs is a political rationality rather than a scientific rationality" (Weiss, 1978, p. 61). In the vignette above, the passage of the welfare reform law did not meet scientific standards of rationality, but may have been rational from a political perspective. For those who designed PRWORA and advocated for it, the process would probably be considered rational because it ended up meeting the stated goals of reducing the welfare rolls.

A Republican representative seen as a rising star in her caucus explained that the policymaking process may seem irrational to academics because academics tend to think "big picture," whereas policymakers' frame of reference is their district. Thus, an action or decision that may seem irrational when considered on a large scale may, in fact, be quite rational for certain subgroups of the population, such as the 55,000 constituents in her relatively homogenous suburban district. When asked what is important for academics to know about the job of being a policymaker, she explained (paraphrased),

> They don't understand the human context in which legislation is made. Legislators have to respond to their constituents. Another thing is that there are philosophical differences in how issues are approached between the two parties. Academics don't understand how there can be differences that go back to our forefathers.

As an example, she cited the founding fathers John Adams and Thomas Jefferson, who disagreed on whether the U.S. Constitution should be based on a federalist (strong national government) or states' rights (strong state government) approach—a philosophical difference that is difficult to resolve based on whether one is more or less rational than the other.

Observation 2: Taking the Politics out of Policymaking Is not Possible, nor Should It Be

If policymakers could teach academics one thing about the policy culture, they would offer this message that emerged over and over again from dozens of interviews over the past 17 years: Policymaking is (gasp) political. Policymakers, often premier communicators who know how to turn a phrase, explained that this is the biggest mistake that academics make in working with them. Republican senator Luther Olsen put it this way: "The State Capitol is loaded with politics. It's not loaded with scientific research." Yet the role of research can be profound. In the words of former president Ronald Reagan, "Information is the oxygen of the modern age. It seeps through the walls topped by barbed wire, it wafts across the electrified borders." It can infiltrate the hallowed halls of power.

One researcher reflecting on his 30 years of experience acknowledged, "There is a lot of mischief and misinformation and politics that drive what happens in policy." According to another researcher with 25 years of experience, most of her colleagues are pretty ignorant about politics "and the burden is on the researcher to figure out how to negotiate the political environment." In dozens of interviews over the years, policymakers gave us an insider's view of why the politics are so central to the policymaking process. After his election, one senator, whose mother had also served in the legislature, observed that most people run for office with idealistic motivations, but then they run into people who disagree with their vision. In his words, "No one runs for the legislature to be adversarial. We run to do good things." But legislators, like the public they are elected to represent, have different visions of what good things are and how they should be accomplished. Among the legislators that we spoke with, *policy* and *politics* were often used interchangeably, as they are in France, where the same word is used for both (Levin, 2003).

Lawmakers frequently cited compromise as one essential tool for getting things done; however, they recognize that outside the lawmaking chambers, compromise may be one of the least understood aspects of the political process. According to a Democrat who worked her way up the legislative ladder from aide to representative to senator, academics have a reputation among her colleagues for looking down their noses at policymakers because the latter compromise in order to solicit broader support for their positions. She explained that compromise is part and parcel of the work policymakers do, citing the current Iraq war as an example. Liberals are mad at and critical of Democrats, who took control of Congress on an antiwar platform and yet have not been able to get the country out of the war. As a politician, she claims to be more realistic: "Do you see a magic wand in my pocket? I totally agree with what some folks say, but the point is that I have to work with others. I have to make compromises to get things done." Another Democrat also illustrated the low regard with which compromise is held outside the lawmaking chambers. Since he was elected 10 years ago, one senator was shocked to find his sharpest critics are (ironically) those constituents and interest groups that share his views, but believe that he compromised too much or made too many concessions.

A Republican legislator provided a specific example of the value of compromise by citing a bill that she sponsored on human trafficking. She found the people that she worked with on this bill to be dedicated to this issue and some of the kindest, most wonderful people she had ever met. Nonetheless, they were clueless about how to write a bill in a way that would actually pass. She explained that it is important to ask questions such as, "What will Democrats say? What will Republicans say? How can we design it so it's not too far left or right?" The supporters of this bill also wanted restitution for victims, but what they failed to understand, according to the legislator, is that this will not fly right now when the state has no extra money. She shook her head in disbelief at their political naïveté and told us once again how important it is for those who want to get involved in lawmaking to understand the political realities of getting a bill passed.

The policymakers we interviewed overwhelmingly viewed the art of compromise as a constructive force in the policymaking process, with one exception. One legislator, with a leadership role in the Democratic caucus, was frank in his assessment that academics err if they think "this place is about policy when really it's about politics. Policy is a stepchild." His comment reflects those who recognize that advances can be made through skillful political compromise, but caution about its potential misuse if principles are compromised (Loewenberg, 2007) or compromises are based only on choosing among competing proposals rather than negotiating across proposals to create new and innovative policy solutions (Lindblom, 1968).

In their initial contacts, researchers were surprised at the extent to which lawmaking is charged by the "alchemy of political influence" (Rabb & Winstead, 2003, p. 22). Tom recalls the adventures of a research scientist at the Institute for Research on Poverty some years ago. He was a labor economist from Australia who was asked to appear before a congressional committee in Washington to discuss his latest research. He left for Washington feeling honored and excited about the opportunity, but was crestfallen upon his return. Quite naive regarding the radical partisan character of politics in DC, he was shocked to discover that there was little interest in his work. He had been invited by the Republican majority and, therefore, was subject to personal attacks by members of the Democratic minority, as were other panelists. Substance did not matter; politics and partisanship did. He thought science would count in the doing of national policy. It never occurred to him that he needed to better understand this new environment into which he was venturing. His reaction is not an uncommon one when researchers first wade into the policy waters.

Yet those who immerse themselves in policymaking on an ongoing basis, such as Mary Fairchild of the National Conference of State Legislatures (NCSL), find the extent of public cynicism toward the policymaking process quite surprising:

> The legislative institution is ... a place where we can have civilized debate, and we want to bring in different views and have those discussions again, in some kind of civilized way, and that is really how public policy is made, by the voicing of all these divergent views in the public body. ... It's always been quite surprising to me, frankly, that people are so cynical about the process.

One reason that policymaking may have gotten a bad rap is the inherent differences between public service and private enterprise. Mark Masters, who has served in both realms as a business owner and chair of a county board of supervisors, explains,

> I came from private enterprise and spent my life doing that. One of my thoughts when I came to the county board was why can't we just manage this business? It took me about three months to realize ... it's pretty easy to understand. You can have as much information as you ever need and you're still not going to manage it any differently than the process that it is. That's the checks and balances that government has in place. Some call it bureaucracy, some call it stupidity, and some call it other things. But it is what it is.

These sentiments parallel those of Carol Weiss, a pioneer of scholarly inquiry into policymakers' use of research. Taking the politics out of policymaking, as rational or desirable as that may sound, is not possible, nor should it be in a system designed for policies to be developed through debate and compromise among those elected to represent constituents with diverse interests and divergent views (Weiss, 1999). This democratic deliberation should not be mischaracterized as an abandonment of one's principles, ideals, or commitment to the common good, according to President Barack Obama:

> After all, the Constitution ensures our free speech not just so that we can shout at one another as loud as we please, deaf to what others might say (although we have that right). It also offers us the possibility of a genuine marketplace of ideas, one in which the "jarring of parties" works on behalf of "deliberation and circumspection"; a marketplace in which, through debate and competition, we can expand our perspective, change our minds, and eventually arrive not merely at agreements but at sound and fair agreements. (2006, p. 94)

Observation 3: Policymaking Is Fluid and Unpredictable

The fluidity and predictability of producing the community's core technology, whether it be research or policy, is another point of friction that can create misunderstandings between the two cultures. The research culture operates under a long-standing tradition of reflexivity, whereas the policy culture rewards reactivity. Researchers, who are trained to be cautious, reflective, tentative, and skeptical, perform their work in a culture so patient and forgiving that it recognizes progress can take years to achieve. In contrast, policymakers are expected to respond quickly to changing circumstances, emerging crises, and unexpected events in a proactive culture that expects, even demands, progress (or at least action) within days or weeks.

In policymaking, surprise dominates. The policy agenda can be driven by the high probability that some low probability event will take over with no warning (Dror, 1986; Levin, 2003). Two prime examples are the school shooting in Littleton, Colorado, and the September 11 terrorist attack in New York City. Both events immediately soared to the top of policymakers' agenda, replacing other priorities, no matter their prior importance, the extent of their political support, or the amount of time and resources already invested. Former state legislator Rebecca Young provided the following example of how a single, sometimes idiosyncratic, event can derail a policy initiative, even when the empirical support is impeccable:

> In Milwaukee, there was something called the intensive sanctions program that was set up in the '90s to substitute for prison time … people would be subject to intensive monitoring while they were out of prison and also able to get certain kinds of training or help with housing and AODA that corrects mental health treatment, the kinds of things that would help them succeed in not committing any crimes. However, one of the persons who was on intensive sanctions did commit a murder. And that was the end of the intensive sanctions program … even though you have the research to show that … this

intensive sanctions program here was quite successful in reducing recidivism compared to time in prison.

The policymaking process responds not only to extraordinary events but also to recurring contingencies such as changes in administration, the timing of the electoral cycle, or the arrival or departure of individuals in key policy roles. For example, the passage of welfare reform legislation was stalled and then fundamentally transformed by the Republican takeover of the U.S. House of Representative in the 1994 congressional elections. Moreover, a whole cadre of advocates, lobbyists, and special interests is continually vying to position issues on the public agenda. Similarly, the media, which prizes itself on reporting novel events, can raise new issues that it argues need immediate attention at the expense of other issues that were once high priorities, but can end up quickly falling from political grace (Levin, 2003).

Even elected officials, who should know lawmaking best, find it difficult to explain the policy process to outsiders, seeming to grasp for words to provide a concrete description of a fluid process with no clear transitions from one state to the next, and one that can halt or even shift directions with little warning. According to one 25-year veteran of the legislature whose office was laden with plaques and trophies of every conceivable shape and size, policymaking can't really be captured in a flowchart because policies do not progress neatly from Point A to Point B. Even after a bill becomes law, it is hard to pinpoint just why it happened as it did.

A newcomer to the Assembly, just completing her second term, explained the elusive nature of policymaking in mathematical terms: "1 plus 1 don't always equal 2"; other factors that are hard to quantify, such as big money and support by outside groups, often come into play. A 10-year veteran of the legislative process from a well-known political family spoke of the policy process not as a flowchart or a mathematical equation, but more like an "art form" where every decision requires some sort of compromise. Because the process of compromise is often long and convoluted, a veteran senator explained, "Change rarely happens swiftly." Yet she immediately underscored the unpredictability of the process by explaining that the biggest accomplishment of her 25-year career was a small legislative change that ironically occurred quite quickly—prohibiting 14- to 17-year-olds from signing themselves out of mental health treatment facilities.

The pace of policymaking is a paradox because it can be both fast and slow. Laws often have to be made within specified legislative deadlines and electoral time frames, so lawmakers can find themselves forced to make decisions quickly even when data are insufficient and analysis is incomplete (Chandler, 2006). One prominent example is the origins of Head Start, which was first implemented with no evidence that it would work on a national scale. Developmental psychologist Edward Zigler believed that he had won a small victory when he convinced Sargent Shriver, chief strategist for the War on Poverty, that Head Start should begin as a small pilot program. But President Lyndon Johnson, "a true Texan with Texas-size ideas," demanded that Head Start begin on a grand scale (Zigler & Styfco, 2002, p. 6). Accordingly, Head Start opened its doors to one-half million children in the summer of 1965, only a couple of months after completion of the planning.

Yet other big, bold ideas may take, not a year or two, but a number of years to be enacted into policy, according to Mary Fairchild, senior fellow at NCSL. Ben Levin, a professor who served as Manitoba's deputy minister of education, had seen policies move too fast and too slow: "Sometimes decisions were made too quickly, without adequate consideration, while at other times choices that seemed obvious were endlessly delayed" (1952/2005, p. 6).

Embellishing its unpredictability, the pace can be uneven, occurring in fits and starts. Gary Sandefur, a sociologist and now dean of Letters and Sciences at the University of Wisconsin–Madison has had extensive experience working with state and federal policymakers on welfare reform. He explained that policymakers may want to move quickly to draft legislation or make a public statement about something, but once this happens everything may grind to a halt:

> In one sense … it's like they hurry up to do something and then they may just drop it after that and move on to something else, so that can be frustrating. So their speed, it tends to be [fast] early on and then … you don't always know what's going to happen after that in terms of actually developing a policy or trying to … draft legislation … it can be a very slow process.

The fluidity and unpredictability of the policy process are captured in that old government saying, "That's final … unless it isn't" (Levin, 1952/2005, p. 16). Even when an agreement has been arrived at, those in the minority may like nothing better than an opportunity to raise the issue again when the circumstances are more favorable to a resolution of their liking.

Observation 4: A Full-Time Opposition Shapes Policy Dynamics

The policy culture differs in several respects that are fundamental both to how inhabitants behave inside the institution and to how policymakers are perceived outside the institution. For example, few other institutions are structured to represent a large body of people who regularly run for office, often with a full-time opposition struggling to beat or unseat them. Lawmaking bodies are indispensable in a democracy in which members are elected *by* the people to conduct business *for* the people. To represent *all* the people, these bodies often have a large number of members, each with an equal mandate to be there but with no reason to cooperate with or respond to the bids of each other (Loewenberg, 2007).

Moreover, each seat is a prize that the opposition would like to claim in the next electoral cycle. To this end, the opposition takes it upon itself to watch members closely and to meticulously point out any mistakes or misjudgments (Levin, 1952/2005). Because each side believes that its approach is surely right and that of the opposition is certainly wrong, these criticisms sometimes can be inaccurate, misleading, or downright unscrupulous. Imagine how the nature of a work environment would change in the face of an opposition whose full-time job it was "to make you look bad" (Levin, 2003, p. 15). Imagine also the cynicism and despair this constant barrage of criticism creates among the public.

Policymakers suggested five ways that the oppositional nature of their culture shapes the dynamics of decision making. First, because policymakers do not have tenure or any assurance they will be around when the next legislative cycle rolls around, the system rewards policymakers for being reactive and responding quickly to emerging issues. One senator explained that policymakers want "quick fixes" so they can solve one problem and move on to the next one in the time frame available, which he quickly quantified as 2 years in the Assembly and 4 years in the Senate in his home state. Social scientists have made similar observations. According to a professor who worked to bring data to policymaking for 20 years (Kaufman, 1993), the surest way a policymaker can jeopardize reelection is by failing to act; even a misguided response can be remedied in the next legislative session if the policymaker is returned to office. The incentive for policymakers, who have no guarantee that they will retain their seat, is to focus their attention and policy efforts "on takeoffs rather than landings" (Weiss, 1978, p. 58).

Second, the tenuous nature of policymakers' jobs also limits their willingness to push too hard on issues that lack popular support. After all, it is public support that puts elected officials into office, and public opinion that decides which policies merit attention. Policymakers will occasionally take unpopular positions, but "staying elected depends on enough people believing that you are doing enough of the right things" (Levin, 1952/2005, p. 18). A Democratic senator explained that if you can't get the majority to go along with you on a bill that you are pushing, you can end up alienating people. If your colleagues don't buy into the idea, you end up "beating your head against the wall and hurting yourself." A previous boss of hers, a state legislator, had mentored her about the importance of backing away from provisions with too little political support: "It's not perfect, but we gotta live to fight another day." In districts like hers that aren't "safe seats," pushing too hard on a bill could end up hurting you in the long run: "Maybe you didn't get the whole pie, but a piece is better than nothing at all. You can go back later and try to get more. And you still will have friends in place to help you."

Third, in the face of a full-time and attentive opposition, policymakers find themselves in the unenviable position of having to focus not only on the long-term goals that motivated them to run for office in the first place but also on avoiding missteps on minor issues that could wind up turning into major problems. The attention of the opposition gravitates toward "perks," especially those that are simple to track and easy for the public to understand, such as the number of gifts accepted, votes missed, per diems claimed, or trips taken. Even the most egregious violations may not be large in their fiscal impact (Levin, 1952/2005), but they could loom large in the public eye by raising questions of character and the dreaded criticism of being labeled *elitist* or *out of touch* with the average voter. Unfortunately, this sets up a dynamic of spending time and energy on avoiding small mistakes, which can drain resources away from the more important work of contemplating and crafting solutions to the pressing problems of the day.

Fourth, because policymakers operate with the perennial cloud of reelection hanging overhead, legislators are forced to consciously consider how they could explain any vote they make to their constituents and political supporters. The importance of these explanations is one of the key findings of a landmark study of campaigning and legislative behaviors of members of the U.S. House of Representatives (Fenno, 1978). The rationale that policymakers use to explain their votes may be as important as the vote itself: "Members believe that it would not take too many unacceptable explanations to cost them dearly at the polls" (Fenno, 1978, p. 342). The clincher is that policymakers have to give attention to the rationale for each vote they cast, never knowing which one may be the hot-button issue used against them in their next campaign.

Fifth, as important as how policymakers explain their votes is whether their votes have been consistent over time. The public values a consistent voting record. Consistency carries with it an aura of a person who is informed and resolute, whereas inconsistency can be cast by opponents as a mark of unprincipled or poor judgment, a definite liability for those elected to make policy decisions (Weiss, 1989). Consistent views and voting records have become even more important in the advent of cable and C-SPAN broadcasting of local policy meetings and floor debates in state houses and the U.S. Congress. Even before lawmakers are sworn into office, they are encouraged to show resolve in their opinions right from Day 1, because any evidence of inconsistency can easily be used against them in the next election.

Why is oppositional politics the sine qua non of democratic decision making? In an interview with a Democratic assemblyman, we explained that we were writing a book on how to infuse research into policymaking. Without missing a beat, he quipped, "Do you think you can?" He went on to explain that we were examining the wrong question. For anyone serious about making policy change, the real power in a democracy lies with elections. "Policymakers get and keep their jobs, only if elected." In three sentences, he put his finger on why the oppositional nature of policymaking is here to stay.

Observation 5: Error-Free Decisions Are Expected to Be Made With Haste

When asked what mistakes academics make in working with policymakers, one 18-year veteran of the Wisconsin legislature said, "Academics don't understand legislators' time constraints. We don't get time to think." A Minnesota legislator expressed similar frustrations: "There is so much to know and so little time that even twelve or fourteen hours isn't enough to do it" (Kerschner & Cohen, 2002, p. 124). Those who work closely with policymakers, like Mary Fairchild of NCSL, concurred that the time of state legislators is "compressed" because of many "competing obligations." Regardless of the jurisdiction, policymakers never seem to have enough time. For example, Ben Levin, who has worked as a professor and a deputy minister, described the pressures on policymakers' time as "enormous and ceaseless": "Politicians are constantly bombarded with requests or demands to do things, stop doing things, increase funding, decrease funding, pass legislation, repeal other legislation, and so on" (Levin, 2003, p. 11).

The pace of legislative activity is just as hectic in Congress. In the 96th Congress, senators served on an average of 10 committees and subcommittees, and representatives averaged 5.5 such assignments. Members of the House are estimated to spend an average of 11 minutes per day reading (U.S. House of Representatives, 1977).

The hectic pace of policymaking is due, in part, to its very nature—any effort that is not a solo act and involves instead moving from individual actions to collective decisions will take time. However, its pace also depends upon several other influences in society, lawmaking institutions, and lawmakers themselves. For example, the societal demand for political action may intensify when citizens become more educated and better organized (Levin, 2003). This strong demand for bills to be acted upon collides with the short supply of days in which to act. Mary Fairchild, a senior fellow at NCSL, explained that the reason the process moves so fast at the state level is institutional—most legislatures are part-time and have to start and finish their job within a finite legislative session. The unrelenting pace of policymaking also may be partially self-imposed, according to one 25-year legislator, who told us that legislators' priorities change from day to day.

The pace influences the policymaking process in a number of ways, such as the breadth and depth of the issues that come before them. For example, a policymaker reasonably can expect to focus on only four or five issues while in office (Levin, 1952/2005), creating a huge mismatch between what policymakers think is personally desirable and what is politically feasible. For those issues that do rise to policymakers' attention, there is never enough time to consider them in the depth they deserve. A 17-year Republican senator explained that serving in the majority, particularly in the state Senate, is a huge responsibility that literally forces legislators to be reactive rather than taking a "big picture" look at issues. According to Levin (2003), "This is not because politicians necessarily like making hurried or uninformed decisions, but because this is what the office requires" (p. 33). In fact, when members of Congress were asked what tasks are important for them to do, studying issues was high on their list, yet it is one of the tasks that appears to get crowded out of their schedule by other demands on their time (Davidson, 1981). In sum, policymakers are forced to make important decisions under tight timelines and without major errors—a next-to-impossible standard the public holds its elected leaders up to.

The time demands that policymakers face not only are physically draining but also take an emotional toll, as explained by Levin (1952/2005):

> Politicians spend a lot of time listening to people, whether colleagues, opponents, constituents, or lobbyists, all of whom feel very strongly about things. They hear horror stories, sad tales, angry complaints. Sometimes they are saddened by what has happened to someone, something they cannot do anything about. Sometimes they are infuriated by someone's stupidity. Often their feelings are stirred. Political discussion and debate, whether in the legislature or in any other setting, runs hot and gets people worked up. When you add to all that an unending work schedule and the sense that there is much more to do than can possibly be done, it is not hard to understand why feelings run high. (pp. 33–34)

The demands are relentless. One male Democratic senator told us that he feels like he is always being pressured to think in a certain way, so he "always has his defenses up." A female Republican senator relayed how annoyed she was to be lobbied after hours at a public swimming pool when attired in her dripping wet bathing suit. Faced with so little down time, such crowded schedules, and ceaseless demands for their time and attention, policymakers can quickly burn out and find they have too little energy and too few new ideas to carry out the agenda that inspired them to run for office in the first place (Levin, 1952/2005).

Observation 6: Policymakers Wrestle With Problems Ranging From the Wee to the Wicked

Researchers sometimes miss the mark in providing useful analysis to policymakers because they are unfamiliar with the number and nature of issues that land on policymakers' desks. As detailed by Lindblom (1968), governments pass laws to build roads, bridges, and dams; care for the aged and disabled; educate citizens; keep the public safe; protect the environment; regulate business and industry; and stimulate the economy. With a portfolio so far-reaching, policymakers must vote up or down on a number of bills, ranging from minor changes in administrative language to sweeping legislation that attempts to redress the most perplexing social problems of our times.

A caucus chair described how he confronted large issues of long-term significance that defy easy or obvious remedies, what we refer to as *wicked* problems (Corbett, 1991, 1993; Rittel & Webber, 1973). However, the majority of his time was taken up with what we call *wee issues*—commonplace, detailed-oriented, administrative matters. The nature of the issue under consideration affected the type of information that was needed:

> The legislature works in incremental moves many, many times, and we have 1,100 to 1,200 Assembly bills introduced every year and 600 or 700 Senate bills, and those are not all big issues. A lot of times they're all very small pieces of state law that need to be adjusted or changed one way or the other. A lot of times the information that might come in might be too broad or too general and not fit those specific needs.

For these technical issues, the information that was forthcoming was often not specific enough or sufficiently targeted to the question at hand. Information was also needed, according to this same long-term lawmaker, when dramatic shifts in policy direction occurred:

> When I was in the legislature, we went through the whole welfare reform issue that the governor had put before us. And there were many, many details on how you would implement sort of a dramatic shift in implementing a major social program. At times like that, it was good to have information available.

When the academy is faced with wicked social problems, such as welfare reform, that entail complexity and uncertainty, its capacity to respond has proved inadequate in a number of ways, three of which emerged in our interviews. For example, one strategy researchers use to make wicked problems more manageable is to minimize and dissect the complexity in ways that are more compatible with the dominant methods of research and evaluation. Granted, such simplification reduces the complexity of the research process, but the wicked problems policymakers confront do not so easily yield to narrow and simplistic solutions, as explained by a former director of the Institute for Research on Poverty:

> In fact, there is a fundamental problem with a lot of the best research as it becomes applied to public policy, in that the experimental method, which is what we use to really uncover truth, works best when you can isolate a specific intervention. Then you can test whether or not that intervention is better than some kind of counterfactual, whether it's a different kind of intervention or business as usual. What we found in the welfare world … is that any particular intervention might work just a little bit … if there was any impact at all.

Another inherent barrier that the academy bumps up against when addressing wicked policy problems is that they do not fit neatly into the academy's disciplinary silos and often exceed the sensitivity of the measures and the sophistication of the methods available to social scientists (Corbett, 1991; Shonkoff, 2000). Wicked problems demand cross-disciplinary, out-of-the-box thinking that can be unfamiliar and uncomfortable for researchers trained to advance a narrow field of study one small step at a time. Instead, what is required is a type of holistic and integrative thinking that academics often do not have the time, training, or wherewithal to engage in. In the words of a member of a National Academy of Sciences panel,

> I think about the world that I've operated in, the welfare world. Academics were more comfortable when the issues were largely economic in character, that is, they were a set of principles, economic principles in terms of guarantees and marginal tax rates and labor/leisure trade-offs that lent themselves to empirical analysis and the development of a set of theoretical propositions. But now welfare is largely about changing behaviors, a much more complex endeavor. And what I found is that a lot of economists, in particular, were most willing to spend a lot of time … when issues were defined in ways that could be dealt with by their discipline. Now that it's a much more complex set of propositions involving individual behavioral changes and the way institutions perform and relate to one another, and so forth, they're not as eager to play in that. Because it's very, very complex, and it doesn't lend itself as easily to the publication of peer-reviewed papers.

Finally, a Republican legislator in her second term pinpointed a fundamental mismatch between the kinds of evidence that are valued in the two cultures. In her work as a policymaker, the kind of information that is most valuable to her is what research says about the people in her district. Even if an issue were widely regarded as a wicked social problem for the population at large, elected officials would be remiss if they failed to consider how this issue affects their own constituencies. What this interchange made obvious to us is that the gold standard of high-quality research—representative samples that provide generalizable data—is not the same as the gold standard of policy-relevant research—localized data on how a policymaker's jurisdiction compares to similar jurisdictions, such as how his or her district compares to other districts in the state or how his or her state compares to other states in the nation (Kaufman, 1993; Riley, 1997).

Observation 7: Policymaking Is One of the Most Complex Undertakings Known to Humankind

Another observation is obvious to those familiar with the policy culture but surprising to those who aren't: Making laws is much more difficult than most people can ever imagine. In fact, researchers who were biculturally competent reached the counterintuitive conclusion that policymakers face more complexity in their jobs than researchers do. One researcher who worked on the 1997–1998 federal balanced budget bill posited that researchers have the luxury of focusing on "small, very well-defined issues that they can reasonably address with the data they have available. Policymakers, by contrast, have to focus on larger questions that tend to be not nearly as well defined." Another researcher with a decade of experience working with lawmakers concurred that the complexity of producing research pales in contrast to that of producing policy:

> Researchers are not dealing with social, complex, political systems. Politicians have to use research in a complex world in which they try and use research knowledge in order to make a difference. They have to be attuned with the political opposition. Research by comparison is so simple. We control for a lot of variables, don't try to change complex systems and organisms. The unintended negative side effects of legislation and policy are so huge, and the weight of responsibility is so great for these people. If I botch my research study, it's going to be buried in a journal. I won't have shaped the nature of the field with my mistake. If you're dealing, for example, with welfare reform and family support, nobody knows yet how this will play out. You can do a lot of damage.

An emeritus professor with 30 years of experience agreed that it is not uncommon for academics to underestimate the complexity of the policymaking process. They often are unaware of all the factors that come into play in any policy, unfamiliar with the dimensions of the decision for which there is no evidence, and unacquainted with the complexities of taking an idea, often untested, and making it reality. Experts or the man on the street often have a solution for policymakers, according to this professor, and they wonder why those "dummies" just can't do X.

> But when you get in there and you try to do X, or Y, or Z, not only are you bombarded by competing visions of what the truth is, but the complexity associated with doing anything, changing bureaucratic cultures, whatever it may be, is enormous, and the specter of unintended consequences is always there. And so you do X, you get it instituted, you make the change, and then you find out that this generation's solution to a problem is the next generation's scandal … sometimes it doesn't even take a generation, it'll take a year or two. And people look back and say "What idiot did that?" just because we can't always anticipate all the blowback and the unintended consequences … this is not

about having a vision of truth and going out and applying it. This is about slogging through thorny issues that have enormously complex trade-offs associated with them.

The origins of this complexity are many, three of which will suffice for our purposes. First, policymaking by its very nature demands that policymakers be generalists, according to a researcher at a prominent think tank: "[They] have to vote on a large number of issues, so they tend to be broad, but not very deep on most issues." Typically, policymakers in any one session are required to vote "aye" or "nay" on issues ranging from minimum wage to mining policy, from taxation to transportation.

Second, policymakers are faced with the formidable task of trying to reconcile visions of truth that are inconsistent with each other and may be inconsistent over time as well. For example, the same constituents who demand lower taxes in one meeting may request more services in the next; later, they may even complain loudly about the consequences of the cuts that they previously lobbied for (Levin, 2003).

Third, the complexity of public policy defies easy and efficient solutions to perplexing problems. Social scientists are much better at documenting "what is" than at making predictions about what "ought to be" (Seeley, 1985) or what "might be." Policymakers, however, are called upon to enact a response to a wicked social problem, which often is untested and may result in unintended, collateral consequences that, like the proverbial Gordian knot, could feed back upon itself. Despite the best of intentions, some policy decisions will later be found to be a mistake, and then policymaking becomes a process of remedying the errors of past decisions (Lindblom, 1968).

Policymakers and researchers have responded by developing strategies for confronting and coping with complexity. One experienced legislator relayed her experience introducing bills that ended up causing problems that she had not anticipated, prompting her to rethink the processes that she uses to design legislation. To gain greater assurance that her bills will bring about the intended change, she now brings to the table those who will be affected by the bill when it is being designed and gives them this charge:

> "You are the practitioner. You will have to work with the legislation. Help me design it." I think that I am a better legislator because I do it this way. I think this is one of the most important things that legislators can do ... the cleaner the bill, the faster it passes. The cleaner it is, the less people there are to fight it.

On the basis of a decade of experience, one researcher has gradually come to appreciate how complex policymaking is and has "become more sympathetic to slowness in the process and the need for pilot and demonstration projects to see if the policy works."

Complexity is one of those cross-cutting themes found in both settings irrespective of whether the primary product is research or policy. A discussion of the complexity of policymaking would be incomplete without mention of an inherent irony in the way that complexity is viewed in the two cultures. Scientists operate in a culture that rewards complex thinking on abstract and esoteric topics, whereas policymakers operate in a culture that shuns complexity because it interferes with the mark of a resolute and stalwart leader—one who takes firm, unyielding positions on issues (Shonkoff, 2000).

Observation 8: The Values of Policymakers and Their Constituents Are Potent Policy Levers

Values are at the core of the cultural clash between knowledge producers and knowledge consumers. It is not that values do not exist among knowledge producers, because everyone has a set of values and priors that they take into any debate or line of inquiry. Instead, the crux of the cultural clash centers on the primacy of values in decision making—being a criteria of prime importance in one culture and subprime importance in the other. The values of policymakers and the values of their constituents are privileged in policy decisions, whereas researchers attempt to keep their decisions as value-free as possible by relying on rigorous research methods and predetermined probability levels. In the words of one experienced researcher, "One has to accept that values are values. We all have them, but as a researcher, my values have no place in my research. But policymakers' values count, and their constituents' values count."

A clash around an issue as fundamental as the criteria for making decisions can impede communication and cooperation between the two cultures. According to a 30-year veteran of the policy process from a land-grant university,

> Policymakers, particularly if they're from the political end of the policymaking process, are really driven and defined by their values, whereas researchers or academics are supposed to be relatively value-free except for the set of values that go into the scientific inquiry per se. So I think that the fact that one tradition or culture has values of prime importance and the other one tries to at least hide their values also makes it a very difficult exchange. So as researchers or policy analysts bring their evidence to policymakers, they're often taken aback when that evidence is filtered through a set of very distinct … priors that sort of shape how the evidence is looked at and used, and sometimes even distorted.

When values dominate science, those socialized into the superiority of research can respond with "a bit of arrogance," according to one professor with stellar credentials in the worlds of research and policy—election by her peers as president of a prestigious political science association and 25 years of experience working with policymakers. When it comes to values, she explained, "It's not an even playing field":

> [If you] make a big announcement, present findings, and don't attend to the fact that a section of the population will object based on value-driven reasons, you won't get as far. Researchers are pretty ignorant in the political space and don't understand where people are coming from. … Now I ask myself, what are the different factions? Where are they coming from? I try to get into their heads.

In her work on politically charged topics such as teenage pregnancy, she learned to reconcile the roles that values played in her work with the roles they played in the work of the policymakers she hopes will use her research. Here's how she does it. She considers her personal values to be irrelevant. What is relevant is that she responds to policymakers' values not by allowing any bias to seep into her research, but by presenting information in ways respectful of diverse values and perspectives.

Those who ply the knowledge broker trade soon learn that research is seldom comprehensive and definitive enough to serve as the sole determinant of a policy decision. Extension agricultural economist Richard Barrows cites the example of a public policy education program that he conducted on an innovative, far-reaching, farmland preservation program that faced the state legislature in Wisconsin in the 1970s. Reflecting on the policy education sessions that he conducted in rural and urban settings for those who were advantaged and disadvantaged by the legislation, he observed firsthand the value that data and objective analysis brought to the debate and eventual enactment of this controversial proposal. Yet he resisted pressure from both his supervisors and state policymakers to provide his personal stance on this issue, because he was fully aware that the decision could not be made on the basis of science alone:

> Scientific knowledge, the wisdom of the university, cannot be used to determine the "correct" policy choice for society because science cannot supply the value judgments that rank the interests of one group as more important than the interests of another. (Barrows, 1994, p. 3)

In sum, science can help identify what is real, but it falls to the purview of values to identify what is ideal (Ross & Staines, 1972). For example, welfare reformers faced the dilemma of balancing two important, yet contradictory, value-based goals: reducing welfare dependency and reducing child poverty. Flinchbaugh cautioned researchers about making value judgments about which of these goals is more important: "Just because you have studied the issue, just because you have a degree behind your name, and just because you may be the 'expert,' does not make your values superior to anyone else's" (1988, p. 224).

Policymakers respect and try to reflect the values of the constituents who elect them to office. Wisconsin state representative Steve Hilgenberg, who ran a successful grassroots campaign to unseat a 14-year incumbent in a leadership position, provides a concrete example of the centrality of his constituents to his role as a state legislator. When constituents stop by his capitol office, he has become well-known for inviting visitors to sit in the chair behind his desk. He explains, "I sit in this chair, but it's not mine. It's yours. It belongs to the district."

In describing his relationship with his constituents, one state senator used the term "intimate" because of how seriously he takes the trust voters have placed in him, an aspect of being a policymaker that he believes is not well understood outside the state house. Policymakers' nagging concern about how the voters will perceive them is no different in the nation's capital, according to then-senator, now-president Barack Obama (2006). He explained that his colleagues, Democrat and Republican alike, come to the Senate fresh off campaigns with

> their mistakes trumpeted, their words distorted, and their motives questioned. They are baptized in that fire; it haunts them each and every time they cast a vote, each and every time they issue a press release or make a statement, the fear of losing not just a political race, but of losing favor in the eyes of those who sent them to Washington—all those people who have said to them at one time or another: "We have great hopes for you. Please don't disappoint us." (p. 133)

Policymakers take very seriously the charge to represent the views of their constituents, despite the enormous complexities of doing so. One senator who had served in the legislature for 25 years put it bluntly: "Our interests are dictated by theirs. If it's not a topic of interest to them, then we don't have time for it." Most policymakers represent a sizeable constituency, so the value stances of constituents often conflict with each other and other prominent policy actors. It falls to policymakers to sort out and to negotiate these varying value orientations—a task that knowledge consumers and knowledge producers alike recognize is one more reason that policymaking is one of the most complex undertakings known to humankind (see discussion in Observation 7).

Observation 9: Policymaking Favors the Status Quo

Press reports tend to revolve around the qualitative shifts that occur in policy direction (perhaps because the press prefers to report on the novel), yet there is always a strong gravitational pull toward the opposite side of the policy coin—the status quo. This dimension does not differ as dramatically between the two cultures, but there is enough of a difference that it can lead to misunderstanding and miscommunication. Academia has been criticized for being mired in disciplinary silos that limit the research questions that are asked, the types of analyses that are conducted, and oftentimes the real-life relevance of the results that emerge. Despite the force of the status quo, there are still institutional incentives for moving beyond the traditional paradigms in the venues of publication, grantsmanship, tenure, and promotion. However, in the policy culture, the predominant institutional pressures are for preserving existing programs and policies, many of which become entrenched in the bureaucracy amidst a throng of vested interests that will defend them to the death (Lynn, 1978). Several legislators spontaneously mentioned this preoccupation with the status quo. One legislator explained it this way:

> These programs end up piling on top of each other. Legislators have to make decisions about what programs to cut and what to expand. It is hard to say "no" to existing programs, even when there is a better alternative.

Despite the fact that most social policies abide by the strong pull toward incremental change, on occasion some qualitatively big jumps do occur. Milton Friedman is credited with saying, "Only a crisis—actual or perceived—produces real changes. When that crisis occurs, the actions that are taken depend on the ideas that are lying around." As an example, Dave Riley cites the birth of Head Start, which was precipitated, in part, by the crisis created by *Sputnik*, which underscored the need to train a competent, new generation of scientists. The conditions required for dramatic policy shifts can be likened to those of a perfect storm—innovative ideas lying around that are picked up by skilled policymakers who shepherd them through the policy process in the wake of a crisis and public outcry for political response. We end where we began. In the words of C. P. Snow, understanding how the policy world ticks is the first step toward making it tick better.

Key Concepts 7.1   How to Leverage Knowledge of the Policymaking Process

- Because policymaking is a political process designed to reach consensus among divergent views, respect the use of compromise as a tool for getting things done.
- Because policymaking is a fluid process, respond quickly to emerging issues and remain patient as issues cycle on and off the political agenda.
- Because of the hectic pace of policymaking and the relentless demands on policymakers' time, schedule briefings at convenient hours and in accessible locations ,and provide information in formats that are easily read and digested.
- Because of the nature of electoral politics, provide evidence on how an issue affects a policymaker's constituents, or how a policymaker's jurisdiction such as a district or state compares with similar jurisdictions.
- Because policymakers are called upon to respond to wicked social problems, avoid miring issues in complexity but portray enough complexity to avert the temptation to legislate simple, "magic bullet" solutions.
- Because values are at the core of the clash between knowledge producers and knowledge consumers, be realistic about what role evidence can and cannot play in policy decisions.

SUMMARY

Lawmaking bodies have been called a "policy development cauldron" (Jonas, 1999, p. 8). *Cauldron* seems an appropriate descriptor for a process composed of a mix of ingredients so paradoxical that it disavows a rational basis for the outcome. Policymaking can leap forward at lightning speed or saunter along at a snail's pace. The resulting decisions can be inspired by statesmanship or fueled by the political calculus of a full-time opposition. No matter the impetus, decisions are expected to be made with haste and without error. Policy problems range from the wee to the wicked, and policy issues range from the commonplace to the complex. Decisions must weigh what facts say are *real* with what values say are *ideal*, while balancing extraordinary forces that push policy in new directions and opposing forces that relentlessly pull policy back to the status quo.

With so many convening and contravening forces, it is no wonder that there is disdain for the policymaking process and disparagement of those involved in it. In large part, Ben Levin (1952/2005) defended government but also acknowledged that government is an imperfect institution:

> [Government] may fail to do what is important or right, and may actually do things that are bad and dangerous. They are sometimes driven by the pursuit of wrong ends: power above purpose, the short-term over the long-term, the interests of the powerful instead of the interests of the majority. Image becomes more important than substance, and personal agendas may dominate public ones. Truth may become a casualty of political convenience. (pp. 6–7)

In keeping with Levin, we see the imperfections, but we also see the potential for policymakers to come together for the common good. For the novice, we fear this chapter may be perceived as a Pollyannaish portrayal given assertions about the efficiencies and effectiveness of the process. Conceivably, the chapter may have an optimistic tone given our reliance on interviews of policymakers who were admittedly interested in using research in their decisions and researchers who had experienced success in communicating research to policymakers. Those we interviewed were obviously familiar with the policymaking process, but it is possible that for reasons unbeknownst to us, they may have focused more heavily on when the policy process worked, as it is designed to, rather than on those instances when it did not. However, we are heartened by the close approximation of our portrayal with that of legendary British political leader Sir Winston Churchill (cited in Langworth, 2008): "It has been said that democracy is the worst form of government except all the others that have been tried."

By no means is this chapter a comprehensive or exhaustive examination of the policymaking process, but our hope is that it will serve to motivate the reader to become a student of the policymaking process—an endeavor that we think is important for a couple reasons. First, we agree with Levin's assessment, based on his experience in Canada, that there is a danger that government will "lose its legitimacy in the eyes of citizens" (1952/2005, p. 7). Troubling trends have also emerged in the United States based on Putnam's analysis (1995, 2002) that in the 1990s voter turnout dropped by more than 25%, and Americans invested less time in public affairs. Yankelovich (1995) documented an increasing disconnect between the public and its political leaders, a trend that was not even evident a decade earlier. Between 1998 and 2004, Americans' trust in government declined for all levels of government (Gallup Organization, 2004). If professionals and the public better understood the inner workings of government, is it possible that they would come to see it as more intelligent, rational, and committed to the public good?

Second, we believe it is fundamental to develop a deeper and more nuanced understanding of the lawmaking process because policymakers operate, not in isolation, but within an institutional culture that sets powerful constraints on what can and cannot be done (Weiss, 1999). We do not contend that policymaking can be reduced to a set of textbook processes that easily can be committed to memory, repeated chapter and verse, and executed by rote. However, understanding the process by which government works brings into sharp relief the core assumptions of the policy culture, which can help researchers cross the cultural divide with more confidence and success. For example, the fact that policymaking is fluid means that successful knowledge brokers must be diligent in determining which issues are on or off the political agenda. Understanding the crowded lives of policymakers prompts the scheduling of briefings at convenient times and the preparation of materials in formats that are easily read and digested. Awareness of how values drive the policy process helps knowledge producers be more realistic about what research can and cannot do.

Now with a clearer understanding of what elected officials are like and how the policymaking process works, we take the next step in our journey to traverse the rugged and rigid terrain into the policy culture. In Chapter 8, we begin with the cultural barriers that knowledge producers encountered in their travels into the policy world and the rewards they experienced when they reached the "Promised Land."

8

Barriers to and Rewards of Cross-Cultural Communication

We are well past the time when it is possible to argue that good research will, because it is good, influence the policy process.

—Ray Rist (1994, p. 546)

Knowing is not enough, we must apply. Willing is not enough, we must do.

—Johann Wolfgang von Goethe (1749–1832)

Sheldon Danziger, who has served as director of poverty research centers at both the University of Wisconsin and the University of Michigan, once lamented, "So much social science, so little policy impact" (2001). But is his pessimistic assertion really true? Aren't there examples where research and analysis have successfully been brought to the attention of policymakers?

Of course there are. The reality on the ground is that the relationship between social science and public policy is neither uniformly good nor uniformly bad. Rather, that relationship is complex, ambiguous, and very contextual. Sometimes science and policymaking connect, sometimes they do not. Sometimes knowledge consumers and knowledge producers communicate well, other times substantial and seemingly impenetrable barriers exist. In this chapter, we dig deeper into what these sources of cultural friction are, specifically what barriers are encountered when those who produce knowledge attempt to communicate with those who produce policy. We examine in greater depth why knowledge producers make the commitment it takes to bring one's research and ideas to the real world and whether this effort really pays off in the long run.

To provide a window into the barriers and rewards of communicating across conflicting cultures, we draw upon the expertise of those who have been successful at doing so. In 2003, we conducted in-depth interviews with 14 social scientists whom we identified through assessments by (a) experts in the field regarding their academic credentials and the policy relevance of their research, and (b) policy-makers regarding their ability to effectively communicate their findings in a policy setting. We intentionally focused on those successful in providing research to poli-cymakers in the hope that what they have learned, often through trial and error, could be synthesized and shared.

We distill the advice of these exemplary policy communicators who cumula-tively account for a combined 274 years of experience working with policymak-ers at the local, state, and federal levels. The sample reads like a "who's who" in family policy, as described in Table 8.1. (See a discussion of the methods of this qualitative study in the appendix and an earlier analysis of these data published by Friese and Bogenschneider in 2009.) These researchers' contact with policymakers consisted primarily of four activities: (a) presenting or testifying before Congress, legislatures, and committees ($n = 14$); (b) responding to individual questions from policymakers and their staff via phone and e-mail ($n = 8$); (c) serving on commit-tees, advisory panels, and task forces ($n = 7$); and (d) writing briefs, memoranda, and contract research reports ($n = 6$). All had experience disseminating research to policymakers at the state level, almost all (13) at the federal level, and 6 at the international level.

Between 2006 and 2008, Karen supplemented these initial interviews with ten 20- to 90-minute videotaped interviews of researchers, university administrators, and presidents of philanthropic and outreach organizations that were nationally known for their ability to communicate with policymakers, 6 of whom we had inter-viewed previously, and 4 of whom we had not. Our informants were not selected on a random basis, given that we had no interest in making population estimates. Rather, we tapped some seasoned inhabitants of both the knowledge-consuming and knowledge-producing communities to elicit the best insights possible.

Drawing upon our community dissonance theory, we asked the original 14 exemplary policy communicators a number of open-ended questions about how their work with policymakers began, what their initial impressions were, whether these impressions changed over time, what barriers they encountered, and which rewards they experienced. (The frequencies in this chapter are based on the stan-dard set of questions included in only the first 14 interviews.) We begin this chap-ter with one of Karen's most memorable policy experiences during her graduate training, a story that she also told in her earlier book (Bogenschneider, 2006). We also refer in several places in this chapter to a talk featuring Emeritus Professor Edward Zigler (Zigler, Phillips, Moorehouse, & Watson, 2009), of Head Start fame, at a recent policy preconference at the Society for Research in Child Development. His reflections over a 44-year policy career, along with Karen's vignette, bring to life many of the barriers that impede policy work along with the rich rewards when these barriers are overcome and policy efforts succeed.

MILK FOR POOR KIDS: AN IMPROBABLE POLICY VICTORY

During Karen's doctoral training, she responded to an announcement seeking a graduate student to work on an advocacy effort concerning a child nutrition issue

TABLE 8.1   Experience, Affiliations, and Policy Credentials of the Study Respondents

Years of Policy Experience	Affiliation	Policy Credentials
20	Land-grant university	Coauthor of an often-cited book on single parenting that had a significant influence on welfare policy
25	Nonpartisan policy research organization	Testified before Congress over a dozen times; currently analyzing changes in Medicaid programs and long-term care in 13 states
10	Land-grant university	Former president of a national organization for family professionals; one of the driving forces of a grassroots family organization
5	Independent research center	Researcher; directs a family intervention named a National Blueprint Program for Violence Prevention by the U.S. Department of Justice that is currently being replicated in 25 communities
16	Land-grant university	Recipient of the American Psychological Association Award for Distinguished Contributions to Psychology in the Public Interest; selected by the governor to direct a $2.5 million initiative to improve child care quality for low-income families in his state
27	Land-grant university	Member of the National Academy of Sciences panel on measuring the effect of changes in social welfare programs; organized a peer assistance network for state government officials to dialogue about welfare reform innovations across state lines
13	Land-grant university	Member of an international team analyzing family policy in the United States, United Kingdom, Canada, and Australia; provides commissioned research, evaluations, and policy papers for a state child support bureau
30	Land-grant university	Work for the U.S. Department of Health and Human Services on prescription drugs was highlighted in a report to the president
23	University	Director of a home visiting program operating in 5 countries and 359 counties in 26 states; responsible, in part, for a law that used tobacco settlement money to provide home visiting for all low-income women in his state
20	Ivy League school	Fellow of a nonpartisan policy research firm; helped evaluate and disseminate the results of a welfare demonstration program for teenage parents
25	Land-grant university	Testified before Congress 16 times and has worked with 14 countries on prescription drug issues; conducted research for the U.S. General Accounting Office, the U.S. Special Committee on Aging, and the Food and Drug Administration
20	Land-grant university	Authored 50 referred articles; testified before three state legislatures on school funding; developed a formula used to distribute revenue to local governments in South Africa

(Continued)

TABLE 8.1   Experience, Affiliations, and Policy Credentials of the Study
Respondents (Continued)

Years of Policy Experience	Affiliation	Policy Credentials
20	Land-grant university	Former director of a poverty center; as assistant deputy secretary for tax analysis at the U.S. Department of Treasury, he worked on changing the official U.S. poverty measure
20	Ivy League school	State, national, and international experience; worked with a governor to shift thinking on the value of family support

in the state. Karen was an unemployed doctoral student at the time, paying her own way through college. Thus, she was able to participate in policy advocacy in ways that she is unable to do in her current tax-supported position as a professor and Cooperative Extension specialist at a land-grant university.

Here was the situation in 1987. A debate had raged in Congress regarding whether poor schoolchildren who received a free or subsidized carton of milk at the mid-morning milk break and again at lunch were "double-dipping" into the public purse. In 1983, Congress voted to eliminate federal support for the morning milk break—a program administered by schools to provide milk for schoolchildren. Through this program, children who could afford it purchased a carton of milk, and poor children received free or reduced-price milk. The consequence of Congress's decision was that the average daily milk consumption of Wisconsin schoolchildren through this program dropped by 80%—from 390,000 half pints in 1981 to only 71,254 in 1985.

Parents did not know about it. Farmers did not rally. Children were unable to speak up for themselves. So the federal morning milk program was phased out, despite a surplus of milk in the state at the time. Somehow, it did not seem right to Karen to eliminate free milk for poor kids, especially in Wisconsin, which prides itself on being the nation's dairy state. Policy work often begins in situations just like this—when enough people believe that *something ought to be done* to make things right.

Karen signed up to work on the project as an unpaid internship, which provided three course credits. (We have always wondered if it is only in the academic culture that one has to *pay* to *work* for someone else.) Karen was supervised by Patricia Mapp, the director of the Children's Audit Project. Pat had previously worked with Democratic and Republican legislators regarding the possible drafting of legislation to reestablish a morning milk program in Wisconsin that would be funded with state dollars.

Karen's first assignment was to gather background information on the nutritional status of children, which seemed a straightforward question, but as with most social policy issues, the evidence was incomplete and the answers proved elusive. After convincing Professor Sheldon Danziger, her instructor in a social policy course, that this analysis would be an appropriate final paper, she produced a 58-page background paper on the issue, including an overview of research on the nutritional status of children, the nutrients available in milk and their supply in children's diets, the impact of hunger on learning, the fit of the special milk program with other child-feeding programs, and the consequences of several policy options for improving children's nutritional status. The paper concluded that reinstating a morning milk program was the most desirable policy option if targeted toward those at the greatest nutritional risk—low-income children. Karen argued that the program was cost-effective, simple to administer, and consistent with prevailing public sentiment that parents should assume primary responsibility for feeding their children. Professor Danziger thought this position was supported well enough to assign the paper a good grade, but he questioned whether the school breakfast program might actually be a better policy option for improving children's nutritional status. (Actually, he proved to be ahead of the times in his thinking, as school breakfast programs gradually have become more widely accepted.)

Undaunted by Professor Danziger's lukewarm response, Karen and Pat met with the Democratic and Republican legislators who were interested in sponsoring legislation on the issue. At the meeting, Karen reviewed the results of her literature review and recommended that the legislation be targeted toward low-income children. After listening to the evidence, one of the legislators pounded his fist on the table as he flatly and firmly declared that he just did not like programs for the poor. With no further discussion, the initial legislation was drafted for all schoolchildren in Wisconsin, with a $3 million price tag.

To begin soliciting the support of policymakers and interested organizations, Karen condensed her 58-page paper into a brochure, but the 4 pages that she came up with (aided by her previous master's degree in journalism) were considered much too long by the legislative aide of one of the Assembly sponsors. This aide then drafted a 2-page fact sheet, which, in keeping with the views of her boss, made no mention of the evidence regarding the elevated nutritional risk of poor children.

Karen's next responsibility was to pull together a statewide coalition of endorsements. Karen knew that the child and family advocates in the states were low budget, sparsely staffed, loosely organized, and less powerful than other interested advocacy organizations. One of the keys to success would be building a coalition with the powerful, organized, and skilled advocates who have the coffers and connections it would take for the bill to have any chance of passage. Karen had a stroke of good luck when a friend linked her up with a well-respected, retired agricultural lobbyist who allowed her to use his name and his little black book with the contact information of every agricultural organization in the state. Eventually 22 organizations signed on to support the bill, including several agricultural organizations, the Children's Trust Fund, the Hunger Task Force of Wisconsin, the Wisconsin Association of School Boards, the Wisconsin Education Association, the Wisconsin Extension Homemaker Council, the Wisconsin Nutrition Project, the Wisconsin Association of School District Administrators, and so forth.

Because Karen and Pat did not get started until April, it was too late to introduce new legislation, so they lobbied to attach their proposal as an amendment to the state budget. The issue was referred to the Democratic Assembly Education Committee, and they promptly targeted a phone campaign on the four members of this body. They coached callers to lobby these four state legislators to include the morning milk proposal in their package of recommendations to the Democratic

Assembly Caucus. If Karen and Pat could persuade this committee to fold the proposal into their legislative package, this would greatly enhance the chances for eventual passage. However, they lost that vote. Undaunted, they expanded their efforts to the entire Democratic Assembly.

A major setback occurred the morning of the Assembly Caucus vote, when their Democratic sponsor changed his mind about introducing the legislation. He actually traded away his sponsorship of the morning milk legislation, now called the *Special Milk Amendment*, to garner political support for another pet project. With some 11th-hour maneuvering by Pat Mapp, Tom Loftus, the speaker of the Assembly at the time, introduced the legislation with an inspiring "Let's do it for cows—let's do it for kids" speech. The caucus passed a scaled-down $820,000 version that targeted free or subsidized milk to poor children. Ironically, the bill that was passed ended up coinciding with the evidence—targeting a morning milk break to poor children who were at the greatest nutritional risk.

Remarkably, the Democratic Assembly passed the Special Milk Amendment 3 months after Karen and Pat had opened the file on the issue and a mere 6 weeks after they had solicited organizational endorsements. They were able to expedite the 5 years that it usually takes to pass a bill in the state for a couple reasons. First, the process was shortened because Pat Mapp and the two legislative sponsors had done some groundwork on the issue during the previous legislative session. They were also able to move more quickly because the organizations that joined the coalition brought to the table their political infrastructure—on-site lobbyists, established phone banks, and existing political connections.

When the budget was passed by both houses of the Democrat-controlled legislature, Karen and Pat felt confident that the Special Milk Amendment would soon be signed into law by the Republican governor. How could he veto milk for poor children? To their surprise, Karen received a phone call from her own representative, who, as fate would have it, had been a college roommate of the governor. He was adamant that the governor did indeed have every intention of vetoing the amendment. Karen immediately called all 22 organizations, many which had well-oiled phone banks, and asked them to contact the governor in support of the amendment. Interestingly, some of the organizations that had been the most helpful with the Democratic Assembly forewarned Karen that they had little influence with a Republican governor. To make a long story short, on July 31, 1987, the governor signed the budget bill into law, including the $820,000 Special Milk Amendment, which was heralded as one of the only new spending initiatives in the 1987–1988 biennial budget. Pat, Karen, and their collaborators celebrated over a tall, cold glass of milk.

However, the public policy process was not over when the law was passed. One of the legislators held some animosity toward the Wisconsin Department of Public Instruction and refused to include in the bill any funds for implementation. In response, Karen wrote a $15,000 grant proposal to a private funding source to ensure that the milk initiative was properly handled at the school and that the program was adequately publicized. She also worked with farm organizations to encourage local farmers to approach their school boards to alert them of this new

TABLE 8.2   Barriers to and Rewards of Cross-Cultural Communication

Barriers	Rewards
Misunderstanding of policymakers	Making the world a better place
Researchers' unfamiliarity with the policymaking process	The excitement of seeing research applied in the real world
Long-term versus short-term time frame	Being respected for their expertise
Scientific language versus policy-relevant language	
The academy's failure to reward policy work	

voluntary program, which was slated to begin just 3 weeks after the budget was passed when the fall school year began.

Embedded in this story are several examples of the barriers and rewards that researchers experience when they wade into the policy world. We describe below these barriers and rewards along with those that emerged from our earlier study and supplementary interviews of exemplary policy communicators (see a summary in Table 8.2).

RESEARCHERS' INITIAL IMPRESSIONS OF BARRIERS TO WORKING WITH POLICYMAKERS

Surprisingly, we found that working successfully with policymakers is not an innate ability that some folks are born with and others are not. Instead, the vast majority of those who eventually became successful in moving seamlessly between the worlds of research and policy described their first impression as one of *culture shock*. For the majority of researchers ($n = 11$), their initial contacts brought into sharp relief cultural differences about which they were previously unaware.

A sociologist whose first experience was testifying on the Family Support Act in the late 1980s was surprised at how little he knew about policymakers: "I think my first impression was that I could never talk to those people because their world was so different than mine, and I didn't want to think the way they had to think." An economics researcher concurred, characterizing research and policy as being "worlds apart." Others described policymakers in disparaging terms such as "not well informed," "unrealistic," and an "old boys' network." A researcher who has a joint appointment at the University of Wisconsin–Madison and University of Wisconsin–Extension aptly observed, "Most scholars would like to contribute to the policy process, but our professional culture drives them to be ineffective."

Consistent with the tenets of community dissonance theory, the researchers identified several specific barriers that served as impediments to interaction and communication across the two communities. The barriers are many, according to Mary Fairchild, a senior fellow with the National Conference of State Legislatures. She contrasts the culture of state legislators with that of analysts, whom she thinks of as folks like her who work in government trade associations as well as researchers and the staff at nonpartisan legislative service agencies:

> And if you look at the analysts, we're interested in completeness and accuracy. Legislators are interested in brevity. That's a very different thing. Analysts [are interested in] number factors, interested in data big time. Legislators are interested in the human factors, interested in people and events. How does this impact my constituency? Analysts move from the part to the whole; legislators move from the whole to the parts. Analysts tend to read everything very carefully point by point ... legislators tend to skim and pause. Another [difference] is analysts are very concerned with the internal consistency and methodology and how the research is conducted ... legislators are interested in the implications—what difference is it going to make? They don't care about your methodology if it can't help them solve a problem. And analysts have an interest in processing that methodology; legislators are little interested in process. And then the other thing is that analysts have relatively consistent attention. At the university, you've got all that time to think. In the legislature ... I don't know any other business ... [where you] ... have to get that much information and that much work done in that sort of compressed time.

In our interviews, researchers raised five specific barriers: misunderstanding of policymakers, researchers' unfamiliarity with the policymaking process, different time frames and languages, and few rewards from the academy. Each is described in turn below.

Misunderstanding of Policymakers

Perceptions are important because they shape the quality and character of relationships. One researcher's first impression was that policymakers "were not well informed ... highly susceptible to the arguments of interest groups, especially provider groups, and a lot of their concerns were constituent driven." Prolonged contact with policymakers helped dispel stereotypes like these, and, importantly, none of the researchers reported that their negative stereotypes were confirmed. One researcher explained that when you come to know policymakers as people, your stereotypes change. On the basis of only 5 years of sporadic contact, she explained that "hanging out with policymakers helps you realize how smart they are. Everybody likes to bash them, and how the media covers them sets that dynamic up. But if you talk to them about their concerns, your view changes."

Another researcher, who worked for 20 years on child care and teenage pregnancy policy and who served as president of a national political science association, said she had "come to appreciate even people who seem radical in their views. If you get to know them, they don't seem quite as extreme. There's some rationale underneath it."

One researcher recognized for his public service by the American Psychological Association initially stereotyped a legislator as a "Republican ideologue," based on the legislator's contention that child care was bad because it helped women take men's jobs. However, later when elected as governor, he was practical, listened to the evidence, and eventually ended up funding a statewide research project led by the researcher on child care quality. In general, the more contact researchers had with policymakers, the more they came to view them as caring, committed, idealistic, intelligent, and rational.

Researchers' Unfamiliarity With the Policymaking Process

Another barrier mentioned by four researchers is unfamiliarity with *the political system and the policymaking process*. Tom recalls the time the Institute for Research on Poverty (IRP) convened a set of briefings for congressional staff in Washington, DC, to explore the pros and cons of devolving welfare and related human service programs to the states. IRP staff spent a great deal of time planning how they would communicate complex research findings in a clear manner. As several IRP staff members were heading over to the Capitol site of the briefings, a senior economist who had done considerable research on child care and other public policies mentioned feeling a certain amount of discomfort. He had never been to Washington, DC, before and had virtually no experience communicating with policymakers. Both Barbara Wolfe, then director of IRP, and Tom found it startling that a veteran affiliate of IRP had managed his career in a way that avoided contact with the policy world. The divide between the academy and the policy world can be wide indeed.

Both researchers and policymakers were frustrated by differences in how problems are defined and decisions are made in the two cultures. For example, one veteran researcher explained differences in how the two worlds define what constitutes a problem:

> Researchers tend by nature to focus on small, very well-defined issues that they can reasonably well address with the data they have available. Policymakers, by contrast, have to focus on larger questions that tend to be not nearly as well defined and expect a precise answer from researchers.

Another cultural difference is how decisions are made in the two communities. Any expectation that good ideas will carry the day or that policymaking is influenced largely by empirical evidence will surely lead to disappointment. In Karen's example of the Special Milk Amendment, ideology initially trumped the data. The evidence that poor children were more apt to benefit from free or reduced-price milk was overruled by a legislator's contempt for programs that benefited only poor children. The initial legislation was drafted to provide a free carton of milk each school day for all children in the state. However, the $3 million price tag drove policymakers to scale back the legislation to serve only poor children. The decision appeared to have been driven more by expense than evidence. Perhaps both played a role. We will never know for sure.

When confronted with insider accounts of how legislation is passed, many academics turn up their nose at the politics of policymaking. According to the president of a national family association, this kind of reaction is naive and perhaps borders on elitism:

> Many academics and professionals disdain the political process out of a kind of naive belief that the world should operate according to what professionals think is important. I've come to appreciate that a democracy has to work with the political process, and that process is about influence, relationships, money … often about money, and that's the nature of the beast, and it's important for me to not think that I'm above this process but to understand that those are the constraints within which I have to operate.

It was obvious to another researcher who had worked with policymakers for only 5 years that the decision-making processes differ in the two communities:

> I don't know what they do. They somehow magically make decisions. I don't know how they make decisions, but I have a feeling that it's not in this careful, step-by-step process that researchers use. The decision-making process is completely different. I think theirs has a lot more to do with critical incidences—something happens out there in the world and that will influence policy.

She attributed differences in decision making, at least in part, to training, which we refer to in our community dissonance theory as *professional culture*. Another researcher elaborated on this same point. Researchers are socialized to be cautious about making any speculations beyond the confines of their data, which allows them to fend off critiques from other scholars. Policymakers, on the other hand, are accustomed to making decisions even when information is incomplete; they become frustrated when researchers are unwilling to make potentially useful generalizations that extend beyond the available evidence.

Another source of cultural conflict for researchers, according to a developmental psychologist, is uncertainty about whether committing time to policy work will eventually pay off, especially when they invest a lot of time. He described the research process as "grindingly slow," but one that did culminate in the accumulation of a body of knowledge. However, with the policy process, there are no guarantees that the time invested would necessarily lead to results. One researcher, recalling his frustrating experience working on a specific piece of legislation, described the dramatic moment when the chair of the House "literally gave [the bill] a thumbs down like in a Roman Circus, and that was a year's worth of work."

Long-Term Versus Short-Term Time Frame

One barrier to bringing research to bear on policymaking, mentioned by eight researchers, is differences in the temporal nature of their work environment, which we refer to in our community dissonance theory as *institutional culture*. Researchers approach their work from a long-term perspective, whereas policymakers have to react to issues that often arise with little warning. Take, for example, the Wisconsin Special Milk Amendment, which was passed into law in 6 weeks as an add-on to the biennial budget. Policymakers deal with a myriad of issues and often are called upon to react to the crisis of the moment or respond to issues so wicked that the prospects for resolution are uncertain at best. Conversely, researchers can work on a small project over a long period of time, chipping away at one question and making progress that is slow but typically steady.

In addition, there is a sequence and timing to policymaking that researchers can largely avoid. In the words of an economist who worked for a time in the U.S. Department of Treasury,

> Academics take time to get things right. Policymakers often aren't in control of the questions that need to be asked and are rarely in control of the timing. We have control over questions and time. Policymakers have no control.

"It can be hard to get the two roles in sync with each other," according to one researcher, who has spent a lifetime working with policymakers beginning during his days as a graduate student. When policymakers call for information they need in a day or two, you can easily get caught up in "the tyranny of the urgency" of the policy agenda.

The short-term time frame through which policymakers often view issues can also be a barrier for those who would traverse the two communities. One researcher found it difficult to work with policymakers on persistent and perplexing problems such as poverty issues or family policy where it is likely that it will take a long time to see benefits to the bottom line. Policymakers may leave office or lose interest long before the issue has generated enough support to be acted upon.

Scientific Language Versus Policy-Relevant Language

Another barrier is that researchers and policymakers speak different languages. Half of the sample ($n = 7$) acknowledged that language is a problem and voiced frustration about policymakers' lack of understanding of scientific methods and/or the solid body of evidence it generates. For example, Ed Zigler quipped that when he first started working with policymakers, many of them thought that "Piaget was a watch" (Zigler et al., 2009).

Researchers are at fault here, too, according to an Extension specialist, because they are socialized to "use jargon, a passive voice, don't know how to be succinct … [and] every conclusion … has a caveat or an exception." A social work researcher aptly stated how language can be a literal blockade to communication across the two cultures: "Policymakers want a yes–no, good–bad answer, and we are incapable of providing such a thing." Karen encountered the importance of brevity firsthand in her work on the Special Milk Amendment when the legislative aide that she was working with told her that a 4-page summary of the evidence was way, way too long.

Karen also recalls making a phone call to a researcher at a major think tank to clarify the meaning of a word in his writing that she was summarizing for a briefing report. He scoffed that anyone should understand what the word meant. Nonetheless, as they spoke, he checked online before having to admit that it was a word that he had coined. Thus, its meaning would be clear only to a small, narrowly focused group of his peers.

The exemplary researchers we interviewed took it upon themselves to transcend the language barrier by avoiding jargon, abbreviating the methodology, explaining in lay language what good evidence is, and omitting some of the subtleties in the findings such as subgroup or demographic differences. Yet one academic expressed some discomfort in doing so, noting the tension between being respected by one's academic peers and simultaneously being useful to those engaged in the business of translating research for policy purposes. When presenting to a lay audience, he thinks about "what language can I use to flag for my academic peers that I do understand the differences, but that I'm glossing over them for the moment to give a useful response."

The Academy's Failure to Reward Policy Work

Barriers are also put up by the academy, according to one half of the researchers (*n* = 7), even though each worked at a land-grant university that operates under a century-long tradition of translating research for public consumption. Based on their experience in the academy, policy work was considered time-consuming and too often "an extracurricular activity." There are few incentives to take one's research to the next level, and policy work ends up taking time away from activities that would lead to pay raises. One department chair at a land-grant university was blunt—policy work brings "no prestige, no dollars." Professor Ed Zigler, whose long career focused on policy, provided a concrete example. He recalled one of his academic peers telling him, "You'd make a first-rate child psychologist if you would just give up this policy stuff" (Zigler et al., 2009). This lack of respect for policy work was also observed by a former director of a poverty institute at a land-grant university:

> If you are an academic, there are no rewards for policy work, and I don't care what they say at the top, public service is simply not given any respect. You have to make up time you spend working with policymakers. It doesn't matter how important the issue is … whether you … create peace in the Middle East—it's not going to mean anything to your academic colleagues. … I missed out on certain academic rewards, such as promotions and more money. … Academics get rewarded for publishing in peer-reviewed journals.

He went on to explain that land-grant universities, in particular, strive to elevate the rewards of taking integrative, cross-disciplinary work out into the real world. However, the reality is that disciplines within the academy are set up to reward narrowly focused work published in peer-reviewed journals that appeal to a specialized set of colleagues. Similarly, Emeritus Professor Edward Zigler, retired from Yale University, expressed dismay that publishing an article in *Child Development* that will be read by 300 colleagues is highly prized, whereas writing an article in *Parenting* magazine that will be read by 3 million subscribers is considered "prostituting" yourself (Zigler et al., 2009). The confinement of academic rewards to scientific publications is no different at public universities, according to an emeritus professor at a land-grant institution: "And so when you begin to go down a different path, you have to appreciate the fact that you're pushing against those dominant values in the academic culture." For him, working between these two worlds was like walking on a tightrope. With almost 30 years of experience under his belt, it has become easier, and he thinks that he is respected in both worlds but not without costs: "You sacrifice something. You need different skills, different language, you only have so much energy to go around. It's difficult to do everything well."

Ed Zigler echoed these same sentiments recently at a policy preconference. He described the advice that he has given to his graduate students, protégés such as the successful Georgetown University professor Deborah Phillips, coauthor of *From Neurons to Neighborhoods*. He explained that incorporating policy expertise into one's professional training is not easy, which means that you will have to work twice as hard. To be successful in a university setting, you need a specialty area of study, and policy becomes an add-on. He underscored the importance of this policy expertise by poking fun at himself when he first started working with Congress. He explained that he could only describe his first two months on the job as "absolutely appalling." He confessed to making more mistakes than anyone could possibly imagine. We need to teach our students the nature of policy, he concluded, so that we don't send any more "stupid Ed Ziglers to Washington, DC" (Zigler et al., 2009).

One researcher at a land-grant university had also experienced the inevitable rub of trying to straddle the academic and policy worlds. In fact, he clearly perceived research and policy as two separate communities with little overlap between them:

> The main frustration is not getting people's attention, especially when issues are complicated. In part, that's a choice that I made. ... I could have been more aggressive in setting up meetings with them, and tried to push ideas. ... I haven't made the kind of commitment that it would take, but the cost would be high, because it means not authoring articles and not doing my job here.

The rigidity and narrowness of the academy is nowhere more apparent than it is for junior faculty, who must weigh how pursuing policy-relevant research may affect their prospects of getting tenure. One researcher reflected on his 30-plus years in policy work and contemplated whether it is possible to have policy relevance in one's work and peer-reviewed publications as well: "It's definitely possible to do both [but] hard to do as a junior faculty member, who should get tenure first, and tread lightly in the policy environment until you've done that." Another health researcher with 25 years of policy experience also concluded that it is possible to be an academic and work with policymakers, but was quick to point out that it is a different path: "I don't think the two inherently have to conflict, but if one doesn't consciously understand the differences and work to resolve them, it will become a conflict."

University administrators can advertently and inadvertently put up barriers. For example, administrators, especially those at publicly funded institutions, worry about what messages might be conveyed and whether they could be portrayed in ways that could reflect adversely on the university. One Extension specialist relayed his indignation with a chancellor who requested a copy of his comments in advance to guard against being caught in a situation where the administration might be contradicted or the university embarrassed. Also, the infrastructure in higher education is set up to provide resources, support, and technical assistance for generating research, with little thought given to the infrastructure needs of those involved in disseminating research.

Another institutional barrier noted by one researcher is that over time most faculty members find it hard to resist being pulled into the enticing culture of academia with its incarnate expectations, reward systems, and values. Many professionals choose the field of family studies, psychology, sociology, social work, or other social science disciplines because they want to make a difference in the lives of individuals and families. However, one researcher observed that over time that ambition takes a backseat to the more immediate pressures of acquiring a PhD, landing a job, getting tenure, securing merit-based raises, and earning the respect of one's peers.

Summary of Barriers

With barriers so seemingly impenetrable, it should come as no surprise that researchers' initial forays into the policy culture were overwhelmingly negative. In the words of one researcher at a renowned research institute,

> You feel stupid a lot of the time. You're potentially out of your area. They want you to draw conclusions that you don't want to draw. You feel like a nerd. … Presenting at a conference is less stressful than it is to talk to high-powered legislators. Presenting to policymakers gets your heart rate up. Sometimes you present something that you think is relevant, and it becomes obvious that it is not at all interesting to them.

Why would anyone want to invest the time and human capital necessary to understand a culture so foreign that it obviously would entail a steep learning curve to successfully navigate its borders? One reason is that researchers' initial perceptions tended to evolve over time with more exposure to and experience with policymakers, as we discussed extensively in Chapter 6. Moreover, as the quality of their interactions improved, the rewards of relaying research to policymakers became more apparent. This is the topic we turn to next.

THE REWARDS OF RELAYING
RESEARCH TO POLICYMAKERS

Interwoven in researchers' stories of the difficulties of engaging policymakers were examples of the various rewards, three of which we cover here, namely, the exhilaration of making the world a better place, the excitement of seeing research applied in the real world, and the satisfaction of being respected for their expertise. We asked explicit questions about the rewards of working with policymakers in the first 14 researcher interviews only.

Making the World a Better Place

Most researchers ($n = 11$) agreed that they are motivated by a desire to make the world a better place. Some researchers noted specific policy goals such as better treatment for kids with serious problems, whereas others spoke more globally about benefits for families and society. One researcher, partially responsible for a state law that used tobacco settlement money to make home visiting available to all low-income women, said his "goal is not just to do science but to make a difference for families and children. Science is a means, not an end." Another researcher who was successful in passing a premarital education law in his state agreed:

> It's a way to do potentially good for many, many families as opposed to helping individual families. It's a way to have a potentially broad impact. It's also a way to change the culture. In participating in the conversation at the policy and political level, it becomes a public conversation. I find that I have access to the media when I'm involved in the policy area in a way that I don't have otherwise.

Three researchers were motivated by pragmatism, noting that policymakers control the "purse strings." One 20-year veteran of the policy process said,

> I don't have a lot of interest in doing research for research's sake. I do what I do because I'm hoping that the knowledge we gain will make the world a better place for kids, [and] for families, and if I don't work with policymakers, I stand very little chance of having my work make any difference.

The Excitement of Seeing Research Applied in the Real World

The application of research was rewarding to the majority of researchers ($n = 10$), as exemplified in this comment: "I do it because I want policy to be better." In the words of a researcher who wrote a book that continues to have an impact on welfare reform over a decade after it was published, "Part of it is the desire to make a difference and to influence policy. That's partly why I became a sociologist." Another researcher, who is a social worker by training, says that he works in the policy world because he was socialized to speak for vulnerable groups and to help ensure that their voices have a place at the policy table:

> Policy will be made; policy will be changed. Programs will be implemented. I think that should be done in the context of a knowledge base. I do it because I want policy to be better. ... I don't think that the policy process will ever be driven solely by what the research shows, but it can be informed by it.

In several instances, these researchers were able to affect the enactment or implementation of a policy. For some, the rewards were seeing the political process work, especially for vulnerable populations. For example, in her work on the Special Milk Amendment, Karen found it reassuring to observe how effective the political process can be when well-meaning people join hands around an important cause. For others, the reward was seeing the interest of policymakers in research and analysis. "Policymakers are looking for good evidence," according to one researcher with 28 years of experience. "When we can deliver good evidence, there is greater receptivity there than I originally expected." Ed Zigler's conclusion was similar based on his extensive experience with federal policymakers in both the legislative and the executive branches of government. What became clear to him is that "knowledge is power," no matter whether the policymaker is a Democrat or Republican (Zigler et al., 2009). However, even when a policy failed to pass, researchers thought their efforts were worthwhile because providing information to the media through public forums, such as talk shows and public radio, is a way of shaping public dialogue on high-profile issues.

When asked about the rewards of policy work, one researcher who is a national expert on welfare reform finds it stimulating to work on something as complex and challenging as policy:

> The challenges make it worthwhile. Occasionally something becomes reality. You see some effects or you have some sense (it might be delusional) of shaping the debate. Or sometimes you can stop bad ideas, at least what you consider a bad idea. ... It's stimulating to bring [research] to the real world.

Several researchers acknowledged the difficulty of measuring any impact on policymaking, but they take pride in having a hand in the political process, with several characterizing it as gratifying, invigorating, and stimulating. One researcher, who worked to change the official U.S. poverty measure, said, "Academics get so excited when something is statistically significant, when substantively it means very little. It's stimulating to bring it to the real world."

Being Respected for Their Expertise

Another reward, mentioned by half ($n = 7$) of the researchers, is feeling flattered that the value of their work was recognized by the policy community. For example, one researcher who has been working with policymakers since the 1970s has received phone calls from congressional staff for technical advice; been invited to one-on-one meetings in Washington, DC; been asked to testify at hearings or consult with task forces; and written reports that were never published in the traditional peer-reviewed literature, but were circulated to policymakers and probably received "more visibility than anything I ever published." The demand for one's expertise beyond the walls of the academy is rewarding, according to another researcher who worked for the assistant secretary for planning and evaluation: "The biggest reward is seeing the relevance of your work and seeing your work taken seriously."

This is in sharp contrast to the reception one's work receives in the research community, according to a veteran researcher and associate dean, where everyone has expertise, and nobody gives it any particular respect:

> People outside the university often respect our expertise more than people inside the university. They see us as experts and communicate that respect. That's very rewarding. It invigorates me as a researcher to see the utility of our knowledge.

Another researcher, who is currently serving as a dean of the largest college in a land-grant university, concurred that one of the main rewards is public acknowledgment of one's expertise:

> … a sense of satisfaction of being asked to give your opinion. It's an ego thing, and my ego won't let me pass up that opportunity. So I think it's largely the ego. You also hope that something you say has an influence.

In sum, researchers were explicit about the many rewards for delivering research and analysis to the policymaking process. These rewards were not guaranteed, they were infrequent, and by no means were they predictable. Yet the pull of these rewards was so strong when they did occur or when there was even a likelihood that they could occur that once these researchers were involved, they stayed involved. A health researcher explained that he found policy work to be self-motivating: "Personally, I find it very rewarding, and the more success I've had with it, the more rewarding I find it. So, I work a lot harder." How can would-be boundary spanners break through the cultural barriers? Several pointers for becoming cross culturally competent are detailed in Key Concepts 8.1.

Key Concepts 8.1   Cross-Cultural Communication: Breaking Through the Barriers

- When you traverse into the policy world, be ready to experience culture clash.
- For successful collaborations with policymakers, treat them as the caring, committed, intelligent, and rational partners that experienced boundary spanners have found them to be.
- Given the long-term nature of policymaking, be patient in expecting results.
- Given the lack of rewards from the academy, be self-rewarding in identifying success.
- To become biculturally competent, plan to work twice as hard to learn the attitudes, knowledge, and skills it takes to succeed in a different culture.
- Becoming biculturally competent requires an investment of time and effort, but those who stay the course find it exhilarating, exciting, and satisfying. In the words of master communicator Edward Zigler (Zigler et al., 2009), "You can lose 100 times, but you only have to win once, and then you have it."

SUMMARY

These interviews corroborate the basic tenets of community dissonance theory— that underutilization of research in policymaking is due to misperceptions and miscommunications between researchers and policymakers who operate in different professional and institutional cultures. Research utilization in policymaking was perceived not as a problem that lies with policymakers, but rather as a two-way process that requires communication and collaboration between policy-minded researchers and research-minded policymakers. In these interviews that focused on the researcher end of the utilization process, these exemplary social scientists identified cultural barriers they encountered when communicating research to policymakers—misunderstanding of policymakers, unfamiliarity with the policymaking process, different time frames and languages, and few rewards from the academy. Surmounting these barriers brought no guarantee of success, but engaging policymakers could bring several rewards, namely, the exhilaration of making the world a better place, the excitement of seeing research applied in the real world, and the satisfaction of being respected for their expertise outside the academy.

For those researchers who contemplate whether to wade into the policy arena, the cultural barriers are formidable. For those researchers who do wade into the policy arena, the rewards can be rich. But just what is it that happens betwixt and between the barriers to policy work, on one side of the research utilization equation, and its rewards, on the other side? We asked a number of researchers who had worked long and hard at becoming biculturally competent what advice they would offer for those interested in mustering up the wherewithal to embark on the perilous but promising journey from the culture of research to the culture of policy. Their 10 recommendations follow in Chapter 9.

AUTHORS' NOTE

Chapter 8 expands upon an earlier publication by Friese and Bogenschneider (2009).

9

Communicating With Policymakers
Insights From Policy-Minded Researchers

It's a totally different world, government, from academics. In academic life, there's no premium on time, the premium is on getting it just right. In government, if you haven't got the right answer by four o'clock this afternoon when the president meets with the prime minister, that perfect paper you get in a little bit late is an "F."

—Joseph Nye (as cited in Williams, 2006, p. 4)

Nothing could be more irrational than to give people power and to withhold from them information, without which power is abused. A people who mean to be their own governors must arm themselves with the power which knowledge gives. A popular government without popular information or the means of acquiring it is but a prologue to a farce or a tragedy, or perhaps both.

—James Madison (1751–1836)

Despite their initial insecurities and misgivings, the rewards of making the world a better place, seeing research applied in the real world, and being respected for their expertise outside the academy proved irresistible to many researchers. With these rewards as the light at the end of the policy tunnel, we now turn to the heart of the book—an attempt to put flesh on the bones of our community dissonance theory. Although we are far from the first to try navigating the murky territory between the worlds of knowledge producers and knowledge consumers (Smith, 1991), what we bring to this discussion are the insights of those who have been successful in bridging the wide gulf between research and policy. We asked our exemplary policy communicators what advice they would have for those who might follow in their footsteps. Their advice is summarized in the 10 recommendations that follow, which we present along with corroborating evidence (where it exists) from the published literature on disseminating research to policymakers. Our researcher informants recommended the knowledge that is needed, approaches that work, skills required, and the attitudes it takes to bring research to bear on policymaking.

WHAT ADVICE CAN RESEARCHERS OFFER ABOUT COMMUNICATING RESEARCH TO POLICYMAKERS?

The available social science evidence on research utilization, albeit limited for the policy community (Nutley, Walter, & Davies, 2007), has been conducted in different settings (e.g., congressional committees, executive agencies, local health and social service organizations, policy intermediary settings, and welfare-to-work demonstrations) and draws from the perspectives of a range of disciplines (e.g., business, education, economics, health services, political science, psychology, public administration, public affairs, and sociology; Jacobson, Butterill, & Goering, 2003). Disseminating research to policymakers is not an exact science, yet it can be informed by science, specifically the literature identifying variables associated with its utilization, as summarized in Table 9.1.

These studies reveal which variables are associated with research utilization. However, they are seldom based on direct observations of the phenomenon (Beyer & Trice, 1982) and provide little insight or guidance for how social scientists might actually translate the variables into pragmatic strategies for infusing research into policymaking. To fill this gap and build a better sense of what these variables mean for the real world, we turn to our interviews of exemplary knowledge producers who have developed a level of bicultural competence. This chapter is based on 14 interviews of exemplary policy communicators (see the description of the sample in the appendix and Table 8.1 and an earlier analysis by Friese and Bogenschneider, 2009). This initial data set was supplemented with ten 20- to 90-minute videotaped interviews of researchers, university administrators, and presidents of philanthropic and outreach organizations, four of whom we had not interviewed previously.

We also ask our informants to reflect on their successes and to offer recommendations for others interested in disseminating research to policymakers. We refer to these skills, attitudes, and approaches as "tricks of the trade" that are needed to transfer research findings from the laboratory to legislative bodies. The 10 recommendations follow and are summarized in Table 9.2.

Recommendation 1: Conceptualize Policy Work Not as Disseminating Research to Policymakers, but as Developing Relationships With Them

Looking back over a decade of experience working with policymakers, one researcher said the change in his thinking could be likened to a paradigm shift. He no longer thinks about disseminating information *to* policymakers, but instead focuses on developing relationships *with* them. When a relationship exists, a mutual

TABLE 9.1   Variables Associated With Research Utilization by Policymakers

Variable	Description
Accessibility	The ease with which policymakers can find research (Nelson, Roberts, Maederer, Wertheimer, & Johnson, 1987; Nutley et al., 2007; Oh, 1997)
Affiliation of the intermediary	The nonpartisan reputation of the information purveyor or how closely the purveyor conforms with the ideology and value system of the policymaker (Dunn, 1980; Nelson et al., 1987)
Applicability to questions of interest to policymakers	Results pertain to issues policymakers care about (Beyer & Trice, 1982; Zigler, 1998)
Credibility of the information source	Policymakers feel they can trust the researcher or intermediary (Feldman, Nadash, & Gursen, 2001; Hird, 2005; Nutley et al., 2007; Oh, 1997)
Development of appropriate infrastructures	Ongoing opportunities for researchers and policymakers to interact and develop partnerships with each other (Weiss, Murphy-Graham, Petrosino, & Gandhi, 2008)
Engagement in the research process	Policymakers have some investment in results (Nutley et al., 2007)
Narratives or anecdotes	Results communicated in a way that touches or reaches policymakers and that they can use to reach their colleagues and constituents (Nelson et al., 1987; Nutley et al., 2007)
Presentation	Results are communicated in a clear, concise manner (Beyer & Trice, 1982; Feldman et al., 2001; Greenberg, Linksz, & Mandell, 2003; Greenberg & Mandell, 1991; Nelson et al., 1987; Nutley et al., 2007; Weiss & Bucuvalas, 1980)
Relationship between producer and consumer	A relationship of trust exists (Bimber, 1996; Hird, 2005; Huberman, 1987; Innvaer, Vist, Trommald, & Oxman, 2002; Nutley et al., 2007; Oh, 1997; Weiss et al., 2008)
Timeliness	Results available when decisions are made or issue is politically salient (Beyer & Trice, 1982; Feldman et al., 2001; Greenberg et al., 2003; Innvaer et al., 2002; Nelson et al., 1987; Nutley et al., 2007; Weiss & Bucuvalas, 1980)
Type of organization	Institutional support for generating and disseminating policy-relevant research (Beyer & Trice, 1982; Dunn, 1980; Hird, 2005; Nelson et al., 1987)
Use of economic indicators	Recognition of financial implications such as the cost to taxpayers of implementing a policy and bringing it to scale (Huston, 2002)

sharing of knowledge naturally occurs, and the better the relationship, the more relevant the flow of information will be. In the words of a professor and former president of a national family professional association,

> Disseminating information to policymakers is really not how I think of it anymore. I think of it as developing relationships. Develop a relationship and there is information that gets exchanged in these relationships; the better the relationship, the better the partnership, the more relevant they will see us. That kind of relationship only gets formed when we learn from them.

TABLE 9.2 Recommendations From Exemplary Policy Communicators: Translating Community Dissonance Theory Into Practical Advice for Policy Communicators

Domain of Community Dissonance Theory	Recommendation of Exemplary Policy Communicators
Interactional preferences (Domain IV)	1. Conceptualize policy work not as disseminating research to policymakers but as developing relationships with them.
Targets of interest (Domain II)	2. Take the initiative to contact policymakers or policy intermediaries.
Cognitive frameworks (Domain III)	3. Learn about the target policymaker audience.
	4. Communicate research findings in ways that meet policymakers' information needs.
	5. Use clear, careful language when dealing with myths about vulnerable populations.
Contextual preferences (Domain VI)	6. Familiarize yourself with the policymaking process.
Focal interests (Domain I)	7. Provide a timely response to the questions driving policy debate.
	8. Learn how to approach policy work as an educator rather than an advocate.
Feedback loops (Domain V)	9. Show respect for policymakers' knowledge and expertise.
	10. Be patient and self-rewarding in defining success.

Note: The domains of community dissonance theory are defined and discussed in Chapter 5 and in Table 5.4.

A 30-year veteran of the policy process noted that nothing is more important in working with policymakers than developing a sense of trust that is nurtured in the context of a relationship:

> Develop relationships. Nothing is going to better both prepare you to work in the policymaking world as well as ease your transition in and make you more effective than if you develop relationships with policymakers and begin to develop a trust that goes both ways. Learn how to talk with them. Learn how to listen to them. Learn how to interpret the kinds of pressures they are under. Learn what's ... important in their world and try to communicate to them what's important in yours as well. All that takes time, all that takes dialogue, but that's the price you have to pay unless you simply want to issue your reports, send them into the policymaking process, and have them hit the floor with one resounding thud.

Those successful in crossing the research–policy divide explained to us why relationships are so important in the policymaker's world. For example, Mary Fairchild, a senior fellow at the National Conference of State Legislatures, explained that the reliance on relationships in lawmaking bodies is "huge." Policymakers rely on trusted relationships, in part, because there is so little time to make decisions that can run the gamut from farming to family leave, from taxation to transportation. In Fairchild's words,

> I think relationships are huge, and the reason for it is [that] there's so much that goes on in the legislative process. You know, in many states there isn't a limit on the number of bills you can introduce. I'm a liaison to the Montana legislature, and they meet for 90 days every 2 years. They don't have a limit on the number of bills they can introduce, so last year, there were over 2,000 bill requests. For a legislator to read 2,000 bills in 90 days and understand them, it's impossible. You can't do it. So, they specialize. That's one of the reasons we have a committee system ... the ... other thing is ... people will listen to people they trust: colleagues, other legislators, advocates, researchers—you know, people who have a reputation as being able to help solve a problem.

Earlier Tom mentioned his work with a Wisconsin welfare reform committee headed by Democrat John Antaramian. They developed a close working relationship. Long after the committee ended its work, John continued to call upon Tom for advice and counsel on welfare issues. Trust and credibility are not easily earned but are priceless in the policy arena.

The more time sensitive a policy decision is, the less likely that policymakers will have time to seek out new sources of information and the more likely that they will turn to those they already know and trust. On the basis of Weiss's (1989) experience in Congress, national experts may be less influential than experts from think tanks or the policymaker's hometown university with whom staffers already have a relationship. Ruby Takanishi (2002), president of the Foundation for Child Development, observed this firsthand when she served as a congressional fellow:

> Most important, I learned that relationships with key staff and building trust and credibility over time matter a great deal ... there are so many competing interests, so many competing sources of information, and so little time to make decisions that may affect the lives of many. To have any hope of being effective, a person must be available, ready to respond quickly and briefly. ... When you examine the situation, being in the right place at the right time and having the necessary relationships can make all the difference. It is not only knowing relevant research findings, but knowing when and how to use them to inform policy, and typically as quickly as possible. (pp. 21–22)

One recurring theme in our interviews is that these relationships are exorbitantly important, but extraordinarily difficult to develop given that they span two distinct cultures. A former director of the Institute for Research on Poverty (IRP) describes some of the missteps and miscommunication that can occur when academics and policymakers first make contact, much of which stems from stereotypes each hold of the other:

> There is a problem that comes out of the insecurities that both parties feel. I have seen academics who are very confident when they are dealing with other academics become tongue-tied and very uncertain of themselves when they are dealing with politicians and/or policymakers. And that leads in some cases to an exaggeration of their worst sort of predispositions or dispositions. So they become more technical, they try to impress them, or they try to overwhelm the other party with how much they know. Or they may even communicate their lack of respect for the policymaking process and demean it. ... On the other

hand, policymakers often look at academics or researchers and say, "Oh my God, I have to deal with this egghead … they're going to talk in ways that I'm not going to understand. They're going to try to intimidate me with technology and statistical jargon that I'm going to find overwhelming." … The basic lack of confidence that both parties bring into that room can be a huge problem.

Through these culture-spanning relationships, knowledge producers reported gaining a richer, more nuanced understanding of the types of decisions policymakers have to make, the complexity of their role, and what researchers can contribute to the policy process. One researcher had "gotten better at understanding where [policymakers] are coming from and how they like to get information." Another researcher relayed that because of the rapport he had established, policymakers "come to [him] earlier in the process to help develop policy approaches," and he "can have input early on rather than the forest fires that you hit at the end."

When long-term working relationships with policymakers were established, they were characterized by increased mutual understanding, which one researcher likened to a "partnership." One former president of a political science professional association described her relationships with policymakers as both a push and a pull. Policymakers sometimes pushed her research findings in a direction that she would not have taken them, and sometimes she was pulled by policymakers to consider new ideas and ways to frame research questions to make them more policy relevant. She found that her relationships with policymakers evolved over time:

> It's much more of a comfortable give-and-take. There is an assumption that we look at common problems, but from a very different perspective, and the challenge for both of us is to find the middle ground where we are mutually supportive of the other's agenda.

Karen has been involved in bringing research to Wisconsin policymakers through the Family Impact Seminars for 16 years on topics state legislators identified as pressing issues that could benefit from social science knowledge. However, it began to feel even more like a partnership when Karen began asking the legislators who advise the Family Impact Seminars to help her better understand policymakers and the policymaking process (e.g., what is important for academics to understand about the job of being a policymaker, what is the biggest mistake that researchers make when working with policymakers, and what advice could they offer for academics interested in providing objective information to policymakers). Through this line of questioning, which squarely placed policymakers in the expert role, it became obvious that we were starting from different vantage points, but we were working toward a common goal—to improve the quality of policy decisions. We each had expertise that could support the other's agenda.

Recommendation 2: Take the Initiative to Contact Policymakers or Policy Intermediaries

We have observed repeatedly that it is up to researchers to take the initiative in contacting policymakers; perhaps no better example exists than the following experience. Tom recalls the moment when he listened to then-governor Tommy Thompson talk about welfare reform at a luncheon held at the governor's mansion in Madison, Wisconsin. Governor Thompson had earned a national reputation as a welfare reformer, pioneering the much admired and equally feared Wisconsin Works (W-2) initiative. This notoriety, plus a number of other policy successes, helped Thompson launch two tries for the U.S. presidency and certainly played a role in his securing the position of secretary of Health and Human Services under George W. Bush in his first term (2001–2005).

At the luncheon, the governor talked about how he came to some of the core ideas embedded in his reform concept that, at the time at least, was the most work-focused initiative in the country. He stressed how he had invited welfare recipients to working lunches at the governor's mansion to ask them what it would take for them to exit welfare for the world of work. They said they needed help with child care, transportation, and health care coverage for their family, which they risked losing by exiting the welfare rolls. Motivated by these insights, he put together a set of building blocks for a strategy that would insist recipients choose work over welfare where feasible, and then provide the supports they needed to make work a reasonable option. (See Mead [2004] for one inside story of how W-2 was developed.)

All well and good, Tom thought. But it occurred to him, as he sat there listening to the governor's narrative, that Thompson could have called any one of a number of researchers at the University of Wisconsin, where IRP had been established in 1966 as part of the federal government's War on Poverty. They had access to myriad studies, evaluations, and analyses that arrived at the same story line presented to him by actual recipients and with far more breadth and detail than could possibly be gleaned from a few selective testimonials. These research products could have brought a wealth of insights and substantiated evidence both to understanding the issue and to developing possible responses.

Why didn't Thompson pick up the phone and call the so-called *experts*, those who devote their professional lives to the creation of knowledge? After all, the University of Wisconsin was the home of the Wisconsin Idea—the simple concept that it is the academy's responsibility to bring its expertise to bear on issues affecting the public good. Perhaps the governor was suspicious of the political dispositions of those at the university. Perhaps he had experienced awkward interactions with researchers in the past. Perhaps the thought never occurred to him. We may never know.

What we can assert is that this is not an isolated incident. Governor Thompson was not any kind of outlier in his behavior. Most decision makers (i.e., knowledge consumers in our framework) do *not* turn to research and researchers as a primary information source as they go about their business. We simply are not on their radar screen. On the basis of our own experience and the conventional wisdom of so many others who have thought about these things, we conclude that those who dedicate their lives to understanding the world and those dedicated to making the world run a bit better enjoy an awkward, tentative relationship. It is up to researchers to take the first step, to do the courting (if you will) to explore further a professional "marital" relationship.

Our sample was selected based on the researchers' track record in working directly with policymakers. Another approach raised by one respondent is to work through policy intermediaries who have developed relationships in the policy world and already possess the prerequisite expertise that effective policy work entails. We describe each approach below.

Researchers described how they first made contact with policymakers. Almost half (*n* = 6) of "first contacts" resulted from a request from an interest group, professional organization, or policymaker. Four researchers reported that the initial contact was part of their job, 3 of whom had previously worked in state government. Three made their initial contact as an undergraduate or graduate student. Surprisingly, in only one instance was the first contact self-initiated with a researcher contacting the policymaker. Overall, the researchers in our sample did not proactively seek out policy work; instead, they responded to being tapped on the shoulder with a request to get involved.

The most predominant avenue for gaining access was a request from an interest group or a professional or government organization. One researcher was invited by the surgeon general during the Carter administration to talk with staff about using his program model for a federal initiative. Another researcher, who was successful in helping pass a premarital education bill in his state, explained that his initial contact with policymakers occurred when he was asked by a county Cooperative Extension agent to give a presentation on marriage. The session was attended by a state senator who had been trying to promote marriage-friendly legislation but heretofore had experienced little success. The senator asked the researcher to provide academic support for what he was doing and connected him with a member of the House of Representatives, and together they became a team that worked on premarital education legislation.

For four others, contact with policymakers was an integral part of their job. Three researchers started out working in state government, which entailed considerable contact with legislators. One researcher was invited to join a day care advisory board at the Department of Health and Family Services in his state. He was unsure how this came about, but he speculates that he was recommended by one of the contacts he had made when first arriving in town; he deliberately made the rounds to introduce himself, took key people in the child care network to lunch, and contacted those in leadership positions in Head Start and other professional societies.

Three researchers first made contact as part of their undergraduate or graduate studies through involvement in a student organization, undergraduate job, or the encouragement of an advisor to present dissertation findings to policymakers. One researcher was elected national president of a student professional society and through this contact developed a network of legislative staffers that would call him for advice even before he graduated. Another worked as an undergraduate at the Brookings Institution and found himself in meetings with high-level politicians such as senators Edward Kennedy and Philip Hart, which was "very heady, very exciting." One of the best ways for young people to make contact with policymakers, according to Ruth Massinga, former president and CEO of Casey Family Programs, may be to volunteer to work for them on areas of mutual interest:

Sometimes I think one of the easiest things to do, but people don't think about it, is to volunteer if you can to work with a policymaker. Offer to help him or her formulate ideas around areas of interest to you that you know are interesting to him or her. If you volunteer, you come up with a product that that person is interested in or pursues his or her line of interest or inquiry. Then you have more of an opportunity to become a trusted, a reliable resource for that person. There's no substitute for hard work. You've got to work it … but I think for a young person, developing a relationship, becoming a reliable resource for a policymaker is an invaluable way to really understand how that policymaker thinks, how other policymakers think, and how you may be of use and then how your interests and their interests may come together.

Finally, we were surprised that only one of these exemplary communicators initially gained access by taking the initiative to approach policymakers. One researcher volunteered to help Michael Dukakis when he was campaigning for governor of Massachusetts. Along with someone from the Kennedy School of Government, the researcher helped develop a formula to allocate money to local governments based on need. After Dukakis was elected, the researcher met with the chief of staff and the legislature, and the formula eventually was adopted and enacted into state law.

If researchers are ever to become competent and confident in two cultures, they need to take the initiative and begin building relationships with policymakers or policy intermediaries. During our interviews, three strategies for gaining access emerged. Dave Riley, a professor and Cooperative Extension specialist at the University of Wisconsin–Madison, recommended that professionals intentionally create opportunities to put themselves in close proximity to legislators:

It's true, just the physical propinquity, how close we work to each other, turns out to be important. And here in Madison, Wisconsin, we actually have one of the best relationships of the university with the legislature anywhere in the country, and largely it has to do with our being located a half mile away from each other joined with State Street. It's just the accident of geography that has helped us more than anything else. Still that half mile can be a problem because I don't bump into my legislators in the café I go to for lunch; it's a half mile apart. So we need to find occasions to rub elbows more often, not just on formal occasions even. And we can take responsibility for that. We can invite legislators to talk in our classes, to give lectures on campus. I think we ought to be asking them every year to come to campus and tell us what they wish we were doing research on. I can tell you even if we never followed their advice, they would feel so much gratitude in being asked that it would change the relationship in a positive fashion.

Researchers also recommended attending conferences situated between the two worlds (i.e., research conferences that are policy-relevant, and policy conferences that are research-relevant). Such occasions are perfect opportunities for initiating relationships.

Gary Sandefur, who worked with policymakers, first as a professor and now as a dean at the University of Wisconsin–Madison, explained that another avenue for gaining access to congressional representatives is through making contact with staffers:

> The one thing that I think some people don't understand … is how important staffers are. And it's important in my role now. You know, you may think you want to talk to the congressperson or the governor, but talking to their staffers and getting their interest in your problem and getting their confidence … that's what you really need to do. And if you overlook those people, or treat them as if they're not important, then you're never going to get the access that you want to have.

A prescription drug researcher, who worked at the federal level, concurred that staffers are "a critical group to understand and get connected with." On the basis of our experience, staffers are typically the gatekeepers in gaining access to policymakers. However, we have found that their influence depends upon the size of the staff and their level of experience, which varies considerably from Congress to the state house, from state to state, and from office to office (e.g., whether policymakers are in the majority or minority party and whether they serve in a leadership role or chair a committee).

One final avenue for gaining access is contacting those who already have access—policy intermediaries. One knowledge producer decided to work with intermediaries after repeated frustrations when her policy attempts failed—her papers were ignored, presentations missed the mark, and press conferences were poorly attended. Similarly, another knowledge producer explained that researchers often do not have the translation skills or the time and desire to develop them: "You either have to take it to the next steps yourself or make sure that the work gets into the hands of the brokering organization, like the Family Impact Seminars, who force that marriage." If knowledge producers lack the prerequisite skills, Kristin Anderson Moore, former president of Child Trends, warned that working directly with policymakers can backfire:

> For a whole variety of reasons, researchers may not want to go directly to policymakers, or they may not be the best people to go directly to policymakers; they may not know how to do it. But there are still many things they can do. Certainly, one of the most important things they can do is good, policy-relevant research. Do it, get it reviewed, get it published, and then it becomes a part of the knowledge base. And then they can work with organizations, like Family Impact Seminars, of course, and make that information available. … I think that is an easier way for maybe an academic to make their work available than … trying to do it independently. It's very tricky. It can backfire. It can blow up. So I think you want to work with people who know the "ins" and the "outs."

As an example, when IRP was planning congressional briefings on the devolution revolution in social policy taking place in the 1990s, Barbara Wolfe, then IRP director, asked Wendell Primus, a former congressional staffer, what he would suggest as the best approach to setting up these briefings. He suggested that IRP secure the assistance of an experienced intermediary, recommending Theodora

Ooms, the DC veteran who had developed the Family Impact Seminar model as a way of bringing quality research to the policy process.

Recommendation 3: Learn About the Target Policymaker Audience

Learning about the target audience is not a new concept. A social policy professor pointed out that this tradition dates back to the old social work adage of beginning where the client is, and an Extension specialist emphasized that knowing your audience is a general principle of good teaching, which is as true for policymakers as for other target audiences. In the words of Dave Riley, an endowed chair at the University of Wisconsin–Madison, "To be a good teacher, you start by knowing what does the learner know, and then you start there and begin to grow outward from what they currently know."

For those inexperienced in the policy world, researchers explained those aspects of the policymaker audience that are important to understand—knowing whom to target, at what level, and with which strategy. When considering whom to target, knowledge producers typically think first of Congress, according to Child Trends researcher Kristin Anderson Moore, even though an enormous amount of the legislation, policy, and regulations that affect children and families happens at the state or local levels. So, one of the initial steps for those venturing into the policy world is to determine whether the issue of interest falls under the jurisdiction of local, state, and/or federal policymakers. Another researcher cautioned against thinking about policymakers too narrowly, as the only actors who enact laws, without considering the influence that policy administrators have in developing the rules and procedures through which policies are implemented. For example, one family researcher who testified at a hearing that would give marriage and family therapists access to Medicaid, relayed his impression that

> most of what was going on was happening off stage and … all the reasonable arguments that I could make were undone by a fiscal note that was developed by somebody in the health department who was not interested in the legislation.

After researchers figure out whom to target, it is important to think generally about what level of information is best suited to a policy audience. According to Professor Gary Sandefur,

> So it's not your professional peers. It's not your fellow social scientists. And it's also not your freshman class. It's somewhere in between there. It's very knowledgeable people who, in some cases, know a lot more about the topic than you do. That is, they know about the policies that exist, the history and development of those policies, and what the possibilities for change are.

Child Trends' Kristin Anderson Moore also suggested spending some time sorting out the best way to reach this target audience, which sometimes introduces a whole new set of mechanisms that are not always initially apparent:

For example, you might want to do a newsletter column in a newsletter that reaches the audience you want to reach. So in other words, it's not necessarily getting something into the *New York Times* or *Washington Post*, but reaching the audience that you really want to reach. So you need to think through, "Well, who are those people and what is it that I know that I need to share with them and how can I say that succinctly?" and then go for that exact mechanism.

Because policymakers are not a homogeneous group, six researchers recommended doing some homework or "reconnaissance" on the specific policymaker to be approached rather than making a cold contact. For example, one researcher advised that knowing their position is important because the higher the policymaker is on the pecking order, the briefer your response has to be: "If you ever get a chance to write a briefing paper for a president, it's going to be one side of one piece of paper, that's it, because a lot of paper crosses their desk." A 25-year veteran of policy work recommended preparation that is even more specific. He actually tries to figure out the knowledge level of the particular policymaker that he will be dealing with:

> Within a body of legislators, there are usually two or three people who know something really well, and the rest rely on those two or three. You need to understand at what given level the policymakers are at and what's their role. Is this their area of expertise or are they just trying to get up to speed?

In citizen-based lawmaking bodies, many policymakers bring with them their own profession and area of expertise, according to Mary Fairchild of the National Conference of State Legislatures, but there is likely to be a learning curve on many other policy issues. One researcher provided a compelling account of how not having this insider information can render research useless to the policy process. He had been asked to provide cost estimates of guaranteed child support and decided to focus on why it would be good to start small because large effects had a high cost. Unbeknown to the researcher, the request emanated from a person running for governor, who wanted to show a big effect regardless of the cost. In the researcher's words,

> I missed the question. ... I actually had the tools to answer the question that he wanted to know but hadn't prepared for it because I thought he was asking a different question ... it's really important to get the question right—to understand what the policymaker's hoping for, to understand the kinds of policies that are under consideration, and what the person's ... value-schema is: how they evaluate the trade-offs between cost and coverage, between maybe efficiency and effect, or whatever trade-offs there are. The more I can understand what the policymaker's hoping for, the more information I can provide.

The gubernatorial candidate decided not to make child support a part of his campaign, and the researcher still wonders to this day what might have happened if he had taken time to investigate whom the request had come from and what he wanted to know.

Recommendation 4: Communicate Research Findings in Ways That Meet Policymakers' Information Needs

Learning to communicate with policymaking and academic audiences can be likened to becoming bilingual or bicultural, according to Professor Daniel Meyer of the University of Wisconsin–Madison, who has worked with policymakers in this country and abroad for almost 20 years:

> You're trying to write to one audience, trying to understand what that audience wants and needs and the way they interpret information, so that's the kind of information you're trying to provide for them; and then, you turn around the next week and try to write to a different audience, understanding where they're coming from, the culture in which they work, trying to speak ... with the language that they understand.

This new language, which we refer to as *policy speak,* requires that communication be concise, pithy, and clear. The first advice off the lips of half (n = 7) of these exemplary policy communicators was "You have to be brief." As aptly put by Cooperative Extension specialist Dave Riley,

> If they give a question, an 8-minute answer is way, way too long. You need a 30-second answer. Every answer you give ought to be like a 30-second elevator answer to a stranger. ... So you have to learn to be really brief, cut it down.

Two veterans of the policymaking process, Joel Rabb and Donald Winstead (2003), provided an example of how a brief message was helpful in enacting Florida legislation that secured federal waivers for a welfare reform demonstration program: "Deep and persistent poverty is bad for kids" (p. 36). When the take-home message can be stated in eight words, "even someone with an attention span measured in nanoseconds could understand that" (p. 36).

Being fluent in policy speak also requires being pithy. Ten researchers advised simplifying the message by focusing only on what's relevant: "Cut to the chase quickly" and "Distill the message without overwhelming policymakers with too much detail. You need to be able to boil down a 20-page paper into 2 pages or 3 minutes on the phone." By frequently testifying before Congress, one researcher learned to process the analysis to the point that "the first thing out of your mouth is what we know and what it means to them." Another researcher thinks of it as delivering "information in a quick and concise way that passes the 'So what?' test." What policymakers care about is the bottom line, not how the bottom line was arrived at.

Finally, communication for policymakers needs to be clear, which can be particularly challenging when the presenting problem is complex. One researcher cited the example of child support payments, which can be calculated in dollars or as a percentage of income. To figure out which approach is best, policymakers often ask about the size of the payment in each. However, this is the wrong question because child support orders based on percentages are most often used in cases of low-income folks, who are more apt to default on their payments. The researcher explained that it takes careful language to explain that the simple answer is not necessarily the right one, and to describe how statistical techniques can correct for income differences.

Policymakers also often have unrealistic expectations of research, such as seeking "panaceas where they don't exist," according to a researcher at a renowned nonpartisan think tank. When research does exist on an issue, Kristin Anderson Moore of Child Trends describes how she explains to policymakers and the public what the findings actually mean:

> A lot of people want to know what to do about their individual family or they want to know … what to do about a specific law. And research is really about averages. So it's very hard to say exactly … what people should do. And so what we can do is we can share what we know clearly and succinctly, but with those caveats.

Clear communication can also be challenging for academics who have been socialized into a culture of discussing their research with appropriate nuance and caution using discipline-specific jargon and methodological precision. When the audience is policymakers, researchers must resist the temptation to try to impress the audience with the sophistication of their language or the complexity of their analytic techniques. A poverty researcher offered the following cautionary tale:

> You should really emphasize being clear as opposed to obfuscating what you're trying to say. And that sounds a little, I suppose, humorous, but in some ways, some academics feel that if fewer people understand what they're saying, that must mean they're being very profound. So there's almost a counterproductive character to the way at least some academics perform. If you're working with policymakers, you want to boil things down as neatly and as clearly and as coherently and as succinctly as possible.

One researcher learned from his own mistakes how important it is to consider the choice of words. He learned that terms such as *welfare regimes* or *policy schemes* have an accepted meaning in the academic culture but carry an entirely different connotation in the policy culture:

> I tend to talk about welfare regimes or policy regimes. And when I use that term, I use it in a neutral sense to describe a cluster of policies trying to do a, more or less, coherent thing. … When I've used that word in writings, sometimes policymakers have said to me, "Don't use that word to describe our policies. *Regimes* means something very negative to us. It means an inflexible set of policies and that's not … the image we're trying to project." A similar word is *scheme*. So I sometimes use that term, very neutrally. "The policy scheme" is to do a particular thing … policymakers have said, "We don't have schemes here. We have purposes. We have policy objectives. We have clusters of policies. We have similar policies trying to achieve the same objectives, but we don't have policy schemes." The language matters. Learning their language is important.

The choice of language takes on an additional layer of complexity when communicating to policymakers in a venue that may also include academic colleagues. Speaking with policymakers requires being brief. This entails ignoring a lot of the intricacies in the findings such as exceptions to the rule, or limitations in the populations to which findings apply, or whether alternative explanations for the findings are plausible—all caveats that your colleagues would expect to hear. Professor Dave Riley explained that he has learned what language to use to flag for his academic peers that he understands these caveats, but is omitting them in the interest of distilling out what is useful to policymakers:

> I learned the skill while doing live radio call-in shows on our national or our statewide public radio network, where I'd get a phone call on a question I hadn't anticipated ... and of course my colleagues might be listening in. And so to give an answer that's brief and general and summarizes, but also doesn't make your colleagues slap their foreheads wondering what's wrong with you is ... a skill you generate over time. ... Sometimes you put little flags in, and those little flags are for your colleagues. And you might say, "Of course, there are differences for boys or girls or people in different social classes for this finding, but in general this is what we find." And so, that will be a case where you're speaking first to the one audience—your scholarly colleagues—and then to the listening public and kind of covering yourself. ... You're aiming for that simple, general, most important take-home message in a way that still doesn't embarrass your colleagues with how stupid you've become in ignoring the depth of detail in your findings. But the depth or detail—you shouldn't go into that. That is a mistake.

Researchers raised several special challenges of communicating with policymakers—finding ways to package the information, display findings in a visual way, explain statistics to nonscientists, and deal with null findings or inconclusive evidence. We deal with each in turn.

First, one researcher, who developed a formula used to distribute revenue to local governments in South Africa, relayed that the more experienced he becomes, the more time he spends thinking about how to package the information. The need for user-friendly packaging was obvious to him because he deals with complicated fiscal matters that you cannot summarize for policymakers by writing a complex mathematical equation on the board. One way to bring a human face to data is with case studies or personal stories (Rabb & Winstead, 2003), which are particularly useful if policymakers can be assured that they represent a sizeable portion of the population rather than the idiosyncratic experiences of one or two people. At the Family Impact Seminars, we think of research illustrated with representative case studies or personal stories as a "one-two punch." With the convincing story, you get a left! With rigorous research, you get a right! With a convincing story and rigorous research, you get a knock-out punch.

Second, a common mistake is putting research out in a format that is "delightful to academics but dreadful for policymakers," according to a researcher with 20 years of experience. In general, policymakers prefer percentages or means and simple graphs or figures that visually portray the findings and do not require a lot of explanation. Professor Dave Riley, who has been nationally recognized by the American Psychological Association for his distinguished contributions to psychology in the public interest, has developed a simple formula for writing for policymakers. He aims for policy briefs short enough to be posted with a refrigerator magnet. The ideal is one page on a single topic with (a) a question (e.g., which is better, X or Y?) in a bold-faced, 20-point headline at the top of the page; (b) two or three sentences that answer the question of interest; and (c) a picture or figure to illustrate the data (no decimal points allowed).

Third, researchers have found it challenging to explain how much confidence policymakers can have in their findings using statistics that are easy for nonscientists to understand. Even explaining basic concepts can be challenging when the Holy Grail in the research culture is statistical significance, whereas in the policymaker culture, substantive significance is what matters. In the words of a member of a National Academy of Sciences panel,

> There's a huge difference in how academics and policymakers view the issue of significance ... researchers get very excited when they can find something that's statistically significant. And they often then bring that to the policy world, and are amazed that policymakers don't drop everything else and then change the world based upon the fact that they found something that was statistically significant. Well it doesn't take a rocket scientist to realize if you have a big enough sample size, you can find a lot of things that are statistically significant. But whether or not something is substantively significant is a different matter entirely. ... And in addition to that, you have to take into account what are some of the costs of changing the world. There are always opportunity costs whether it's in terms of tax dollars or in terms of opportunities that are not taken or ... unintended consequences that we don't see at the outset. I think policymakers are much more attuned, in fact, at anticipating a lot of these other costs. ... I think that gap between statistical and substantive significance is a big one.

Another veteran researcher advised that researchers should "avoid technical jargon" but still signal to nonscientists the rigor used to produce the findings:

> It's important for them to trust in us that we did this rigorously. It's important for people to trust you. They want to know important nuances, they want to know that I've done this right. There is always a crisp way to let them know that I've done that with care.

A researcher who works for a major think tank explained that he never discusses methodology, and he does give policymakers some numbers but not a lot. The key, of course, is providing those numbers that are most relevant to the policy question under consideration.

Finally, researchers offered advice on dealing with situations where there were null or inconclusive findings. For one researcher, a major teenage pregnancy demonstration project did not prevent pregnancy as intended. Her advice about how to handle this unexpected result was explicit: "It's very important to deal upfront and proactively with no findings":

> We did not succeed. The way to deal with that is to make sure that when we did the research, we went deep enough with the research to start to understand what was wrong with our theory. The theory was that if we gave them access to contraception, they wouldn't want more kids. We learned more about how services were delivered and how mothers responded. The way we dealt with this when we presented the findings was to put it upfront and say that this isn't about access and information but about finding ways to be supportive and validating.

When the findings don't tell a clear story, a researcher from a major policy think tank explained how he proceeds. He tells them when there is mixed evidence, but keeps in mind that policymakers typically have a low tolerance for ambiguous results: "I don't dwell on ambiguity, but I don't fudge the ambiguity." Similarly, Kristin Anderson Moore recommends relaying to policymakers

> some sense of your certainty … you may not be absolutely certain. There hasn't been a randomized trial, but the best evidence indicates that—always using very careful words.

These concrete strategies can help overcome some of the challenges of learning how to communicate in ways that meet policymakers' unique information needs. One researcher explained that he had learned from his mistakes when people were gracious enough to point them out to him. He also took several proactive steps to learn the language of the policy world:

> So sometimes what I've tried to do is read the Web sites of the state legislatures, or the National Governors Association, or of the [political] parties. And once you read the platforms, you get some sense of the kind of language that people are using, what the buzz words are … if I can understand that well enough to know how I can best communicate using their buzz words from time to time as appropriate, I think I can connect with them in a different way. But I do have to work, so it's like learning a new language.

Others recommended turning to examples of testimonies and policy briefs written specifically for the target audience. Others were able to get a crash course on working with policymakers by asking for advice and feedback from experienced people inside and outside policy settings. The Family Impact Seminars often turn for advice to analysts who work for policymakers such as the staff employed in nonpartisan legislative service agencies.

Recommendation 5: Use Clear, Careful Language When Dealing with Myths About Vulnerable Populations

Policymakers find it particularly difficult to access research on vulnerable children and families, yet ironically these are the very populations most likely to come to their attention (e.g., developmentally delayed children and disadvantaged families; Scott, Mason, & Chapman, 1999). One researcher found policy work frustrating because of the stereotypes he encountered, particularly about vulnerable groups. These stereotypes are troubling, because myths tend to be treated as fact in policy debate (Flinchbaugh, 1988; Heckman, 1990).

The myths that exist in the policy world were apparent to one researcher when he testified before a legislative committee on welfare reform. The committee members were "very polite, but it was so clear to me that their view of people on welfare was that there was something wrong with them" and the problem was giving them a "free ride." Similarly, a book that he coauthored was sometimes misused to stereotype single parents as being "bad for the country," when his intent was to "point out the difficulties of single parents and how we need to help them." Yet despite some mischaracterizations, much of the research was correctly interpreted, and his book ended up having enormous impact on welfare reform, in part, because the writing was clear and the statistical analyses were easy to understand.

To build understanding of vulnerable populations, researchers suggested being quite explicit about how families in a study might correspond to the policymakers' own life or that of their constituents. One researcher explained how he generated enthusiasm for a premarital education bill by getting policymakers to draw on their own personal preparation for marriage. Another researcher felt that her research was dismissed, not because of its quality, but because of a misperception she could have addressed if she had anticipated it: "[My state] is seen as a rural state, and when I presented in New York, they didn't understand how that would relate to teenagers in New York. The assumption is that what worked there will not work here."

Researchers also offered advice on dispelling myths that policymakers may hold. One recommended being "willing to talk in a straightforward way about very complicated issues ... that you usually wouldn't have to explain to other researchers." Another explained, "I try not to present things in an ideological good-guy, bad-guy kind of framework because a lot of what they think they know is wrong." This is particularly important in overcoming myths that policymakers sometimes hold about fragile families, low-income individuals, or other vulnerable populations.

One researcher who has analyzed family policy in four countries advised choosing language carefully after policymakers pointed out his use of terms such as *illegitimate births* may have fed into negative stereotypes about children born to single parents. His terminology may have conveyed a meaning he had not intended and may have inadvertently signaled to some policymakers that he held a particular political perspective. Researchers are well advised to carefully choose language for describing vulnerable families because these words can reinforce existing stereotypes rather than provide a new frame for thinking about how public policy can provide support or produce change in these families.

Recommendation 6: Familiarize Yourself With the Policymaking Process

Unfamiliarity with the policy process was a barrier mentioned by four researchers in our exploratory study. It is easy for professionals and the public alike to condemn politics and criticize the policy process out of a naive belief that the world should operate according to what they think is important. Over time, those serious about bringing research and evidence to the policy process became more aware of the premises underlying policymaking, more cognizant of how the process worked, and less critical about how policy decisions are made.

Most agreed that the burden falls on the researcher to figure out how to negotiate the political process and adapt to the policymakers' culture. Several approaches to learning about the policy process emerged from the interviews. For example, one researcher recommended "getting closer to the policy process yourself." She explained that a year spent in Washington, DC, was "transformative" and made her a better researcher. As researchers learned about the policymaking process, they became increasingly aware of its political nature and more adept at adapting to the budgetary and political constraints that policymakers face. As aptly put by Mark Masters, the chair of a county board of supervisors in a rural Midwest county,

> We are struggling with finding dollars, as everybody is, but I think it's more acute now than ever. So we'll always ask, "Where is it coming from, how much is it going to take, and what are we going to substitute and not provide for somebody else?" So a lot of decisions, as good as they may be, can't happen because there's no money. I guess what I'm trying to say is you can spin your wheels a lot and not make any progress because there won't be dollars. You need to understand how we're going to provide for this program and the policy. And that becomes a real political battle.

One researcher was politically astute in considering the fiscal impacts of a bill he was working on to reduce the marriage license fee for those who completed a premarital education course:

> The challenge is the short-term perspective. Keep emphasizing the long-term investment and be willing to give them as much cover as possible to help them when others say, "Why are we spending the money?" For example, with the premarital bill, we worked out a formula to raise the standard marriage license fee for everybody by $5, and then we estimated that no more than 20% would enroll in marital courses, and the cost would be made up by the increase. We worked on making it cost neutral instead of just saying, "Darn it, they should understand that this will prevent divorces later on, save child support, and all those things."

Researchers also learned to adapt to another potential sticking point between the two cultures—the lightning pace of policymaking. One researcher in pharmaceutical economics likened policymakers' urgent requests to being an emergency room physician. He devised ways of dealing with these time-sensitive requests without overtaxing his busy schedule:

I learned to identify major issues in the policy world, economic trends, et cetera. I track those trend lines and catalogue them. When I get one of those forest-fire emergency calls from the policymaker, I have most of the research already organized, ready to answer the question. If I had to do all the work when I got the call, I'd never make it. ... I'm usually ahead of the game on most of the issues. I have research done when most other people are just beginning to think about it.

Recommendation 7: Provide a Timely Response to the Questions Driving Policy Debate

According to nine researchers, a big mistake that many knowledge producers make is not promptly addressing the issues driving policy debate. Responding to policymakers' questions in a timely manner is critical, according to one researcher, whose efforts over a 15-year time span helped put affordable drug therapy on the policy agenda:

When the crisis happens, you have to be willing to drop everything else in your life and work on it if you want to have impact. Timeliness is critical for effectiveness, and if you can't do that, then you lose access over time and lose opportunity to provide technical advice. That's very stressful in one's life with family and everything.

Researchers provided us with specific examples of the payoff of providing relevant research "just in time" for policy debate. By making time to respond when a governor and his cabinet asked for advice, one researcher was able to shift thinking on the value of family support in a state. Another researcher coauthored a book on single parenting that ended up having a major impact on the debate of welfare reform. In reflecting on why this book was so influential, he humbly attributed its success to "just kind of serendipity that we happened to write a book on the right topic at the right time." A major reform of the welfare system had piqued political interest in single parenthood at the very time his book, with its clear story line, hit the press.

Several researchers attributed the impact of research to more than its timing, explaining that it also depends on how closely the research maps onto the questions policymakers are discussing. What researchers think are interesting questions and what policymakers find relevant are often not the same thing at all, according to one researcher with policy experience at the state, federal, and international levels. A researcher at an evaluation firm concurred: "You have to think of what legislators are interested in and need, rather than what you're interested in and need." In the words of another experienced researcher, no matter how good the research techniques and technology are, "if you get the question wrong, the research is useless." One 25-year veteran of policy work recommended focusing on issues currently on the plate of policymakers:

If you want to get the attention of policymakers, identify the problems they are dealing with ... so you always frame it in the context of what problem of society or problem for the policymaker can I solve. … If you don't understand that, you get ignored.

In fairness, one researcher presented a dissenting view. An economist, who had worked in the U.S. Treasury Department early in his career, explained that he did not think it would be good for him personally or for policy-oriented scientific inquiry for researchers to try to better anticipate the specific needs of policymakers. Instead, he recommended that academics push their frontier forward in the hope that policymakers will draw from this base of knowledge if they are interested. This researcher correctly pointed out the value of basic research that, on occasion, rockets into relevance in the face of changing and unpredictable circumstances. Yet the vast majority of these exemplary policy communicators concluded that relevant research is most apt to arise when the questions reflect the real-world issues to which policymakers must respond.

Researchers also suggested ways to transform one's scholarship from research questions that are mundane to ones that are germane to policymakers, three of which we mention here. First, one researcher recommended thinking upfront about how the research questions will resonate with policymakers: "Right from the beginning of designing a study, I'm thinking about how this can be used and how it might influence [policy] when it's done." Second, a researcher whose program is being implemented in 5 countries as well as 240 counties in 23 states explained how identifying policy-relevant questions is necessary but not sufficient. Policy relevance also entails selecting outcomes that can easily be explained to and understood by those outside academia.

Researchers not only have to ask the right questions but also have to make sure that the measures or outcomes that they are looking at are policy relevant. For example, Sara Watson (Zigler, Phillips, Moorehouse, & Watson, 2009), senior officer at the Pew Center on the States, recommended that researchers collect data on outcomes that their grandmother would care about. It's more important to talk about behaviors and conditions that are of immediate social concern than scores on a paper-and-pencil test.

Finally, it can be difficult to focus on the problems that policymakers are facing if research questions are driven primarily through a conventional, disciplinary lens (Van Langenhove, 2001). Research that slowly and surely builds on the findings of previous studies can be likened to looking at the world through the "rearview window." According to a videotaped interview of Tom,

> I think a lot of research tends to build upon research that was done in the past. You're looking for a slightly different way to either collect the data or run a different analysis. You're looking for a little niche that you can find that you can fit into. So that it's very rearview-mirror oriented. … And I think when you get out and work in the real world with real policymakers, you might get a better sense of what's coming down the road in front of you. I have seen a lot of my colleagues developing research questions that to my mind are very dated because they represent the world as it was 10, or 20, or 30 years ago. And I want to encourage them to get out and see what's going on today, or what policymakers think will be the emerging issues 5 or 10 years down the road.

To stay up on the politics, six researchers emphasized soliciting feedback ahead of time on what is policy relevant from analysts and staff who track issues. They can familiarize you with problems on policymakers' radar screen, provide the political context for your research, and identify policymakers who specialize in and provide leadership on the issues of interest. Also, researchers and policymakers can try to talk to each other about policy-relevant questions, but those who had done so offered a word of caution. If the conversation is to flow smoothly and the interchange is to be productive, it takes a certain set of communication skills and an acknowledgment of what knowledge and expertise both parties bring to the table. An emeritus professor at a land-grant university emphasized how difficult the conversation can be when two parties socialized in two starkly different cultures sit down across the table from each other:

> Too often when you get academics or researchers and policymakers in the same room, they don't know how to talk to each other … researchers will ask, what do you want to know? And it will be silence because policymakers don't sit around and think about, "Well what are going to be my research questions or questions of what I would call *management uncertainty* over the next year?" So you have to engage in a dialogue that's not as pointed and focused on the research question. You have to really talk [and] dialogue with these policymakers, and out of that … will emerge and evolve the kinds of things that you should be focusing on. And it takes a bit of training. It takes kind of a trained ear. You have to listen to what they say and then perhaps reflect back something like, "Oh, what I hear you saying is" and you may get "Oh yeah, that's it" or "That's not quite it. I think what I'm really concerned about is Y not X." And so I think it's through this back-and-forth that you can begin to identify and craft research questions that have some relevance to what policymakers really want to know, even if they can't articulate it all the time, as opposed to what researchers thought the key research questions were.

Those researchers who had honed their communication skills offered advice on ways to talk with policymakers, what kinds of information are reasonable to expect to emerge from these conversations, and how to interpret the advice they offer. First, Ruth Massinga, former president and CEO of Casey Family Programs, underscored how important it is to engage in a broad-ranging discussion of the policy issues but also to narrow in on defining the question well.

Tom agreed that it is imperative that the policy question be clearly articulated, which he illustrated with an example of how an unclear or shifting definition can make the debate confusing and incomprehensible. He and his colleagues were asked whether low-income families would relocate to Wisconsin to take advantage of the state's more generous welfare benefits. Initially, the question seemed quite straightforward, but as the debate ensued, it became less clear whether the preeminent policy concern was (a) the in-migration of welfare-motivated individuals, (b) those likely to end up on welfare regardless of motivation, (c) the poor in general, or (d) minority families in particular. Each different population invites different questions, different policy responses, and different processes for answering them. Several policy analysts joined in the debate of this controversial issue, often focusing on a different segment of the population, which resulted in a conflicting set of policy recommendations (Corbett, 1991).

The phrasing of a policy question can also serve to defuse controversial issues, which Kansas Cooperative Extension specialist Barry Flinchbaugh (1988) illustrated with the story of two public policy educators. They were asked many decades ago to help the state of Indiana decide whether to establish a social security system. At that time, social security was associated with New York liberal Franklin D. Roosevelt and was viewed by many as "pink at best and downright communist at worst" (p. 223). Defining the policy problem as "should we or should we not have social security?" would clearly have had a polarizing effect and immediately pitted the liberals against the conservatives. Instead, these astute public policy educators defined the issue by focusing on the true underlying problem: "How do we take care of old folks? Whose responsibility is it and what is the government's role?" So instead of focusing on a single controversial solution, they focused on a problem that few could disagree with, which helped establish a climate more conducive to constructive dialogue and seeking common ground (Flinchbaugh, 1988, p. 223).

Researchers also cautioned that policy questions cannot be thought of in isolation but must be conceptualized as part of a policymaking process that is incremental in nature, extends over time, and is not necessarily irreversible (Weiss, 1978). According to Lynn, Jr., "Social problems are seldom 'solved' by a single act or policy deliberation, even if it seems so at the time" (1978, p. 17). So knowledge producers must listen for the specific policy questions that policymakers express, which may have a short time horizon, but also listen for how this particular issue fits into the evolution of the larger issue over time, which may be more conducive to the time-consuming nature of knowledge production (Lynn, Jr., 1978). In the words of Ruth Massinga, who started her career as a caseworker before becoming secretary of the Maryland Department of Human Resources and finally CEO and president of Casey Family Programs,

> Yes, policy happens in increments, and we have to dissect that, and we have to understand that so that we're not asking the ultimate question when actually we're just starting a process. So we have to be fair to both the consumer and the policymaker and the researcher that we're not biting off too much too soon. But if we're practical and thoughtful and far-reaching in the way in which we see the potential, not the real change today, but the potential, I think we can make important strides in making sure that the conversations are legitimate conversations and that the findings are findings that we can be proud of no matter how modest.

In addition to knowing how a specific question fits into a larger debate, it is also important to know where a particular policy or proposal fits in the legislative pipeline. On the basis of her congressional work, Weiss (1987b) recommended that knowledge producers consider the trajectory of the issues. For example, she recommended trying to reach policymakers and their staff in the months before specific bills are being introduced because the longer one waits, the more conceptual premises have already been established and the more compromises have already been reached. Professor Daniel Meyer recommended trying to assess the trajectory of decision making on the issue, specifically whether or not policymakers have already made up their mind:

> I think some issues have already become very politicized, and so many policymakers already have a position. And to the extent that I can, I try to stay out of those questions because the timing is not right. In some ways, the timing is too late. What I would hope to do and what I would encourage others to do is to try to have their antennae out for issues that are coming, where there's unknowns that the researcher could provide some answers to early in the policy process before people have already taken positions. One of the things that I think is a particular strength of the Family Impact Seminars is ... working with policymakers to identify the issues that are just coming on the horizon so that we can figure out what the unanswered questions are and assist with the policymaking process before it's become so politicized that the groups aren't listening.

At the Family Impact Seminars, we believe any topic can be effective, but the real key to effectiveness is *when* the topic is presented and how it intersects with the interests of policymakers and the policy process. Because legislators have so many issues to consider, we believe that it is not fruitful to provide research on "back-burner" issues that have not caught the attention of policymakers and have not yet emerged on the legislative agenda.

To identify timely policy topics, the Family Impact Seminars strive to simultaneously consider the importance of the trajectory of the issue and the trajectory of decision making on the issue—a concept that we first heard discussed by Rick Kordesch when he directed the Family Impact Seminars at the Pennsylvania State University in the early 1990s. As shown in Figure 9.1, we have mapped out legislative interest in a topic on the vertical axis, which ranges from low to high. On the horizontal axis, we specify the process of issue development, which includes issue identified, legislation debated, law passed, administrative rules developed, and laws implemented. We believe that the optimal time to discuss research that is most conducive to its consideration and utilization is when the policy issue is moving onto the radar screen of policymakers (as indicated by the star in Figure 9.1) but before they have made up their mind about how to vote. Paraphrasing the memorable words of public policy educator Barry Flinchbaugh (1988), when the trenches are dug and the guns are aimed, it's time for war, not education. Because not all bills that are introduced have momentum behind them, we use Kingdon's (2003) theory of open policy windows to identify issues for which research may have the best chance of influencing a policy outcome (see the Seminar process for selecting topics in Chapter 11).

Recommendation 8: Learn How to Approach Policy Work as an Educator Rather Than an Advocate

An important consideration is not only *what* information to provide to policymakers but also *how* to provide it. Almost half (*n* = 6) of the sample said one key to success

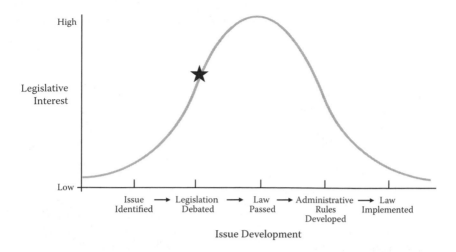

Figure 9.1   Identifying topics at the time information is most useful to policymakers.

is approaching policymakers as an educator who presents policy alternatives rather than as an advocate who lobbies for a single desired policy option (see also Chapter 10). Three reasons emerged for this recommendation. First, a factual, scientific approach can be a unique niche for researchers in policy settings, because it allows them to "become political without being politicized in the process" (Wong, 2007). One researcher, who began policy work as a student 25 years ago, explained,

> There are too few people who have prepared and made themselves available as technical advisors to policymakers and that remain independent enough to do that with credibility. All the trade organizations are glad to send their people in, but they all come with a direction.

Daniel Meyer, a social work professor, never takes strong advocacy positions. Instead, he assumes an educational role that is unique in shedding light on questions that policymakers have and illuminating some of the trade-offs they inevitably face. By helping them understand a factual basis on which to determine policy decisions, any necessary trade-offs can be made from a knowledgeable perspective. Another researcher with a decade of policy experience explained that he gradually came to recognize how powerful this education approach can be: "Over time ... I learned ... of the power of the role of a person who brings a balanced view to the table."

Second, a family researcher explained that those who assume an advocacy role may be limited in *which* policymakers and political parties they can work with. Researchers can be effective as advocates, according to another researcher, but not without consequences: "They write good op-eds. They'll never be invited to testify because one half of the committee will love them and the other half will hate them." Another researcher, who was tapped by his governor to improve child care quality in his state, concurred:

> To be able to communicate through your interactions that you do not pretend to be a policymaker, that you're not telling them what to think or what policies to promote, but rather are a scientific staff person ... that means a willingness to be useful for all political parties.

This education approach, by its very nature, requires researchers to focus not on promoting their own predilections or trying to please policymakers, but rather on being honest about what the data do and do not say. On the basis of 25 years of experience, one researcher put it this way:

> I tell them what will really happen whether they like it or not, and if they try it out and find that I was pretty accurate, they'll come back. It's better to be tactfully honest and give them the best advice you can, and don't try to be a pleaser because that will burn both of you. You can sell your reputation, but you can only sell it once. Don't put yourself in a situation where you're someone else's mouthpiece unless you expect it to be your last time. You will lose your credibility.

Finally, a researcher, who has received national awards for the contributions of his research to society, views the education approach as a way of communicating respect to policymakers for the expertise they bring to the table. He views advocacy as an expert-based attitude, where you tell others what decision is best rather than let them decide on their own.

> Scholars who know a lot about an issue and feel strongly about it are often unwilling to allow others to make their own mistakes. That's an antidemocratic attitude. That's an expert-based attitude. If you believe in democracy, you have to allow the majority to make up their own minds. Most academics have a very hard time with that.

Another researcher reflected on how adopting the educator role was central to her most memorable experience working with policymakers in the past 20 years. She recalled one time, when she worked in a close setting with policymakers who had a keen interest in welfare-related issues, as an "incredible teaching and learning experience on both sides." The policymakers listened to what the researchers said, partly because they had practical experience and partly

> because we didn't come at them with prescriptive recommendations but rather with factual information that would help inform them ... I felt that I had perhaps done something useful ... and that it would have an impact on policy. And even more important, it was an interactive process. I was feeding into the process.

Recommendation 9: Show Respect for Policymakers' Knowledge and Expertise

What became clear from these exemplary knowledge brokers is that success takes more than the vast knowledge they had attained and the sundry skills they had gained. The most common piece of advice from our sample and others as well

(McCall, Groark, & Nelkin, 2004) is to show humility and respect for policymakers and their expertise. One researcher was blunt: "If you're cynical, you won't be effective." Success in the policy world requires a certain sense of humility regarding what research can bring to the political fray and a respect for the role that policymakers play. One 30-year veteran of policy work had seen academics taken aback when the world didn't change as they thought it ought to when they had tried to overwhelm policymakers with their data or the findings of the literature:

> [Academics] oftentimes will cite the literature as if they were evoking the Bible or some other ... absolute truth. And, of course, there are so many interpretations of the literature, it is very often like the Bible. There aren't that many areas, particularly in the social sciences, where everyone agrees both on what is in the literature and how one should interpret it and how one should apply it. So when academics come across as if they're bringing revealed truth to decision makers and policymakers, that can be very off-putting. And they oftentimes don't bring their insights with enough caution and reverence, if you will, for the fact that policymakers are dealing with very, very complex environments, and they have to deal with a lot of different stakeholders who represent very diverse positions. And that evidence ... [is] only one input into the policymaking process. Researchers and academics tend to think it ought to be the only input, but in fact that's an arrogance that I don't think that they fully appreciate that they have... until you really ... arrive at a balanced position that I think puts evidence in its proper place, and in which the results or these insights are delivered with enough caution and humor and balance and kind of in a holistic way, at least you acknowledge the fact that there are other factors that go into the decision-making process. Until you get to that point, you're probably going to be dismissed somewhat.

On the basis of her experience with federal policymakers, Weiss (1983) echoed the need for an attitude of humility regarding the influence of research and the researcher: "Be modest in your expectations of influence. Do not expect your study to catapult you into the position of advisor to the prince" (p. 241). You set yourself up for failure, according to two researchers in our sample, if you approach policymakers with the attitude that you are "God's gift to the world" or "I know best." In contrast, Dean Gary Sandefur advised being open and willing to listen:

> You really have to try to understand how they're approaching and thinking about a problem and listen to their questions so that you don't give them the answer you want to give them ... you really try to be responsive to their needs and their questions. So I think ... the primary thing is to be open and to listen and then try to be helpful, if you can. ... So I think openness, listening—those are important attitudes to have.

In some respects, these attitudes come instinctively, according to a national expert on welfare reform. However, one must be continually vigilant about how attitudes that may be apropos in the research culture may be inappropriate in the policy culture:

> If you play the same games that you play with your academic colleagues, you're going to turn off the policy folks. And when I say games I mean by trying to one-up people with the sophistication of your technique … do any of that crap and you're dead. Treat them as though they are doing important work and that you're interested in what they are doing. You have to show them respect, first and foremost. You have to be interested in what they are doing, in societal questions of public good, and justice.

Dean Sandefur concurred that behaviors that would be accepted and perhaps even embraced in academic settings could be devastating for building relationships in the policy world:

> Check your ego at the door. You can't feel that your opinion is more valuable and more important than all the other opinions. Check your opinion at the door. Don't feel offended when they cite someone else even if you thought you gave the better testimony. Listen to them and learn from them. I learned a lot from working with congressional staff because sometimes they ask questions, research issues that I never thought about.

Humility and respect are essential to building a genuine partnership with policymakers, according to a researcher who served as president of a national family organization:

> It takes an appropriate degree of humility, bringing a sense that policymakers have wisdom, knowledge, and experience to bring to the table, and that is no less than [the researcher's] knowledge and experience. See them as collaborators and that they have constraints on them that are different from the constraints on me. A genuine partnership is what I am looking for.

Showing humility and respect for policymakers can be easier when you realize that democracy means "the people," according to Professor Dave Riley, and that's just who policymakers are.

Recommendation 10: Be Patient and Self-Rewarding in Defining Success

Policy work clearly is not a walk in the park. The story of doing policy work would be incomplete without mentioning the frustrations that even the best-intentioned and most well-prepared scholars experience. Five researchers described one of their policy experiences as "frustrating," particularly when politics dominates the science. One case in point was one researcher's experience working on the failed Clinton health care reform. Another researcher, when asked to testify at state or congressional hearings, felt like he was being used as part of "political theatre": "People aren't particularly interested in your perspective; they're there to ask certain questions and make certain statements, and so you're kind of like a bit player in their efforts to make a public impression on people."

Perhaps the most frequent frustration, expressed by 10 researchers, is not knowing whether your efforts will pay off. No matter how promising or effective a policy might be, a random political event can stall progress or even shift policy in the opposite direction. Professor Dave Riley likened policy work to a "crapshoot":

> Doing research is like putting money in the bank at 4% interest. It isn't much, but you can count on some return. In the policy arena, however, there is no guaranteed payoff. You can lose everything. You can lose your shirt.

Professor Riley described a gamble he took when he got involved in helping his state set up a five-star rating system for child care quality. To him, this idea had political promise. It would appeal to liberals who wanted to improve the quality of child care, and it would appeal to conservatives because it was a market-based system that provided quality ratings to individual consumers so that they could choose which child care option to use. Given the promise of this policy, he conducted applied research on the topic, taught informational sessions on quality ratings systems in communities across the state, and provided a range of implementation options for the executive agency officials responsible for establishing and administering the system.

> That was a two-year effort with a staff of about seven people working with me, and we generated a large amount of consensus in several communities that it was a good idea. … And then for purely political reasons, it got squashed. It got squashed because it became a program promoted by the governor. … The legislature was the opposite political party, and if it was the governor's idea, they didn't want it. And I slapped my forehead on that one. I should have been finding a way for both political parties to take credit for it. And so it was 2 years of work on a really promising idea. … And we had some research evidence for how to do it efficiently and effectively. And it died. It's gone. … I may try to resurrect it, or I might not. … Five years from now we might find that it was important in eventually getting this thing passed, or it just may never happen. It might just be an investment, a risk I took. It was an investment I made, and the investment didn't pay off. That happens.

Despite his disappointment, Professor Riley went on to say that sometimes it is "still worth taking the risk" because the random political events do line up right:

> The rational science is never enough to make a policy. It's never sufficient, but sometimes it's necessary. … I like to think of Head Start as a good example of that. There was about 15 years of really good child development research that led to the idea that "Gee, maybe early experience is really important. Maybe we need to invest in those earlier years." And then it just happened that the people who were in the Kennedy administration in the early '60s were the right group of people with the right kind of political value commitments that lined up with that research, and so then Head Start happened. And it wouldn't have happened without both being true. And so you do the research because it's necessary, but you just have to remember, it's never sufficient.

One of the original planners of Head Start, Edward Zigler, an emeritus professor from Yale, recommended taking the long view. He explained the way the policy game works: "You can lose 100 times, but you only have to win once, and then you have it" (Zigler et al., 2009). We heard over and over again in our interviews this theme of being patient and realistic about the time it will take for research to percolate up into public and political consciousness. In the literature, several researchers acknowledged that policy often moves incrementally, and changes do not occur as rapidly as they would have liked (Chandler, 2006; Takanishi, 2002; Weiss, 1978; Zigler & Styfco, 2002).

One emeritus professor pointed out that the slow progress of policymaking should not be too off-putting to researchers: "After all, as an academic, you're used to dealing with a timeless pursuit of truth. Well, the policymaking process can be a timeless pursuit as well." Only this one researcher was willing to provide some parameters for how long it might take for an investment to begin paying off:

> It depends what you're trying to ... accomplish, but I think it is relatively accurate to say that you're probably safe if you try to give your most conservative or pessimistic scenario of how long something will take, double it, and then you'll fall halfway short, in terms of the time it'll take to accomplish something.

For those on the outside of the policymaking process looking in, this can be very off-putting. In the words of Mary Fairchild of the National Conference of State Legislatures,

> It may look like nobody's paying attention, it may look like, you know, people don't care about the issue, when ... that's really not what's going on at all. They're dealing with 10 issues, and you're focusing on your one. It's just a different environment.

Fairchild explained that policymakers oftentimes must weigh several issues that are competing for scarce resources. This translates into tough decisions about where the money for your issue will come from, whether from education, Medicaid, or transportation—all issues with their own constituencies informing them of evidence that comports with their positions. For particularly big ideas, Fairchild said, "It's not just a year. It's not just 2 years. ... They do take a number of years to become an enacted policy, and don't be discouraged by that."

Given the snail's pace of policymaking, one 20-year veteran said early on that he was frustrated when he would talk to policymakers and they would end up doing whatever they wanted to do anyway. He learned how seldom you can claim that a particular testimony led to legislation, but overtime he came to realize that repeating the same thing eventually begins to have an impact. These researchers cautioned that policy work can be "hard" and a "marathon race," but "if you stick with it, you will eventually see results."

SUMMARY

The voices of our experienced researchers corroborate the basic tenets of our community dissonance theory—that underutilization of research in policymaking is due to misperceptions and miscommunications between researchers and policymakers from a number of disparate communities who operate in distinct professional and institutional cultures that shape their communication styles, decision-making criteria, questions of interest, reward systems, salient constituencies, and time frames. Research utilization is perceived not as a problem that lies with policymakers but as a two-way process that involves both policy-minded researchers and research-minded policymakers.

In this chapter, we focused on the research end of the utilization process. These exemplary social scientists identified cultural barriers they encountered when interacting with policymakers and provided several pragmatic strategies for communicating and collaborating across these conflicting cultures. Consistent with the cultural dimension of *interactional preferences*, the data suggest a paradigm shift in the way we conceptualize research–policy connections. Instead of thinking about disseminating research *to* policymakers, the data suggest focusing more heavily on developing relationships *with* them. Given a long-standing oral tradition in lawmaking bodies (Weiss, 1989), policymakers rely more on the spoken than on the written word (Smith, 1991), yet researchers have often failed to capitalize on this knowledge in their attempts to engage the policy community. The efforts put into communicating directly with policymakers pale in comparison to other pursuits; instead, what has prevailed is the tradition of writing papers and policy reports. Gaining entrée may entail moving away from expert-driven models of research dissemination and toward more collaborative relationships that validate the expertise each brings to the table (Kellogg Commission, 1999).

Consistent with the cultural dimension of *targets of interest*, that is, to whom policymakers pay attention, researchers are not a salient stakeholder. We are not on their radar screen. Thus, researchers cannot wait to be tapped on the shoulder. Surprisingly, that is exactly what most of these exemplary communicators did, with only 1 of 14 proactively making an initial contact with a policymaker. If researchers who move seamlessly between the research and policy communities are ever to become the rule rather than the exception, they need to take the initiative and begin building relationships with policymakers or policy intermediaries. To do so, researchers can encourage students and colleagues to present their research in policy settings and seek out policy internships. They can also take the initiative to invite policymakers to serve as resources in campus classes and professional meetings, and to consult with experienced knowledge brokers.

The insights shared in this chapter also lend support to the cultural dimension of *cognitive frameworks*. Researchers explained the importance of learning about targeting the policymaking audience, and about how to communicate research findings in ways that are consistent with how policy decisions are made. Moreover, consistent with the dimension of *contextual preferences*, researchers recommended learning about the policymaking process and how the political context shapes another dimension, *focal interests*. For example, the researchers emphasized the fast-paced nature of the policy context and the importance of providing timely responses to the questions driving policy debate. In addition, in the policymaking context, most information that policymakers receive is agenda-driven, or at least agenda-influenced, so providing research-based information free of values and stock solutions makes policymakers sit up and take notice.

The insights also support the dimension of *feedback loops*, specifically what the rewards are and how success is defined. With increasing exposure, researchers came to respect policymakers' knowledge and expertise, and to identify common rewards they share with policymakers when collaborating to solve complex social problems. As they gained experience, researchers came to realize the importance of (a) being patient in expecting results, given the long-term nature of policymaking, and (b) self-rewarding in identifying success, given the lack of extrinsic rewards from the academy.

Key Concepts 9.1 captures some of the chapter's insights about getting started in policy work. Do the insights suggest that working with policymakers is a set of pragmatic processes and procedures that can be learned over time? We believe so, at least for many knowledge producers and knowledge intermediaries. Will anyone who takes the time to acquire this knowledge, build these relationships, and develop these prerequisite skills and attitudes be successful? That is less likely. We write this book with a spirit of humility given that the complex, value-laden, and idiosyncratic processes through which policies are made make it difficult to develop a specific, quantifiable, and transferable set of recommendations that professionals can unfailingly use across situations to bridge the gap between research and policy. Moreover, these data derive from a small, nonrepresentative sample composed of the best and the brightest based on (a) expert assessments of the quality of their publications and their reputation in the field and (b) policymakers' appraisal of their ability to successfully communicate research and draw policy implications.

Key Concepts 9.1   Getting Started in Policy Work: First Steps

- To acquire the attitudes it takes to succeed, move your mind-set away from expert-driven models of research dissemination to one of more collaborative relationships. Success in the policy world requires humility regarding what research can bring to the political fray and a respect for the role that policymakers play.
- To get started, do not wait to be tapped on the shoulder—researchers are not on policymakers' radar screen.
- To gain entrée, find occasions to rub elbows with policymakers— invite them to give presentations, attend their conferences, participate in their listening sessions, and make appointments to meet with them.
- To figure out where to start, determine whether the policies you are interested in fall under the jurisdiction of local, state, or federal policymakers. Then tap into the power of constituency by making an appointment to meet with your elected representatives. Inquire about their policy interests and ask which policymakers provide leadership on your policy interests.
- To get their attention, frame your communication with policymakers around the problems that they are dealing with.

- To develop realistic expectations, remember it is not necessary to be a master before you begin. According to exemplar policy communicator Dave Riley, "Hurry, go out, start making mistakes." Building relationships with policymakers is a developmental process that becomes easier over time.

This sample was heterogeneous in terms of substance, focus, and approach. It was composed of developmental psychologists, economists, family scientists, pharmacists, and sociologists experienced in communicating with policymakers at the local, state, federal, and international levels through a range of communication vehicles encompassing the spoken and written word. However, the sample was homogeneous in one very important regard—all of these social scientists got involved, stayed involved, and experienced some success in communicating research findings to policymakers. Conceivably, given the nature of the sample, there is the very real possibility that the findings overstate the potential to effectively communicate research to policymakers and understate some prerequisite attitudes, skills, or personality traits that are so ingrained that they did not seem to bear mentioning. For example, one emeritus researcher elaborated on some basic orientations to the world that may make policy work an endeavor too innately frustrating, too seemingly futile for some social scientists to take on:

> And a lot of it depends really on your basic personality. If you see the world as black and white and if you see most issues in those stark terms and you define success in those climactic ways, you may not want to be in public policy because it's going to be too frustrating for you. Things are not that clear. Constituencies and stakeholders are constantly evolving, and the unintended consequences are enormously complex and sometimes difficult to predict ... there are these inherent trade-offs in the policymaking process that you can't get around. Someone is going to end up with the short end of the stick sometimes when someone else is satisfied. And so you have all these inherent, I think, limitations and things that should caution you about being too exuberant and optimistic. And if you can live with all that, then it's worth entering the field of play.

Similarly, Snow (1961) mentioned differences in the intellectual and moral temperaments of those who work in science versus those who work in government. To succeed, scientists, particularly in their formative years, have to "think of one thing, deeply and obsessively, for a long time" (p. 72), whereas government officials must think about a great many things and their interconnections for a short span of time. Granted, there may be other elements of personality or temperament that our sample inadvertently overlooked but that may be fundamental for knowledge brokers who would work with distinction in the policy vineyards.

Finally, one clear message from our interviews is that building relationships with policymakers is a developmental process that eventually becomes easier and more rewarding. Initial contacts were not always positive, suggesting it takes time to develop the necessary skills and to overcome false stereotypes about policymakers.

Yet Professor Dave Riley cautioned that there is really no substitute for going out and starting to work with policymakers:

> And my last piece of advice is the most important probably. You shouldn't think that you have mastered this before you start doing it. I always like to quote from the best how-to book ever written on any subject ... by Nicolaides, *The Natural Way to Draw*, and it is a book that if you read it, it'll teach you how to draw. ... And Nicolaides says, on the first page, you will not learn to draw until you make your first 10,000 mistakes. So hurry, go out, start making mistakes. It's the advice we all need, and no amount of listening or reading about working with policymakers is a substitute for going out and starting to make your own mistakes, so I encourage that.

Even less-experienced social scientists can move far beyond the novice stage by tapping into the 274 combined years of experience of the 14 exemplary policy communicators in our initial sample and the 10 supplemental interviews we conducted. By building collaborative relationships with policymakers, social scientists can diminish the gap between knowledge producers and consumers by building the capacity to bring evidence to bear on policy decisions. In the words of a member of a National Academy of Sciences panel,

> If I had to do it all over again, I wouldn't change anything one bit. I think it's the rare person who can do public policy from an academic perch. ... Not everyone can do good policy work and feel comfortable with it. But if it is in your heart to do it, go for it. There is nothing more important than doing that ... well, and by God, the world needs it!

The world needs knowledge producers and intermediaries who dedicate time and energy to communicating with knowledge consumers, broadly defined. Success depends on deciding not only what to communicate but also how to do so. We touched above on the approach to use when working with those in the policy community, but we believe it is so important and so little understood that we devote the whole next chapter to it.

AUTHORS' NOTE

Chapter 9 expands upon an earlier publication by Friese and Bogenschneider (2009).

10

Approaching Policymakers
Moving Beyond "What" to "How"

Scientific knowledge, the wisdom of the university, cannot be used to determine the "correct" policy choice for society because science cannot supply the value judgment that ranks the interests of one group as more important than the interests of others.

—Richard Barrows (1994, p. 3)

If we are serious about making our science relevant to policy development, we need to cultivate the highest degree of respect and credibility ... that means that we must take care both in drawing the line between science and politics, and then not crossing it.

—Steven Breckler (2006, p. 22)[1]

Anyone who has ever played golf will understand the rationale for this chapter. Playing golf entails knowing not only *what* to do but also *how* to do it. Clearly, it is not enough to know the goal—getting the ball in the hole with as few strokes as possible. It is also necessary to know how to translate this knowledge into effective action.

This chapter addresses an age-old question, one that dates back to the origins of scientific research and continues to perplex both social scientists and their professional societies to this day: What is the most reasoned approach for working with policymakers to turn good research into sound policy? When knowledge producers venture into the policy culture, they first conduct an empirical scan to locate research relevant to the questions at hand. Sometimes overlooked, but no less important, is an analysis of which approach to use to provide research to policymakers. When approaching those in power, some knowledge producers use their expertise to advocate for the policy directions they deem most desirable. Others argue that social scientists must maintain their objectivity at all costs and recommend a dispassionate or education approach (Breckler, 2006).

This question of approach shadows all aspects of doing policy, including communicating with policymakers, developing relationships with special interest groups, organizing seminars, preparing press releases, testifying at hearings, or writing reports. Conversations, relationships, seminars, press releases, testimonies, and reports each can be approached from an advocacy or an education perspective. After laying out clear definitions of these two alternate approaches, this chapter looks to examples of how individuals and organizations have approached policy work and what success they have experienced. Then we identify why knowledge consumers and knowledge producers alike believe the education approach is most effective for working with policymakers. Finally, we consider some of the prominent objections to the education approach and offer advice about how to best implement it.

DIFFERENTIATING THE ADVOCACY AND EDUCATION APPROACHES FOR WORKING WITH POLICYMAKERS

In our experience providing technical assistance on which approach to use for policy work, we have found that discussion can be muddied by absent or ambiguous definitions. Thus, we start by defining the term *advocacy*. Some individuals or organization advocate for families, youth, or the poor. This we think of as advocacy with a small "a" because it entails bringing the needs of a particular group to policymakers' attention, but without lobbying for a particular policy option. Advocacy with a capital "A" means examining options in light of one's own value system using a personal interpretation of the scientific evidence with the aim of promoting a single policy option that is determined to be most desirable for society (Barrows, 1994; Bogenschneider, Olson, Mills, & Linney, 2006; Nye & McDonald, 1979). Put simply, the intent of the advocate is to persuade.

The essence of advocacy is captured in the words of the director of research at a prominent, advocacy-oriented think tank in Washington, DC: "We are combatants in the battle of ideas. We are on one side, and we make that clear. We are not just for better government and efficiency, we are for particular ideas." Terms like *combatants* capture how advocates jockey for political advantage as they engage in policy debate "in line with a preconceived set of ideas or principles rather than simply to pursue research questions in whatever direction they may lead" (Smith, 1991, p. 206).

Advocates come in all stripes and flavors—conservative, liberal, libertarian, populist, and so on. Their Web sites often claim that they are a nonpartisan purveyor of balanced information, but of course they handpick the studies and results that reinforce their principles, positions, and political preferences. When the scientific evidence is incomplete, advocates do not shy away from drawing conclusions about the character of a social problem or an optimal policy response.

In contrast, educators do not lobby for a single policy option. Instead, they attempt to inform political discourse by clarifying the potential consequences of various policy alternatives. Whereas the aim of the advocate is to persuade, the aim of the educator is to inform by presenting research objectively minus any mention of personal preferences. The value judgments and ultimate decisions are entrusted to the policymakers elected to make such choices rather than to the expert such as Plato's philosopher king (Barrows, 1984, 1994). The expert feeds into decision making by supplying objective information on the issue and building understanding of a range of policy options. Educators must trust the democratic process enough to give up control, which, of course, they never have anyway (Barrows, 1994).

The education approach forms the basis of the Family Impact Seminars and the Welfare Peer Assistance Network (WELPAN) that we have been involved in and is also used by some think tanks and several long-standing legislative support bureaus such as the Congressional Budget Office, the Congressional Research Service, the General Accountability Office, and similar units in many state governments. The educator can also serve as a consultant to advocacy organizations or coalitions of citizens interested in specific issues. Educators deliberately strive to work with groups with vastly different political persuasions and offer evidence on all sides of an issue. In contrast, advocates would limit their work to like-minded coalitions and provide only information that portrays the group and its views in a favorable light.

ADVOCACY AND EDUCATION ACROSS THE AGES

To breathe life into the advocacy and education approaches, we provide a number of examples, some contemporary and others dating back to an era when so-called university expertise first emerged. In 1890, only 400 doctoral degrees were awarded in the United States; some of these newly minted PhDs served for a short time in government, but quickly gravitated toward more prestigious academic careers (Smith, 1991). Since these earliest days when science was in its infancy, experts have disagreed about the role that science could and should play in the body politic.

The Policy Approaches of Lester Ward Versus John Commons

Some experts envisioned a direct link of science to policy akin to the advocacy approach. Take the example of Lester Ward, a self-taught man who worked his way up to the chief paleontologist post in the U.S. Geological Survey in 1892. Ward was so enamored with how the methods of science could be used for social and economic development that he coined the term *scientific lawmaking* (Commager, 1950). In stark contrast to the laissez-faire economic thinking of his time, Ward "envisioned legislatures that would operate like laboratories, where laws would be enacted as a 'series of exhaustive experiments' " (Smith, 1991, p. 32). His utopian vision of a symbiotic relation between the laboratory and the legislature never became reality, yet Ward's intellectual influence is unmistakable. He was elected the first president of the American Sociological Association in 1907, and his thinking is said to have had a profound impact on the administrations of Woodrow Wilson and Franklin D. Roosevelt and the formation of the modern Democratic Party (Commager, 1950; "Lester Frank Ward," 2008).

This can be contrasted with the approach of economics professor John Commons, an influential figure in Wisconsin policymaking, whom we first introduced in Chapter 3 for his role in the development of the first workers' compensation law in the country and the nation's first unemployment compensation policy. Commons's close work with lawmakers became so well-known that Theodore Roosevelt asked to meet him during an appearance in Madison to address the legislature (Stark, 1995). Author and public servant Frederic C. Howe (1912) was so inspired by Commons's policy work and that of his Wisconsin colleagues that he claimed, "I know of no place in America where officials work with more devotion than they do in Wisconsin. There is an enthusiasm for public service that is unique" (Howe, 1912, p. 50).

In contrast to Ward, Commons was adamant in his memoirs that his role was that of an advisor and educator to leaders, not an advocate: "I never initiated anything. I came only on request of legislators, of executives, or committees of the legislature" (Commons, 1934, p. 110). Commons held a pragmatic outlook about whether policymakers used or disabused his advice. He believed that policymakers alone could determine the utility of his advice by running it through the filter of their own practical experience and that of their followers.

> The leaders alone had the long experience of success and defeat. It was they who took the risks of defeat and deserved the credit of success. … If you furnished a worker-leader or a political leader with any material he could use, he alone could tell how much of it he could use, when and how, if it was to "get across" to his followers. Hence I always accepted philosophically what they rejected of my hard work, and stuck to them nevertheless. They were leaders. I was an intellectual. (Commons, 1934, p. 88)

A Contemporary Example of Education Versus Advocacy: The Sad Story of the Child Support Assurance Concept

A clear and compelling example of the tensions between education and advocacy emerged in 1979, when a legislated group called the Wisconsin Welfare Reform Study Advisory Committee tapped the Institute for Research on Poverty (IRP) for input and expertise on how to make major changes in the state's child support system. Irwin Garfinkel, an economist and IRP director, had been thinking about child support since the mid-1970s when officials at the U.S. Department of Health and Human Services had encouraged him to pursue research in this area. Borrowing some ideas from Harold Watts, IRP's first full-term director, and some programmatic ideas from Sweden, he began to formulate the concept of an assured child support system.

Though an idealist, Garfinkel was not naive. He realized that any extension of an income entitlement must be accompanied by aggressive plans for enhancing private child support payments.

The Welfare Reform Study Advisory Committee was a perfect platform for developing and advancing a comprehensive Child Support Assurance System (CSAS). The concepts were endorsed by a public body and received considerable public and political attention. Still, concepts that are elegant on paper raise many questions in the real world. Though the advisory committee's report received praise for being imaginative and bold, much work remained. The new governor, Lee Sherman Dreyfus, affirmed that the state was prepared to undertake fundamental reform and appointed an interdepartmental task force to design and implement various recommendations. Some notable success was achieved with the creation of a state refundable tax credit. However, progress on the child support front was slow, stalled by strong opposition from fathers' groups along with questions of cost and the proper role of government in child support enforcement.

Recognizing that turning the CSAS principles into a real program would be a marathon, not a sprint, and would require more research and analysis, the state of Wisconsin entered into a formal relationship with IRP in the early 1980s. Tom recalls sitting down with Sherwood Zink, staff attorney for the Department of Health and Social Services to develop a contractual arrangement.

There was no precedent for such a relationship, so each provision of the first contractual agreement had to be carefully crafted. Because both parties were still operating within their own political cultures and pressures, there were many thorny issues to resolve—how would data privacy be handled, who would have proprietary ownership over research or evaluation products, and, in the final analysis, who really was in charge? At the end of the day, language was agreed upon that established a contractual working relationship between IRP and the (then) Department of Health and Social Services, who would function as partners in an effort to transform the child support system. That agreement became the template for a contractual arrangement that remains in effect to this day, more than a quarter century later.

Over the next decade, an intensive, wide-ranging struggle was waged to enact CSAS. The university brought its expertise and national capacity to tap into the best and brightest academics. The state brought its political authority and practical knowledge. A third ally proved to be Tom Loftus, who served on the initial Welfare Study Committee and was now rising to a leadership position in the state Assembly.

The early child support struggles were on the collection front. A firestorm of protest arose from fathers' groups. State and legislative allies provided some cover, and the university muted certain concerns through rigorous analysis: Who would pay how much? How did payments differ under alternate scenarios? Would the children be better off economically and otherwise? In the face of extreme emotion, numbers and rational analysis often proved persuasive.

The tensions between science and power came to head during an effort to experimentally evaluate the elements of the CSAS. There were to be 10 experimental counties that would use the new way of setting and collecting child support and 10 control counties that would serve as the counterfactual. Wisconsin, however, has a tradition of strong local control. Therefore, the county board in each experimental county had to agree to participate. The first county to vote was Racine, a semiurban county located south of Milwaukee with a significant blue-collar, working-class population. Irv Garfinkel, Tom Loftus, and other state officials were there for the vote, and so were hundreds of angry men, some of whom had done their strategizing at local taverns. Of course, the vote never took place, and the sheriff asked the intrepid reformers in attendance if he might escort them back to their cars. When they replied that they did not think it necessary, the sheriff replied that he thought it was essential.

In the end, cooler heads prevailed. The innovations were introduced, evaluations conducted, laws passed, and reforms brought to scale. The evaluation results were persuasive, sometimes compelling. However, further analyses revealed other problems. No arena of social policy is ever simple. In response, further reforms have flowed, and some of the original innovations have been changed, sometimes radically. Yet through all this, knowledge producers and consumers worked together to continuously assess and innovate and evaluate.

The clash of cultures was most manifest on the Assured Benefit (AB) side of the ledger (i.e., the public guarantee of a minimal child support benefit when the noncustodial parent could not or would not contribute enough). It was the most dramatic reform in the package. At the same time, its cost was unknown. It seemed like another entitlement when existing entitlements were under attack. To Governor Tommy Thompson, it looked like an expansion of the cash welfare program at a time when he was looking for ways to minimize the scope and reach of welfare.

The story of the AB is long and convoluted (see Corbett, 1992; Loftus, 1994). Battles raged on all levels throughout the 1980s and into the 1990s. The conflict was conceptual. Was the AB another name for welfare or something fundamentally different? The battle was theoretical. How would people behave? Would mothers quit work if the transfer were available? Would absent fathers pay more or less? The battles were logistical. Could an effective program be designed that was administratively practical and operationally feasible? Above all, the battle was political. Whose vision of reform would prevail? On one side, Tommy Thompson was poised to make a national name for himself by radically changing the face of welfare by heading in a very different direction. On the other side, Tom Loftus and a growing body of academics (including conservatives such as Lawrence Mead and Charles Murray) argued that the AB would mitigate the ravages of child poverty, while actually reducing reliance on welfare-type assistance.

For awhile, progress was made. One huge issue was obtaining a waiver of federal rules and getting permission to use part of the federal contribution to Aid to Families With Dependent Children to defray the costs of the AB. In 1984, legislation was passed in Congress authorizing Wisconsin to try out the AB concept, subject to a rigorous evaluation and other conditions. The authority ran from 1986 to 1994. The clock was ticking. Some of the key paperwork necessary to put the waiver into effect sat on the incumbent governor's desk on his last day in office. He chose not to sign the papers, leaving that decision to the man who would succeed him, Tommy Thompson.

Work continued as if the AB would be implemented, at least on a trial basis. Wisconsin supporters were further energized by the fact that a welfare reform committee report authorized by Governor Mario Cuomo also proposed a child support package including an AB. In 1991, the National Commission on Children called for a national experiment of the AB concept.

Despite all this national attention, the concept died with a whimper rather than a bang. By mid-1989, the initiative had become a partisan issue. Assembly speaker Loftus had made it clear that he intended to run for governor, with welfare reform and child support as two of his major issues. Governor Thompson sequestered the funds for the administration of the AB pilots. In the fall of 1989, the legislature passed a bill directing the governor to spend these funds, but the governor vetoed the bill. With continuing resistance from the governor, and now the concept fully politicized, the game was up, and planning gradually ceased.

Irv Garfinkel really wanted the AB concept to work. He was an academic and would be guided by numbers. But he was also a visionary who felt passionately about his ideas. In retrospect, that passion may have led him and others, including Tom, to forget certain fundamentals in the push for reform. It was easy to tie the project's fortunes to a powerful legislative ally, Tom Loftus. But in doing so, partisan neutrality was sacrificed. Not enough energy was expended in reaching out to Thompson and others in his administration early on. Later, when the effort was made, the preconceptions were firmly set. These academics were seen as liberals, or Democrats, or simply not to be trusted.

WHICH APPROACH IS THE MOST EFFECTIVE WHEN RESEARCHERS WADE INTO THE POLICY COMMUNITY?

Historically, Americans have been intrigued by how expertise might be used to improve the way we govern ourselves, but little consensus has emerged on which approach should govern the efforts of knowledge brokers (Smith, 1991). The evidence is incomplete on whether social scientists have met with more success with advocacy or education in their policy work.

We cite three sources of data here, which are admittedly inconclusive yet nevertheless informative—the reflections of a researcher socialized as a basic scientist who, as fate would have it, unexpectedly ended up spending his career as an applied scientist; the experience of an organization that has been well served by the education approach but only after being poorly served by the advocacy approach; and a study of how the approach used by policy think tanks contributed to their success in bringing information and analysis to policymakers and journalists.

Reflections on a Life at the Crossroads of Research and Social Policy

Edward Zigler is an emeritus professor at Yale University and recipient of the American Psychological Association's highest award for Outstanding Lifetime Contributions to Psychology. Among his many contributions, Zigler served as one of the original planners of Head Start, was appointed by President Nixon as the first director of the U.S. Office of Child Development, and became chief of the U.S. Children's Bureau. Early in his career, when he received a call to join the Head Start Planning Committee, he was the youngest person to be invited and the only one without an applied background. He had been trained in what he termed a "scientist's science" in contrast to a "public science" (Zigler, 1998, p. 532). He had a traditional background in methodology, hypothesis testing, and theory building. Some of his mentors advised against accepting the Head Start job instead of a more prestigious job in basic science at this early and pivotal point in his career. He made the decision with "trepidation" (Zigler & Styfco, 2002) but ended up accepting the job. He reflected 25 years later on the wisdom of this decision:

> I certainly found that by trying to change the experiences that affect poor preschoolers, I gained a better grasp of the dynamics of human development. All told, I became a better scientist because of this very practical exercise. (p. 6)

At first, he found this new assignment daunting. Well socialized into the academic culture, he expected to be teaching college students in lecture halls and publishing research and theory in the traditional scientific outlets. Instead, his students were high-ranking policy officials who needed research distilled to bullet points on what was policy-relevant. He found policymakers to be eager learners who called him "Professor Zigler" and referred to his meetings with them as "lectures." He came to know them as dedicated public servants interested in what research could relay to help them reach better policy decisions: "Policymakers welcomed me as an interpreter and tried to act on what I taught them" (Zigler & Styfco, 2002, p. 13).

Zigler described many disappointments across his 44-year career, the biggest one being Nixon's veto of the 1971 Comprehensive Child Development Act. However, he also articulated many successes that he had a hand in. Zigler has been recognized for his many contributions to the long-term sustainability of Head Start; his tireless commitment to assessing the impact of Head Start, particularly its "sleeper effects"; his efforts to raise the quality of Head Start with the first set of truly enforceable child care standards; his proposal for infant care that eventually emerged from Congress as the 1993 Family and Medical Leave Act; and his role in establishing other innovative programs such as Home Start, the Child Development Associate program, and the Twenty-First Century (21C) Schools. His efforts benefited countless children and families across the country, while at the same time enriching scientific understanding of fields such as early childhood development, program intervention, and family support (Zigler & Styfco, 2002).

When asked to reflect on his remarkable career in policy, his response was informative. He focused not on *what* research he conveyed to policymakers but rather on *how* he did so:

> Thinking back, I attribute my success in having some influence over national social policies to my posture as an educator, not an advocate. As I learned over my time from planning Head Start to advising its administrators, developmentalists can accomplish much more by telling policymakers what we know and admitting what is not yet known, separating our facts from our opinions. I believe officials have listened to me over the years because they see me as a scholar, not as an advocate who has some other agenda. My only agenda, the one that has guided me throughout my career, is to serve the best interests of children and families. (Zigler & Styfco, 2002, p. 14)

Zigler's policy agenda parallels our earlier definition of advocacy with a small "a." Zigler brought the interests of children and families to the attention of policymakers but without lobbying for a particular policy option. Zigler (1998) believes that it is the role of scholars to use research to *inform* policy (similar to our definition of policy education) in contrast to advocates who use research to *shape* policy (similar to our definition of policy advocacy with a capital "A"). This approach guided his thinking and his actions as well. Many who have worked with him, including Wade Horn, assistant secretary for children and families in the U.S. Department of Health and Human Services in the George W. Bush administration, commended Zigler for his ability and willingness to move beyond partisan politics (Kersting, 2003).

An Organization's Transformation From Advocacy to Education

The Wisconsin Taxpayers Alliance (WISTAX) is a nonpartisan organization that state policymakers from all political perspectives often tell us is an authoritative voice for nonpartisan information on how Wisconsin government works, taxes, and spends. This organization originated as an offshoot of a meeting of Wisconsin business leaders convened in 1931 by Governor Philip F. La Follette. In response to their recommendation to form a statewide organization to study taxation and spending, WISTAX was established in 1932. Initially formed as an advocacy organization, WISTAX developed policy proposals for cutting taxes and curbing government spending, and worked to organize local groups of county-based, dues-paying members that supported their mission. This initial approach was abandoned when WISTAX reports lacked credibility among those who disagreed with their point of view and when members of their county organizations became involved in political contests.

In 1934, WISTAX reorganized under an education umbrella and, since then, has successfully built a nonpartisan reputation. WISTAX conducts objective research and provides policymakers and the public with accurate, unbiased information. For example, when we recently interviewed a number of Wisconsin policymakers about the usefulness of the broad array of newsletters they receive, the one newsletter that consistently received accolades from the left and right alike was a modest-looking, one-page, one-color newsletter issued by WISTAX.

This nonpartisan reputation is no accident, as the WISTAX Web site makes clear that it avoids any affiliations with other organizations and does not engage in lobbying, endorse candidates for public office, or take positions on issues. After its initial foray as an organization formed to advocate for specific causes, WISTAX picked itself up, brushed off any remnants of advocacy, and reincarnated itself with an education approach. This approach has better positioned the organization to achieve its goal of efficient, responsible government.

Policymakers' Use of Expertise From Public Policy Think Tanks

Public policy think tanks provide another window into our examination of different approaches for working with policymakers. Think tanks have grown in number and influence, quadrupling in size between 1970 and 1996 from fewer than 70 in the late 1960s to more than 300 by the mid-1990s. Think groups have also grown in variety, becoming increasingly diverse and often more ideologically driven and market-oriented (Rich, 2001). Because they vary substantially in their motives and modes of operation, these information outlets comprise a natural experiment of sorts, with some that seek to be a servant *of* the policymaking process and others that strive to impose a particular perspective *on* the policymaking process.

Andrew Rich (2001) conducted a study of a random sample of 66 public policy think tanks drawn from a sample of 200 nationally focused think tanks in 1996. He stratified them according to ideology (i.e., conservative, liberal, centrist, and no identifiable ideology) and location (i.e., inside or outside Washington, DC). Overall, 61% were based in Washington, DC, and the rest were situated elsewhere in the country. The think tanks were of all sizes and ideologies, with 30% that were centrist or of no identifiable ideology (e.g., the Brookings Institution and the Washington Center for China Studies), 29% conservative (e.g., the Heritage Foundation and the Center for Education Reform), and 17% liberal (e.g., Worldwatch Institute and the Council on Hemispheric Affairs). Market orientation was assessed by the intended audience, amount and proportion of resources devoted to promotion and marketing, and background of the staff.

Among the many findings of Rich's (2001) study, congressional staff and journalists rated think tanks as more credible if they were not market-oriented and of no identifiable ideology, compared to their market-oriented and ideological counterparts. Moreover, policy actors were able to discern these ideological orientations. Think tanks that were nonmarket-oriented and with a centrist or no identifiable ideology were more likely to be paired on congressional committee with others viewed as credible or authoritative, such as university researchers; in contrast, those that were more market-oriented more often testified with special interest groups. Also, when think tanks testified with other think tanks on congressional panels, they were most likely to appear with those that were like-minded; for instance, conservative think tanks were more likely to be paired with other conservative-leaning organizations, centrists with other centrists, and so forth.

When policymakers or the media needed authoritative sources of expertise, organizations with a centrist or apparent absence of ideology were sought out. Congressional staff and journalists most often turned to sources that offered the most careful research and neutral analysis, particularly when the source was located close at hand. However, one exception did emerge: When the purpose was to build political support for a particular idea such as in staged congressional hearings or on the editorial pages of newspapers, more aggressive and ideological sources of expertise were tapped.

Summary

In sum, the experiences of the public-policy-oriented individuals and organizations described above converge around the value of the education approach (a) for informing policy decisions and (b) for promulgating the attention, respect, and trust of those who make policy decisions or are in a position to influence them. This evidence and these experiences suggest that observers may overestimate the potential of the advocacy approach for working with policymakers and, at the same time, underestimate the power of the education approach. This assertion raises the compelling question of why the education approach carries the cachet it does in policymaking, the topic that we turn to next.

WHY IS THE EDUCATION APPROACH EFFECTIVE?

A scan of the literature identifies several possible reasons for the effectiveness of the education approach stemming from the cultures that policymakers and researchers are socialized into and operate within, its affinity with the political nature of the policymaking process itself, and its consistency with the information needs of policymakers in a modern democratic society.

Responsiveness to What Policymakers Say They Need

What policymakers need, according to a psychologist elected to Congress, is not more information but more objective and valid input (Strickland, 1996). From our experience, particularly with the Family Impact Seminars and WELPAN, a hunger for objective information does exist. Tom recalls the last time he spoke before a state legislative committee on welfare reform. Listening to speaker after speaker provide largely agenda-driven opinion, subjective analysis, and selected evidence in entirely predictable presentations, he wondered how the committee members managed to maintain their sanity. After giving what he hoped was a balanced presentation, several legislators expressed their thanks for someone who was there to *inform* rather than *influence* the committee.

In a recent study of state legislative service agencies, John Hird (2005) surveyed 773 legislators in 19 states (response rate = 25%). In an institutional culture that legislators see as highly politicized, almost 9 in 10 (88%) preferred facts and objective analysis with the political decisions being left to them—a preference about as popular as free beer or mom's apple pie. Policymakers express this penchant for objective information in their own words in testimonials about the Family Impact Seminars. For example, one state agency official likened seminar information to a "breath of fresh air." A conservative Republican legislator commended the approach used by the Seminars: "[The] ability to present and prepare unbiased research based on objective analysis and without political taint is truly refreshing." Qualities of information that are expected and as natural as the air we breathe in the research culture are so unexpected and unnatural in the policy culture that they are described as *refreshing* and *a breath of fresh air*.

Those who work closely with policymakers also see the valuable role that objective information can play in the policy culture. Following a Family Impact Seminar for Wisconsin policymakers on health care coverage, an analyst from a nonpartisan legislative service agency wrote the following comment on an anonymous evaluation: "The fact that the room was full—a great sign that the topic is timely. Interest in objective information is high." An aide working in the office of a state legislator wrote the following positive comment regarding a recent seminar on prisoner reentry: "Objectivity—research was presented in a way that speaks to reality, which transcends political lines." The value of evidence was evident in federal policymaking as well according to Ruby Takanishi, president of the Foundation for Child Development. When she was awarded a Congressional Fellowship early in her career, she found herself on the receiving end of lobbying. The limits of moral arguments quickly became apparent to her.

Why do policymakers and those who work with them value objective information in a policy culture overly crowded with information? A poverty researcher explained the richness of objective information and why it, like cream, rises to the top of policymakers' preferences:

> Policymakers are desperate for honest brokers. That sounds funny because they have access on the Web and Internet to tons of data, but what they need is information, not just data and not just research reports. They really need people who can bring good information to them in a dispassionate way that does not look agenda-driven. If they smell an agenda, they will be instantly suspicious. Now sometimes that agenda will conform to their prior values and you may get a foot in the door, but that's not serving them real well.

In the limited research available, policymakers and decision makers alike rank information that is unbiased as one of the top three qualities of research that make it useful in their jobs from a list of 29 characteristics in the Weiss and Bucuvalas (1980) study and 19 characteristics in Karen's exploratory study (see Chapter 2). Policymakers are always on guard wondering which experts can be trusted and which are disingenuously cloaking themselves in the "authority of science" (Bimber, 1996, p. 12).

In a curious sort of way, objective information is also valued for reasons of political expediency. Analysis that is nonpartisan may be more convincing to the public as a rationale for action and also may broaden its appeal to and support from a wider spectrum of policymakers. As an example, the Congressional Budget Office (CBO) has used an approach much like the education approach discussed here. CBO analysts first identify the range of competing policy proposals and the available evidence for each. Policymakers can use this type of analysis for a wide range of purposes—to support their own position, to thwart opposing positions, and, when they are moved to change their position, to choose wisely among the remaining alternatives (Weiss, 1987b).

Consistency With Researchers' Socialization in the Scientific Method

The education approach is consistent with the scientific method, which lies at the very core of the research culture. Advocacy often entails making a case on one side of an issue, whereas the scientific method embodies an evenhanded consideration of facts on all sides of an issue. Interestingly, some of the most well-received Family Impact Seminars presentations have been made by researchers who have presented findings that they acknowledge forthrightly have surprised them by contradicting their initial hypotheses. Policymakers' enthusiasm for the Seminars and for WELPAN-type networks may be based, in part, on the novelty of being exposed to input grounded in sound research methods rather than the more fungible, idiosyncratic factors sometimes employed in the policy culture.

Socialization in the scientific method sometimes brings with it an enthusiasm for basing policy decisions on the best available knowledge rather than the "junk science" sometimes provided by those with a political agenda or a personal stake in the outcome (Bimber, 1996). Yet research is seldom comprehensive and definitive enough to serve as the sole determinant of a policy decision. As an example, many school districts face the issue of whether preschoolers are entering kindergarten ready to learn. In these situations, policymakers often look for facts to determine whether school readiness is a problem. Imagine a scenario where a local school district commissions a study that finds one third of 5-year-olds in the district are not school-ready. Policymakers and their constituents may have legitimate disagreements on whether this "fact" is correct. Questions arise on what the appropriate benchmarks of school readiness are and how well researchers are able to measure them.

Reasonable people can also disagree about the interpretation of this fact. For example, if it is accepted as true that one third of the 5-year-olds are not school ready, is this number small or large? If large, is it important enough to warrant a public investment of tax dollars?

Even in situations where the facts lead to only one interpretation—that taxes should be used to help ensure that children enter school ready to learn—different value orientations may lead to different policy responses. Citizens can legitimately disagree about whether this is an issue that is best handled in the privacy of the family or whether there should be a broad-based community response. Would it be best to fund education programs to involve parents in the academic success of their offspring, which conceivably could benefit the target child and his or her siblings as well? Or would it be better to invest in a community-wide response such as 4-year-old kindergarten that may be broader in its reach and more consistent in its impact?

Even when science can provide evidence-based data on parent education programs or 4-year-old kindergarten, a study cannot provide the value judgments about which program is the most politically feasible and more in keeping with local priorities and values. A Minnesota state legislator articulated the importance that values play in policy decisions, particularly on hot-button issues such as abortion or the right to die:

> For me, those are issues that I have some very strong feelings about. … It doesn't matter what my party says, you know, I have some very strong opinions that are based on my sense of the world. … Some issues that are defined as health care issues are, I would say, for me sort of bottom line, personal, ethical or conscience decisions. … And so while I listen to all sides and read things, that will be what will decide my decision on some of those things. (cited in Kerschner & Cohen, 2002, p. 121)

In sum, the weight of evidence occasionally may fall on the side of one particular policy option; however, for the vast majority of issues, the facts are not all known, they can be interpreted in more than one way, and one's value system may lead one to favor one policy alternative over another. Even the most rigorous, reliable, and challenge-proof data cannot supply indisputable facts, the only correct interpretations, and ideal value judgments (Barrows, 1994).

For most issues, education is the paragon of approaches for researchers because they have not been trained in "the unscientific art of advocacy" (Barrows, 1994, p. 11) that entails believing strongly and unwaveringly in a single policy proposal. To the contrary, they have been socialized by the scientific method to be skeptical and open to alternative explanations, which makes it more difficult to be a true believer in one optimal policy response (Takanishi, 2002).

Fundamental to a Long-Term Commitment to Working With Policymakers

The education approach may be more effective for anyone who is making a long-term commitment to working with a number of policymakers on a range of issues. In a political process built on making decisions through debate and compromise, issues do not rise on the public radar screen unless there are differences of opinion. Taking sides on an issue, as advocates do, can undermine future credibility with the opposing interests. Each stance may alienate more individuals or groups, which over time could limit a person's ability to build the credibility and form the political alliances on which successful policy work depends (Barrows, 1994).

Approaching policy work as an educator indicates a willingness to be useful for all political parties and helps ensure one's effectiveness regardless of which party is in control. For example, since we have been conducting seminars in Wisconsin, the governor's office has changed party, and the majority in the Assembly and the Senate has shifted from one party to the other and back again.

This commitment to working with policymakers irrespective of party or political perspective is particularly important for those who work for public institutions. Professor Dave Riley, an employee of the tax-supported University of Wisconsin–Madison, knows this firsthand:

> You have to be neutral. You better be able to talk to any politician who wants your advice and be able to communicate that to them, especially if you work for a public institution like I do. You are a public professor. That means you work for everybody in the public, not just those whose political beliefs you agree with … you have to have a willingness to do that.

When tax-supported employees are perceived as advocating for a particular position, it can backfire. The consequences are not always as transparent as they were when a Cooperative Extension community development agent in the 1970s was conducting a policy education program in his county on a controversial land-use issue. A proposed four-lane highway was deemed to be beneficial for the county's depressed economy. However, it would be detrimental for many farmers whose family farms would be torn asunder and whose fertile fields would be paved under. The county agent tried to approach the highway issue as an evenhanded educator laying out the various policy options and the potential consequences of each, but his personal support of the highway project became known in the course of the program. This gave the impression that he was an advocate dressed up in educator's clothing. Karen will never forget an irate farmer coming to the office the next morning complaining about the way the program was handled and threatening to eliminate the Extension agent's job. When this agent retired, the position was eliminated. It took more than a generation to restore it.

The approach knowledge producers choose to use also affects how policymakers view research and researchers. For example, when scientists approach policymaking as an advocate, it can raise questions about the objectivity of research. The mystique of the scientist stems, in part, from this training in the scientific method that enables one to remain dispassionate and objective in the midst of the political fray. If scientists become involved in advocacy, it raises questions in the minds of policymakers about the trustworthiness of the research messengers: Are they really dispassionate scientists, or are they at heart nothing more than "hired guns"? Are they reporting the real raw data, or do they "cook" the numbers and massage the message to validate their personal views or the political predilections of their employers or funders (Smith, 1991)? Almost instinctively, when reading about new "science" that contradicts the existing consensus on controversial topics such as global warming, policymakers immediately look to see who supported the work or with whom the messenger is institutionally located. These are clues as to whether he or she, along with the "evidence," can be trusted.

The Ability to Facilitate Consensus Building

Policy often emerges from conversation, compromise, and consensus building among divergent views. Building bridges across these diverse perspectives is more easily accomplished by educators and organizations without a partisan agenda who are respected by those on all sides of an issue. A liberal Democratic legislator explained that she serves on the board of a child and family advocacy organization. In her words, even though this organization "has strong, solid research with a spotless record," it is "seen as left-leaning" and is "automatically written off" by many of her colleagues. In her work on the Family Impact Seminars, Karen has seen how a reputation as an impartial arbiter can bring together some of the state's most liberal and most conservative legislators. In the policy culture, if a liberal group sponsors a meeting or issues a report, only the liberal-leaning legislators pay attention, and when a conservative group is the source, it is tracked only by those with conservative credentials. This ability to bring together policymakers who do not always see eye to eye on issues is unusual, according to former Wisconsin legislator Daniel Vrakas, who chaired the Assembly Republican caucus:

> One of the things I've noticed over the years about the Seminars is that sometimes you have some of the most diverse legislators that actually want to tackle some of these problems that the Family Impact Seminars has presented on, and I find that tremendously interesting.

In fact, these opportunities are so out of the ordinary that when asked what was best about a 2005 Family Impact Seminar on health care quality, one anonymous state legislator scrawled on the evaluation form that it was a "bi-partisan legislative event."

At a recent seminar, the attendees included policymakers from all political persuasions—a legislator who introduced a single-payer health plan, the sponsor of a bill allowing teachers to carry guns to school, the representative who cast the deciding vote against allowing citizens to carry concealed weapons, and a legislator widely recognized as one of the most vocal opponents of the university. When these disparate legislators come together and when they hear authoritative information that is well respected on both sides of the aisle, it does not guarantee that consensus will occur, but it does provide a forum for discussing issues across party lines and for seeking common ground where it exists. A Democratic senator explained how the iron curtain of ideology can sometimes yield when open discussion occurs:

> Well, do you remember that Family Impact Seminar when such and such presenter talked about this and, you know, we are doing just what he told us not to do or this is … congruent with what that particular presentation was. And because we're able to engage in discussion on strictly a policy matter as opposed to sort of an ideological way … I think we've been able to discuss the issues in a more responsible way and actually come to more responsible conclusions as a result.

These opportunities may be so valuable today not because there is not enough information but ironically because there is too much. Policy analysis has become a growth industry (Dunn, 1994) that has produced a glut of information—the sheer volume and complexity of which has overwhelmed even the most conscientious policymakers, who lack the staff and time to keep informed on all the issues that confront them. As observed by a member of a National Academy of Sciences panel,

> Washington, DC, … is now a town that is built around inertia because [for] anyone who advances a position, there are a set of countervailing forces out there … think tanks … policy analysis organizations, advocacy organizations, whatever, some of which are purporting to be objective, but they're not. … In the old days … [when] an issue would come up, the government would produce a white paper, and this would be the distillation of the best thought on this topic. There would be today a thousand white papers or their equivalent on any particular issue if it was controversial and meaningful. And each of those white papers would have its own outlets and ways of diffusing out into the public conscious. … So what decision makers really need now is a way to find safety in a place, kind of a private space, in which they really can think about things and get good information that's given to them in a reasonable way because the rest of their world is just really crowded.

A society as good as ours is at marshalling data on all sides of an issue needs to become equally as good at providing venues to "encourage that continual and fearless sifting and winnowing by which alone the truth can be found" (taken from an 1894 report of the University of Wisconsin–Madison Board of Regents, as cited in Herfurth, 1949).

Capacity to Counteract Superficial Media Analysis

The approach that knowledge brokers use to provide research and analysis to policymakers cannot be considered in isolation from the modern industrialized society in which it occurs. The media industry floods the marketplace with information, providing widespread access to Americans in all walks of life. For example, in 2000, 98% of households had a TV (Television Set Ownership, n.d.), 99% of households had a radio (U.S. Census Bureau, 2006), and 53% of households received a newspaper, a percentage that has declined from 100% saturation in the 1970s as newspapers have become accessible online and other media have become more widely available ("Newspaper," 2008). In 2005, 97 million adult Internet users sought news online (Bergman, 2006), and by 2007, 73% of all U.S. households had computers (Nielsen Media Research, 2007). The appeal of the media is that it allows policymakers and policy pundits to efficiently reach large audiences with a consistent message, but the downside is that the medium may shape the message, as McLuhan and Watson (1970) warned almost four decades ago.

The media creates a policy environment "open to spin," according to candidate and now-president Barack Obama (2006). Reporters are socialized to get the facts so they can back up what is written or aired as being fair and objective. Under the constant pressure of tight deadlines and the continual competition for ratings and market share, one convenient way to appear objective is to publish the talking points of each side with little or no attempt to sort out which is closer to the truth. So what happens is that the Bush White House releases its deficit projections. This is followed by a reaction from a liberal analyst who questions the numbers and a conservative analyst who swears they are right on the mark (Obama, 2006). Notably absent is information that may be the most credible—those in the center with no ideological axe to grind (Rich, 2001). This point–counterpoint type of journalism often overplays the conflict between the parties and underplays any way to convey which perspective is closer to the truth.

In the absence of an authoritative figure like Walter Cronkite or Edward R. Murrow, politicians like Barack Obama realize that there is no great reward in store for those who tell the truth. In fact, truth telling may leave one more open to attack, especially when the truth is complicated and less amenable to the 30-second sound bite:

> Facts alone can't always settle our political disputes. Our views on abortion aren't determined by the science of fetal development, and our judgment on whether and when to pull troops out of Iraq must necessarily be based on probabilities. But sometimes there are more accurate and less accurate answers; sometimes there are facts that cannot be spun, just as an argument about whether it's raining can usually be settled by stepping outside. The absence of even rough agreement on the facts puts every opinion on equal footing and therefore eliminates the basis for thoughtful compromise. It rewards not those who are right, but those ... who can make their arguments most loudly, most

244 EVIDENCE-BASED POLICYMAKING

frequently, most obstinately, and with the best backdrop. … The politician may still, as a matter of personal integrity, insist on telling the truth as he sees it. But he does so knowing that whether he believes in his positions matters less than whether he looks like he believes; that straight talk counts less than whether it sounds straight on TV. (Obama, 2006, pp. 127–128)

Congressman Robert F. Bennett, a Republican senator representing the state of Utah, makes a similar observation based on his experience interacting with both policymakers and the press. He characterizes the speeches that he hears in the Senate as being "political sloganeering." Similarly, op-ed pieces written by political reporters are "very compelling and very easy to understand" but oftentimes "wrong" (Bennett, 1997, p. 1). He provides this compelling story about how expertise is needed to tackle thorny problems such as identifying what steps it would take to stimulate the U.S. economy:

The chief executive officer of the company … calls his people together and says to them, "We have a deficit in this company of about $1 million a month. If we cannot solve that deficit problem, we will go bankrupt. What can we do to deal with a deficit of $1 million a month?"

His first expert steps up and says, "Mr. Chairman, I have examined this issue very carefully, and I can tell you what it is we need to do. Without question, we can solve our problem if we simply raise our prices. We are selling $50 million a month worth of our products. So if we raise our prices two and a half percent, we will make enough money to cover our $1 million a month deficit. Case closed. All you need to do is to raise your prices."

The next expert stands up and says, "Mr. Chairman, raising prices is absolutely the worst thing you could do. I know the answer to our problem. We must cut prices. Our problem is that our competition is cutting into our market share. We are losing sales right and left because our prices are too high. If we simply cut our prices by 5 percent across the board, the increased volume will do two things for us. Number one, our total sales will go up; and number two, our cost of sales will come down as we get economies to spread over a larger number of units. So I disagree absolutely with the first expert. He says raise prices, and I say cut prices."

Then the third expert stands up and addresses the chairman in our boardroom, and he says, "No, they are both wrong. The price structure is just fine. What we must do is spend more money on plants and equipment. Our factory is outmoded; our costs are enormously high in the factory. If we spend another $50 million on the factory and retooling and new equipment, we will cut our overall cost of manufacturing by more than $1 million a month."

When he sits down, the fourth expert stands up, and she says to the chairman of the board, "Mr. Chairman, they are all wrong. We do not need to raise prices or cut prices. We certainly do not need to increase spending. All we need to do is cut spending, cut the overhead. Our overhead is running about $11 million a month, and if we cut it 10 percent that would give us the $1 million a month we need to come to a break-even position."

So there sits the chairman of the board. He has four groups advising him. The four groups are saying to him, "Raise prices. Cut prices. Increase spending. Cut spending." He thanks them all for their efforts. They leave. He is there, left alone with an assistant who does not have a great deal of experience in the business.

The assistant looks at the chairman of the board and says to him, "OK, you have four options. Which one are you going to take?" Because we are dealing with a wise chairman who has a great deal of experience in the free market system, he smiles at his assistant and says, "All four."

When you manage a business that is constantly changing from day to day, as every business is, you cannot put it in a static pattern, and then leave it forever. You have some products that are not price-sensitive, and you can raise the price and thereby increase your margins without having any punishment in the marketplace. You have some other products that are overpriced, or need a lower price in order to increase their hold on the market, so you cut the prices on those products. You have some increased spending needs for plants and equipment, research and development; it is the future of your business that depends on your increased spending in those areas. Finally, of course, you have areas where you have to cut spending.

In government terms, what we are saying with this pattern is that there are some areas where you would cut taxes, some areas where you would raise taxes, some areas where you would cut spending, and some areas where you would raise spending.

It is not the simple either/or circumstance. … It is a very challenging management problem … of trying to figure out how to … make the right kind of investments for the future. (pp. 2–3)

Both these politicians, one Democrat and one Republican, agree that expertise is needed if society has any hope of solving the complex problems that confront and confound it. Both agree that an impartial arbiter may be needed to help sort out competing claims, each containing elements of truth. Bennett cited the example of the perennial debate about which president was responsible for the largest tax increase in U.S. history. Predictably, the Republicans point a finger at Bill Clinton, and the Democrats accuse Ronald Reagan. Who is right? If the measuring stick is nominal dollars, the Clinton tax increase was the largest in history, but if the metric is constant dollars, adjusted for inflation, then the tax increase pushed through by Reagan was the largest (Thompson & Bennet, 1997). In the current environment of fast-food journalism, the educator can play an important role in helping policymakers, the press, and a confused public sort through these dueling versions of the truth.

Clearly, educators can never claim to speak only truth, but they can provide standards for judging what is more and less accurate. The niche that the educator can fill is reminiscent of a story told by the late senator Daniel Patrick Moynihan when he was on the verge of winning a heated argument with a colleague. In frustration, the other senator blurted out,

"Well, you may disagree with me, Pat, but I'm entitled to my own opinion."
To which Moynihan frostily replied, "You are entitled to your own opinion but you are not entitled to your own facts." (cited in Obama, 2006, p. 126)

Demonstrates a Personal Commitment to the Democratic Principles Upon Which the Country Was Founded

For researchers, who are experts on an issue, using the dispassionate education approach in policy work seems like an unnatural act. Upon reflection, however, it is consistent with the two principles upon which our democracy was founded and still functions today—democratic decision making and enlightened self-interest.

The elaborate machinery of our democracy—the Bill of Rights, the built-in system of checks and balances, federalism, the separation of powers—was designed to make policymaking a deliberative process with decisions arrived at through debate and compromise in the public arena among those elected to represent diverse interests (Flinchbaugh, 1988; Obama, 2006). Thus, in a pluralistic society such as ours, there is "no single public interest and no optimal policy choice" but rather multiple interests represented by policymakers with a range of political and value perspectives (Barrows, 1994, p. 3). Policymakers are elected to represent the views of their constituents and can be removed from office if they fail to adequately do so.

The educator's role is to provide policymakers with the best available research and analysis of the problem, available policy alternatives, and consequences of each. The ultimate decision of which alternative is most desirable is left to policymakers elected to make these value judgments. The difficult task of the educator is to refrain from making personal value judgments about what policy alternative is most desirable, which takes a real commitment to democratic decision making. Professor Dave Riley described the conflict many researchers face when they must squelch the attitudes and beliefs that fueled their interest in policy work in the first place:

> The most important attitude or belief is kind of a paradox. And that is, you get into this kind of work if you're interested in policy. And you're usually interested in policy because you have some strong ideas about it, you're motivated. But in order to be successful at it, I think you have to have a stronger commitment to democracy than to your own political beliefs. And by that I mean, you have to be committed to the idea that you might tell them everything that your field knows and they might make a decision different than yours, because they have different values than you. They were elected and you weren't, and you have to be okay with that. You have to say to yourself, "I did my job. I told them what our science knows. It's not my job to make the decision. I'm happy that democracy works even when it makes decisions other than my own." And so it takes this real fundamental commitment to democracy, which is the opposite from a commitment to your own political ideas, and yet it's your own political ideas that probably got you interested in the first place.
>
> That's not easy. A lot of faculty cannot do that. A lot of faculty ... only understand the advocate role. And I'm talking about something very different from the advocate role. I'm talking about a role where you don't pretend that you are the one to make the decision. You're just the fair broker of information who can work with either political party and tell them what we know. They get to make up their own minds, and, in fact, I like to think of democracy as being a form of government that ensures that each of us is allowed to make our own mistakes.

The Founding Fathers believed that the democratic process is a better form of making decisions than "administrative fiat or the dictates of a single individual" (Barrows, 1994, p. 4). For example, the United States is one of the only countries in the world without a specific mention of the word *family* in its constitution. This silence on families was not accidental, but a deliberate attempt by the Founding Fathers to avoid a patronage system based on lineage or wealth as existed in the English monarchy against which they were rebelling (Rice, 1977). One common impulse of the Founders is a rejection of all forms of absolute authority, whether it be family lineage or the king, theocrat, oligarch, dictator, or, we would add, expert:

> It's not just absolute power that the founders sought to prevent. Implicit in its structure, in the very idea of ordered liberty, was a rejection of absolute truth, the infallibility of any idea or ideology or theology or "ism," any tyrannical consistency that might lock future generations into a single, unalterable course, or drive both majorities and minorities into the cruelties of the Inquisition, the pogrom, the gulag, or the jihad. (Obama, 2006, p. 93)

The education approach makes sense in a democratic system where there is no single source that is the ultimate authority and where the knowledge producer is not considered "all-wise":

> Their creative minds and imaginations may lead to research pregnant with potential for fundamental social change, and their recommendations may occasionally urge basic reforms in the institutions of society. But a democratic society, through its duly constituted representatives, has a say about its destiny. It has no more obligation to accept the data and dicta of social scientists than it does to listen to shamans, astrologers, or television commentators. (Weiss, 1978, p. 61)

The education approach is also aligned with the democratic principle of enlightened self-interest. People, if given good information, will make the right decision most of the time. Researchers must restrain their passion and rest assured that the democratic process works for the patient and persistent. Using the education approach takes both a sense of hubris about how well democracy works and a sense of humility about what research and the researcher can contribute.

SOME PROMINENT OBJECTIONS TO THE EDUCATION APPROACH

Critics of the education approach question both the objectivity of research, no matter how carefully it is generated, and the political neutrality of policy education, no matter how dispassionately it is disseminated. We address below four questions we are frequently asked.

First, is science value-free? Few would argue that science is wholly objective. To borrow a phrase from Nagel (1986), scientists are unable to climb out of their own mind. Yet Sternberg and Grigorenko (2002) warned against jumping to the conclusion that science is wholly relative:

> We think it is dangerous to lapse into believing as do some people ... that because all of science is value laden, it is all relative anyway. Science is unique among approaches to knowledge in that it is self-correcting. Through strong empirical research, good theories gain support and bad theories sow the seeds of their own destruction. (p. 1130)

Because research is self-correcting, it is a form of evidence that is more likely to result in truth. Finding truth is what policymakers repeatedly tell us is what they are seeking. Even though policymakers may be unable to fully articulate it, this self-correcting feature of research may be one reason they value it.

Second, is objective, bias-free policy education ever possible? Of course not. Along the knowledge-translation continuum, there are ample opportunities to exercise discretion, such as the choice of topics to target, framing of issues, explanation of ambiguous data, and presentation of results (Bimber, 1996). Because complete objectivity is not humanly possible, critics question the legitimacy of even striving to be objective, which policy educators liken to throwing out the baby with the bathwater. Educators, however, do not reject the ideal of objectivity, as is fashionable in some intellectual circles, just as the ideal of justice is not abandoned because it cannot be perfectly attained (Glenn, 1993). In the political culture where most information comes with a direction, efforts that conscientiously aim to be objective and unbiased are usually recognized and respected for striving to rise above the politics (Barrows, 1994).

The objectivity ratings of the Wisconsin Family Impact Seminars are informative in this regard. Despite attracting some of the state's most liberal and most conservative legislators, the objectivity rating of the Seminars on a scale of 1 (*poor*) to 5 (*excellent*) has never dipped below 4 for any of the 26 seminars (since we have been collecting objectivity data).

Third, if education is as objective and unbiased as possible, does that mean it is a politically neutral act? No policy effort is ever politically neutral. Providing information on an issue, no matter how objectively, favors some groups over others. For example, even perfectly objective information on a tax referendum favors passage, because people who are informed are more apt to vote "yes" than their uninformed counterparts (Barrows, 1994). Policy education is inevitably more advantageous to individuals and groups who are less informed than to those who are more knowledgeable. In some situations, providing objective education on an issue builds understanding of different points of view, which can foster compromise and consensus. Thus, policy educators strive for objectivity, fully recognizing that complete objectivity is never possible and that, even if it were, education is not a politically neutral act (Barrows, 1994).

Fourth, is it possible to work with policymakers as both an advocate and an educator? Serving in both roles is difficult and perhaps impossible. Once you cross the line from education to advocacy, policymakers are likely to remember your advocacy stance (after all, they operate in a political environment that keeps track of such things) and to view all information from you as tainted and potentially biased. Once you have written an op-ed piece, it may not be possible to go back to being an educator. It is hard to unring the bell.

As an example, a Cooperative Extension agent in a small, rural county advocated for the use of federal funds to establish a local child care center. This advocacy effort made it literally impossible for her to later serve as an educator on policy alternatives to help employed parents consider how to best care for their children. No matter how reliable the research and how objective her presentation of child care alternatives, the community knew that she once supported child care centers. Using both approaches is difficult because it requires you to be upfront as to whether you are wearing the hat of an advocate or that of the educator. The danger, of course, is being accused of cherry-picking the data and disguising an advocacy effort under the mantle of education, which would destroy your credibility. Effectiveness as an educator rests on credibility and a nonpartisan reputation.

HOW CAN EDUCATORS ESTABLISH AND MAINTAIN A NONPARTISAN REPUTATION?

Attaining credibility as an objective educator does not come easily. It takes conscious effort on several fronts. For example, to attain and maintain the objective and nonpartisan reputation of the Family Impact Seminars, Karen has established a balanced legislative advisory committee that includes an equal number of Democrats and Republicans and, within the parties, a range of those considered liberal, moderate, or conservative. In the early days of the Seminars, she was criticized for not having any "real Republicans," which in "policy speak" meant conservative Republicans. This bipartisan committee of policymakers is used to identify seminar topics that have support from both sides of the aisle, so we do not inadvertently play into a partisan political agenda. We consider the topics at hand carefully, trying to run them through the filter of how a conservative or liberal might view them. To work effectively with policymakers, Jere Bauer Jr., a 22-year analyst in the nonpartisan Wisconsin Legislative Fiscal Bureau, relayed that it is fundamentally important to remember that policymaking is political:

> One of the pieces of advice that I would have, and this gets to the nonpartisan nature, is to understand the partisan nature of the legislature that you're going into. Because if you go into a legislature, and you think you're being nonpartisan, and [*spreads his hands far apart*] covering the issues here and here [*points to two points close to his left hand*], but really, this is the scope of what you're looking at [*again spreads his hands far apart*], you're going to be considered partisan, no matter if the word in front of your name is nonpartisan. You have to, absolutely have to, understand that partisan nature of the legislature. And understand the scope of the issue, whatever the issue is.

Karen screens seminar speakers carefully to check for a partisan reputation, any authorship of op-ed articles, and a record of working only for Democratic or Republican administrations. The Seminars strive to present a range of policy options that are currently being debated or discussed on both sides of the aisle.

To establish a safe, nonpartisan environment that fosters the seeking of common ground, we do not invite lobbyists or the media to the seminars.

On a personal level, Karen has found it difficult to separate her actions as a private citizen from her role as a public policy educator. She has made a conscious decision to refrain from any political activity off the job that might interfere with the nonpartisan reputation that she has meticulously built on the job. For example, she avoids personal campaigning that might align her with a particular candidate or political party—no bumper stickers, yard signs, or campaign donations. At the university level, she is firm (some would say rigid) about avoiding any involvement in what she calls "budget boosterism." She has turned down invitations to participate in Lobby Days to support the university budget, refused requests from the chancellor for the names of legislators who attend Seminar events, and declined publicity for awards to the Seminars for fear that the program would come to the attention of lobbyists and the media.

The trade-offs Karen has made may seem drastic to some and draconian to others, but she believes they are well worth it. Maintaining credibility as an educator requires an objective, unbiased reputation. Such a reputation takes constant tending but, once earned, is golden and allows effective policy work over time and across issues with policymakers of all perspectives and political persuasions.

The facilitators of WELPAN also took pains to eliminate ideology and partisanship from the network's proceedings, even though state executive agency officials tend to be somewhat less driven by values than politicians are. The members made all important decisions: what topics to deal with, what resource people to invite in, even who could sit around their table as they discussed policy and programmatic options and directions. Nothing was published in WELPAN's name unless all members signed off first. It was this sense of objectivity that members prized, continuously reporting that this was a safe place where they could vet ideas and information absent pressure and lobbying.

SUMMARY

This chapter moved beyond the "whats" of bringing evidence to bear on public policy to the "hows" of doing so. We examined examples of individuals, organizations, and think tanks with enviable records of working with policymakers. We have come to the conclusion, surprising to many, that public policy education, which is deliberately dispassionate in its approach, has proved disproportionately powerful in its effect. We attribute this counterintuitive claim to a number of factors residing in the research and policymaking cultures, the nature of the policymaking process itself, and the larger context in which research is used in modern democracies. In particular, we believe that the objective, nonpartisan information that is part and parcel of the education approach is prized (a) in a policy culture where the vast majority of information comes with a direction and (b) in a research culture where scientists are trained to be skeptics who weigh the facts on all sides of an issue.

The education approach seems best aligned with a political process where long-term effectiveness requires (a) working with a number of policymakers on a range of issues and (b) building consensus by bringing together policymakers from opposing parties and perspectives. In particular, the education approach is effective in a modern society in which the media relies on a point–counterpoint type of journalism that does little to sort out the truth. Finally, it is consistent with the principles on which democracies are founded—that policy decisions are made not by experts, but rather by policymakers elected to represent the values and views of their constituents and who will make the right decisions most of the time if given good information. Advice on operationalizing the education approach is outlined in Key Concepts 10.1.

Key Concepts 10.1   Operationalizing the Education Approach

- Aim to inform policymakers rather than influence them.
- Tell policymakers what is known and what is not yet known, always separating fact from opinion (Zigler & Styfco, 2002).
- Help sort out competing claims by providing standards for judging what is more and less accurate.
- Strive to be a fair broker of information who can work with either political party.
- Provide private, safe venues for policymakers to receive and reflect on relevant evidence-based information.

Because education and advocacy are new to many of our readers, we intentionally portrayed them as black-and-white approaches that are quite distinct from each other. In accord with Ben Hunt, we believe that when learning something new, "it is almost impossible not to absolutize it in some way" (as cited in Doherty, 1995, p. 165). In reality, however, the distinctions are not this clear-cut, and the two approaches can overlap to some extent. For example, the policy educator can never be totally objective, and the most effective advocates often alert policymakers to the downsides of their positions. As explained by a seven-term state legislator, "I know the best lobbyists that come into my office are the people that educate me about an issue."

At the Family Impact Seminars, it is true that we advocate for families in the small "a" sense by raising the perspective of an underrepresented group that has little voice in the arena of policymaking. However, we cannot be accused of advocating with a capital "A" because we do not present family solutions to social problems as the only or the best alternatives, but rather as one of many competing political responses. Our mission is to raise questions rather than give answers about whether families are involved in the problem, whether they should be involved in the solution, and whether family policies are more effective than those that focus on individuals.

Such subtleties are salient in ideologically sensitive settings where there should be "no confusion between research and advocacy" (Rabb & Winstead, 2003, p. 36). In practice, it is seductive to mix the two approaches, a temptation that should be actively resisted. In the words of Breckler, we must draw a line in the sand between science and politics and not cross it:

If we want to play the role of scientists, then we need to keep our own politics out of it. If we want to express our political ideology, then we must do so without the pretense of offering objective scientific evidence. (2006, p. 22)[1]

These thoughts are not meant to be the final word. They are proposed with a sense of confidence of their consistency with our experience and the experience of others. Yet empirical evidence on how evidence is used in policymaking is surprisingly slim (Nutley, Walter, & Davies, 2007), as is evidence on the effectiveness of policy education. Generating evidence on efforts to disseminate evidence to policymakers is a consuming passion of the organizers of the Family Impact Seminars. In Chapter 11, we provide some lessons that we have learned over the past 16 years.

ENDNOTE

1. Copyright 2006 by the American Psychological Association. Adapted with permission. The official citation that should be used in referencing this material is Breckler, S. J. (2006) Crossing the Line. *Monitor on Psychology, 37*(11), 22. No further reproduction or distribution is permitted without written permission from the American Psychological Association.

11

Generating Evidence on Disseminating Evidence to Policymakers

KAREN BOGENSCHNEIDER, HEIDI NORMANDIN, ESTHER
ONAGA, SALLY BOWMAN, and SHELLEY M. MACDERMID

Directors of the Family Impact Seminars in Wisconsin,
Michigan, Oregon, and Indiana

We should be on our guard not to overestimate science and scientific methods when it is a question of human problems; and we should not assume that
experts are the only ones who have a right to express themselves on questions
affecting the organization of human society.

—**Albert Einstein (1949)**

The current lack of evidence about the impact of research on policy and practice
outcomes reflects more an absence of evidence rather than evidence of absence.

—**Sandra Nutley, Isabel Walter, and Huw Davies (2007, p. 3)**

Over the past 20 to 40 years, calls for evidence-based policy and practice
have become so commonplace in North America, Europe, and other
developed countries that Aletha Huston characterized them as "routine"
in her 2007 presidential address to the Society for Research in Child Development
(2008, p. 9). Take, for instance, the 2002 No Child Left Behind law that mentioned "scientifically based research" 111 times. Like Huston, we are taken with
how quickly the lexicon of evidence-based policy appears to have caught on with
policymakers. Consider the enthusiasm expressed by Republican senator Carol
Roessler, a 25-year veteran of the Wisconsin legislature, about passing policies and
enacting programs that are evidence based:

> The legislature absolutely more and more is looking for outcome-based, evidence-based information. Not simply opinions. We are looking for the facts, and we are looking to support programs that have effective outcomes and that have a proven track record and, again, are evidence-based. I know that that's something that I have used in terms of information to support legislative initiatives that I have presented and passed. And that I think has been, in probably the last 3 to 4 years, a greater concentration on what are the definitive outcomes, how do we know this works, and elimination of programs that don't have good outcomes.

Yet the irony of the current state of affairs deserves mention. Policymakers say they want more science, but we still have scant evidence about effective ways to deliver that evidence. The time has come, according to Harvard's Jack Shonkoff (2004), when the dissemination of research should be considered a science unto itself, particularly in the policy context where the evidence is more limited and less robust than in other practice settings (Nutley et al., 2007).

We take stock in this chapter of the complexities and challenges of generating evidence about efforts to disseminate evidence to policymakers. To help shed light on what can best be described as the "black box" of how policymakers access and use evidence, we propose a theory of change that articulates seven key elements of how evidence is thought to influence policy decisions. We also present our preliminary attempts to evaluate each element of this theory, drawing upon the literature and our extensive experience conducting the model for bringing research to the attention of policymakers referenced throughout this book—the Family Impact Seminars that each of us spearhead in our respective states. We believe that some of the lessons learned may have relevance beyond the Seminars for evaluating other research dissemination efforts as well.

WHAT IS KNOWN AND UNKNOWN ABOUT DISSEMINATING RESEARCH TO POLICYMAKERS

Scientists' response to evaluating the dissemination of research to policymakers has been mixed. Brodkyn reacted with pessimism, contending that it is futile to even think about causality because when evidence is invoked to justify policy decisions, it is tainted by politics in inscrutable ways that defy rational explanation (cited in Weiss, 1995). Others are similarly cynical but cite methodological impediments (Segal, 1983). For example, some reject the study of questions that do not readily conform to randomized experiments as unevaluable and unworthy of the evaluator's time (Brown, 1995). Others criticize the overvaluing of randomized experiments, which they believe have led to an undervaluing of alternative methodologies even when they may be more appropriate for certain research questions (McCall & Green, 2004).

We wrote this chapter because we are compelled to evaluate our own efforts to move evidence from the hallowed walls of the academy to the harried halls of the state house. We borrow from common principles, models, and methods of evaluation (Coffman, 2007), but we consciously push against dominant academic perceptions that evaluation research methods are static and relatively stable (Collins & Overton, 2006). We believe that methods continuously evolve in response to different programs, purposes, contexts, and stakeholders. In our view, evaluating socially significant work such as research dissemination should be a high priority and not "handcuffed" (Harvard Family Research Project, 2007, p. 14) because we lack perfect approaches, measures, and methods.

This chapter is a humble first step to push the evaluation envelope. It was written in the spirit of hypothesis generation that we hope will lead to hypothesis testing. We have not arrived at definitive answers, but we feel confident that our experience familiarizes us with impediments faced by the field and raises questions evaluators need to ask and issues they need to resolve. We illustrate the complexity of the challenge before us with some real-life stories about how policymakers have put evidence to use in their work.

Vignettes of How Evidence Is Used by Policymakers

We present three vignettes here, including one based on the experience of a nonpartisan organization providing technical assistance to members of Congress, one that derives from an experimental evaluation of a welfare reform initiative, and a third that stems from one state's experience providing research to policymakers using the Family Impact Seminar model. These examples bring to light many of the dizzying challenges that confront and confound evaluators. Even when it appears that policymakers use evidence, the interim steps whereby research influences policy remain largely a mystery.

The Congressional Office of Technology Assessment (OTA). The rise and fall of OTA, described in a 1996 book by Bruce Bimber, is particularly relevant for two reasons. First, 75% of its staff were researchers, and second, it is one of the only nonpartisan legislative service agencies that Congress voted to enact and, then 23 years later, voted to ax. OTA's mission was to provide information and expert analysis to Congress on technology policy, but also on such issues as defense, energy, the environment, health care, and land use. OTA produced about 20 to 30 reports annually, with each study taking about 2 years to complete. Its studies were designed, conducted, and reported in ways that were relevant to and readable by busy policymakers. Albert Gore Jr., jokingly nicknamed "Senator Science," is alleged to be the only known member to have been spotted carrying around a full-length OTA report on the floor of the Senate. Most policymakers became familiar with OTA studies by reading the one-page summaries or by being briefed by OTA staff.

Threats to the agency's existence in 1975 prompted efforts to trace the use of the agency's research and analysis in congressional decisions. The most direct and obvious ways to document the impact of the agency—linking legislation or laws to an OTA study—came up empty-handed. In interviews of policymakers, congressional staff, and agency personnel, not one vote cast by a member of Congress could be traced to an OTA study. In a content analysis of the congressional record, including oral statements, revisions to these statements, and even written insertions, the influence of the agency is nearly absent. In the 1980s and 1990s, of the

535 members of Congress, references to OTA studies occurred less than once a month. After striking out on these three visible and verifiable fronts—legislation that passed, votes cast, and comments amassed—it seems safe to conclude that OTA had little, if any, influence on policy in its 23-year history. Reviewing this questionable track record, a San Diego newspaper penned an article titled "The Office of WHAT?" (Bimber, 1996, p. 38).

Upon further examination, however, Bimber (1996) concluded that dismissing OTA's influence was misleading, if not downright mistaken. In a broad analysis that gathered anecdotal evidence on a number of bills, Bimber (1996) concluded that OTA's influence on the policy process was both rhetorical and analytical. On several occasions, members of Congress such as Representative Pete Stark and Senator John Tower used OTA studies to back up their rhetoric on issues ranging from pharmaceutical prices to energy policy. Observers do not believe that these elected officials came to their views as a result of OTA studies, but tactically used the studies as ammunition for persuasively convincing others of their previously held positions.

In other instances, OTA studies performed more of an analytic function. In 1974, James Schlesinger, the secretary of defense, requested funding for Counterforce, the nuclear weapons targeting strategy. Central to this decision were estimates of the casualties that might result from a nuclear exchange between strategic sites rather than population centers. Several members of Congress questioned the estimates provided by the Department of Defense (DOD) and asked OTA for estimates. The OTA study criticized the DOD numbers, which provided a rationale for the chair of the Senate Foreign Affairs Committee to request revised estimates. So, in this instance, OTA helped Congress better grasp whether a problem existed and what the policy responses might be.

Many major bills (e.g., the Brady Bill and the appropriation for the Strategic Defense Initiative) and dozens of minor bills bear OTA's impact, although the influence of OTA was not immediately apparent. This is instructive for four reasons. First, this example illustrates that evaluators should think about *when* to look for the influence of evidence on policy decisions. For this nonpartisan purveyor of information, the influence occurred earlier in the policy process when issues were being framed and the policy agenda was being set. For example, in one bill that required chemical markings in the marketing of commercial explosives, the subcommittee labeled the three policy alternatives as "OTA Option 1," "OTA Option 2," and so forth. Second, this example indicates the importance of considering *where* to look. OTA staff did not always communicate directly with elected officials but often provided information indirectly to aides. Obviously, these indirect lines of communication would not be reflected in voting records, bill sponsorship, or the Congressional Record.

The example also illustrates *what* to look for. Votes cast by policymakers may not be the best indicator of the effectiveness of an agency charged, not with providing voting recommendations, but rather with producing policy options for policymakers to consider. Finally, the OTA example illustrates *how* fine-tuned indicators need to be if they are to detect influences that may be modest rather than monumental in impact. No reasonable person expects that policy decisions would be based solely on what evidence indicates or an expert recommends. Rather, evidence is one of many influences in a multiply determined process in which no single factor prevails over all the rest. In addition, once scientific evidence is incorporated into a policymaker's knowledge base, it becomes difficult to decipher where it actually originated from (Tseng, 2008).

The New Hope Project. The New Hope Project was a pilot antipoverty initiative developed by nongovernment individuals in Milwaukee to test whether a make-work-pay strategy could increase the labor supply of the urban poor and lift them out of economic destitution. At the core of the initiative was a clear offer. If a previously low-income participant was willing to work at least 30 hours per week, the project would guarantee a wage supplement that would lift the family out of poverty, ensure health care coverage, and provide child care.

The policy question raised by New Hope was straightforward. If society could guarantee that full-time work would enable those at the margins of society to escape poverty and have access to affordable child care and health care, would those folks participate in mainstream society as productive citizens? Even if the answer were positive, however, the subsidies for wages, child care, and health care were costly. Thus, the results, if there were any, had to be rigorously reached and had to be substantively significant.

New Hope contracted with MDRC to conduct an experimental evaluation. It also appointed a national advisory board that included such research luminaries from the academic world as Rebecca Blank, Gary Burtless, David Ellwood, Larry Mead, Michael Wiseman, and so forth. It also expanded the evaluation team to include Greg Duncan from Northwestern University and Aletha Huston from the University of Texas.

The sponsors were willing to subject their program to a rigorous experimental evaluation. Eligible families walking through the door were assigned to either an experimental group or a control group, a process the sponsors found logistically inconvenient and normatively stressful. They did it anyway, however. They took the science of what they were doing very seriously. They took the risk of failure very seriously. There would be no fudging the numbers, no whitewash of the results.

The results turned out to be positive. Project participants worked more and escaped poverty in significant numbers. Their children performed better in school and had fewer problems, compared to those in the control group. New Hope turned out to be a rare social policy reform success, and the evidence was unambiguous. It was good science. These results were consistent with evidence from similar initiatives in Minnesota (the Family Independence Initiative) and Canada (the Self- Sufficiency Initiative). That is, the evidence that so-called make-work-pay strategies would work did exist. Moreover, the results were widely disseminated in numerous forums, with Michael Laracy of the Annie E. Casey Foundation leading the way in getting the news out to the policy world.

So, did governments rush to replicate New Hope or its twin initiatives? The answer most likely would be *no.* But did New Hope and similar make-work-pay initiatives influence the policy dialogue about welfare policy? The answer to that may well be *yes.* Over the past decade, we have seen a significant expansion of wage subsidies, subsidized child care, and public health coverage for poor children and their parents. Thus, no one replicated a "junior" New Hope as such, but elements of the New Hope concept witnessed a dramatic swing in political popularity. Good evidence brought to policymakers in various forms over a number of years did seem to have an effect. It may not be immediate. It may not be direct. In the end, however, science did seem to matter, though not to the extent hoped for by proponents of the make-work-pay paradigm.

The Oregon Family Impact Seminars. Oregon's first Family Impact Seminar was strategically conducted early in the 2001 legislative session. The seminar featured two speakers, one being John Karl Scholz of the University of Wisconsin–Madison, who provided the latest evidence on the consequences of several policy options, including providing tax credits to the working poor. Scholz has published extensively on Earned Income Tax Credits, directed the Institute for Research on Poverty at the University of Wisconsin-Madison, and served as assistant deputy secretary for tax analysis at the U.S. Department of Treasury.

Six legislators (in a body of 90 members) and 64 members of the public, who heard a 60-minute presentation and received a briefing report with the latest research and relevant policy implications. This Family Impact Seminar, held in conjunction with an Oregon House Revenue Committee. The session was also broadcast live over the Internet and on closed-circuit television throughout the capitol building. Also, in a follow-up discussion session, Scholz met with top personnel from the Legislative Revenue Office, legislative staff, and representatives of key advocacy groups to examine the effect of policy options such as tax credits on the working poor. In end-of-session evaluations, participants' knowledge of Earned Income Tax Credits significantly improved.

The Republican chair of the House Revenue Committee and a Democratic representative ended up introducing HB 2716, a bill to establish refundable child care tax credits for low-income, working families. Before the session adjourned, the bill was passed by a Republican-controlled legislature and signed into law by a Democratic governor. Under the law, families who paid for child care but did not earn enough to pay state taxes received 40% of their costs as a refundable child care credit. Previously, the credit could be taken only as a deduction on a family's state income taxes, which limited its reach to only those earning enough to pay taxes. The chair of the House Revenue Committee credited the Family Impact Seminars because it "raised the level of the conversation and helped us keep tax credits in the forefront."

How can the effectiveness of a Family Impact Seminar, like this one, be evaluated? How much credit, if any, can the seminar organizers take for the law that was passed? Without a counterfactual, is there any way to determine if the law would have passed in the absence of the seminar? Without random assignment, would another legislator have sponsored the bill if the chair of the House Revenue Committee was assigned to the control group? Without causal evidence regarding the seminar's influence on lawmaking, should the program be abandoned, or does it merit the investment of continuing time and resources?

The Complexities of Evaluating Efforts to Disseminate Evidence to Policymakers

The most important program evaluation questions are often the most difficult to answer (Shonkoff, 2004). As the vignettes lay bare, evaluating efforts to disseminate evidence to policymakers introduces several additional layers of complexity regarding such issues as the stakeholders, outcomes, methods, and time frames (Corbett, Danziger, & Werner, 2005). Below we review empirical and experiential evidence regarding each.

Stakeholder complexity. At the heart of stakeholder complexity are differences about what constitutes evidence. Take the example provided by Thomas Guseky, author of 12 books on research and evaluation, 2 of which have earned him the National Staff Development Council's Book of the Year Award. When he asked administrators and teachers to rank order 15 indicators of student learning, the results were almost exactly reversed. Administrators gave high marks to state and national test results, whereas teachers endorsed their own, more immediate indicators that students were grasping the concepts being taught in the classroom (Kreider & Bouffard, 2005).

The standards of evidence that policymakers use were exemplified by Tommy Thompson, a former governor in Wisconsin and former U.S. secretary of Health and Human Services. In a talk that he gave at the Heritage Foundation, he described Wisconsin's experience transforming welfare from an income-support program to a system based on work and self-sufficiency with accompanying reforms in child care, child support, and work preparation. As evidence of the success of his initial reforms, Thompson explained that caseloads dropped by 60% statewide and 32% in the largest urban center, Milwaukee. According to his estimates, families were earning $5,000 more per year by working than they had previously received on welfare, and the state's payments to welfare recipients dropped from $46 million per month in 1987 to $21 million per month in 1997. Drawing upon Kids Count data from 1986 to 1993, the time period when the welfare reforms were launched, Thompson claimed that child poverty in Wisconsin dropped 13% and child abuse declined by 15%. In addition, he read a letter from a welfare recipient who had kept in touch with him after he helped her land a job several years earlier:

> Governor Thompson, I want you to know where I'm at. Me and my daughter have left our beloved Wisconsin. We are now living in Phoenix, Arizona. And I just got promoted and I had to leave Wisconsin for this promotion. Now, I'm running the office in Phoenix, Arizona. And I want you to know that the next time you come to Phoenix, I want to take you out for lunch, and I can afford to pay for it. (Thompson & Bennett, 1997, p. 9)

According to Thompson, this letter brought tears to his eyes. For him, it was the most convincing form of evidence:

> A letter like this made everything that I had been doing to reform welfare realistic. It put a face on welfare reform. And I knew from this letter and from her example that we were indeed going in the right direction. (p. 9)

It is apparent that evaluations can have disparate purposes, and stakeholders can look to different standards of evidence (Patton, 2001; Weiss, 1972). Policymakers such as the former governor want to know if a program works and whether its benefits are worth the costs to the taxpayer. But what do we mean by the term *works*? As our studies and others have shown, policymakers find anecdotes and stories to be convincing evidence for colleagues and constituents (Nelson, Roberts, Maederer, Wertheimer, & Johnson, 1987; Nutley et al., 2007).

Researchers are interested in whether something works, and whether the results can be attributed to the program and replicated in other settings. Because researchers are interested in rigor, they prize the "gold standard" of evaluation—experimental methods that allow them to attribute causality and rule out alternative explanations. Program administrators are looking for better ways to serve their clients, so they want to know if, how, and under what conditions the program is working (Weiss, 1972). Thus, program administrators are less impressed with experimental studies because they explain little about *what* elements of the program work and *how* each contributes to the program's success (Weiss, 1997). To cut through the complexity, evaluators first need to get a firm fix on the purpose of the evaluation: Who are the stakeholders, what questions do they want answered, and which types of evidence do they value?

Outcome complexity. On first blush, the critical outcome for measuring effective dissemination of research to policymakers seems obvious—whether evidence-based policies are passed. Yet there are several problems with this seemingly straightforward approach. It is based on faulty assumptions about policymakers, about the character of the legislation itself, about the approach used to disseminate research, and about the political environment in which the dissemination effort occurs. We consider each in turn below.

First, it is a faulty assumption that policymakers agree that policy decisions should be evidence-based. Not all policymakers agree. To cite one example, congressional staffers on both sides of the aisle worked for many years to publish the *Green Book*, a compilation of vast amounts of data and research related to a number of social programs that constituted the social safety net in the United States. The *Green Book*, which ran well over 1,000 pages (using very small print), was widely known as the "Bible" to policy wonks and academics interested in social policy. Wendell Primus, on the Democratic side of the aisle, first put this publication together. After the Republicans assumed power in 1994, Ron Haskins, representing the new party in control, made sure the *Green Book* was updated on a periodic basis. Unfortunately, bipartisan support did not make the publication immune from ideological attack. Tom recalls watching a congressman on C-SPAN rip into the *Green Book* as a "Socialist plot." To this congressman, these numbers, regardless of their source or rigor, were suspect. If the numbers showed that income inequality was growing or that wage growth was slowing, then that evidence might support arguments for more public resources for disadvantaged populations. For this policymaker, such data were inherently dangerous. Is the incorporation of evidence into policy decisions a reasonable outcome when a significant number of the target audience do not value evidence and are prone to discount it, no matter how relevant, high-quality, or well presented?

Even if policymakers agree that evidence-based policy is a desirable end goal, they can have legitimate disagreements about how to best reach the desired end (Weiss, Murphy-Graham, Petrosino, & Gandhi, 2008). Karen worked with a governor's Commission on Children and Families, a broad mix of policymakers and the public from different walks of life, many of whom were appointed by a conservative governor. The members of the commission agreed that an important policy direction for the state would be supporting children growing up in single-parent families. Karen reviewed 29 evidence-based policy solutions with the committee that were described in a Family Impact Seminar briefing report on that topic (Bogenschneider, Kaplan, & Morgan, 1993). How many of these options did the commission decide to endorse? To Karen's great surprise, not one. The evidence-based alternatives were largely government solutions to a problem that commission members believed were primarily private in scope and cultural in nature.

The passage of a policy is a reasonable outcome only if the legislation is supported by available evidence. In some cases, evidence is used to defeat a policy or eliminate a program (Coffman, 2007). For example, given evidence of the DARE program's limited success in reducing drug use (Ringwalt, Ennett, & Holt, 1990), an informed policymaker would vote against any additional funding. Even when a policy proposal is consistent with existing evidence, it may be shortsighted to count program replication as the only valid outcome. For instance, the successful New Hope Project was not adopted carte blanche, yet its evaluation influenced the terms of policy debate, and several components of the program ended up becoming politically popular.

Policy enactment is also a problematic measure of success when knowledge brokers use an education approach to disseminate research (see Chapter 10). If the aim of the effort is to inform policy by providing the potential consequences of alternative policy options (including the status quo), is the passage of a particular outcome a logical measure of success?

Finally, policy enactment may be unrealistic given the number of policy levers in the political culture. As illustrated in the earlier example of the Office of Technology Assessment (Bimber, 1996), research is only one of many policy drivers that include ideology, values, political interests, and other influences that are beyond the reach of the knowledge broker (Weiss, 1999). Thus, if a policy fails to pass, is it fair to conclude that the research dissemination effort was ineffective? Conversely, if an evidence-based policy is enacted, is it reasonable for the research disseminator to take all the credit, some credit, or any credit at all?

If systemwide impacts (Weiss, 1972), such as the enactment of laws by an entire legislative body, seem too grandiose an outcome, could we instead assess more immediate outcomes short of ultimate legislative approval? Are there intermediate outcomes for building policymakers' capacity to use research in their decisions, such as measures of knowledge gained, attitude changed, or relationships built? Would efforts to disseminate research be considered effective if individual policymakers use evidence to evaluate existing legislation, draft new legislation, or develop policy positions? What if they incorporate research into speeches, discussions with colleagues, or replies to constituent questions? Could evaluators look for evidence that research has been used to shift the (a) salience of issues, (b) frameworks for thinking about them, (c) solutions for addressing them, (d) tactics for implementation, or (e) reallocation of resources? (These uses of research are defined and discussed in Chapter 5.)

Looking for individual effects calls into question a common evaluation practice—seeking average effects of a program or policy across the entire sample. Drawing from the Oregon vignette, the Family Impact Seminar appears to have reached 6 legislators out of a total body of 90 members. Even if the program had a large effect on such a small segment of the sample, the average effect is likely to be insignificant. However, the vignette reveals that the program had a "whopper" effect on 1 state legislator—the chair of the House Revenue Committee, who later introduced legislation on a child tax credit that was eventually passed and signed into law. From a traditional evaluation paradigm, a program that failed to produce a significant average effect across the sample would be considered a disappointing failure. From a pragmatic policy perspective, a program that played a part in enacting legislation that will benefit thousands of families across a state would be considered a substantive success.

In sum, to avoid looking for the wrong kinds of influence in the wrong places (Weiss, 1999), evaluators should ask such questions as the following: Is the program aimed at individual effects, system effects, or both? Is it reasonable to expect the same effect for every policymaker irrespective of his or her prior positions and philosophical predilections? Is there a larger set of outcomes than simply policy change that might indicate the impact of a policy dissemination effort? What might these outcomes be? For these outcomes, what is a meaningful impact—the number affected or the size of the effect (Riley, 2008)? Do we look only at so-called positive policy outcomes—new laws and programs? What if research is used to stop an ineffective policy or program from being adopted? Does that count or not? Looking further down the road, when research actually affects policy decisions, should we assess the efficacy and effectiveness of those policies? If so, how should we do so?

Methodological complexity. In the research and evaluation communities, the basic ground rules are clear. In 1993, Michael Wiseman summarized this conventional wisdom as follows:

> "Rigorous evaluation" has come in general to mean an evaluation of effects based upon an implementation plan that assigns some randomly selected subset of recipients affected by the innovation to a control group treated with the pre-experiment system. Outcomes such as welfare receipt, employment, and childbearing for the "treatment" group participating in the new program are then compared with outcomes for families treated contemporaneously with the pre-reform program. The random assignment experimental design assures that, aside from differences attributable to chance, the units in the two groups will be on average the same with respect to demographic characteristics and external circumstances other than those varied for the purposes of the experiment. As a result, differences in outcomes between the experimental and control groups are reasonably treated as products of the innovation. (p. 19)

Jack Shonkoff (2004) and Deborah Phillips are a shining success story of how to translate research for public consumption. They began by reviewing the evidence on early childhood development in the National Academy of Sciences book *From Neurons to Neighborhoods* and then took the next step of working with communication experts to craft language that frames this issue in ways that attract policymakers (Shonkoff, 2007). Shonkoff (2004) aptly described the inherent difficulties of using randomized, controlled trials for program evaluation:

> The limitations of nonexperimental and quasi-experimental designs have been well described; the imperative of randomized, controlled studies to answer causal questions has been hammered home again and again. The logistical and financial barriers that must be scaled to successfully conduct high-quality longitudinal studies are legendary. The ethical concerns about random assignment … have been debated endlessly. (p. 4)

What is an evaluator to do if this tried-and-true method for "rigorous" evaluation does not neatly map onto the question at hand? We agree with those who place the focus on the phenomenon of interest, so that the research questions come to drive the methods rather than the reverse (McCall & Green, 2004; Sternberg & Grigorenko, 2002). The nature of one's worldview and one's research questions go far in determining what methods are plausible and possible. If you see the hypodermic metaphor as the way research is used (Pettigrew, 1985) and have narrow policy questions of interest, perhaps classical experiments could work (perhaps). If you see the limestone metaphor as more apropos (Bulmer, 1987) and are trying to affect policy more gradually and globally, a theory-of-change approach with interim outcomes might make more sense.

Ideally, researchers would conduct evaluations using an experiment in which participants are randomly assigned to either a treatment condition or a control condition. Yet for a research dissemination effort in the policy world, is it feasible to assign policymakers to a "treatment" or "no treatment" condition? What are the practical implications and political ramifications if some legislators are invited to a presentation of the latest research on a high-profile topic and others are not? Even if it was politically feasible, can contamination be avoided in an institutional culture that operates on trust, where members come to rely on colleagues who develop specialized expertise on specific issues? Are these "go-to" or "cue-giving" policymakers (Matthews & Stimson, 1975) likely to contaminate their colleagues assigned to the "no treatment" condition? Could randomization actually lead to inappropriate and perhaps even false conclusions (McCall & Green, 2004)? For example, do those who choose to participate in educational seminars have different preexisting characteristics about the value of research, attitudes toward the university, and so forth that would make it inappropriate to generalize to those unmotivated to attend?

Moreover, what is an evaluator to do when finding an appropriate counterfactual is unlikely? As director of a national project operating in 28 states and the District of Columbia, Karen has considered comparing how an issue moves forward in one state that conducts a Family Impact Seminar on a particular topic to other states that do not. The upside of a counterfactual is the many benefits such a comparison would bring to the rigor of an evaluation and the confidence in any claims of impact. The downside is that each state is an N of 1, which yields a maximum sample of 49 if every state could be considered a legitimate comparison. Obviously, they cannot. States differ from each other in many obvious and not-so-obvious ways that are likely to have real-world consequences for research utilization by policymakers:

- state characteristics (e.g., size, region, and population demographics),
- the lawmaking institution (e.g., length of legislative session, which varies from 1 month every 2 years to full-time bodies; the number of members; whether service is part-time or full-time and term-limited),
- political history and configuration (e.g., Blue State or Red State, similarities or differences in the party of the legislature and the governor),
- availability of and access to information inside and outside the legislature (e.g., existence and extent of nonpartisan service agencies, scope of efforts to disseminate research to policymakers, saturation and activism of advocacy groups),
- the quality of the dissemination effort (e.g., legislative involvement in design and execution of the effort, quality of research, skill of the research presenter, marketing of the initiative, its timing), and
- the salience of an issue (e.g., availability of funding, a crisis or serendipitous event that creates interest in an issue, local champions who push issues).

States, like other political jurisdictions, vary in many respects. With each state being considered an N of 1, could a counterfactual be created with enough states to provide sufficient power to detect significant differences when they exist? When differences emerge, how confident can we be that they emanate from the intervention rather than differences in program implementation and the political environment? How can evaluators account for unanticipated changes over time across even matched counterfactual sites (Hollister & Hill, 1995)?

Moreover, should a randomized experiment be the method of choice when the program itself makes no claims of causality? Even when research of the highest quality and utmost objectivity is disseminated to the right policymakers at the right time in the right way, knowledge brokers would make no claim that a single influence operating within a multidetermined process such as policymaking would "cause" a particular policy decision. After all, research might be used by both sides on a given issue, or one provision may be evidence-based but not another, leading to no legislative action or to a legislative outcome that some favor and others believe an abomination. How do we assign value to the dependent measure in such situations? In policy contexts, is a randomized experiment truly the "gold standard," or is this seemingly simple truth really no more than "fool's gold" (Gueron, 2007)? Are there other methods that might be more appropriate, such as time series analysis or regression discontinuity designs that would allow evaluators to compare the program against itself over time (Corbett, Danziger, et al., 2005)? Does it make sense to follow the trajectory of policymakers who value, seek out, and use research in their decisions? As hinted at in our policymaker typology in

Chapter 6, can *Enthusiastic Nonusers* of research become *Enthusiastic Users* if presented with research that is credible, accessible, and timely?

To settle on methods for evaluating programs that disseminate research to policymakers, evaluators need to consider a number of questions: Is random assignment feasible? What kind of counterfactual can be constructed? Are there alternatives to the randomized experiment that might be more suitable given the constraints imposed by the political context? Can trajectories of policymakers' research utilization be traced over time to see if increased exposure leads to more or less respect for and use of research in decision making?

Time complexity. One of the most confounding complexities is time. We think of timing as a "fickle factor" in the policy culture. Policy issues rise and fall on the political agenda, policymakers are sworn in and "term limited" out, and the prevailing political winds can shift direction at the voters' discretion in every election. Evaluators must choose a time frame over which to assess whether research dissemination has been effective. From a theoretical perspective, the slow way research seeps into policymakers' frame of reference has been referred to by Bulmer (1987) as the "limestone" model and by Weiss as "enlightenment":

> [Research] brings new information and new perspectives into the policy system. It often shows that old shibboleths are misguided and it punctures old myths. Over time, the ideas from research seep into people's consciousness and alter the way that issues are framed and alternatives designed. Assumptions once taken for granted are now re-examined. Issues that used to be given high priority are now seen to be less important. New issues, previously unrecognized, move up the policy agenda. The slow trickle of enlightenment is hard to see and harder still to identify as the product of social science. But the cumulative effect may be a major recasting of the policy agenda and the embrace of a very different order of policy. (Weiss, 1999, p. 195)

From a pragmatic perspective, examples abound of just how long it can take for this redefinition, recasting, or reframing to occur. On the basis of a 22-year career, fiscal analyst Jere Bauer Jr. explained that "certainly over time, a low dose, low dose, low dose" of good information eventually does have an impact. One researcher explained that it took 15 years for affordability in drug therapy to become part of the policy agenda. Kristin Anderson Moore of Child Trends described how the importance of fathers has gradually become recognized and how positive development has slowly but surely become part of policy debate. In her words, it does happen, but it is rare to see something change the world directly and immediately:

> I think the thing that was really a surprise to me earlier in my career was presenting testimony on teen childbearing ... and actually getting into the newspaper and having that affect policy and then realizing, "Oh, that doesn't happen every year." Many years go by before that happens again. ... It is a very long-term kind of a commitment; it becomes a lifestyle. ... So I think it becomes really a strong commitment. And you have to just accept the fact that those kinds of mountain-top moments where you feel like you've really gotten something across clearly, and they heard it and it had an impact, that those moments are pretty rare for any of us.

Some issues lend themselves to quicker action than others, but for controversial issues, you could spend a lifetime on them and not see the changes you hoped for. An academic with 30 years of experience working with policymakers explained the slow pace of policy change, drawing on the country's half century of experience with health care:

> If you were someone who really thought that this country ought to have publicly supported health care for everyone, you probably would have gotten excited when Franklin Delano Roosevelt included that in his charge to the committee that developed the Social Security Act and thought, "Ah, we're going to have that now." And you would have been excited when Harry Truman raised the idea again, and when Lyndon Johnson eventually pushed through Medicaid and Medicare, and when Bill Clinton revisited the topic during his presidency. ... And, of course, your career would have long been over, and you would have now been dead and not seen that come to pass. And yet slowly we have seen an increase in public coverage of children and family and other individuals piece by piece by piece. So a lot of it depends on how you define what the issue is and how you define progress. If your solution was a single-payer system, publicly funded and administered, you would feel probably betrayed and very discouraged having spent the last 65 years working on this. Yet if you could be satisfied with inexorable progress, a little bit here and there, sometimes a step back, sometimes two steps forward, you might look back on your life and say, "Hey, we left it somewhat better off than where we started" ... there are seldom opportunities or moments when you get very clear transitions or changes in course that say, "Ah, this is it! We've reached the Promised Land!"

Timing raises two primary questions for evaluators. First, *when* to look for whether research has arrived in the Promised Land. For example, the Early Head Start program for children aged 1 to 3 was launched, in part, by the accumulation of decades of research on the importance of the early years to human development (Zigler, 1998). If the influence of these studies had been evaluated too soon, the impact would have been said to be minimal. What criteria can determine the best time for assessing the influence of research on policymakers and policymaking? Second, *how* can the evaluator detect small effects that accumulate over time? When looking for blockbuster effects, even imperfect measures can detect them; however, fine-tuned indicators are needed to ferret out the more subtle enlightenment functions served by research such as projecting ideas into political discourse and framing the terms of policy debate (Weiss, 1999). What kinds of measures can evaluators use to track modest effects that add up to something over time?

BABY STEPS FOR EVALUATING EFFORTS TO DISSEMINATE EVIDENCE TO POLICYMAKERS

Given our active involvement in the business of bringing high-quality and objective research to policymakers since 1993, the Family Impact Seminars have wrestled with the challenges of program evaluation, in general, and the complexities of stakeholders, outcomes, methodology, and timing, in particular. In response, we developed a theory of change to guide our evaluation efforts. To help contextualize the theoretical framework that follows, we expand on the methods and purposes of the Seminars described earlier in Chapter 3. We also detail the preliminary protocols and procedures we use to evaluate each element of our theory of change.

The Family Impact Seminar Methods and Protocols

As detailed in Chapter 3, the Seminars are a series of presentations, discussion sessions, and briefing reports for state policymakers designed to (a) build greater respect for and use of research in state policy decisions and (b) encourage policymakers to examine the family impact of policies and programs. The Seminars are currently being conducted in 28 states and the District of Columbia. Since 1993, these sites have conducted over 145 seminars on a wide range of topics identified by state policymakers, including 30 on family health, 22 on family poverty and economic security, 13 on families and schools, 13 on juvenile and adult crime, 9 on child abuse and family and youth violence, 9 on teen pregnancy, and 8 on early childhood care and education.

We are presenting the evaluation experience of Indiana, Michigan, Oregon, and Wisconsin—four of the first sites conducting Family Impact Seminars in their state capitals. The Seminars provide high-quality, objective research and dispassionate analysis on current family issues. The traditional format of the 2-hour seminar consists of two or three 20- to 30-minute presentations given by a panel of premier researchers, program directors, and/or policy analysts. For each seminar, a background briefing report summarizes policy-relevant research on the issue in a succinct, easy-to-understand format. The presentations are followed by discussion sessions that provide a neutral setting outside the political environment for policymakers to discuss issues and seek common ground where it exists. To foster consensus building, we do not typically invite lobbyists and the media (see Chapter 3 for a full description of the methodology).

Evaluation Protocol and Procedures Employed by the Family Impact Seminars

A common evaluation protocol has been developed. Our data are based on five evaluation procedures: careful record keeping, end-of-session evaluations, phone interviews, testimonials, and tracking of seminar issues as they progress through the policy process. The stakeholders for the evaluation data are many, including policymakers we try to attract to seminar activities, funders we strive to persuade to underwrite the seminars, university and legislative partners we seek as collaborators, and university administrators whom we want to assure that our time is well spent and that the university is well represented. For policymakers, telling stories about how research is used in policymaking has proved to be the most believable, trusted, and influential evidence. For our colleagues and for advancing the body of theoretical and empirical knowledge of research utilization, more objective and statistically based methods are employed (Patton, 2001; Weiss, 1997). Because we have multiple purposes in mind, several kinds of evaluation data are collected.

Using a Theory of Change to Guide Policy Education Efforts

When we first began, our goal was to evaluate the Family Impact Seminars in a way that moved beyond bean counting—adding up the number of presentations delivered, discussions held, and publications produced. According to Weiss (1995), one of the key reasons why assessing program effectiveness stumps evaluators is that the assumptions undergirding programs are poorly articulated. In addition, David Olds (2009), developer of the Nurse-Family Partnership program, contended the assumptions undergirding the problem itself are often poorly understood:

> Are we here to promote a particular program or are we here to solve a problem? It's a fundamental question; in fact, it's an issue that I had to struggle with when I first began this work. And I eventually came to realize that I was not here to promote a program; I was here to solve a problem. ... It's also important for us to realize that ... you have theories, you have ideas of how this is going to work.

Consistent with these insights of Weiss and Olds, we developed a theory of change, which is defined as a tool for developing solutions to complex social problems (see Anderson, n.d., 2004; Weiss, 1995). Our theory of change articulates how and why we thought a policy education effort like the Seminars might address an important societal challenge—policymakers' underutilization of research in policy decisions. Specifically, we attempted (a) to unpack the processes that we believe occur when policymakers do use research to guide their decisions and (b) to detail what indicators need to be assessed to document this process in a systematic fashion. We doubt that we have identified every relevant element in the research utilization process, and we realize that our measurement of these elements is preliminary. Nonetheless, we found it enlightening to take a vague, mysterious process such as research utilization and break it down into a number of discrete early and intermediate steps that must occur if the long-term goal—policymakers using research and a family perspective in their jobs—is to be realized (Anderson, 2005).

As a point of clarification, a theory of change differs from a logic model, which is a more tactical, program-level explanation of program inputs, outputs, and activities for producing outcomes. In contrast, the theory of change is a more "strategic picture of the multiple interventions required to produce the early and intermediate outcomes that are the preconditions of reaching an ultimate goal" (Anderson, 2005, pp. 12, 19). A theory of change could encompass several logic models that explain programmatically how to produce each outcome.

THE FAMILY POLICY EDUCATION THEORY OF CHANGE

The *Family Policy Education Theory of Change*, as we have dubbed it, has seven key elements that can help knowledge intermediaries assess whether the time and resources they are expending on policy education will achieve the anticipated long-term outcomes of having policymakers take research and a family perspective into account in their jobs. This theory of change draws upon several theoretical traditions: constructive theories of learning, Kingdon's open policy windows, social learning, and community dissonance theories (e.g., see Walter, Nutley, & Davies, 2005). Moreover, the theory embodies several types of research use because we recognize that research is seldom used in a direct or linear way. We attempt to measure conceptual and instrumental uses of research (see Nutley et al., 2007; Tseng, 2008) as well as some new concepts for research utilization raised earlier in Chapter 5, such as framework shifting, solutions shifting, and allocation shifting.

The theory details what we believe are some of the early and intermediate outcomes essential for a policy education effort such as the Seminars to realize its long-term goal. As visually depicted in Figure 11.1, the early outcomes entail engaging policymakers and experts to identify family issues and then providing research on these issues in ways that attract the policy community to dialogue in a nonpartisan, educational setting. Intermediate outcomes include knowledge gained, attitudes changed, and relationships built. That is, providing research on timely issues in a nonpartisan setting begins a process whereby policymakers gain

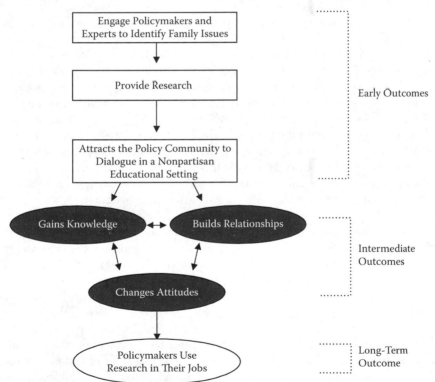

Figure 11.1   Family Policy Education Theory of Change: How policymakers use research in their jobs.

knowledge on both research and the family impact of policies, which, in turn, changes their attitudes about the value of research and a family perspective in policymaking. These attitude changes subsequently increase their propensity to build relationships with researchers and their colleagues in ways that are useful in their jobs.

We believe that this process is multidirectional, but we are not always certain of the direction of effect. Conceivably, this process may begin with policymakers building relationships with researchers; in the context of these trusting relationships, policymakers may seek out research-based knowledge and, in so doing, change their attitudes about the value of research and a family perspective in policymaking. Or it could be that the process begins when policymakers gain knowledge of research and how it affects families from seminar activities, which prompts them to build relationships with researchers and colleagues and, in turn, contributes to changes in attitudes about the value of research and a family perspective in policymaking. The long-term outcome is that policymakers use research in their jobs in a number of ways such as sharing it with their colleagues and constituents, as well as using it to draft legislation and enact laws that support families.

The Family Policy Education Theory of Change has the potential to inform other policy education efforts in several ways, three of which are described here. First, the theory introduces some early and intermediary outcomes in the research utilization process that are sometimes overlooked. For example, policy educators tell compelling stories about the impact of their efforts on policy change (California Research Bureau, n.d.; Mayer & Hutchins, 1998; McClintock, 1999; Melton, 1995; Wilcox, Weisz, & Miller, 2005). Many of these existing evaluations describe the implementation process with no mention of outcomes, or sometimes outcomes are claimed with no evidence of the process whereby they are realized. Sometimes policy educators leap ahead from research being provided to laws being enacted, without considering what might occur in the black box between research delivery and policy change. Because it can take years for evidence to seep into policymakers' consciousness or for a policy to pass, this means that policy educators face the challenge of maintaining support from funders and other stakeholders with little or no interim evidence that their efforts are having any impact.

Second, we believe this theory of change may have applicability beyond the Seminars, because it is framed not from the perspective of "program testing" but rather from that of "variable testing" (Weiss, 1972). The variables we test and the early, intermediate, and long-term outcomes we identify could apply to any effort to disseminate evidence to policymakers.

Third, this theory can help policy educators identify which theoretical elements are being measured and which are not. For example, we constructed a grid that included, on one side, the elements of our theory of change detailing how policy education contributes to policymakers' research utilization and, on the other side, the evaluation protocols that we were using. The gaps between the two sides of this grid visually pointed out which elements were not being evaluated, prompting us to develop new questions and procedures to ensure examination of every theoretical link.

In this section, we present the underlying rationale and the empirical evidence for each element of the Family Policy Education Theory of Change. Then for each

TABLE 11.1   Evaluation Strategies for Assessing Each Component of the Family Policy Education Theory of Change

Component of the Theory of Change	Program Evaluation Strategy
Engage policymakers and experts to identify family issues	Examine whether program organizers take the following steps to identify issues for policy education: (a) contacting policymakers to identify the problem, (b) consulting with experts to generate evidence-based policy solutions, and (c) recontacting policymakers to assess the political viability of the policy solutions.
Provide research	Items in a postsession questionnaire assess whether the research presented at the program is relevant, useful, objective, practical, innovative, economically feasible, and politically feasible.
Attracts the policy community to dialogue in a nonpartisan educational setting	Careful record keeping of attendance at the program and discussions track how many policymakers are reached and whether the information reaches influential policymakers such as committee chairs, bill sponsors, legislative opinion leaders on the issue, and so on. End-of-session evaluations assess the usefulness of the discussion sessions.
Gains knowledge	Retrospective pre- and posttest items in the end-of-session questionnaire assess participants' perceptions of their understanding of the research presented at the program and how it affects families.
Changes attitudes	Attribution questions in phone interviews 6 to 8 weeks after the program examine changes in attitudes about the value of research and the importance of a family perspective in policymaking.
Builds relationships	Phone interviews 6 to 8 weeks after the program track attitude change about how approachable researchers are, contacts with researchers and colleagues on the program topic, and the ability to identify others interested in the issue. Testimonials are shared about the dialogue created among policymakers of opposing parties and between researchers and policymakers.
Policymakers use research in their jobs	Follow-up phone interviews 6 to 8 weeks after the program assess research utilization and participants' ratings of the usefulness of several information sources, including one's own program. Track policy issues to assess if and how the information was used. Rely on existing evaluations to assess whether laws that are enacted are effective and supportive of families.

component, we explain which indicators we use, how we operationalize them, what evaluation protocols we have put in place to collect the relevant data (see Table 11.1), and the preliminary evidence in support of the theory. Figure 11.2 is an expanded schematic of the theory of change, which includes each indicator assessed in the evaluation as we specify below.

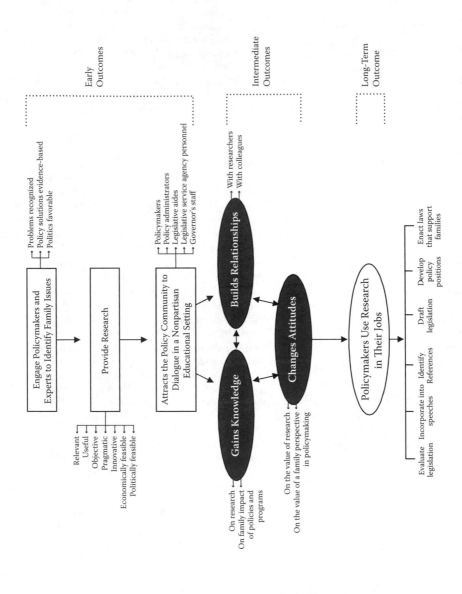

Figure 11.2   Detailed map of Family Policy Education Theory of Change: Measuring policymakers' use of research in their jobs.

Engage Policymakers and Experts to Identify Family Issues

Policymakers, who are elected for 2- to 4-year terms, are faced with literally hundreds of issues that they must vote on each session. Because not all bills that are introduced have momentum behind them, we use Kingdon's (2003) theory of open policy windows to identify the issues for which research may have the best chance of influencing a policy outcome. When policy windows are open, the conditions are right for social change on an issue, and policymakers are willing to invest their time, energy, and political capital because their efforts may succeed.

The opening of a policy window usually occurs with the convergence of three separate streams: problems are recognized, policy solutions are available, and the political climate supports change. No single stream is likely to place an item on the decision-making agenda. For example, a problem without a solution, a solution without a compelling problem, and problems or solutions that are politically unacceptable at the time quickly result in the closing of a policy window. Typically, more visible policy participants such as the governor or legislators set the legislative agenda, whereas hidden participants such as academics, legislative service agency personnel, and state agency staffers identify policy alternatives.

Following Kingdon's framework, the Family Impact Seminars use a three-step planning process for linking problems with policies and politics (see Figure 11.3). First, we interview a bipartisan group of legislative and gubernatorial advisors to identify the single most compelling problem with bipartisan interest. Second, to identify evidence-based policy solutions, we form a seminar planning committee composed of those with expertise on the issue, including academics, state agency representatives, and staff from the legislature's nonpartisan service agencies. Third, to assess the political feasibility of these policy solutions, we recontact our legislative and gubernatorial advisors to rank the policy solutions that will be featured in the presentations, discussion sessions, and written materials.

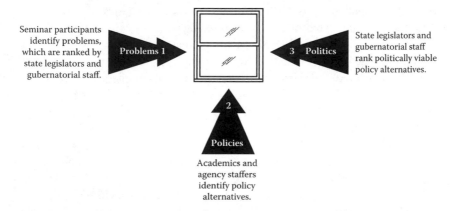

Figure 11.3   Planning timely Family Impact Seminar topics: Identifying open policy windows. *Source.* Adapted from *Family Policy Matters: How Policymaking Affects Families and What Professionals Can Do,* 2nd ed., p. 260, by K. Bogenschneider, 2006, Mahwah, NJ: Lawrence Erlbaum.

One way to evaluate a research dissemination effort is a simple check to see if the appropriate planning steps were taken to ensure that a policy problem is addressed with evidence-based solutions that are consistent with the prevailing political climate. These three steps are (a) contacting policymakers to identify the problem, (b) consulting with experts to generate evidence-based policy solutions, and (c) recontacting policymakers to assess the political viability of the policy solutions.

Republican Senator Carol Roessler, who advised the Wisconsin Family Impact Seminars about topics for seven different seminars, explained how important this element of the theory of change is:

> As I look at how we've worked with the Family Impact Seminars, it's been … bipartisan, both parties participating and identifying what the issues are we see coming up this session. If you were just to think about it from the outside, I don't think that you would have the inside feel for what we would identify as areas that we need information on now because we'll be making decisions on that particular issue in the course of this legislative session.

Democrat Representative Tamara Grigsby, chair of the Wisconsin Assembly Committee on Children and Families, characterized the planning process as "well thought out" and "very impressive":

> I really appreciate being able to be part of the process. I really appreciate the process for going around and finding a bipartisan team of legislators that can give input and feedback … [on] what should be prioritized and what's the most relevant and timely issue. … I really respect that process.

We also have some anecdotal and empirical evidence that the usefulness of seminar information depends on whether the policy conditions are ripe for research and policy analysis. Wisconsin's first 16 seminars were divided into two groups: those on topics with legislation pending (e.g., welfare reform, long-term care, prescription drugs) and those on topics that were identified by legislators as a high priority, but no legislation was pending (e.g., child support, youth resilience). We then compared these two groups by (a) analyzing legislative attendance and (b) running t tests on the participant's overall rating of the seminars along with its objectivity, relevance, and usefulness. First, seminars that addressed topics with pending legislation attracted 50% more legislators than seminars on high-priority issues with no pending legislation. In end-of-session evaluations, no significant differences were found in the seminars' overall rating or their relevance and objectivity; however, legislators rated seminars on topics with pending legislation significantly more useful than those with no legislation pending ($t = -2.57, p = .01$). A Republican legislator described how he was able to apply information from a Family Impact Seminar, which he attributed in part to its timing:

> Prescription drugs was an excellent … seminar that we had because we dealt with it shortly afterward, and we heard from folks saying, "This is what you

should do, and this is what you should not do," and we tailored some of our legislation in this area.

Provide Research

In the highly politicized world of policymaking, research evidence may not play a decisive role, but it still plays an important role (Hird, 2005; Huston, 2008; Mooney, 1992; Weiss, 1999; Weiss & Bucuvalas, 1980). One Republican legislator eloquently expressed the uniqueness of research-based information in the policy-making institution:

> The reason that I go to the Family Impact Seminars is they bring in speakers that we normally never get to hear from in the state capitol. The state capitol is loaded with politics. It is not loaded with scientific research or people who have studied these issues from across the country. So what happens is we hear from a number of well-respected folks who know the issue inside and out, and we get information that we never ever get an opportunity to hear otherwise.

When working with policymakers, however, not just any research will do. As discussed in Chapter 2, policymakers appear to apply three tests to determine their likelihood of using research: a "credibility test" that screens research for its scientific quality, a "timeliness test" that assesses whether research is available when decisions are made, and an "accessibility test" that apprises its brevity and understandability. The credibility and timeliness tests are important indicators of the kind of research that should be presented in a policy education effort like the Seminars.

Each Seminar site uses a common end-of-session evaluation to assess a seminar's overall rating along with ratings of its relevance, usefulness, and objectivity. The relevance and usefulness ratings are proxies for the timeliness of the research presented at the seminar. Objectivity is a credibility test, of sorts, that indicates the trustworthiness of the research or perhaps the researcher who gave the presentation. We calculated the mean participant ratings of relevance, usefulness, and objectivity for the 43 Family Impact Seminars held in Indiana, Michigan, Oregon, and Wisconsin (88% of the seminars are included). On a scale of 1 (*poor*) to 5 (*excellent*), the relevance ($M = 4.33$) and usefulness ($M = 4.12$) ratings provide a favorable indication of seminar timeliness. The mean objectivity rating across these seminars in four states was 4.35, which is an amazing figure given that the seminars are attended by some of a state's most liberal and conservative policymakers.

The value policymakers place on objectivity is expressed by a veteran Republican legislator, Senator Luther Olsen, who is a partner in a farm supply and grain dealership in central Wisconsin:

> That's the best part of the Seminars, they're nonpartisan, they are research based. ... It really makes no difference if you're Republican or Democrat. The information is good, and it is very, very well balanced. That's very important in being a credible source. You have to, in my estimation, [give us] just the facts ma'am, just the facts, as they used to say in *Dragnet*.

The valuing of objectivity transcends party lines, as evidenced in this comment about the Seminars from Representative Tamara Grigsby, a social worker who represents an inner-city Milwaukee district:

> It's objective. It's neutral. It's not an advocacy approach. It's here's the information. Here's the data. Here are some things that have worked some places. Here are some things that haven't. You make the decision. That really leaves people feeling very comfortable that they're not in a partisan environment. And that no one's lobbying them, which is naturally what everyone ... expects everyone is trying to do in this building.

To examine the utility of the information within the constraints imposed by the institutional culture of lawmaking bodies (Webber, 1986), evaluation questions assess whether policy options are discussed, how practical and innovative they are, and to what extent they are politically and economically feasible. After a Wisconsin seminar on corrections policy, 56 respondents (67% response rate) provided the following ratings on the policy options presented at the seminar. Overall, 85% (N = 44) reported that the seminar included at least one policy option defined as *a program, law, bill, or legislative action*. On a scale of 1 (*poor*) to 5 (*excellent*), participants rated the options across four different dimensions: *practical* (4.1), *innovative* (4.0), *economically feasible* (3.9), and *politically feasible* (3.6). Of the 168 ratings across these four dimensions, most were rated 3 or higher, with a total of only four ratings of 1 or 2.

Providing research that is relevant and is at the right level of detail is a challenge for those who organize seminars. Sometimes legislators find seminar information is too technical (e.g., "this was over my head," "too much started from an assumed knowledge base that most don't have"), and other times it was not technical enough (e.g., "not very much meat in today's seminar; just an overview, not very deep"). Other legislators report that the seminar information was not tailored enough to the state and did not offer enough policy solutions and new ideas.

Attracts the Policy Community to Dialogue in a Nonpartisan Educational Setting

Too often, the hundreds of sophisticated studies being produced and the volumes of first-rate policy reports being written never reach policymakers in a position to apply them to policies and programs (Huston, 2008). Simply spewing out written reports seldom changes practice. Instead, consistent with constructivist theories of learning, meaning is arrived at through interaction. The most effective research dissemination for policymakers appears to be seminars and workshops that provide opportunities for dialogue (Nutley et al., 2007; Walter et al., 2005).

Thus, a fundamental step in evaluating any policy effort is often overlooked—knowing whether you are getting the information to the right people in the right way. Assessing whether information is reaching actors in the policy community entails careful record keeping and tracking of seminar attendance, requests for reports and information, and Web usage statistics. For example, the 18th Family

Impact Seminar in Wisconsin was attended by 110 participants: 28 legislators came to the morning seminar alone or with an aide, 5 additional legislators came to a legislator-only luncheon discussion, an additional 26 offices sent an aide to the seminar, and 15 more offices ordered the briefing report or audiotape. Overall, this seminar reached 74 legislators and their staff—over half of Wisconsin's 132 legislative offices along with 19 state agency officials, 5 legislative service agency staffers, and 2 university faculty.

Another evaluation strategy is tracking whether the seminar reaches influential policymakers. According to Mary Fairchild, senior fellow at the National Conference of State Legislatures, one of the biggest mistakes people outside of the legislature make is that "they develop a relationship with a friendly legislator. Somebody who is their friend ... and that person may not have an ounce of influence." So, we track not only how many policymakers come but also who comes, such as committee chairs, bill sponsors, and legislative opinion leaders on the issue. For example, of those offices with a staff member specifically assigned to child, family, or human service issues, two thirds attended one of two Wisconsin seminars on prescription drugs, participated in a discussion, or ordered a briefing report. At a Wisconsin seminar on early childhood education and care, a luncheon discussion included many of the key players on the issue: the chairs of the Education Committee in the Senate and the Assembly, the chair and ranking minority member of the Assembly Children and Families Committee, and the Assembly Democratic caucus chair.

Another way to evaluate a policy effort is its ability to provide information or opportunities that are unavailable in other settings. According to Smith (1991), the most valuable service a professional could provide policymakers may not be generating novel policy ideas. Rather, it might be providing a neutral space for dialogue outside the contentious, interest-group-dominated environment in which policymaking typically takes place. By operating outside the political pressures of the policymakers' usual environment, research dissemination efforts can provide a neutral forum that appears to be more conducive to seeking common ground and reaching compromise.

In one example, 14 legislators attended a roundtable discussion on health care costs. On a scale of 1 (*poor*) to 5 (*excellent*), legislators rated the usefulness of the discussion as 4.3 (response rate = 93%). When asked how useful the discussion was in helping make contacts with colleagues on the other side of the aisle, legislators assigned a rating of 4.2. Senator Mark Miller, current cochair of Wisconsin's powerful budget committee, explained the value he finds in seminar discussions for building understanding of different policy perspectives:

> The other thing that I really, really like is the fact that legislators from different political persuasions who are sincerely interested in dealing with that particular policy issue get a chance to understand what the concerns of the other members are. We oftentimes don't understand people on the other side of the aisle because we don't get a chance to talk to them just on policy, and that's one of the real benefits of the Family Impact Seminars.

Gains Knowledge

Our theory of change proposes that policymakers must understand the research that is presented if they are going to act on it. To assess policymakers' understanding of research on the issue and how it affects families, we use the retrospective pre- and posttest methodology first proposed by Campbell and Stanley (Lamb, 2005). At the end of the session, participants report their understanding of the same items *before* and *after* the seminar.

The retrospective pre- and posttest methodology is not considered a perfect evaluation tool because of a potential bias when respondents want to appear like a "good subject." However, in previous studies, little difference has been reported between the results of evaluations using retrospective pre- and posttests and traditional pre- and posttests (Lamb, 2005; Pratt, McGuigan, & Katzev, 2000). Retrospective pre- and posttest methodology can be useful in situations in which more traditional methods are difficult to use, four of which we consider here specifically in relation to policy settings. First, this method is appropriate when a less complex and time-consuming evaluation is desirable. Busy policymakers might not be willing to commit the time to complete the two evaluation protocols required in a typical pre- and posttest. Second, Professor Laura Hill (e-mail communication, June 3, 2009) recommended this method when you are asking people to rate their knowledge on items that they do not grasp, but think they do. Thus, pretest results can be inaccurate when participants initially think they know more than they do (read myth). Myth and the propensity of policymakers to treat myth as fact is well documented in policy settings (Flinchbaugh, 1988; Heckman, 1990).

Third, one goal of the evaluation of policy education is exactly what the retrospective pre- and posttest evaluation does—to explain change in knowledge as experienced subjectively by participants (Hill & Betz, 2005; Pratt et al., 2000). For some stakeholders such as legislative advisors and funders, knowledge change stated by policymakers may be one of the most persuasive forms of data. Finally, a retrospective pre- and posttest helps avoid "response-shift" bias by clarifying misconceptions in terminology before participants complete evaluation protocols. After the concepts are explained at the seminar, participants assess their new level of understanding and then reflectively assess their understanding before the event (Lamb, 2005). In policy education efforts, it is not unusual for research presentations to include new terms and innovative policy proposals that are previously unfamiliar to many policymakers.

Figure 11.4 displays the results for six items assessing perceived knowledge change from a Michigan Family Impact Seminar on Medicaid. Paired sample *t* tests examined whether the pre- and posttest means differed significantly. Overall, 61 participants (57% response rate) reported significant ($p < .01$) increases in knowledge on every item, including knowledge of both (a) the research presented at the seminar and (b) the family impact of policies and programs.

We have some circumstantial evidence that this retrospective methodology is valid. Looking within states, the results are not always significant, and they are sometimes significant for some participants (i.e., legislators) but not others (i.e.,

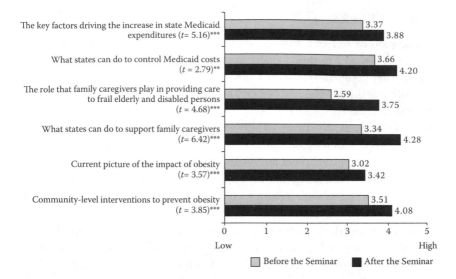

Figure 11.4   How participants rated their understanding of research and the family impact perspective. *Note.* Based on responses from 35 participants (57% response rate) attending a 2005 Michigan Family Impact Seminar, "Supporting Children and Families While Controlling Medicaid Costs." $^{oo}p < .01$, $^{ooo}p < .001$.

legislative staff). In addition, consistent with our expectations, legislators typically report lower pretest knowledge on the seminar topic than do more specialized state agency staff. Looking across states, we have noticed that pretest knowledge is considerably lower in some states than others, particularly those states with less access to and support from nonpartisan legislative service agencies.

Legislators have explained to us what these knowledge gains mean to them. For example, one Republican legislator reported that seminar information "raises the level of understanding across different issues in the Capitol. So I use it to question what we are doing, to say, 'You know this is a good thing.'" Anecdotal evidence indicates that evidence-based information destroys myth. For example, a Republican legislator commented after a seminar on parenting, "I wasn't sure that government had a role in parenting, but now I am sure we can no longer stick our head in the sand." Similarly, a legislative aide wrote on an end-of-session evaluation that the seminar "put many of our presumptions in a new light."

Another indicator of how legislators value knowledge is comments from legislators when they are unable to attend seminars. Democrat Mark Miller put it this way: "I know I have missed some of the sessions that our [Family] Impact Seminar puts on, and it just kills me." Similarly, Republican Senator Carol Roessler explained what it means to her to miss a Family Impact Seminar:

> We know we're going to miss information. We know we're not going to have the knowledge that, first of all, was given and that some of our colleagues will have. We consider ourselves really engaged in this particular issue, and we're not able to be there. ... Other colleagues are going to have that [information], and we would like to be engaged with them.

Changes Attitudes

The utilization of research may depend upon policymakers' attitude toward the usefulness of research in their work (Caplan, 1979). Empirical evidence, albeit limited, finds that policymakers most likely to use social science research report the most positive attitudes about its value (Bogenschneider, Johnson, & Normandin, 2009; Webber, 1986).

No known study documents the extent to which policymakers consider in their decisions the impact of policies on family well-being. However, some evidence exists that policymakers recognize the importance of families to a strong and vital society. In a study of the leaders of state legislatures that included Democrats and Republicans, liberals and conservatives, they rated family issues as a "sure-fire" vote winner (State Legislative Leaders Foundation, 1995). In the past three decades, progress has been made in the theoretical (Minuchin, 1974) and programmatic rationale for family-centered prevention and intervention. Program approaches that focus on families have proved more effective than programs that target only individuals in fields such as enhancing children's academic achievement and emotional development, promoting positive youth development, and preventing violence, delinquency, and disease (Brooks-Gunn & Duncan, 1997; Brooks-Gunn, Klebanov, & Liaw, 1995; Kumpfer, 1999; Spoth, Kavanagh, & Dishion, 2002).

To assess attitudes about the value of research on family issues, participants are asked to attribute changes in attitudes to the Family Impact Seminars (see this approach in Riley, Meinhardt, Nelson, Salisbury, & Winnett, 1991). These items were developed from anecdotes about how the Seminars had benefited them and are written in a way that asks respondents to attribute causality (e.g., "Because of the Family Impact Seminars, I am more likely to consider how pending legislation might affect families"). Because policymakers are called by staff associated with the Seminars, the results could be threatened by social desirability bias—the tendency of respondents to paint themselves in a favorable light or to respond in ways that they think will please the interviewer. We address these concerns, in part, by using a 3-point response scale of *not at all*, *a little*, or *quite a bit*. The response *a little* gives participants a socially desirable way to indicate that the Seminars have not benefited them very much. Thus, we consider *a little* as a negative response; only respondents who report *quite a bit* are counted as affirmative. We conducted phone interviews of 15 state legislators (88% response rate) who attended a 2006 seminar on long-term care. Because of the Seminars, policymakers reported being *quite a bit* more likely to (a) consider how pending legislation might affect families (73%), (b) see the practical value of research (73%), and (c) consider how new legislation that they were developing might affect families (60%). The results are displayed in Figure 11.5.

Participants often comment that the Seminars help them come to appreciate the value of a family perspective in policymaking. For example, one state agency section chief wrote,

Because of the Family Impact Seminars, I am "quite a bit" more likely to:

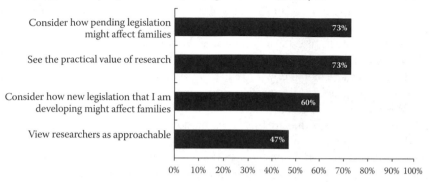

Figure 11.5   Percentage of legislators reporting attitude changes as a result of the Family Impact Seminars. *Note.* Based on phone interviews of 15 Wisconsin legislators (88% response rate) following the 2006 long-term care seminar.

> The Family Impact Seminars are something we make time for. Many people from around the department, including division administrators, attend regularly. Most important, this is the only time such a broad group gets together to really discuss family-related issues in an atmosphere that encourages good public policymaking over politics.

As noted previously, one Republican legislator articulately expressed in lay language the value to policymakers of receiving research on representative studies of families:

> In the Capitol, we get removed three or four steps from the folks who actually have to deal with a lot of the laws that we pass. We don't have to meet them at the counter when they go to the family services department at the county or the city or the school. ... [The Seminar] gives us an opportunity to see through studying how this affects large groups of people, because if we do get involved, it is usually anecdotal information, and so we deal with one or two people that talk to us about an issue. But we don't have the numbers and research to say how does it affect folks in a large scale, and that is very, very important.

Builds Relationships

Drawing from our community dissonance theory introduced earlier, the lack of communication between researchers and policymakers stems from differences in the cultures of researchers and policymakers, none more important than preferences for accessing information. One of the most consistent findings in the research utilization literature is policymakers' preference for the spoken word over the written word, based on a long-standing oral tradition in legislative bodies (Smith, 1991; Weiss, 1987a). Thus, research dissemination is more apt to be successful if conscious efforts are made to increase opportunities for face-to-face interaction (Walter et al., 2005). We have some evidence that the Seminars may help researchers initiate relationships with policymakers and reciprocally help policymakers initiate relationships with researchers. On the basis of unsolicited feedback from speakers and policymakers, the Seminars appear to dispel stereotypes that both policymakers and researchers hold of each other. Researchers report being impressed by how informed and perceptive policymakers are, and policymakers report being surprised at how practical and down-to-earth researchers are.

These perceptual shifts translate into more frequent contact. Following two 2001 Wisconsin seminars on prescription drugs, 30% of policymakers reported contacting researchers for further information (N = 11, 55% response rate). Legislators also contact staff of the Seminars to help them identify experts on issues of interest, find resources on specific questions, and provide written materials to help them prepare for speeches or hearings. These contacts appear to affect the attitudes that policymakers hold about researchers. On the basis of data from interviews following the 2006 Wisconsin seminar on long-term care (N = 17, 88% response rate), almost half (47%) of the legislators interviewed said that because of the Seminars, they are *quite a bit* more likely to view researchers as approachable (see Figure 11.5).

Consistent with social learning theory, studies of research utilization reveal that policymakers rely upon their colleagues for information (Walter et al., 2005). One unexpected benefit of the Seminars is the unique opportunity that they provide for some of the state's most liberal and conservative legislators to sit down together and discuss policy alternatives. We have been surprised by reports from state legislators that they have few opportunities to become acquainted with their colleagues on the other side of the aisle.

The role of the Seminars in building collegial relationships has emerged from both quantitative and qualitative data. In qualitative phone interviews of legislators following two seminars on prescription drugs, 78% reported sharing the information with colleagues, and 64% reported that the seminar helped them identify others interested in the issue (N = 11, 55% response rate). One Democratic legislator commented that seminar information was particularly useful for partnering with Republican colleagues because it does not carry partisan baggage and is accepted by members of both parties. Because the Democrats were in the minority at the time, he explained that seminar discussions helped him identify potential partners in the majority party who were in a much stronger position to move issues forward.

Senator Mark Miller, in a presentation to a gathering of knowledge brokers in the summer of 2008, explained how the Seminars indirectly affect policy change through the dialogue created between policymakers of opposing parties:

> Now interestingly enough, in the 10 years that I've been in public office, I've also come to realize that we tend not to make decisions either as voters or as legislators based on facts. We tend to make them based on emotion. Emotion tends to override reason. So we need to find ways of delivering facts, information, and research in a way that breaks down those barriers, that opens our minds to what the research tells us. And that is the challenge I think that you're all going to face as you try to implement these kinds of programs in your

communities. How do you break down the ideological and the partisan barriers that prevent us from communicating effectively? I think that institutional frameworks such as the Family Impact Seminars is extraordinarily beneficial in making that happen … in creating that institutional framework by which we can have a discussion across the partisan and ideological divides that often separate us, unnecessarily. Because what I find … is that we have more commonality than differences. But our differences are what keep us from coming to effective solutions. And you can help them get that together.

Accolades such as these were also expressed by Republicans, such as then-Assembly Majority Caucus Chair Daniel Vrakas, a 14-year veteran of the Wisconsin legislature who had been elected by the widest margin of any Republican in the Assembly. He explained how the Seminars helped him develop a reputation as a "problem solver" and work more effectively across party lines:

I am one of the leaders in the Republican side of the aisle. However, I think that I'm viewed and well respected by members on the other side of the aisle. I really think one of the reasons why that is the case is because of things such as the Family Impact Seminars where you're really trying to reach across the aisle, reach across the great divide to people and other legislators that may have a completely different worldview of how you solve these difficult problems. So it has helped me tremendously in terms of building my credibility and integrity with members in the other party. So for that, I have to thank the Family Impact Seminars.

Policymakers Use Research in Their Jobs

Sometimes it is (falsely) assumed that research is ignored by policymakers when, in fact, research may slowly seep into the policymaking process over time (Weiss, 1999). The end-of-session questionnaire administered at a seminar can tap immediate changes in knowledge, but it is not able to measure the longer-term impacts of seminar information. On each end-of-session questionnaire, we list the past five or six seminars and ask respondents to retrospectively report how they may have used information from prior sessions. Following some, but not all seminars, we conduct 10- to 30-minute phone interviews to find out how useful the information has been to policymakers after they have had some time to reflect on it, and the issue has had time to wind its way through the legislative process.

In 2001, about 2 months after two Wisconsin seminars on prescription drugs, we conducted phone interviews of participants, including 11 legislators (55% response rate). Of these legislators, 100% used the information to evaluate legislation, 82% to incorporate into speeches or presentations, 80% to identify references for further information, 27% to frame budget proposals, and 10% to draft legislation. The extent of use across several aspects of a policymaker's job indicates the potential of the Seminars to provide research that is useful and policy relevant.

Self-report data raise concerns about social desirability bias. To partially address this concern, we created contrast groups against which the reporter can compare the program (Riley, 2008). In interviews, we asked participants to rate several sources of information on child and family issues (see Riley et al., 1991). We intentionally place the Family Impact Seminars last on the list so the respondents have a frame of reference in mind before they complete the rating. We hypothesized that the information sources would be rated in the same order as in interviews of legislators attending an earlier seminar. We conducted a trend analysis to examine whether the mean ratings followed the hypothesized trend shown in Figure 11.6 (from the most useful on the top to the least useful on the bottom). Legislators rated the Seminars as the most important information source followed by committee hearings, constituents, lobbyists, media, and Web sites. Given that committee hearings and the Seminars were almost tied in the earlier ratings, it is no surprise that the means did not align exactly as we hypothesized; however, the means were close enough so that the linear trend analysis was still significant, $F(1, 13) = 49.67$, $p < .001$.

In written questionnaires, interviews, and testimonials, policymakers report that seminar information influenced their policy decisions, sometimes to enact laws and sometimes to defeat legislation. For example, legislators reported using seminar information to develop positions on cigarette tax and welfare reform legislation. A senator reported that a seminar presentation on the evaluation of the state's long-term care services helped put long-term care reform on the legislative agenda. In follow-up phone interviews, typically one or two legislators report that they used seminar information to draft legislation, and the vast majority used it to evaluate pending legislation. One Democratic legislator explained how seminar information gets incorporated into policy decisions:

> Because of the Family Impact Seminars, we are able to engage in discussions on a policy as opposed to an ideological level, and I think that we have been able to discuss the issues in a more responsible way and actually come to more responsible conclusions as a result.

Again, these testimonials shared with staff of the Seminars raise questions about social desirability bias. One potential avenue to avoid this potential bias is to turn to key informants who can compare the Seminars to other similar programs. For example, Dave Riley, associate dean of outreach in the University of Wisconsin–Madison's School of Human Ecology, described the Seminars in this way:

> In Wisconsin history, this is the only successful, ongoing, educational seminar series provided by the state university for state legislators and agency heads. Of the 10,000+ faculty in the UW system, it would be hard to point to more than one or two who could claim as great an impact on Wisconsin state policies as Prof. Bogenschneider has had through these seminars. Certainly, no other professor has done more to show state government leaders the value and utility of their state university and of research-based knowledge generally.

We also have evidence of policymakers explaining the value of the Seminars to key informants *not* affiliated with the program. Take, for example, this testimonial

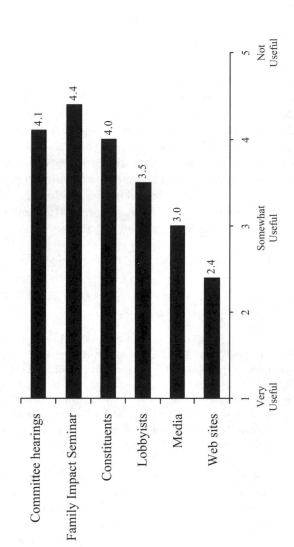

Figure 11.6   Average legislator usefulness ratings of information sources about child and family issues. *Note.* Based on a linear trend analysis from 15 legislators (88% response rate) attending a 2006 Wisconsin Family Impact Seminar on long-term care, $F(1,13) = 49.67$, $p < .001$.

by Peyton Smith, assistant vice chancellor, and coordinator, Wisconsin Idea Project, at the University of Wisconsin–Madison:

> I have been told by both Republicans and Democrats about the good work of [the] Family Impact Seminars. In fact, [*names four Wisconsin legislators*] specifically mentioned we should do more along the lines of Professor Bogenschneider's Family Impact Seminars in early January when I asked them how UW–Madison could improve its relationships with the state. Those testimonials are not easy to come by.

We also track how Family Impact Seminars information may be acted on in the legislative process. For the reasons discussed earlier, though, we make no claims that the seminars, in and of themselves, *cause* a policy change. Several examples exist where policy decisions *may* have been influenced by the Seminars. Following a seminar in Nebraska on ways to support low-income families, the legislature passed a state Earned Income Tax Credit discussed by a seminar speaker. In Indiana, after a middle school violence seminar, the legislature passed a law requiring public schools to have a safety specialist. A Michigan seminar featured a program that was included in the governor's State of the State address and in legislation introduced in the U.S. Senate by a Michigan senator. In Wisconsin, several features of other states' prescription drug programs that were presented at two seminars were incorporated into a prescription drug law enacted shortly thereafter.

As an advisor to the Wisconsin Family Impact Seminars, one of the roles Senator Carol Roessler played was to help identify seminar topics. She explained how a 2006 Family Impact Seminar contributed to passage of long-term care legislation the following year:

> We had started working on it, but the availability of the federal government giving us permission to wasn't there yet. But yet I had heard from insurance folks in my district how this had been done. I looked at some of the research of the other states, how they had saved maybe $13 million in one state from their Medical Assistance funds. I was able to use that research as well as what the [seminar] presenter brought to us, and we have now effectuated that change in our legislative policy this last session. That came about because of expressing an interest in this particular topic area.

To date, we have relied upon the research of others to assess whether policies reasonably influenced by the Seminars are effective, in general, or supportive of families, in particular. For example, the Earned Income Tax Credit, passed after a Nebraska seminar, is widely considered an effective antipoverty program because of its work-incentive features, low administrative costs, and targeting on taxpayers with wages in the bottom quartile of workers with children (Hotz & Scholz, 2000).

SUMMARY

This chapter attempts to move the evaluation of policy education beyond "bean counting"—merely adding up the number of presentations delivered, discussions held, or publications produced. Evaluators of policy education face a daunting task given the complexities they face regarding who the stakeholders are, what the long-term goal is, what early and intermediate outcomes to measure, which methods to employ, when to assess impact, and how to assess small impacts that accumulate overtime. We designed a theory of change for family policy education that specifies how research comes to bear on family policy decisions. Our theory also proposes some alternative methodologies to examine whether our work with policymakers is reaching its intended goals of (a) building greater respect for and use of research in policy decisions and (b) encouraging policymakers to examine the family impact of policies and programs. This theory of change has improved the evaluation of the Family Impact Seminars and may have the potential to inform the evaluation and implementation of other policy education efforts in at least four ways.

First, our theory of change helps identify what to measure by surfacing previously unstated program assumptions. This theory extends previous seminar evaluations (California Research Bureau, n.d.; Mayer & Hutchins, 1998; McClintock, 1999; Melton, 1995; Wilcox et al., 2005) by building on several theoretical traditions (i.e., constructive theories of learning, Kingdon's open policy windows, social learning, and community dissonance theories) to specify the whys and hows of turning good research into sound policy. Each theoretical link (i.e., short-term and intermediate outcomes) must operate in concert if the long-term goal is to be realized (i.e., policymakers using research in their jobs). Our theory identifies the short-term outcomes that policy educators must achieve—providing research on family issues (identified by policymakers and experts) to the policy community in a nonpartisan educational setting that encourages open dialogue. These initial outcomes lead to the unfolding of a series of multidirectional intermediate outcomes—the policy community gains knowledge, which changes its attitudes about the value of research and a family perspective in policymaking that, in turn, increases its propensity to build ongoing relationships with researchers and colleagues. This knowledge, when acquired in the context of established relationships and positive attitudes about the value of research, can achieve the long-term goal—policymakers using research in their jobs. They use this research in such ways as sharing it with colleagues and constituents, drawing on it to draft legislation, and using it to enact policies that support families.

In our articulation of the theory of change, the process appears to unfold in a linear-like fashion from awareness to knowledge gain to attitude change and ultimately to application in the policy process. We believe, though, that the process is much more iterative (Walter et al., 2005) than our description implies. We are uncertain where it begins and ends, how it accelerates or stalls, what all of the interim steps are, and whether some steps are more or less important than others.

Second, we attempt to bring together several different types of research use, including knowledge gain, attitude change, incorporation of evidence into speeches, drafting of legislation, development of positions, and enactment of laws. These indicators attempt to embody previous conceptualizations of research use (e.g., instrumental, conceptual, tactical, imposed, and process; Nutley et al., 2007; Tseng, 2008; Weiss, 1979). For example, changes in knowledge and attitudes are clearly conceptual uses, whereas legislation drafting and position development conform to instrumental uses (Walter et al., 2005). The theory also incorporates constructs that we raised earlier in this book such as salience shifting, framework shifting, solutions shifting, tactics shifting, and allocation shifting. For example, changes in the valuing of a family perspective in policy decisions is clearly framework shifting, whereas drafting legislation could be conceptualized as both solutions shifting and allocation shifting. Undoubtedly, in future iterations of the theory, we will try to capture these constructs more deliberately. We view this merely as a beginning attempt to disentangle the different ways that research is incorporated into the jobs, daily functioning, and decision making of policymakers.

Third, in keeping with the tenets of empowerment evaluation (Wandersman et al., 2005), developing a theory of change can also be an exercise in capacity building. For example, when things go wrong, program organizers can turn to the theory to see if components of the theory were overlooked or not followed meticulously enough. It might help them sort out whether additional elements are needed to avoid a similar failing in the future. When things go right, organizers can analyze what features accounted for the success and whether these features are adequately reflected in the theory. The intent is to monitor short-term performance and to build long-term sustainability by a continuing and critical examination of the viability of each element of the theory (Weiss, 1995).

Fourth, this theory of change can help prevent program drift (Fixsen, Naoom, Blasé, Friedman, & Wallace, 2005). The organizers of the Family Impact Seminars share a powerful vision of connecting the research community (which is producing hundreds of studies on issues that policymakers are debating) and the policymaking community (which does not have the staff or time to gather evidence on all the complex issues confronting them). This vision helps organizers stay the course, but a theory of change can help guarantee that the vision is operationalized as intended (Brown, 2003). For example, in their zeal, organizers can stray from the educational approach and begin advocating for the policy option that best represents their own values and interpretation of the scientific evidence, or they can lapse into thinking that experts are in the best position to know what topics policymakers *should* be thinking about. Without a theoretical map of how evidence winds its way through the policymaking process, organizers can inadvertently sabotage their own efforts by skipping a component of the theory of change, each of which is essential to program success. The value of a family policy education theory of change is summarized in Key Concepts 11.6.

Key Concepts 11.1   Is Taking the Time to Develop a Theory of Change Worth Your Time?

- Conducting even the most promising policy education program takes more than believing in your heart that it works. You can add "precision to your passion" (Pittman, 2008, p. 19) if you take the time to specify the early and intermediate outcomes that are expected to occur when a program provides research to policymakers to guide their decisions.

- Developing a theory of change can move evaluation beyond bean counting—adding up the number of presentations delivered, discussions held, and publications produced. Theory-based evaluation forces you to raise and respond to the critical questions of who the stakeholders are, what the long-term goal is, what early and intermediate outcomes to measure, which methods to employ, when to assess impact, and how to assess small impacts that accumulate over time.
- A theory of change can help build capacity for short-term performance and long-term sustainability by a continuing and critical examination of the viability of each element of the theory. When things go wrong, programmers can look to the theory for clues to avoid a similar failing in the future. When things go right, organizers can analyze what elements accounted for the success and whether these elements are adequately reflected in the theory.
- A theory of change can help prevent program drift by providing a theoretical map of the elements that contribute to program success. Periodically examining adherence to each theoretical element helps ensure the program is operationalized as intended.
- Specifying the whys and hows of turning good research into sound policy has benefits for our empirical understanding of research utilization that extend well beyond a single policy education program.

Our experience evaluating a policy education program in several states has taught us that a theory of change is necessary for a good program, but it is not sufficient. Having a theory of change in hand, no matter how good, does not ensure program fidelity (Philliber, 1998). In a sense, practitioners "redesign the program each day by what they do and how they do it" (Weiss, 1997, p. 517).

The Family Policy Education Theory of Change that we propose here has several limitations. First, a theory of change, no matter how accurate, cannot attribute outcomes to a program like the Family Impact Seminars. Even when data are consistent with the theory, the test is not based on a randomized trial, and, therefore, claims regarding causality cannot be made (Philliber, 1998). We cannot claim with confidence that the same laws or policy outcomes would not have occurred in the absence of the seminar. Conceivably, such outcomes could have resulted from any number of unmeasured factors or misspecification of links between measured factors (Anderson, 2004). That is, at this stage of development, if the long-term outcomes are not achieved, it is unclear whether this is from a failure of the program (i.e., the program did not activate the specified process) or from a failure of the theory (i.e., our understanding of the research utilization process is incomplete or inaccurate; Weiss, 1972).

Second, the evaluation data provided here are far from conclusive, but using a theory of change can provide insights that even the most sophisticated experimental evaluations fail to do. We potentially can explain what factors are responsible for program success or lack thereof (Weiss, 1997). The data do provide some evidence in support of our proposed theory of change. However, we are presenting some of the best data on each evaluation strategy, so the results demonstrate the potential of policy education even though not every seminar reaches this potential.

Third, the results reported here cannot rule out the possibility of selection bias—whether seminar participants are more apt to value, seek out, and use research in their decisions than nonparticipants (Hollister & Hill, 1995). Fourth, we have not fully capitalized on the evaluation potential offered by the 28 sites that are affiliated with the Policy Institute for Family Impact Seminars. These sites provide a natural experiment that potentially can be tapped to test whether there are disparate conditions in different states that are not adequately reflected in the current theory of change (Weiss, 1995). Fifth, for reasons of brevity, the results reported here focus on elected officials, although equally important is research use by other policy actors (e.g., state agency officials and legislative aides). Finally, the outcomes of the Family Impact Seminars must be interpreted with caution given that they result from evaluation of one's own program. The validity of such self-evaluations depends on programmers' ability to raise alternative hypotheses and interpretations, and their willingness to acknowledge failures and shortcomings (Brown, 1995).

The evidence on the success of the Family Impact Seminars reported here, albeit not definitive, is promising. However, we cannot carry out even promising programs such as the Seminars because we believe in our hearts that they work. We must continue to submit them to rigorous evaluation. In the words of Pittman (2008), we need to add "precision to our passion" (p. 19).

Yet the path to precision is strewn with multiple and seemingly impervious impediments that we believe may be just one more artifact of the cultural barriers that divide us. Perhaps we can begin to build an evidence base on disseminating evidence to policymakers by convening a meeting of the minds. We should bring together knowledge brokers who have the experience and expertise to bring research to the attention of policymakers, policymakers who are in the best position to know how they access and use research in their decisions, and evaluators who are able to envision the next generation of scientific methods. Bringing together these communities may spark the insights and innovations essential to better evaluate programs that fall between the cracks of social relevance and scientific rigor.

12

Where Do We Go From Here?

Some books are to be tasted
Others to be swallowed
And some to be chewed and digested.

—**Francis Bacon (1561–1626)**

To understand is hard. Once one understands, action is easy.

—**Sun Yat-sen (as cited in Cohen, Manion, & Morrison, 2000, p. v)**

*T*he desire to advance what we have come to think of as evidence-informed policymaking is widespread. Everywhere we turn we encounter frustration with our failure to bring quality research and dispassionate analysis to those doing public policy. No stakeholder is more sensitive to this challenge than the philanthropic community, which invests large sums on nurturing quality research in the somewhat quixotic hope of improving the effectiveness of public policies. Not surprisingly, many philanthropists are acutely aware of just how elusive this philanthropic objective remains.

The W. T. Grant Foundation, with a focus on youth policy development, is quickly moving to the forefront in addressing this challenge. In a recent internal briefing paper, Vivien Tseng (2008) noted the following:

> When we review our portfolio of grants over the last few years, we are pleased that our grantees have produced high-quality research evidence that is relevant for policymakers and practitioners in areas such as after school, mentoring, K-12 education, juvenile justice, welfare, and health. We are aware, though, that many findings that appear relevant and useful are not being used in policy and practice. We also know that policymakers and practitioners are often frustrated that research that is relevant and could inform their work does not exist or, if it does, is not accessible or easily understood. We want to better understand when, how, and under what conditions research evidence is used in policy and practice that affect youth, and how its use can be improved. (p. 12)

Foundations are not alone in their dissatisfaction with the current state of affairs. Members of the academy, certainly many in research universities, too often look upon the policy process with ill-disguised distaste. They are aghast that evidence plays such a small role or is manipulated to advance partisan or ideological positions. Even those in the media occasionally call for an end to partisan paralysis, criticizing politicians for failing to pursue more evidence-based policymaking. Of course, they do so even as they pit one point of view against another and spark further gamesmanship by focusing on who wins and who loses in the daily partisan struggle. Pundits express exasperation with the endless partisan bickering among political players, while so little progress is apparent on seemingly intractable social challenges such as health care, poverty, and educational performance disparities . among racial groups, to name just a few. Of course, we are not totally naive. Some in the academy are surely tempted to selectively employ evidence in ways that advance their own personal agendas, the media has been known to exploit information for ratings advantages, and pundits gain attention by exacerbating partisan or ideological tensions.

This failure to bring science to policy is particularly acute for what we think of as *social policy* concerns. As suggested earlier, a more comfortable fit appears to exist between the policy world and the harder sciences. In that arena, the underlying policy and research questions are more technical in character, and the issues are less subject to conflicting values and partisan divides. As with everything else, there are exceptions. Science has not been able to decide for us the precise inception of a human life, nor has it generated a complete consensus about the reality of global climate change. Still, despite the complexity involved, our attention has been more fully engaged by what we call *social policy* and *social research*.

THIS BOOK—A SMALL STEP FORWARD
IN A LONG JOURNEY

In the preceding chapters, we covered a good deal of ground. We initiated our journey by revisiting the thoughts of a number of pioneers who grappled with this question in the past (Caplan, 1979; Shonkoff, 2000; Snow, 1961), particularly in Chapters 1 and 4. They pointed us in the direction of the distinct communities and cultures between knowledge producers and consumers, and we made some effort to articulate a more complex understanding of the research and policymaking worlds. Rather than thinking only about two or three distinct and separate worlds, we laid out a more continuous institutional architecture ranging from academics located in pure research settings to a complex of settings covering applied researchers, intermediaries who bridge the research and policy worlds, and government workers who perform research functions. We then extended that architecture to encompass practitioners, managers, policymakers, and those public functionaries who support them. The bimodal world that dominated earlier thinking was simply too simplistic.

We also took some time to think through whether we were really tilting at windmills. If policymakers evidenced no interest in research and researchers demonstrated no interest in the policymaking world, perhaps our efforts are all for naught. We found quite the contrary in our interviews with representatives from both ends of the spectrum, those who produce and those who consume knowledge. We found, in fact, that policymakers express considerable interest in using research (see Chapter 2), sometimes for policy purposes (to help make good decisions and avoid making bad ones) and sometimes for political purposes (to earn the respect of colleagues and constituents, and to build support for legislation they want to pass). We also tapped the views of researchers, even in academically oriented settings, who have witnessed their work contribute to the resolution of real-world issues (see Chapters 3 and 8 for examples) and who have tasted the (addictive) rewards that such contributions bring. Indifference alone does not explain the breakdown between these worlds. We had to look elsewhere, at least in part, to explain the failure to communicate.

In Chapters 4 and 5, we started with the work of our predecessors who focused on the concepts of *community* and *culture*. Not surprisingly, we revisited the very notion of *research use*. Building upon prior thinking of pioneers such as Nutley, Walter, and Davies (2007), Weiss (1979), and others, we identified several dimensions in which research and empirical evidence essentially shifts our thinking in the real world of doing public policy. We posit that sound research, when viewed through the lens of knowledge consumers and when brought to policymakers in effective ways, can perform the following functions: alter how resources are distributed (*allocation shifting*), how policy/programs are designed and administered (*tactics shifting*), which policies/programs are pursued (*solutions shifting*), how we basically think about certain social issues (*framework shifting*), how much importance we give to an issue (*salience shifting*), and even how we think about doing policy (*awareness shifting*).

With these potential functions in mind, we fully engaged the concept of *culture* and slowly erected a theoretical foundation that we label *community dissonance theory*. Our thesis is simple. There are many legitimate reasons why research cannot answer all policy questions. But even where research can play a seminal role, we find that communications between knowledge producers and consumers is fraught with failure and peril. At the heart of this disconnect we place the concept of *culture*. With care, we elaborate on our notion of *culture* along two related dimensions—professional contributions and institutional contributions. The former taps the socialization process built into the way individuals are trained and incentivized. The latter taps into the organizational locus in which they currently function and how a whole set of interactional patterns in the workplace shape thinking and behavior.

Our discourse on community and culture plays out in a discussion of how these influences inform our ability to communicate with others. Again, we build on prior contributions to think through how key inputs from our professional and institutional cultures shape the way we see the world and others. We identify six domains, each with two dimensions: *focal interests* (what do we think are important questions), *targets of interest* (which constituency groups catch our attention), *cognitive frameworks* (how we process input and make decisions), *interactional preferences* (how we like to interact with others), *feedback loops* (to which environmental signals are we particularly sensitive), and *contextual preferences* (deep background factors such as how we think about time and where we are most comfortable). Taken together, these domains constitute the basic ways in which members of each community can differ and make communication possible at best and improbable at worst.

Much of the remainder of the book is devoted to insights and tactics that help us circumvent the limits of the cultural milieu in which each of us operates. In short, we cannot, and should not, deny who we are. The research culture and the policy culture, along with all the permutations where elements of both cultures intermingle, constitute legitimate professional expressions and ways of doing things, each playing a role in moving policy forward. Still, we can learn to be sensitive to the idiosyncrasies of our own cultural milieu and, in doing so, learn much more about those with whom we want to communicate. Knowledge and sensitivity are the initial steps toward enhanced communications and mutually beneficial interactions.

In Chapters 2 and 3, for example, we explore examples where some success in wedding research to policy has existed, particularly from the policymaker perspective. In Chapters 6 through 9, we focus on members of the research community. What do they need to know about policymakers, about the policymaking process, and about tactics that might make it possible for them to influence the policymaking community? Interspersed throughout the book, but especially in Chapter 9, are lessons and insights for achieving cross-community communication. For example, if you are a researcher who wants to work with policymakers, then don't act like a researcher. Rather, learn what policymakers want and deal with them accordingly. Find out what they want to know, when they want to know it, and how they want the information. What impresses your colleagues is not what will necessarily impress those in the policy community.

Ironically, one of our more salient insights is researchers have more influence when they try to exercise less influence. That is, objectivity and the dispassionate dissemination of information are critical elements of any effort to reach out to policymakers. Those successful in the policy world often *educate* rather than *advocate*. That perspective is explored in Chapter 10. Those doing policy are surrounded by lobbyists and interest groups. What most policymakers hunger for, at least the better among them, is access to honest information brokers who will tell it like it is and who will communicate with them in a direct and nonagenda-driven manner.

We fully recognize, however, that we do not have a corner on expertise. Our experience and prior work with members of both the knowledge-producing and the knowledge-consuming communities provide us with many insights. Still, so much more rigorous research is needed on so many fronts. In particular, generating evidence on disseminating evidence to policymakers is not easy. Doing policy occurs in a complex, multidimensional environment. It is not easy to impose the kind of gold standard experimental methods that we use to assess simpler research questions. As we detail in Chapter 11, we must be more ingenious here, must think through underlying theories of change, and must measure what we can to determine if we are headed in the right direction. No challenge is more daunting than figuring out how best to research the very question of using research.

WHAT RESEARCHERS COULD DO
AND WHY IT IS SO HARD

Surely, with even a little thought, we can generate a long list of research questions, some merely information gathering in character, some analytical, and others foundational. At the very center of this quest, we believe, is getting a better handle on the processes through which policymakers access research and incorporate it into their decisions. Such knowledge can expand our empirical understanding of this understudied phenomenon, and also help us build better theoretical frameworks for explaining why research is passed over or, conversely, why it is put to use in policy decisions. Such knowledge is central to developing programmatic strategies for communicating research to policymakers. Such knowledge is fundamental to evaluating the effectiveness of such efforts.

Research could also provide a deeper, more nuanced understanding of community members (i.e., knowledge producers, consumers, and intermediaries). Exactly what set of priors do the communities and subcommunities bring to their interactions with one another? Are some researchers naturally better at doing policy-relevant work, and are there others who would be more effective working through intermediaries? As hinted at in our pilot studies, are there personal or contextual factors that make some policymakers more receptive to evidence, and could a better understanding of these differences inform our policy education efforts? Is it possible that policymakers' appetite for research could be nourished over time by giving them a taste of timely, high-quality research in a digestible format? What can we learn from intermediaries who have an intensive focus on and commitment to communicating evidence to policymakers?

This field is hampered at its very core by methodological limitations, none more important than measurement. What does research utilization mean to knowledge consumers? What really are our dependent measures of interest? What analytic methods can legitimately be brought to bear on this complex topic? Stemming from various disciplinary cultures, some scientists feel that causal inferences can be arrived at only through formal experiments. Others are comfortable dealing with unobserved differences between treatment and nontreatment populations through various statistical techniques. Still others are quicker to accept causality and focus on teasing out explanatory and contextual factors associated with perceived impacts. Such differences emerge from very basic feelings about what constitutes believable "evidence." This list could go on.

Finally, we do not neglect some of the more or less objective reasons why research and rigorous analysis are discounted in the making and doing of policy. For example, research results do not always present a clear and compelling answer to complex or controversial policy questions. Results legitimately can vary given differences in the way models are specified, key variables measured, data collected, and analyses carried out. The sheer magnitude of research and analysis often makes it improbable that decision makers can isolate and sort through relevant work. And, of course, empirical evidence simply is not the only legitimate input into a policymaking body in a democratic society that represents diverse interests and divergent views. Values, self-interest, and power also play substantive roles in the rough-and-tumble of a democracy.

Even when politics and values do not trump the science, dispassionate policymakers might well arrive at dramatically different conclusions as to the meaning of available research. In the final analysis, we are not overly concerned about such differences in interpretation and use. Well-meaning observers looking at the same evidence can draw quite disparate conclusions about their policy import. Our primary focus has been on a whole range of what might be termed *cultural* and *communication barriers* that limit the use of science in doing policy. For example, how do knowledge producers and knowledge consumers view themselves and their work? What is it about their professional preparation and the institutional settings in which they function that can interfere with positive working relationships? In short, why don't they communicate better?

The answer always leads us back to our core notion of *culture*. Members of various groups along the production–consumption continuum possess their own language and their own communication styles. Even within the knowledge-producing community, each group marches to different disciplinary drummers, with goals and aspirations and methods that do not easily overlap (Cook, Shadish, & Wong, 2005). Knowledge producers are exposed to distinctly different institutional cues and signals that further impede their ability to communicate. In fact, too often knowledge producers feel penalized for seeking a relationship with knowledge consumers. Knowledge producers often see the time and energy required to develop relationships with policymakers as a professional cost in the ongoing race to maintain their scholarly reputation.

Knowledge consumers, on the other hand, often fail to see much comparative advantage in reaching out to knowledge producers. They can find it difficult to relate to researchers, who often are looking at yesterday's problems rather than today's priorities, who behave in alien ways, who are frequently elitist and arrogant, and who speak in obscure, jargon-infused language.

From the production side of the equation, we find the current state of affairs particularly puzzling. True enough, the primary imperative of science is to build upon and extend our theoretical knowledge base. Still, many scientists instinctively want to contribute to how the world works. They would love to see their research used by policymakers and practitioners. They would be most gratified to find their work actually being applied to improve the well-being of society. There is no greater reward, according to our exemplary policy communicators, than seeing their research and ideas translated into policy. At the same time, many located in intermediary organizations devote resources and energy to shaping public discourse but with degrees of success that have not been documented. They support original research and produce reports that translate good science for the makers and doers of policy. Yet, are these good intentions enough?

Despite all of this apparent interest, little systemic attention is paid to the science of bringing rigorous analysis to the policy world in ways that it might actually be used. To our knowledge, there exists little rigorous empirical work on the factors that facilitate or impede the use of science in the public arena. We do not host theoretical or research conferences on this topic. We do not encourage researchers to focus on the utility of their work for policy, nor do we think about incentives for those doing policy to alter their own attitudes and behavior. Our research universities expend little energy preparing the next generation of social scientists to interact with policymakers or to really understand how the policy world operates. Even as our land-grant institutions of higher learning espouse efforts to extend knowledge beyond the walls of the academy, the target population for such efforts is seldom policymakers.

Think about the following for a moment. The United States continues to spend more than other countries on research and development to support our remaining competitive advantages in the global market place. We also spend large amounts on research to maintain our military technological advantages and to advance our scientific leadership in such areas as alternative fuels development, global warming, and the space program. We establish formal mechanisms (e.g., the National Council of Economic Advisors and the research arm of the Federal Reserve) for bringing rigorous research to bear on economic challenges. We have some 250 graduate programs dedicated to training professionals interested in public policy. Yet, at the end of the day, some of our most pressing social issues are thrown into the policy arena with only haphazard attention paid to extant research and analysis. Somehow, solutions to some of the most complex questions we face as a society are left haphazardly to the vagaries of the political marketplace.

Public agencies do have research capabilities and budgets. But as suggested in Chapter 1, support for this function has eroded dramatically over time. Certainly, the philanthropic community does a lot, trying to pick up in the face of government retrenchment on the research front. Foundations spend millions on preparing thick, glossy reports but less on strategies for ensuring that these reports are read and used. They host conferences where research is presented to other researchers and interested policy wonks, but virtually nothing to develop innovative means to move beyond mere exposure to research results. It is not likely the current situation will turn around by publishing more reports or experimenting with techniques for issuing findings that are briefer and contain more pictures. Similarly, the media laments the state of contemporary public governance. There is too much partisanship with reasoned debate being replaced by political jockeying. The long-range public good is sacrificed to short-term personal or ideological gain. Yet the visual media drifts toward screaming matches where hard-core partisans vie to shout each other down. The printed media, with some exceptions, tends to slide toward glitzy and simplified pieces on complex topics, replacing substantive discussion with short, tabloidlike presentational styles using big print and dramatic colors. Besides, obituary notices for serious journalism are now part of our daily news diet. In its place, Web-based opinion and agenda-driven "evidence" flower, but with negligible safeguards established to ensure accuracy and balance.

Presidents and provosts in the academy issue hortatory statements encouraging faculty to engage in public service. University administrations assert that organizing, synthesizing, and transmitting knowledge for the public good is a legitimate academic endeavor and should be so rewarded. At the end of the day, no faculty member at a research university is fooled. At best, public service might well rank even lower than undergraduate teaching in the hierarchy of valued activities at top research universities. You can do it if it is done with the effortlessness of Gods, but don't spend too much time at it or intimate that you actually enjoy the experience. If you do, your dedication to scholarship will be questioned.

NEXT STEPS: EXPLORING AN ACTION AGENDA

We must look deeper, and more honestly, at the long process of bringing these two communities together. Underpinning any intervention strategy ought to be a research agenda that rigorously explores both the nature of the challenges and the efficacy of plausible responses. We looked at the challenge of advancing the evidence-based policymaking agenda as an opportunity to build on the work of others. Walter, Nutley, and Davies (2005, p. 341) suggested five key mechanisms to underpin any overarching strategy for promoting research utilization:

- *dissemination:* simple circulation or presentation of research findings to potential users, in diverse and more or less tailored formats;
- *interaction:* developing stronger links and collaborations between the research, and policy or practice communities;
- *social influence:* relying on influential others, such as experts and peers, to inform individuals about research and to persuade them of its value;
- *facilitation:* enabling the use of research through technical, financial, organizational, and emotional support; and
- *reinforcement:* using rewards and other forms of control to reinforce appropriate behavior.

These mechanisms are all well and good. They seem intellectually sound enough, and all make intuitive sense. Yet we know from our extensive discussion throughout the book that any realistic agenda for moving toward an evidence-informed policy world must not only aim to bring knowledge producers and consumers together, but reach deeper and more profoundly into the factors that separate them. We must address the very cultures in which they operate.

No action could have more effect than making research use a priority issue across all relevant communities. Research utilization is not a panacea to problems associated with doing public policy, particularly in the social policy area where value conflicts, theoretical disputes, and tactical differences are so prevalent. Moreover, as suggested throughout, there are severe limitations in just how well science can deliver unambiguous answers to complex social challenges. Still, we can do better. All actors, no matter whether they identify with the knowledge-producing, knowledge-consuming, or various intermediary communities, can think harder and more creatively about how to bridge the communication gap.

Below, we lay out a framework for a potential action agenda. It is not a panacea but a start, a way to get our thinking caps in gear. We organize this agenda around four themes. In the first theme, we push for more empirical input about the nature of the challenge and about effective solutions. In the second theme, we suggest adding the results of this future research to what we already know in order to alter the ways in which knowledge producers think about public policy and to change the contours of the culture in which they operate. In the third theme, we apply this research (along with what we already know) to strategies oriented toward improving the knowledge-consuming communities' interest and use of good science. In a final theme, we explore possible actions that might transform the intersection of the science and policy worlds on a more systemic level. These four themes, taken together, comprise an action agenda for the future, as outlined in Key Concepts 12.1.

Key Concepts 12.1   An Action Plan for the Future

Theme 1: Establishing Research Utilization as a Research Question

- Develop a consensus about what the salient research questions are.
- Pay particular attention to how policymakers use (or fail to use) research on vulnerable populations.
- Explore core research strategies to be pursued more deeply in the future.
- Initiate forums to facilitate cross-community dialogues.
- Attract new scholars to the study of research utilization.
- Develop a philanthropic infrastructure to facilitate such research.
- Develop more systemic strategies for promoting the use of policy-relevant research.

Theme 2: Changing the Cultural Milieu in Which Knowledge Producers Function

- Develop venues where researchers can tap emerging policy issues and questions.
- Examine incentives within academia for doing policy-focused research.
- Develop tutorial materials and Web sites for those wanting to do more policy-relevant research and outreach.
- Encourage faculty in research universities to work with students aspiring to become policy scholars.
- Develop more curricula that focus on the doing of policy-oriented research.
- Develop more opportunities for students and young scholars to work with policymakers.
- Facilitate cross-fertilization of ideas about teaching policy-relevant research and outreach.

Theme 3: Changing the Cultural Milieu in Which Knowledge Consumers Function

- Involve intermediary organizations more fully in enhancing policymakers' access to research and their research literacy.
- Develop tutorials and other products to help policymakers communicate with researchers.

- Focus more attention on translating research for policymakers.
- Sustain and improve efforts to disseminate research to policymakers.
- Provide more forums for policymakers and researchers to dialogue about future research agendas.

Theme 4: Exploring Systemic Changes

- Develop opportunities for knowledge producers and consumers to build relationships.
- Convene forums to stimulate cross-community dialogue.
- Enhance public and private support for policy-relevant research and its application.
- Encourage the philanthropic community to shift their focus from the new to the tried and true.
- Make the promotion of evidence-based policymaking a national issue.

Theme 1: Establishing Research Utilization as a Research Question

We recommend the development of a comprehensive research agenda exploring the reasons for underutilization or inappropriate utilization of research. This constitutes a sound preliminary step toward improving the use of research in policymaking and management. Executing such a research agenda is not a straightforward proposition, however. For a variety of reasons, there are conceptual, methodological, and cultural challenges that need to be addressed.

We need to develop a consensus about the character of the research questions to be addressed regarding how research is used in policymaking and what challenges exist. There are numerous research issues that require discussion and resolution, too many to fully explicate here. For example, one foundational question is how to define research use. We suggest taking care to view research utilization, not from the public or professional perspective, but through the lens of policymakers, where the research rubber hits the road. Another question that we argue is foundational to increasing research utilization is figuring out the basic processes through which policymakers access and use research to inform their decisions. It is well-known that lawmaking bodies operate under a long-standing oral tradition, yet policymakers' use of research has seldom been studied from a social network perspective. How does research come to policymakers' attention, and how much does its use rely on transfer from trusted colleagues? How do the "go-to" legislators, who policymakers tell us are so important, influence research utilization? How do policymakers calibrate the value of research alongside the other policy inputs that come to their attention, under what conditions do they take research into account, and when and why is it discounted?

Have we defined our target populations of interest well enough—who are the knowledge consumers that we should focus on? Are some policymakers more receptive to research, and how can we build on that interest? Extrapolating from the policymaker typologies in our earlier study, are there ways that *Enthusiastic*

Nonusers of research can be converted into *Enthusiastic Users?* Which strategic delivery strategies should we examine? The list could go on and on.

We need to pay special attention to how policymakers use research relevant to vulnerable populations. In our interviews of exemplary policy communicators, they found communicating research on vulnerable children and families to be frustrating because of the many myths and stereotypes they encountered. Vulnerable children and families (e.g., developmentally delayed children, delinquent youth, foster children, and fragile families) are the very ones most likely to come to the attention of policymakers (Scott, Mason, & Chapman, 1999), yet ironically they are often the most misunderstood. What languages and approaches are needed to communicate research on vulnerable children and families in ways that dispel myths and overcome stereotypes? Do we need special strategies to advance child and family policies that seldom result in immediate economic impacts? Can we develop strategies to communicate economic impact, when it exists, and to strategize about ways to provide political cover for policymakers, when it does not?

We need to think about core research strategies to be pursued. In this book, we rely upon the existing literature and our interviews of researchers from across the country; policymakers, policy administrators, and policy analysts from Wisconsin; and policymakers from New York. We recognize that we have barely scratched the surface in tapping insights potentially available from key stakeholders. We need to launch a broader and deeper dialogue with samples drawn from various communities discussed in this book—knowledge producers, knowledge consumers, and intermediaries. In addition, we should commission a series of in-depth case studies of efforts to wed science and policy. Much can be learned from those who have labored to make this potential marriage work, both those who have succeeded and those who have not. What methods are best suited to investigate the questions of interest? Are experimental methods appropriate for all research questions? For some, the methods may be transparent, for others, problematic. Before launching a major research agenda, we could profit from an in-depth dialogue into these and other foundational questions.

We need forums designed to facilitate cross-community dialogue about how to stimulate a broad interest in doing studies on research utilization. As a prelude to launching this research agenda, we suggest engaging representative members of all relevant stakeholder communities in a dialogue that vets various research issues (as introduced above), but also stimulates interest within the research community. We suggest a series of forums where knowledge consumers, knowledge producers, and intermediaries can dialogue among themselves and across their respective communities. These forums should be organized around policy questions that could benefit from research. Although papers might be commissioned, the organizing principles would focus on a peer dialogue devoted to arriving at reasonable strategies for moving ahead.

We need to attract promising new scholars to the study of research utilization. We believe the best way to initiate a longer-term research agenda on disseminating research successfully to the policy community is to attract younger scholars. We need to interest them early on in this topic. Identifying specific research questions that lend themselves to dissertations or that might constitute the early research foci of young scholars would stimulate additional related work as their careers mature.

We need to develop a philanthropic infrastructure to facilitate such research. Launching a research initiative does not occur in a vacuum. It demands four things: vision, direction, resources, and an infrastructure. The vision should emerge from forums described above that lay out the whys and hows of the emerging agenda. Direction demands quality leadership that gives the effort a grounded center of gravity. A policy-centered research agenda, however, also needs resources. As with other policy issues such as family preservation and fatherhood, philanthropic organizations may need to take the lead and draw attention to the resource-deficit issue. For example, major philanthropic leaders are in a position to convene meetings on this question, attract relevant government leaders, and spearhead a collaborative effort that would combine their fiscal resources and expertise.

We need more systemic strategies for promoting the use of policy-relevant research. We must take steps to help ensure that policy-oriented research is used. The principle end users and sponsors of such research should be involved in all phases of the work. What we *do not* need is more professional conferences where a couple "token" policymakers are invited to participate in an event organized to appeal to those from a research culture. What we *do* need is more conferences organized for those in positions to apply lessons learned. These venues should be designed to maximize discussion of the results and to seek practical applications. In addition, we have the capability to create a demand for such research. In part, this means creating new outlets for this type of publication that is explicitly written for and marketed to nonacademic audiences rather than "common denominator" publications marketed to both audiences that do not suit either very well.

Theme 2: Changing the Cultural Milieu in Which Knowledge Producers Function

Much of the material in prior chapters deals with how the culture of the knowledge production community (or communities) mitigates against research utilization. We believe, for example, that researchers (and many of their close compatriots) do not understand the policy world. They don't know how to intervene in the policy process, approach policymakers, or communicate effectively when they do interact with them. How might we begin to change things? We start with the following possibilities.

Develop venues where researchers can tap into emerging policy issues and questions. We start here because getting the question wrong is the biggest mistake that knowledge producers make, according to our researcher informants. The most rigorous study, the most sophisticated analysis, and the most well-honed presentation are all for naught if the research addresses an outdated or irrelevant question. Most academic researchers do not know where to go to keep up-to-date. In fact, they might not be aware of why they need to keep up-to-date. We need to develop opportunities for knowledge producers to ask knowledge consumers about what is going on in the real world. We need to explore venues for this interchange to occur such as conferences, podcasts, Webinars, Web sites, and so forth. These interactions can steer research to current policy questions. What's more, it puts knowledge consumers in the expert role, a position of respect upon which enduring relationships can be built.

Examine incentives within academia for doing policy-relevant research. Now, we touch upon a truly Herculean challenge. What can we do to reward researchers for doing policy-relevant work? This is not what the academy respects or rewards. Perhaps we can develop awards or forms of recognition for the best work in various policy areas, much like Harvard's Kennedy School of Government rewards innovative public programs or the MacArthur Foundation has its "genius" awards. The real work, however, must come within the academy itself. How do you change a culture that rewards a publication in an obscure journal that will be read by a few peers more than a significant contribution to the public good? How do you effectively incentivize academics to reach out to the policy world? Could the academy devote the same resources, support, and technical assistance for disseminating research as it does for generating research? Those engaged in disseminating research need copy and layout editors, conference organizers, evaluation consultants, graduate assistants, grant coordinators, Web developers, and so forth.

Develop tutorial materials and Web sites for researchers wanting to conduct policy-focused research or to communicate with policymakers. We have researchers out there who need help today. Let us say we have an academic researcher who primarily has communicated with other academics but now is working with government officials. Who can he or she turn to for help? Are there Web sites that can offer guidance? Are there trainings or tutorials that teach how to write for government officials as opposed to other academics? Where can one get a sense of how public agencies view research questions, how they think about research findings, and how they do their everyday business? We need to develop such Web sites, such tutorials, such trainings. They need to be widely publicized and accessible. And we need to make room at conferences and workshops so that attendees can be exposed to such materials.

Encourage the existing stock of faculty in research universities to support those students who aspire to become policy scholars. Researchers in training are very dependent upon the faculty with whom they work. These are their primary role models. At the same time, such faculty quite naturally expect their students to emulate them and to follow in their career trajectories. Unfortunately, the top of the knowledge-producing pyramid is reserved for those making brilliant theoretical and methodological breakthroughs when, in reality, the proportion of researchers making such contributions is very small indeed. Perhaps we can work with this generation of faculty so that they communicate to their students that conducting policy-relevant research or engaging in outreach to policymakers is a worthwhile career. Of those social scientists we interviewed who developed the dual capacity to generate and disseminate research to policymakers, just over 1 in 5 got their policy start as a student, often with the encouragement of their advisor. We should think of ways to adjust the culture of the academy to encourage students to think of policy-relevant research and outreach as work that has meaning and significance.

Develop curricula in advanced academic programs that address the challenges and strategies of doing policy-relevant research. Look at any doctoral program in a major research university. What is the typical student's focus? Students concentrate on developing methodological skills, learning how to think like researchers, and mastering the mechanics of conducting cutting-edge research. After all, academics assume that their intellectual progeny will mimic their own professional examples. Virtually no attention is paid to training them to get their work into the policy world. Why don't we encourage more training in user-focused research and on the institutions and cultures that might use their research in the future? Why don't we develop curricula that train students to write for diverse audiences and that prepare them to present their results to nonacademic audiences? These skills will not emerge spontaneously. They need to be nurtured in a conscious manner.

Develop more opportunities for those training to be researchers to work with policymakers and observe the policymaking process. Let us consider another aspect of training for the next generation of knowledge producers. Some students in professional schools do have opportunities to work with policymakers and practitioners as part of their training—students in public policy schools and social work come to mind. But those in training for academic and research careers almost never get this type of exposure. Why not? Some time ago, the Institute for Research on Poverty (IRP) and the Office of the Assistant Secretary for Planning and Evaluation (ASPE; the research arm of the U.S. Department of Health and Human Services) entered into an agreement to help prepare doctoral students to pursue research career trajectories within government. The interested students would take internships at both IRP (to hone their research skills and acquaint them with poverty-related research questions) and then ASPE (to expose them to how a public agency formulated research questions and applied research findings). Surely, we can come up with similarly creative models to expand the training and experiential opportunities for the next generation of knowledge producers.

Make curricula available on the Web to encourage cross-fertilization of ideas about teaching policy-relevant research and outreach. Our experience in teaching campus courses has revealed to us just how isolated college teaching is, particularly for specialty topics such as research utilization or family policy. Web posting of syllabi, teaching techniques, activities, and course readings is one way to encourage a cross-university exchange of ideas and to jump-start a dialogue about how to better prepare the next generation of policy professionals to communicate research to policymakers. As a fledgling effort, the Policy Institute for Family Impact Seminars hosts on its Web site (www.familyimpactseminars.org) a section for instructors teaching college courses on family policy. Currently posted are 14 graduate syllabi, 14 undergraduate syllabi, and 38 class activities and assignments. Contributions to the site emanate from 25 instructors from institutions such as Columbia University, Northwestern University, the Pennsylvania State University, the University of Connecticut, and the University of Maryland.

Theme 3: Changing the Cultural Milieu in Which Knowledge Consumers Function

Transforming the training and cultural development of knowledge producers is only one part of the challenge. Any comprehensive strategy must take steps to modify the dominant culture within the knowledge-consuming community as well.

More fully involve the National Conference of State Legislatures, the National Governors Association, the Policy Institute for Family Impact Seminars, and other such intermediary organizations in efforts to enhance policymakers' access to research and their research literacy. We believe that researchers teaming up with intermediary organizations would be a win–win arrangement. The researchers would gain access to policymakers, and the intermediaries would gain access to cutting-edge research. This collaboration could also advance the concept we term *research literacy,* which involves learning about the core technology of the research community, such as the basic research practices, the meaning of statistical significance, the definitions of descriptive and causal research, and the differences between correlation and causation. We should ask policymakers if they want to become research literate themselves or if they would prefer to find translators they can trust. If policymakers are interested, intermediary organizations or public policy schools could deliver this knowledge and awareness of research practice. We could teach sessions at conferences, offer short workshops, and develop Web-based tutorials for policymakers, legislative staff, executive agency officials, and other inhabitants of the knowledge-consuming community. All such initiatives would focus on a singular theme: How can you get the most out of available research?

Develop tutorials and other products to help policymakers better communicate with researchers. Another challenge focuses on directly helping policymakers in their relations with researchers. On occasion, policymakers interact directly with researchers. Among other things, they commission research projects, participate in hearings where researchers present evidence, or solicit the input of researchers on matters of current interest. We observed that policymakers do not optimize what they get out of these interactions. To the contrary, cultural impediments lead to insecurities or misunderstandings. Perhaps we need training for policymakers in the "care and feeding" of research types. How should you talk to researchers? How can you get them to give you what you need, not what they want to talk about? Why do they act like they do? Are they all as strange as they appear to be? Why don't researchers get what you are up against? In short, better dialogues are possible when participants understand one another.

Focus more attention on translating research for policymakers. We need to think hard about how the knowledge-consuming community perceives what the research community develops for policymakers and to examine how these translation efforts are perceived through policymakers' eyes. As noted earlier, academics interested in public policy still write journal articles that are strong on methodology and almost laughable on the applications of research findings. Evaluation and research firms still write long reports that probably justify their project budgets but have no chance of being absorbed or read by their primary target audience.

A lot of progress has been made. A number of organizations put out policy briefs or user-friendly research compilations on selected topics. All that is good, yet much more can be done. Our preliminary study suggests that policymakers find research useful if it is credible, timely, and accessible. Yet so little is known about policymakers' preferences for research characteristics, communication venues, presentation styles, and, in the case of written communications, the optimal length, format, and writing style.

In our view, one of the most promising new translation strategies is strategic frame analysis, which builds on the latest communications research and cognitive theory. Jack Shonkoff and his colleagues have worked with the FrameWorks Institute to apply these strategies to developing communication messages around early childhood education that resonate with and are meaningful to the public and policymakers. On the basis of their experience, when the communication is effective, people tend to frame issues in more effective ways, not as problems of individual children or families, but rather as social issues that need public policy to produce change (see Center on the Developing Child, 2007; FrameWorks Institute, 2002, 2005). Our exploratory study of policymakers hinted at how important political considerations are for the most enthusiastic users of research. We can develop methods that do a better job of framing research for policymakers in ways that are more useful in the political culture in which they operate.

Sustain efforts and energy on disseminating research to policymakers. For policymakers, accessing relevant research that is objectively and clearly summarized and that coherently addresses real-world practicalities is a daunting task. Savvy policymakers might be successful, but they should not find it that hard to get the input they need. Accessing objective research drawn from different sources, and that has been prescreened in terms of quality, is even harder to do.

We could do a lot more to examine the optimal avenues for bringing research to policymakers. Does it make sense to build the knowledge, skills, and attitudes so that researchers themselves can translate their studies for policy consumption? Perhaps we should rely more heavily on those who have the access and the skills to be effective purveyors of research, such as knowledge brokers and those who work for and with policymakers in agencies such as the Congressional Budget Office, the Congressional Research Service, state legislative services agencies, and so forth.

Could we do a better job of developing Web-based sites that are organized around the needs of policymakers? Barbara Blum and her colleagues at the National Center for Children in Poverty and Barry Van Lare in his work on the Welfare Information Network are examples of two efforts to bring research on welfare reform to policymakers. Both experimented with ways to organize and publicize their sites to make the information accessible and relevant. The problem, however, is that these sites were seen as focused primarily, if not solely, on welfare reform. When that topic faded from the front burner, so did support for their pioneering efforts. This agenda should be driven not by a substantive issue that is hot for a moment, but rather by the deeper need to wed science and social policy.

Provide more forums for policymakers to dialogue with knowledge producers about future research agendas. Few attributes of the current state of affairs have struck us as so disappointing as the tendency of the knowledge-producing community to do "rearview mirror" research, to focus on yesterday's questions. In effect, the real world often changes faster than researchers realize. So the culture of welfare offices changes, and researchers still develop research questions assuming nothing has changed. Developing future research agendas is too important to be left entirely to researchers. Rather, future agendas should emerge from an intense dialogue where members of both the knowledge-producing and knowledge-consuming communities really have an opportunity to interact around some of the most pressing problems of the day.

Theme 4: Exploring Systemic Strategies

Finally, there are action steps to be considered that cut across all stakeholder communities or are more general in nature.

Develop opportunities for knowledge producers and knowledge consumers to build relationships. On the basis of our data and experience, we need a paradigm shift if research is ever to flow more readily and seamlessly between the research and policy communities. Instead of disseminating research *to* policymakers, we need to think of developing relationships *with* them. The challenge of bringing knowledge producers and knowledge consumers together is not easy to overcome. Their worlds do not easily intersect. Researchers and policymakers do not work in the same settings, attend the same conferences, read the same reports, or eat at the same restaurants. Interactions will not occur naturally, so bringing them together will require some unnatural acts. We will need to think strategically about ways to create opportunities for communication to naturally occur—inviting policymakers as resources in classes and conferences, participating in their office hours and constituent feedback sessions, attending policymaker conferences, and putting ourselves in places that policymakers frequent (e.g., coffee shops, Fourth of July parades, campaign rallies, and community meetings). Among our sample of researchers who developed into exemplary policy communicators, only 1 of the 14 gained initial access by taking the initiative to contact a policymaker. These relationships are so key that we can no longer leave them to chance. We need to be planful in making these contacts more certain, more deliberate, more frequent.

Convene forums and other workshops to stimulate a dialogue across all relevant communities about the nature of the problem and possible solutions. Above, we suggest a series of forums that might be convened around specific topics such as developing a research agenda, bringing research-specific findings to policymakers in more effective ways, or evaluating the effectiveness of efforts to disseminate research to policymakers. Here, we shift our focus to a more general level of concern. We believe that communication and dialogue are essential to understanding this issue and successfully advancing any remedial set of initiatives. Clearly, there are members of each community who care about this issue. They should be brought together in a series of carefully designed workshops. Each workshop might be organized around discrete dimensions of the overall issue. Some might focus on exploring the causes of communication breakdowns, other forums could focus on possible solutions, and still others might focus on specific target communities (e.g., intermediary organizations and the role they play). On the basis of our experiences with WELPAN, the Family Impact Seminars, and other similar venues, we strongly believe that a great deal of wisdom can be uncovered when smart, well-meaning people are brought together in environments that encourage open dialogue among participants who do not normally interact. As much as we think we know, so much more can be tapped with a little effort, initiative, and investment.

Develop more avenues for public and private support for policy-relevant research and its application to real-world problems. By some measures we are going in the wrong direction. More social research is being done today, relative to the heyday of evidence-based policymaking in the late 1960s and early 1970s. Much of that increase has come from private (philanthropic) sources. But government-sponsored research, and government capacity to use social research, is retreating. As pointed out in Chapter 1, the size of the research arm of the U.S. Department of Health and Human Services is a fraction of what it was 30 years ago. As budgets are stretched, investment in R & D is likely to be further threatened. The irony is that research is needed even more when public budgets are tight. We need a healthy debate on expanding social research and what government can do (e.g., invest more in data infrastructure development such as the American Community Survey) and, in particular, to invest more to develop the capacity to use quality research in public policymaking.

Encourage a shift within the philanthropic community from a focus on the new to the tried and true. We have been particularly struck by what we see as shortsighted tendencies within the philanthropic community. Foundations want to be innovative and accountable—not a surprising demand from their boards. This drives them to chase what are seen as new approaches to impress their boards, to focus on narrow policy questions viewed as doable, and to demand measurable impacts in the short term. These directions can put the philanthropic community in direct conflict with the reality of the policy world where change is incremental and problems are complex. To the cynic it appears that society has complex problems, whereas universities have disciplines, legislatures have committees, and foundations have program priorities (Kellogg Commission, 1999). Most social problems are not so easily divided and compartmentalized.

Venues such as WELPAN and the Family Impact Seminars have proved remarkably successful in getting research to policymakers in ways that they can use. The philanthropic world must appreciate that investing in tried-and-true strategies that bridge the gap between knowledge consumers and producers over the long run is a critical investment, even if it does not seem to "fit" within their immediate, short-term portfolios. One of the most challenging aspects of organizing seminars for policymakers is the mismatch between what it takes to do good policy work and what it takes to do good fund-raising. For policy education to be effective, it must focus on the issues that policymakers are debating or discussing, whatever they may be. If topics are selected to fit a foundation priority, they may fall flat with a policy audience if the timing is not right. If Seminar topics are identified too early, the issue may have been resolved or fallen off the policy agenda before the program materializes. By waiting to identify topics, however, organizers of the Seminars often miss grant deadlines or miss windows of opportunity because the turnaround time is too long.

At the same time, we are cognizant of the very real difficulties associated with generating the rigorous evidence foundations need to warrant their investment. Given how the complex world of doing policy operates, philanthropists need to think of their investments as funding capacity rather than an ensured outcome. Substantive policy challenges are more like marathons than short sprints. Policy work needs to be thought of as building up the potential of longer-term dialogues and understanding between worlds that have too long been separate. The importance of this cannot be overstated.

Make evidence-based policymaking a national issue. At the end of the day, nothing is more important than getting this issue on the nation's agenda. Occasionally, a National Research Council initiative looks at the issue, or conferences are organized around the state of social research in the country. But we need something that is broader, more sustained, more inclusive, and independent of any current agenda. Self-interest, ideology, and partisan advantage will always have a place at the policy table. The challenge is to find a more prominent role for dispassionate evidence in doing public policy, or at least our best effort at objectivity, particularly in the social policy arena. We need to get that issue on the public agenda and keep it there.

Summary of Reasonable Steps

The above are tentative suggestions based on what we think are reasonable steps that might be taken. We, however, have no monopoly on wisdom here. Ideally, any such action agenda should be driven by sound theory and supportive empirical evidence. Our agenda is premature in that sense. We recognize, however, that analysis can be paralysis in this context. We must act and assess as we go along. In effect, action drives the need for theory and vice versa. Moreover, we may have to develop and refine our evaluation methods as we go. Researching research use is an extraordinarily difficult challenge. As we overview in Chapter 11, we do not even have a consensus on how to think about the concept of use. For this reason, and others, our action plan is put forward with great humility.

SUMMARY

Challenging the way the world works is an undertaking always fraught with potential disappointment. Many wise observers have cautioned against the conventional wisdom that science and rational analysis are an unambiguous positive good. A number of thoughtful scholars have argued that the virtues of rational policy analysis can be oversold. Doing public policy with an overreliance on rigorous empirical data interpreted by remote elites is antithetical to our desire for a full play of all values and perspectives in our policy process. Moreover, it is replete with adverse, unintended outcomes (Banfield, 1980; Lindblom & Cohen, 1979).

Hird (2005) is particularly cautious about how far we can go in advancing the evidence-informed agenda. His work stresses the very nature of partisanship in making policy. He noted that term limits have shifted power centers within state legislatures toward staff and made identifying key actors even more difficult. And he stressed that emerging technologies serve to proliferate the ways policymakers can be exposed to undigested "evidence" where quality and meaning are highly suspect. His cynicism is even deeper, however. Referring to skeptical academics, Hird (2005, p. 21) noted the following:

> These scholars lament the pernicious effects of policy analysis which, under the guise of objectivity, erode democratic impulses, invest excessive power in policy analysts who are far removed from the problems of the average citizen, and ultimately promote what Harold Lasswell calls a "policy science of tyranny."

Such cautions are not to be dismissed lightly. The scientific community does not have a monopoly on wisdom, nor can members of this community assert any special claim to dispassionate objectivity. Experts are human too. They have values that may or may not comport with the broader public good, self-interests that they want satisfied, personal idiosyncrasies and preferences that color their judgment, and blinders that hinder their vision about the ultimate value of their work. Rational analysis, grounded in sound empirical methods, is not a guarantee of good government. We have spent too much of our adult professional lives within the academy not to see its faults and limitations up close and personal.

On the other hand, there is a growing sense that we need to do something to elevate the general tenor of policy dialogue these days. A former ambassador to Norway and longtime legislative leader in Wisconsin reflected on his time as a state legislative leader as follows:

> A legislature can be an institution where individuals act collectively for the public good. A legislature can also be a cesspool of individualism. Unfortunately, the latter describes many state legislatures in recent times. I will not say that individualism has been the sole reason for scandal, gridlock, public disgust, and the popularity of term limits, but it is a monster that will destroy the community that is the legislature. (Loftus, 1994, p. 166)

In conversations with another past majority leader of the Wisconsin state assembly, Terry Willkom, he reflected on how political discourse has degenerated since he held his leadership position in the 1970s. Then, like now, there would be spirited partisan debates for public consumption. Then, unlike now, there were enough statesmen and stateswomen in both parties that would work across the aisle, often outside of the public eye, to compromise and find solutions with a goal of serving the overall public good. Enough politicians cared about good government to make good government a reasonable prospect. Public service was not an oxymoron but something that was held up as a noble avocation. The American people hunger for such acts of integrity and courage, according to Mark Helprin (1998), writing in the *Wall Street Journal*:

> The American people hunger for a statesman magnetized by the truth, unwilling to give up his good name, uninterested in calculation only for the sake of victory, unable to put his interests before those of the nation. What this means

in practical terms is no focus groups, no polls, no triangulation, no evasion, no broken promises, and no lies. These are the tools of the chameleon. ... Nonetheless, after and despite it betrayal, statesmanship remains the manifestation, in political terms, of beauty, and balance, and truth. It is the courage to tell the truth, and thus discern what is ahead. It is a mastery of the symmetry of forces, illuminated by the genius of speaking to the heart of things.

The pursuit of the public good cannot be left solely to the interplay of power and self-interest. We need some set of rules, some ways of looking at issues and challenges that can elevate our public discourse above the political fray that is too often defined by partisan and ideological positions. We do not deny the reality that evidence and rational analysis cannot be the final determinant of public policy. The human element is critical and unavoidable. Certainly, however, science as a way of framing questions and thinking through possible resolutions should play a much bigger role. It is not the total answer, but it can play a substantive role in moving beyond the paralysis and gridlock that seizes up our political institutions.

We believe that any successful strategy for advancing the evidence-based policy agenda will center on the role of relationships. Knowledge producers and knowledge consumers must get to know one another. They must learn each other's worlds and how each other thinks and behaves. It may not solve all our problems, but it will be a start. Eugene Smolensky, former director of the Institute for Research on Poverty and dean of the School of Public Policy at the University of California–Berkeley, shared with Tom his experiences in Washington, DC, working on welfare reform in the Carter administration during the 1970s. Like a lot of academics, he came away with a much deeper awareness of just how difficult it is to do public policy. The easy academic answers sometimes proffered within the academy are not always defensible in the extraordinary complexity of the real world. He expressed awe of Joseph Califano, then secretary of the then U.S. Department of Health, Education, and Welfare. Smolensky marveled that Califano's head "didn't explode" given the scope and complexity of the issues under his aegis. For Smolensky, exposure to the real-world policy process deepened his understanding and appreciation of both the policy process and the people who do this hard work. That is an epiphany that many academics who have ventured into the real world share.

In the end, an evidence-informed policy world is possible. In important ways, it already exists, even if it is hard to find sometimes. We do not have to await the Platonic ideal of a government composed of rational, altruistic elites. Empirical evidence and rigorous analysis can play a larger role if we take the time and care to do things right. It is up to us to make it happen more often and to greater effect. If we don't take advantage of our comparative advantages in science and technology, our inaction may have repercussions that reverberate on future prospects for addressing the wicked social problems of the 21st century. The need is there. The interest is there. The science is there. As many have pointed out, a journey of a thousand miles starts with the first step. We challenge the reader to take that step. In the words of T. S. Eliot, "the end is where we start from" (*Little Gidding*, Part V, line 3).

Appendix:
Methodological Notes

W e liberally referenced our own studies and interviews throughout the book. We describe them in detail only here for reasons of efficiency (to avoid repeating the methods in several places) and effectiveness (to improve the flow of the writing).

The analyses constituting the foundation of this work are based on the decades of experience the two authors have had working directly with policymakers to improve the quality of policy decisions. Between us, we have accumulated exhaustive experience gained through our work in and with government at the local, state, and federal levels. We have worked with think tanks, advocacy organizations, and broad segments of the philanthropic communities. We also have collaborated with other intermediary organizations such as Child Trends, the National Conference of State Legislatures, the National Governors Association, and the nonpartisan service agencies in state legislatures.

We conducted an extensive review of the applicable literature and the theoretical work of those who have written about this topic over the years. We thought hard about how this existing body of literature might help us understand what we have observed in our work with both policymakers and researchers.

Throughout the book, we draw heavily on our two models for bringing research to policymakers—the Family Impact Seminars and the Welfare Peer Assistance Network (WELPAN). The Family Impact Seminars are a series of presentations, discussion sessions, and briefing reports that provide high-quality research and dispassionate analysis to state policymakers. Currently, 28 states, affiliated with the Policy Institute for Family Impact Seminars, are planning or conducting Seminars in their state capitals. The Seminar methodology and the existing evaluation data are discussed extensively in Chapters 3 and 11.

WELPAN is a group of senior welfare administrators from seven states that met periodically to dialogue about their experience in designing, implementing, and evaluating welfare reform. WELPAN occasionally brought in resource people to meet with the group, but basically it employed a horizontal strategy of bringing together similarly situated peers who face like challenges to dialogue about their experiences and share what worked in their respective locales. Several assessments of WELPAN have been done, with one independent review in 2001 (SAL Consulting, 2001). These evaluations have focused primarily on the Midwest group but also on the experiences of the shorter-term West Coast and southern networks. Additional detail on WELPAN can be found in Chapter 3.

Our names are on the cover of this book, but our thinking has been shaped immeasurably by a number of very smart people whom we have had the pleasure of working with over the years. For example, as director of the Policy Institute for Family Impact Seminars, Karen has had the distinct honor to work with the directors and several staff involved in the Family Impact Seminars in Alabama,

Arizona, the District of Columbia, Florida, Georgia, Hawaii, Illinois, Indiana, Iowa, Kentucky, Louisiana, Maryland, Massachusetts, Michigan, Minnesota, Mississippi, Montana, Nebraska, New Mexico, North Carolina, Ohio, Oklahoma, Oregon, Pennsylvania, Texas, Utah, Virginia, and Wisconsin. Since 1999, the first 20 state affiliates have conducted over 140 seminars on topics such as child abuse, domestic violence, early childhood care and education, family health issues, family poverty and economic security, families and schools, juvenile and adult corrections, strengthening families/parenting, teenage pregnancy, and welfare reform. Typically, about six to eight phone conferences have been held annually to facilitate cross-state dialogue and peer mentoring among the talented professionals that head up the Seminars in each site. Karen has benefited immensely from her continuing collaboration with these courageous souls who engage in the risky and rewarding work of delivering research to policymakers.

In planning the Family Impact Seminars, Karen's understanding of policy has been enhanced through her collaboration with a number of knowledge producers and knowledge consumers in government and academic settings. For example, a number of analysts from the nonpartisan legislative service agencies of the Wisconsin legislature have served on seminar planning committees, written briefing report chapters, and provided consultation on the questions most relevant to current policy debate. Many executive agency officials, too numerous to identify here, have served on planning committees for specific seminars from the departments of administration, the commissioner of insurance, corrections, education, employee trust funds, health and family services, public health, the technical college system, and workforce development. In addition, Karen has collaborated with countless faculty across the country in academic departments including business, child and family studies, consumer science, economics, education, educational policy, educational psychology, law, medicine, pharmacy, population health, preventive medicine, social work, and so forth.

Tom has worked with state-level executive agency officials from Alabama, Alaska, Arizona, Arkansas, California, Idaho, Illinois, Indiana, Iowa, Louisiana, Michigan, Minnesota, Mississippi, Nevada, Ohio, Oregon, Washington, and Wisconsin in peer assistance network settings. He has also worked with countless local and state officials on welfare reform and service integration initiatives, too many to note individually. His local experiences are complemented by a 1-year stint in Washington, DC, working on President Clinton's welfare reform bill. This work brought him in contact with federal officials from several agencies including agriculture, health and human services, labor, treasury, and the White House, as well as numerous congressional staffers and staff from various congressional support agencies. Over his career, he continued working with federal agencies and many national intermediary organizations (including advocacy organizations, the philanthropic community, and think tanks) on various poverty and welfare challenges.

Furthermore, beginning in 2003, we interviewed a number of knowledge consumers and knowledge producers. Because we conceptualize bridging the gap between researchers and policymakers as a two-pronged process, we have strived to better understand both ends of the research–policy equation. We interviewed knowledge producers in traditional academic positions as university professors or

Cooperative Extension specialists, some whose primary responsibility was generating research, and others who were hired primarily to disseminate research. Some of our informants had observed research production and consumption from administrative perches as deans, department chairs, or directors of university institutes. We interviewed preeminent scholars who served on national science advisory panels, who received awards from professional societies for their contributions to science in the public interest, and whose programs had been designated by government bodies and independent evaluators as exemplary models of evidence-based scholarship. We also tapped knowledge producers in less traditional settings who served as presidents of think tanks, analysts in nonpartisan service agencies, and fellows and presidents of both family-focused and policy-oriented professional associations.

On the knowledge-consuming side, we interviewed policymakers of all political persuasions who represented wealthy, suburban districts as well as low-income, inner-city neighborhoods. We interviewed policy implementers in state agencies and policy managers in county government. Across the knowledge producers and consumers, we deliberately sought breadth in the number of roles, differences in areas of expertise, variation in the venues through which interactions had occurred, and diversity in the level of government with a larger concentration at the state level, but representation from those experienced in local-, national-, and international-level policy settings as well.

Another group of informants that Karen has interviewed extensively on repeated occasions over the past 16 years is a group of state legislators in Wisconsin who advise the Family Impact Seminars. Since 1993, when the Seminars began, Karen formed an advisory committee whose membership has increased from an initial 7 members to the current 11. The membership has changed over the years as legislators have lost elections, decided to leave office, or assumed leadership positions, although it has always consisted of one representative of the governor's office and an even split of Democrats and Republicans, strategically drawn from the left, right, and center of the political spectrum. In addition to asking for feedback on emerging seminar topics that might benefit from research and analysis, she also explored related issues such as where state legislators go for information, how useful they find different information sources and delivery venues, which mistakes academics make in working with policymakers, and what advice they would have for knowledge producers interested in providing nonpartisan information to policymakers. Interviews are conducted once or twice a year preceding each Family Impact Seminar. Since 1997, Karen has conducted 94 personal interviews ranging in length from 15 to 90 minutes (response rate = 87%). Some of these advisors have been interviewed repeatedly over the years, and, as a result, the conversation flows more freely and (yes) frankly in the context of a trusted, long-term relationship.

In addition, Karen and her colleagues have conducted two exploratory studies from both the researcher and the policymaker ends of the equation, which we refer to as the researcher study and the policymaker study, respectively. First, Karen and Bettina Friese, formerly a staff member of the Policy Institute for Family Impact Seminars, conducted a qualitative study of the single best speaker at each of the first 17 Wisconsin Family Impact Seminars (see Friese & Bogenschneider, 2009). Each individual passed two screens: (a) a professional screen of the quality of his or her research and (b) a policymaker screen of the effectiveness of his or her presentation. Using a standard set of questions, in-depth interviews were conducted of 14 researchers (response rate = 78%).

To supplement the structured interviews in this qualitative study, Karen conducted ten 20- to 90-minute open-ended, videotaped conversations of knowledge producers who were nationally known for their ability to communicate with policymakers, 6 who had been interviewed previously, and 4 who had not. For each of these supplemental interviews, the participants signed agreements allowing us to use their name and affiliation. This explains why some of the comments interspersed throughout the book are anonymous and others are not.

In 2003, we conducted a study of state policymakers in collaboration with the director of the Family Impact Seminars in New York, Professor Rachel Dunifon. The sampling frame consisted of (a) the entire state legislature (N = 120) in Wisconsin, given two pending elections and one vacant seat, and (b) a randomly selected subsample (N = 67) of the larger New York legislature with a total of 212 members ($\pm$10% sampling error and 95% confidence level). Interviews were completed of 109 state legislators, of which 74 were in Wisconsin (57% response rate) and 35 in New York (52% response rate). In Wisconsin, Karen and her associates conducted a parallel Web-based survey of policy administrators, specifically high-ranking state agency officials. Again, Karen supplemented these interviews with open-ended, videotaped interviews of 8 state legislators and 1 chair of a county board of supervisors, 2 who were interviewed on two occasions. For these interviews, we were granted permission to use the names and affiliations of these knowledge consumers, whereas the interviews of our Family Impact Seminars advisors mentioned earlier were anonymous.

For the interested reader, we provide detailed information on the samples, measures, and analyses of the two exploratory studies cited in this book. The first is the researcher study (see Friese & Bogenschneider, 2009), and the second is the policymaker and policy administrator study (Bogenschneider, Johnson, & Normandin, 2009).

THE EXPLORATORY RESEARCHER STUDY

The *Exploratory Researcher Study* examines what barriers researchers encounter when getting involved in the family policy arena, what rewards they experience, and why they were successful. Qualitative interviews were conducted of researchers who were selected to be speakers at a Wisconsin Family Impact Seminar (see the study results in Friese & Bogenschneider, 2009).

The sample was drawn from the 49 researchers and policy analysts (not program directors) who presented at a Wisconsin Family Impact Seminar on 17 topics over a 9-year period (see the description of the Family Impact Seminars methodology in Chapters 3 and 11). To be a seminar speaker, the researchers had to pass a professional screen of the quality of their research. To be included in the sample, the researchers also had to pass a policymaker screen of the effectiveness of their seminar presentation.

The seminar speakers were chosen by 17 different planning committees composed of experts on the seminar topic, including researchers, executive agency officials, and nonpartisan legislative service agency staff. Committee members selected speakers based on five criteria: (a) scholarly or practice-based reputation, as evidenced by awards, presentations at professional meetings, or recommendations from experts in the field; (b) a record of high-quality research as indicated by publication in prestigious, peer-reviewed journals; (c) a reputation of nonpartisanship; (d) experience presenting research to policymakers or the ability to draw pragmatic policy implications for lay audiences; and (e) the communication skills to present research in an engaging, understandable style (see Bogenschneider, Olson, Mills, & Linney, 2006). Because the aim of the Seminars is to find engaging speakers who conduct high-quality research that is most relevant to the policy questions currently being discussed in a state, speakers were drawn from wherever in the country they happened to be located (see the sample's extensive family policy credentials in Table 8.1).

The sample of 18 critical cases was chosen based on end-of-session evaluations collected to evaluate each seminar (average attendance = 68). The evaluations did not include an assessment of each speaker; however, when participants were asked in an open-ended question what they liked best about the seminar, they often mentioned a speaker. The sample included the most highly evaluated speaker from each seminar so that it would represent a cross section of family policies. One speaker was selected from every seminar, except one (that included only one researcher who was not well received); for two seminars, two speakers were selected because they both received such high marks from policymakers. The study's participants received more positive mentions than any other speaker in their respective seminars with three exceptions—two program directors who were ineligible for the study, and one speaker who was a nonrespondent and thus could not influence the results. Every participant received positive comments on this open-ended question by no less than 5% and up to 41% of the participants; overall, 70% of the sample received positive comments from 10% or more of participants, and 57% received comments from 20% or more.

We completed interviews of 14 researchers (response rate = 78%) spanning such fields as developmental psychology, economics, family studies, health care, and sociology from institutions including Harvard University, the Oregon Social Learning Center, the University of Pennsylvania, and the Urban Institute. The respondents (11 men and 3 women) were employed by universities ($n = 12$) and research organizations ($n = 2$). They had 274 years of combined experience working with policymakers, with an average of 20 years and a range of 5 to 30 years.

Researchers' contact with policymakers consisted primarily of four activities: (a) presenting or testifying before Congress, legislatures, and committees ($n = 14$); (b) responding to individual questions from policymakers and their staff via phone and e-mail ($n = 8$); (c) serving on committees, advisory panels, and task forces ($n = 7$); and (d) writing briefs, memoranda, and contract research reports ($n = 6$). All had experience disseminating research to policymakers at the state level, almost all (13) at the federal level, and 6 at the international level.

Procedures and Analysis

Because Friese and Bogenschneider (2009) were unaware of other protocols, the two communities theory was used to develop open-ended questions tapping the following topical areas: (a) the nature of the initial contacts and how they changed over time, (b) barriers researchers encountered, (c) ways that policy work was and was not rewarding, (d) stereotypes of policymakers and changes over time, (e) differences between the policy and research communities, (f) changes in research mission based on contact with the policy community, (g) attitudes and beliefs necessary for policymaker–researcher collaboration, (h) and recommendations for working with policymakers. Participants were also asked to describe the nature of their policy contacts, where they occurred, and what were their most memorable experiences. To schedule interviews, we contacted participants via letter followed by e-mail. 14 interviews were conducted—6 in person and 8 by phone; all interviews were recorded and transcribed. This study received Institutional Review Board approval from the University of Wisconsin–Madison.

Following Miles and Huberman (1994), we created a codebook to standardize the coding process, which included a priori codes that drew from previous theory and research (e.g., barriers, rewards, and recommendations) and inductive codes not initially anticipated (e.g., specific barriers and recommendations, and subpoints such as brevity in communication). Data were analyzed line by line using an iterative process, with the researchers shuttling back and forth between separate pieces of data, emerging themes, and subpoints. To derive meaning from the data, we (a) clustered the themes into categories (e.g., specific barriers and recommendations), (b) counted the number of times these categories appeared, (c) searched for disconfirming evidence, and (d) drew contrasts where they existed (e.g., contacting policymakers or policy intermediaries). To confirm the validity of the analysis, we (a) reported the findings in the researchers' own voice as much as possible; (b) used theoretical triangulation to corroborate the results with two communities, community dissonance, and structural family systems theories; and (c) relied on intercoder confirmation. That is, one author took the initial pass through the data and coded all interviews. A second author verified these themes and identified new ones; any new themes were subsequently verified by the first author. This process was repeated several times until both authors were confident that the analysis fairly and fully represented the data. The study's findings are interspersed throughout the book.

Of course, we realize the study's limitations. First, the sample was small and targeted only exemplary policy communicators identified by policymakers and professionals. Given the diversity of expertise included in the sample across almost a decade, we can have some confidence that the findings apply to family policy broadly defined rather than to a single family policy issue. Even though the researchers included developmental psychologists, economists, family researchers, pharmacists, and sociologists, further studies are needed to determine if these findings can be extrapolated to research utilization in other fields of social policy. Second, the sample was selected based on the effectiveness of presentations to state policymakers, which conceivably could limit the study's generalizability; however, most researchers had worked with policymakers in several venues, including local, national, and international jurisdictions, and through a range of communication vehicles encompassing the spoken and written word. Third, the value of research in family policymaking may be overstated, given that the sample included only researchers with previous success in this regard. Fourth, the recommendation to approach policy work as an educator, rather than as an advocate, must be interpreted with caution, given that one criterion for selecting Family Impact Seminars speakers is a nonpartisan reputation. Fifth, we recognize that the field would benefit from a parallel study of policymakers. We next turn to our exploratory study of policymakers.

THE EXPLORATORY POLICYMAKER AND POLICY ADMINISTRATOR STUDY

The *Exploratory Policymaker and Policy Administrator Study* was guided by our interest in whether there are characteristics that make some policymakers and agency officials more likely consumers of research than others, and which characteristics of research make it most useful to policy consumers. First, we discuss the policymaker component of the study and then the policy administrator component.

The policymaker manuscript, authored by Karen and her colleagues, Kristen Johnson of the National Council on Crime and Delinquency and Heidi Normandin of the Education Commission of the States, is currently under review for journal publication. The sampling frame consisted of (a) the entire state legislature (N = 129 in Wisconsin, subtracting the two seats pending elections and one vacant seat) and (b) a randomly selected subsample (N = 67) of the larger New York legislature with a total of 212 members (± 10% sampling error and 95% confidence level). These two legislatures are similar in some respects but different in others. Like legislators in nine other states, legislators in these two states serve nearly full-time when elected, compared to their counterparts in hybrid states or in part-time "citizen" legislatures where legislators have other occupations and meet less frequently (National Conference of State Legislatures, 2004). Wisconsin's 33 senators serve 4-year terms, whereas New York's 62 senators have 2-year terms. In the Assembly, Wisconsin's 99 representatives and New York's 150 representatives serve 2-year terms. Neither state's legislators are bound by term limits. Like many other larger states, both states have access to a large number of partisan and nonpartisan staff to help with researching issues, drafting bills, and calculating fiscal estimates. In 2003, Wisconsin had 756 permanent and session-only staff, averaging 5.7 staff per legislator. New York legislators averaged almost three times more than Wisconsin legislators, with 16.2 staff per member (National Conference of State Legislatures, 2003).

Wisconsin and New York have different social policy and political environments. For example, when states are clustered on program approaches for low-income families (Meyers, Gornick, & Peck, 2001), New York is categorized as a *generous* state with above-average income support and in-kind benefits but average enforcement of personal responsibility. In this five-category schema, Wisconsin is categorized as an *integrated* state, providing high income support and benefits yet also enforcing personal responsibility and offering progressive tax policies to support employment.

The two states also have different political cultures. New York is a predominantly individualistic state with a moralistic strain (Elazar, 1984). That is, government intervention in private activities is limited and undertaken to maintain a functioning marketplace, political activity is left to professionals, and new programs are initiated only in response to public demand. In contrast, Wisconsin has a moralistic culture in which government is rooted in the concept of the commonwealth, whereby citizens have a duty to participate in politics, and new programs are initiated even when citizens are unaware of problems.

Staff of the Wisconsin and New York Family Impact Seminars interviewed 109 state legislators, of which 74 were in Wisconsin (57% response rate) and 35 were in New York (52% response rate). For policy actors, response rates of slightly more than 30% are considered good (Browne, 1999). This higher response rate was due, in part, to our track record conducting Family Impact Seminars (a series of presentations, discussion sessions, and briefing reports targeted at state policymakers) for 6 years in New York and a decade in Wisconsin. In addition, we took a number of steps in the design and implementation of the study to ensure legislative response. First, we interviewed 10 Wisconsin state legislators (i.e., members of the Wisconsin Family Impact Seminar Advisory Committee) about the study's methods. On the basis of their input, we abandoned our initial plan of a written questionnaire and instead conducted phone or face-to-face interviews, which we limited to 20 minutes or less. In Wisconsin, legislative leaders in the Assembly and Senate wrote letters commending the Seminars and encouraging their colleagues to participate in the study. Third, reluctant legislators were encouraged by repeated contacts (11.9 contacts for each completed interview in Wisconsin and 6.9 contacts in New York).

Sample Description for the Policymaker Study

Of the 74 Wisconsin legislators, the average time in the legislature was 8.5 years, slightly less than the average of 9.96 years in the 2003–2004 legislature. The average age was 52, close to the average of 51 in the Senate and 49 in the Assembly. Overall, 72% had college or graduate degrees, 70% were male (close to the 73% male makeup of the whole body), and all were White (93% of the Wisconsin legislature were White at the time of the study; personal communication with Jennie Bowser of the National Conference of State Legislatures, December 6, 2007). Of the sample, 60% were Republican, and 40% were Democrat, similar to the legislature's 58% Republicans and 42% Democrats in 2003–2004. Overall, 82% served in the Assembly (compared to 75% of the legislature who served in the Assembly at the time of the study), and 18% served in the Senate (compared to 25% in the legislature).

Of the 35 legislators in the New York sample, the average age was 54, and the average years in the legislature were 10.8 (close to the average tenure of 11.9 in the 2003–2004 legislature). Of the sample, 72% were White, 17% were Black, and

9% were Hispanic, close to the racial/ethnic makeup of the New York legislature at the time of the study—79% White, 14% Black, and 7% Hispanic (personal communication with Jennie Bowser of the National Conference of State Legislatures, December 6, 2007). Four of 5 had college degrees, and 80% were male (close to the 78% that were males in the legislature at the time of the study). Overall, 60% were Democrat, and 40% were Republican (identical to the political makeup of the legislature). In the sample, 80% served in the Assembly (compared to 71% of the legislature who served in the Assembly at the time of the study), and 20% served in the Senate (compared to 29% in the legislature).

Measures for the Policymaker and Policy Administrator Study

These measures drew heavily from the concepts of two landmark studies (Caplan, Morrison, & Stambaugh, 1975; Weiss & Bucuvalas, 1980) and two other influential studies (Kingdon, 2003; Shulock, 1999). Because the two landmark studies were based on agency officials, grant review committee members, and researchers, we pilot tested the constructs used in these former studies with 5 former policymakers and 5 former legislative aides from New York and Wisconsin who were ineligible for the study because they were no longer working in the legislature. Based on these pilot interviews, the reliabilities of all measures reached .7 (which ended up being higher than the reliabilities in the larger study sample), and minor changes were made in the interview instructions and wording of some items.

The final 87-item questionnaire encompassed a battery of measures including the cluster variables (i.e., policymakers' attitudes toward, knowledge about, and behaviors regarding research), research characteristics, and other variables (i.e., who accessed the research and demographic characteristics). During the interview, *research* was defined as "information that is based on scientific studies," and *social science research* was defined as "information that is based on scientific studies on social issues such as poverty, education, families, and so on."

Three variables were used in the cluster analysis to assess whether there are different types of knowledge consumers in state legislatures based on their attitudes (i.e., valuing of research), knowledge (i.e., research access), and behavior (i.e., research use). Table A.1 summarizes the response categories, number of items, means, standard deviations, and reliability coefficients as assessed by Cronbach's alpha.

Valuing of research. This measure draws from studies by Caplan and colleagues (1975), Shulock (1999), and Weiss and Bucuvalas (1980). Respondents assessed their attitudes about the usefulness of social science research with items such as *Social science research is useful for policymaking* and *Social science research can benefit policy decisions.*

Research access. Respondents were asked how often they engage in various means of accessing information on issues important to them (Weiss & Bucuvalas, 1980). Respondents reported on the extent to which they look at program/policy evaluations, read research reports, or ask the nonpartisan service agencies of the legislature for research on an issue.

Research use. This measure assessed the use of research in policy decisions on a high-priority issue (Shulock, 1999; Weiss & Bucuvalas, 1980). Legislators rated

TABLE A.1   Response Categories, Means, Standard Deviations, and
Reliability Coefficients for the Major Study Variables

Variable	Response Categories	Number of Items	M	SD	Reliability Coefficient
Cluster Variables					
Valuing of research	1 (*strongly disagree*) to 6 (*strongly agree*)	5	4.30	1.06	.89
Research access	1 (*rarely*) to 5 (*always*)	6	3.13	0.91	.65
Research use	1 (*rarely*) to 5 (*always*)	3	3.44	0.99	.74
Characteristics of Research					
Action orientation	1 (*low priority*) to 5 (*high priority*)	3	3.42	0.87	.66
New ways of thinking about an issue	1 (*low priority*) to 5 (*high priority*)	4	3.64	0.85	.77
Political framing	1 (*strongly disagree*) to 6 (*strongly agree*)	4	4.88	0.80	.65
Research quality	1 (*low priority*) to 5 (*high priority*)	1	4.82	0.41	
Research presentation	1 (*low priority*) to 5 (*high priority*)	4	4.26	0.59	.65
Timing	1 (*low priority*) to 5 (*high priority*)	1	4.68	0.56	
Unbiased	1 (*low priority*) to 5 (*high priority*)	1	4.71	0.64	

how often they take the results of a study into account when making a decision, talk with their colleagues about research on issues important to them, or use research to justify a decision they had made.

The seven research characteristics included in this study were based on previous studies (Caplan et al., 1975; Kingdon, 2003; Shulock, 1999; Weiss & Bucuvalas, 1980). Three items were rated as some of the most important of 29 characteristics by decision makers when they were selecting which research studies to use in their work (Weiss & Bucuvalas, 1980). Also, we included four of five constructs that emerged from a factor analysis of research characteristics (Weiss & Bucuvalas, 1980) that decision makers said were important in their ratings of 50 research studies. (A three-item measure of "conformity with user expectations" developed for this study had a reliability of .44 and was dropped from the analysis.)

Action orientation. In both landmark studies, one important characteristic of the utility of research was whether it had direct and practical implications for action (Caplan et al., 1975; Weiss & Bucuvalas, 1980). In this study, respondents rated three items including *Research implications are economically feasible* and *Research focuses on factors that legislators can do something about.*

New ways of thinking about an issue. On the basis of the importance of innovative information in Weiss and Bucuvalas (1980), respondents assessed the priority they place on research providing a new way of thinking about an issue. Four items were rated, including *Research findings are unexpected or new* and *Research offers a new way of thinking about an issue.*

Political framing. An important aspect of research utilization (Caplan et al., 1975; Shonkoff, 2007) is whether research is provided in a way that is consistent with the unique information needs of policymakers given the political culture in which they operate. Four items were used to assess political considerations, including *A real life story can mobilize support for an issue* and *A catchy phrase can generate support for an issue.*

Research quality. On the basis of the importance of the quality of research in previous studies (Caplan et al., 1975; Weiss & Bucuvalas, 1980), respondents rated the priority placed on *The scientific quality of the research is high.* To correct for skewing, we performed a reflect and inverse transformation. A value of 1 was added to the largest score in the distribution, and then each score was subtracted from this constant.

Research presentation. One of three top criteria for using research in a previous study was *understandably written* (Weiss & Bucuvalas, 1980). In this study, four items assessed the presentation of research, including *Research findings are understandably written* and *Statistics are not overly technical.*

Timing. Another important aspect of research utilization in previous studies is the relevance of research, specifically whether it is provided when it is needed (see Kingdon, 2003; Weiss & Bucuvalas, 1980). In this study, respondents were asked to indicate the priority that they placed on research findings being available at the time decisions are being made. This item was also transformed using the reflect and inverse method to correct for skewness.

Unbiased. Of 29 research criteria, the third most important consideration for using research was *objective, unbiased* (see Weiss & Bucuvalas, 1980). In this study, respondents rated the priority they placed on *Research findings are unbiased.* Because responses were skewed, the item was transformed using the reflect and inverse method.

In addition to the cluster variables and research characteristics, we also collected data on the usefulness of different information types, who accesses research in legislative offices, and several demographic variables related to research use in previous studies.

Usefulness of different information types. Because we expected policymakers and policy administrators to value different types of information, we asked them to rate the usefulness of 10 different information sources in their work. Based on three theoretical conceptualizations (Bogenschneider et al., 2006; Caplan, 1979, and Shonkoff, 2000), these items were developed to contrast the different institutional cultures of policymakers and policy administrators (see Chapter 5 for an overview of each of these theories). Participants were asked to rate items such as the following on a scale of 1 (*not useful*) to 5 (*very useful*): *A personal story from a constituent about how the policy affected him or her, Information on how to adapt policies or programs to local circumstances, An overview of findings from several research studies,* and *Information on how policies in Wisconsin compare to policies in other states.* Cronbach's alpha was .79 for policymakers and .87 for policy administrators.

Who accesses research. Because the use of research is influenced by who obtains it (Caplan et al., 1975; Weiss & Bucuvalas, 1980), this study assessed whether research was accessed predominantly by staff or by both the legislator and the staff. Four items that assessed the frequency of accessing research (e.g., looking at evaluations of policies or programs, reading research reports) were coded as follows. If the legislator responded *staff only* for two or more items and *both* for two or fewer items, the case was coded as predominantly *staff access*. If the legislator responded *both* for three or more items, the case was coded *both legislator and staff*. Those who answered fewer than three questions ($n = 5$) were dropped from this measure. Research was accessed predominantly by staff in 20.2% of the sample.

Demographics. Respondents reported on demographic factors that previous studies have shown to be important to research utilization: age, tenure in the legislature, education, gender, and political party. In the total sample, the mean age was 53, and the respondents had served an average of 10 years in the legislature. About three fourths of the legislators (74.3%) had a college degree or higher, and one fourth were female (26.6%). The sample was split quite evenly between Democrats (46.8%) and Republicans (53.2%).

Analysis of the Policymaker Study

Cluster analysis, a technique used to classify individuals into groups using multiple variables, is particularly useful for exploratory research (Aldenderfer & Blashfield, 1984). Because no known study has attempted to categorize policymakers on their attitudes toward, knowledge of, and use of research in policy decisions, there were no a priori expectations about the number of clusters or their characteristics. The cluster analyses were conducted in two steps. First, the clusters were identified using the Wisconsin sample. Second, they were validated with the New York sample by fixing the number of clusters to be the same as in the Wisconsin sample and then comparing the similarity of the resulting clusters in the two states (Milligan & Cooper, 1987; Van der Kloot, Spaans, & Heiser, 2005).

The three clustering variables were first standardized using the range method. Next, beginning with the Wisconsin sample, legislators were assigned to clusters using squared Euclidian distance as the similarity (distance) measure (Cabrer, Contreras, & Miravete, 1991; Overall, Gibson, & Novy, 1993) and Ward's method (i.e., increase in sum of squares) as the hierarchical algorithm for combining cases. We obtained similar results using the single linkage (i.e., nearest neighbor) and complete linkage methods (i.e., farthest neighbor; Bartholomew, Steele, Moustaki, & Gailbraith, 2002).

On the basis of changes in the fusion coefficient, we tested the three-, four-, and five-cluster solutions using a form of kmeans analysis that allows the selection of different starting strategies and tests the sensitivity of different case orders (Wishart, 2006). Using the Ward method as the starting point, we ultimately chose the four-cluster solution because it had the smallest value for the Euclidean sum of squares (ESS) distance measure and created meaningful clusters (reproducibility was 32.73% and ESS = 1.58; the solution classified 72 of the 74 cases).

We validated the clusters using the New York data by running a kmeans analysis, fixing the number of groups to be four, as emerged in the initial analysis of the Wisconsin data. Despite the smaller sample size in New York, the pattern of results was remarkably similar. We ran several tests examining whether the clustering variables differed across states. Given the similarity of the clusters across states, we ran the remaining analyses on the two states combined.

This exploratory study has several limitations, four that are noted here. First, the high response rate suggests that the data are likely to be representative of the two states from which they were drawn, but they cannot be interpreted as being representative of policymakers who serve at the federal level or in local municipalities or of legislators in other states. The two states in this study differed in geographic and political character—a small, Midwestern, moralistic state with a substantial rural population, and a large, eastern, individualistic state with an urban metropolis. Yet there are also similarities in that neither have term limits, which may affect research utilization in unknown ways, and both are full-time legislatures with a high number of professional staff. Second, the results are based on self-reports of state legislators about the priority they place on research characteristics, which may differ from the actual credence they place on them when making actual policy decisions.

Third, the findings should be interpreted with caution given the paucity of available measures of research characteristics and research utilization, and the exploratory nature of the measures used in this study. Finally, we are unable to assess the influence of self-selection (e.g., legislators who are more interested in research might be more willing to participate in the study) or social desirability (e.g., the extent to which legislators wanted to please the interviewers or present themselves in a favorable light by reporting greater valuing, access, and use of research than was actually the case).

Methods for the Policy Administrator Study

Between 2003 and 2004, parallel data were collected from a policy administrator sample, specifically high-ranking state agency officials. The state agencies were selected based on two criteria: (a) whether the work of the agency would benefit from the use of social science research and (b) whether the agency makes decisions that affect children and families. In Wisconsin, eight state agencies met these criteria: the Departments of Administration, Corrections, Employee Trust Funds, Health and Family Services, Public Instruction, Revenue, Veterans Affairs, and Workforce Development.

The sample was intentionally limited to high-ranking state agency officials, most appointed by the governor or staff people selected by these appointees. The state agency officials responded to an 87-item questionnaire, similar to that administered to policymakers, that included a battery of measures, including the research characteristics and information types described above. Up to four reminders were sent asking officials to complete the survey. Overall, 56 state agency administrators completed the survey, for a 61% response rate (Bogenschneider & Normandin, 2005).

For further information on the methodology, the reader is referred to Bogenschneider et al. (2009), Bogenschneider and Normandin (2005), Bogenschneider et al. (2006), Friese and Bogenschneider (2009), and SAL Consulting (2001). The reader is also referred to a discussion of the WELPAN methodology in Chapter 3, and the Family Impact Seminar methodology and evaluation in Chapters 3 and 11. Furthermore, the interested reader can direct questions to either author.

References

Aaron, H. J. (1978). *The politics and the professors: The great society in perspective.* Washington, DC: Brookings Institution.

Aldenderfer, M. S., & Blashfield, R. K. (1984). *Cluster analysis.* Beverly Hills, CA: Sage.

Anderson, A. (n.d.). *The community builder's approach to theory of change: A practical guide to theory development.* New York: Aspen Institute Roundtable on Community Change.

Anderson, A. (2004, October). *Theory of change as a tool for strategic planning: A report on early experiences.* New York: Aspen Institute Roundtable on Community Change.

Anderson, A. (2005). An introduction to theory of change. *Evaluation Exchange, 11*(2), 12, 19.

Aos, S., Miller, M., & Drake, E. (2006). *Evidenced-based public policy options to reduce future prison construction, criminal justice costs, and crime rates.* Olympia: Washington State Institute for Public Policy.

Bane, M. J. (2001). Presidential address—Expertise, advocacy and deliberation: Lessons from welfare reform. *Journal of Policy Analysis and Management, 20*(2), 191–197.

Banfield, E. C. (1980). Policy science and metaphysical madness. In R. A. Goldwin (Ed.), *Bureaucrats, policy analysis, and statesmen: Who leads?* Washington, DC: American Enterprise Institute.

Barrows, R. (1984, April). Taking a stand: Extension and public policy issues. *Journal of Extension, 22*, 6–12.

Barrows, R. (1994). *Public policy education* (NCR Extension Publication No. 203). Cooperative Extension Service, Ames, IA: Iowa State University. North Central Regional Publication.

Bartholomew, D. J., Steele, S., Moustaki, I., & Gailbraith, J. I. (2002). *The analysis and interpretation of multivariate data for social sciences.* Boca Raton, FL: CRC Press.

Bennett, R. F. (1997, May 15). How do we manage the economy intelligently? An analysis of our budget, our debt, and our future [Transcript]. *Heritage Lecture No. 584.* Washington, DC: Heritage Foundation.

Berger, S. (1980). *The utilization of the social sciences in policy making in the United States.* Paris: Organization for Economic Development and Cooperation.

Bergman, M. (2006, December 15). *Nearly half of our lives spent with TV, radio, Internet, newspapers, according to Census Bureau publication* [Press release]. Retrieved May 27, 2008, from http://www.2010census.biz/Press-Release/www/releases/archives/miscellaneous/007871.html

Beyer, J. M., & Trice, H. M. (1982). The utilization process: A conceptual framework and synthesis of empirical findings. *Administrative Science Quarterly, 27*(4), 591–622.

Bimber, B. (1996). *The politics of expertise in Congress: The rise and fall of the Office of Technology Assessment.* Albany: State University of New York Press.

Boehnen, E., Corbett, T., & Ooms, T. (1997). The Midwest Welfare Peer Assistance Network (WELPAN): A model. *Focus, 18*(3), 64–66.

Bogenschneider, K. (2006). *Family policy matters: How policymaking affects families and what professionals can do* (2nd ed.). Mahwah, NJ: Lawrence Erlbaum.

Bogenschneider, K., Johnson, K., & Normandin, H. (2009). *Do state legislators value, seek out, and use social science research? Some do, some don't.* Manuscript submitted for publication.

Bogenschneider, K., Kaplan, T., & Morgan, K. (1993, October). What are the effects for children? In *Single parenthood and children's well-being* (Wisconsin Family Impact Seminar Briefing Report No. 2, pp. 18–22). Retrieved March 18, 2008, from the Policy Institute for Family Impact Seminars' Web site, http://www.familyimpactseminars.org/doc.asp?d=s_wifis02report.pdf

Bogenschneider, K., & Normandin, H. (2005, November). *Who is a policymaker anyway and how can we reach them?* Paper presented at the National Council on Family Relations annual conference, Phoenix, AZ.

Bogenschneider, K., Olson, J. R., Mills, J., & Linney, K. D. (2006). How can we connect research with state policymaking? Lessons from the Wisconsin Family Impact Seminars. In K. Bogenschneider, *Family policy matters: How policymaking affects families and what professionals can do* (2nd ed., pp. 245–276). Mahwah, NJ: Lawrence Erlbaum.

Booth, T. A. (1988). *Developing policy research.* Brookfield, VT: Gower.

Boyer, E. L. (1990). *Scholarship reconsidered: Priorities of the professional.* Princeton, NJ: Carnegie Foundation for the Advancement of Teaching.

Breckler, S. J. (2006). Crossing the line. *Monitor on Psychology, 37*(11), 22.

Brooks-Gunn, J., & Duncan, G. J. (1997). The effects of poverty on children. *The Future of Children, 7,* 55–71.

Brooks-Gunn, J., Klebanov, P. K., & Liaw, F. (1995). The learning, physical, and emotional environment of the home in the context of poverty: The Infant Health and Development Program. *Children and Youth Services Review, 17,* 251–276.

Brown, P. (1995). The role of the evaluator in comprehensive community initiatives. In J. P. Connell, A. C. Kubisch, L. B. Schorr, & C. H. Weiss (Eds.), *New approaches to evaluating community initiatives: Vol. 1. Concepts, methods, and contexts* (pp. 201–225). Washington, DC: Aspen Institute.

Brown, P. (2003). A conversation with Prudence Brown. *Evaluation Exchange, 9*(3), 10–11.

Browne, W. P. (1999). Studying interests and policy from the inside. *Policy Studies Journal, 27,* 67–75.

Bulmer, M. (1987). Governments and social science: Patterns of mutual influence. In M. Bulmer (Ed.), *Social science research and government* (pp. 1–23). Cambridge, UK: Cambridge University Press.

Cabinet Office. (1999). *Modernising government* (White Paper CM 4310). London: HMSO.

Cabrer, B., Contreras, D., & Miravete, E. J. (1991). Aggregation in input-output tables: How to select the best cluster linkage. *Economic Systems Research, 3,* 99–110.

California Research Bureau. (n.d.). *The California Family Impact Seminar: Policy research and discussion on issues related to children, youth, and families.* Sacramento, CA: Author.

Caplan, N. (1979). The two-communities theory and knowledge utilization. *American Behavioural Scientist, 22*(3), 459–470.

Caplan, N., Morrison, A., & Stambaugh, R. J. (1975). *The use of social science knowledge in policy decisions at the national level: A report to respondents.* Ann Arbor: Institute for Social Research, University of Michigan.

Carlson, A. (2001). Theodore Roosevelt's new politics of the American family. *Family in America, 15*(10), 1–8.

Carlson, A. (2002). "Sanctif[ying]the traditional family": The new deal and national solidarity. *Family in America, 16*(5), 1–12.

Cartwright, N. (2007). *Evidence-based policy: Where is our theory of evidence?* Washington, DC: National Research Council.

Center on the Developing Child. (2007). *A science-based framework for early childhood policy: Using evidence to improve outcomes in learning, behavior, and health for vulnerable children.* Cambridge, MA: Harvard University. Retrieved March 30, 2009, from http://www.developingchild.harvard.edu

Chamberlin, T. (1890). *The coming of age of the state universities.* (No publisher listed.)

Chandler, S. M. (2006). University involvement in public policy deliberation. *Professional Psychology: Research and Practice, 37*(2), 154–157.

Coffman, J. (2007). What's different about evaluating advocacy and policy change? *Evaluation Exchange, 13*(1), 2–4.

Cohen, L., Manion, L., & Morrison, K. (2000). *Research methods in education* (5th ed.). London, New York: Routledge Falmer.

Collins, A. A. (Ed.), & Overton, W. F. (Series Ed.). (2006). Editors' preface. In K. McCartney, M. R. Burchinal, & K. L. Bub, *Best practices in quantitative methods for developmentalists. Monographs of the Society for Research in Child Development, 71*(3, Serial No. 278). Boston: Blackwell.

Commager, H. S. (1950). *The American mind: An interpretation of American thought and character since the 1880s.* New Haven, CT: Yale University Press.

Commons, J. R. (1934). *Myself.* New York: Macmillan.

Congressional Budget Office. (2007, June). *Federal support for research and development.* Washington, DC: U.S. Congress.

Cook, T., Shadish, W. R., Jr., & Wong, V. (2005, December). *Within-study comparisons of experiments and non-experiments: What the findings imply for the validity of different kinds of observational study.* Paper presented at the French Econometric Society Meeting on Program Evaluation, Paris, France.

Corbett, T. (1991). The Wisconsin welfare magnet debate: What is an ordinary member of the tribe to do when the witch doctors disagree? *Focus, 13*(3), 19–27.

Corbett, T. (1992). The Wisconsin Child Support Assurance System: From plausible proposal to improbable prospects. In I. Garfinkel, S. McLanahan, & P. Robins (Eds.), *Child support assurance: Design issues, expected impacts, and political barriers as seen from Wisconsin* (pp. 27–52). Washington, DC: Urban Institute.

Corbett, T. (1993). Child poverty and welfare reform: Progress or paralysis? *Focus, 15*(1), 1–46.

Corbett, T. (1997). The next generation of welfare reforms: The challenge to evaluation. *Focus, 18*(3), 5-10.

Corbett, T., Danziger, S., & Werner, A. (2005). *Learning from integrated service models: The research challenge* (Concept Paper). Madison: University of Wisconsin–Madison, Institute for Research on Poverty.

Corbett, T., Dimas, J., Fong, J., & Noyes, J. L. (2005). The challenge of institutional "milieu" to cross-systems integration. *Focus, 24*(1), 28–35.

Danziger, S. (2001). Welfare reform policy from Nixon to Clinton: What role for social science? In D. L. Featherman & M. A. Vinovskis (Eds.), *Social science and policymaking: A search for relevance in the twentieth century* (pp. 137–164). Ann Arbor: University of Michigan Press.

Davidson, R. H. (1981). Subcommittee government: New channels for policy making. In T. E. Mann & N. J. Ornstein (Eds.), *New Congress* (pp. 99–133). Washington, DC: American Enterprise Institute.

Davies, H. T. O., & Nutley, S. (2008). *Learning more about how research-based knowledge gets used: Guidance in the development of new empirical research.* New York: William T. Grant Foundation.

Deichtman, S. J. (1976). *The best-laid schemes: A tale of social research and bureaucracy.* Cambridge, MA: MIT Press.

DeLeon, P. H. (1996). Public policy and public service: Our professional duty. In R. P. Lorion, I. Iscoe, P. H. DeLeon, & G. R. VandenBos (Eds.), *Psychology and public policy: Balancing public service and professional need* (pp. 41–55). Washington, DC: American Psychological Association.

DeLeon, P. H., O'Keefe, A. M., VandenBos, G. R., & Kraut, A. G. (1996). How to influence public policy: A blueprint for activism. In R. P. Lorion, I. Iscoe, P. H. DeLeon, & G. R. VandenBos (Eds.), *Psychology and public policy: Balancing public service and professional need* (pp. 263–280). Washington, DC: American Psychological Association.

Doherty, W. J. (1995). *Soul searching: Why psychotherapy must promote moral responsibility.* New York: Basic Books.

Doherty, W. J. (1999). Postmodernism and family theory. In M. B. Sussman & S. K. Steinmetz (Eds.), *Handbook of marriage and the family* (pp. 205–217). New York: Plenum.

Dror, Y. (1986). *Policymaking under adversity.* New Brunswick, NJ: Transaction Books.

Dunn, W. N. (1980). The two communities metaphor and models of knowledge use. *Knowledge: Creation, Diffusion, Utilization, 1*(4), 515–536.

Dunn, W. N. (1994). *Public policy analysis: An introduction* (2nd ed.). Englewood Cliffs, NJ: Prentice Hall.

Dunworth, T., Hannaway, J., Holahan, J., & Turner, M. A. (2008). *Beyond ideology, politics, and guesswork: The case for evidence-based policy.* Washington, DC: Urban Institute.

Einstein, A. (1949). Why socialism? *Monthly Review, 1*(1). Retrieved January 15, 2010, from http://www.monthlyreview.org/598einstein.php

Elazar, D. J. (1984). *American federalism: A view from the states* (3rd ed.). New York: Harper and Row.

Farley, F. (1996). From the heart. *American Psychologist, 51,* 772–776.

Featherman, D. L., & Vinovskis, M. A. (2001). Growth and use of social and behavioral science in the federal government since World War II. In D. L. Featherman & M. A. Vinovskis (Eds.), *Social science and policymaking: A search for relevance in the twentieth century.* Ann Arbor: University of Michigan Press.

Feldman, P. H., Nadash, P., & Gursen, M. (2001). Improving communication between researchers and policymakers in long-term care: Or, researchers are from Mars; policymakers are from Venus. *The Gerontologist, 41*(3), 312–321.

Fenno, R. F., Jr. (1978). *Home style: House members in their districts.* Boston: Little, Brown.

Fiorina, M. P. (2006). *Culture war: The myth of a polarized America.* New York: Pearson Longman.

Fixsen, D. L., Naoom, S. F., Blase, K. A., Friedman, R. M., & Wallace, F. (2005). *Implementation research: A synthesis of the literature* (FMHI Publication No. 231). Tampa: University of South Florida, Louis de la Parte Florida Mental Health Institute, National Implementation Research Network.

Flinchbaugh, B. (1988). Two worms: The importance of facts, myth, and values in public policy. In V. W. House & A. Armstrong Young (Eds.), *Working with our publics: In-service education for cooperative extension—Module 6: Education for public decisions* (pp. 222–226). Retrieved May 29, 2008, from http://eric.ed.gov/ERICDocs/data/ericdocs2sql/content_storage_01/0000019b/80/20/89/07.pdf

FrameWorks Institute. (2002). *Framing public issues.* Washington, DC: Author.

FrameWorks Institute. (2005). *Talking early childhood development and exploring the consequences of the frame choices: A FrameWorks message memo.* Washington, DC: Author.

Friese, B., & Bogenschneider, K. (2009). The voice of experience: How social scientists bring research to bear on family policymaking. *Family Relations, 58,* 229–243.

Gallup Organization. (2004, September 13–15). *The Gallup poll: Government.* Princeton, NJ: Author.

Glenn, N. D. (1993). A plea for objective assessment of the notion of family decline. *Journal of Marriage and the Family, 55*(3), 542–544.

Greenberg, D., Linksz, D., & Mandell, M. (2003). *Social experimentation and public policymaking.* Washington, DC: Urban Institute.

Greenberg, D. H., & Mandell, M. B. (1991). Research utilization in policymaking: A tale of two series (of social experiments). *Journal of Policy Analysis and Management, 10*(4), 633–656.

Gueron, J. M. (2007, June). *Building evidence: What it takes and what it yields.* Robert J. Lampman Memorial Lecture to the Institute for Research on Poverty, University of Wisconsin–Madison.

Harvard Family Research Project. (2007). Pioneers in the field: Four foundations on advocacy evaluation. *Evaluation Exchange, 13*(1), 12–15.

Haskins, R. (2006). *Work over welfare: The inside story of the 1996 welfare reform law.* Washington, DC: Brookings Institution.

Hauser, R., Brown, B., & Prosser, W. (Eds.). (1997). *Indicators of children's well-being.* New York: Russell Sage Foundation.

Haveman, R. H. (1987). *Poverty policy and poverty research, 1965–1980: The great society and the social sciences.* Madison: University of Wisconsin Press.

Haveman, R. H. (2008). The Wisconsin Idea and the La Follette School. *Lafollette Policy Report, 18*(1), 3–6.

Hayek, F. (1989). *The fatal conceit: The errors of socialism.* Chicago: University of Chicago Press.

Heckman, J. (1990). Social science research and policy: Review essay. *Journal of Human Resources, 25*(2), 297–304.

Helprin, M. (1998, July 2). Statesmanship and its betrayal. *Wall Street Journal.*

Henig, J. R. (2007, May). *The evolving relationship between researchers and public policy* [Transcript]. Presentation at the American Enterprise Institute Conference, Washington, DC. Retrieved May 29, 2008, from http://www.aei.org/events/filter.,eventID.1455/transcript.asp

Herfurth, T. (1949). *Sifting and winnowing: A chapter in the history of academic freedom at the University of Wisconsin.* Retrieved May 21, 2008, from http://www.library.wisc.edu/etext/WIReader/WER1035-Chpt1.html

Hill, L. G., & Betz, D. L. (2005). Revisiting the retrospective pretest. *American Journal of Evaluation, 26,* 501–517.

Hird, J. A. (2005). *Power, knowledge, and politics: Policy analysis in the states.* Washington, DC: Georgetown University Press.

Hollister, R. G., & Hill, J. H. (1995). Problems in the evaluation of community-wide initiatives. In J. P. Connell, A. C. Kubisch, L. B. Schorr, & C. H. Weiss (Eds.), *New approaches to evaluating community initiatives: Vol. 1. Concepts, methods, and contexts* (pp. 127–172). Washington, DC: Aspen Institute.

Holzer, H. (2009). *Low wage earners in a tough economy: An interview with Harry Holzer* [Audio download]. Retrieved June 4, 2009, from http://explore.georgetown.edu/news/?ID=40301

Hotz, V. J., & Scholz, J. K. (2000). Not perfect, but still pretty good: The EITC and other policies to support the U.S. low-wage labor market. *OECD Economic Studies, 2000*(31), 26–42.

Howard, M. (1988). *How to help your teenager postpone sexual involvement.* New York: Continuum.

Howe, F. C. (1912). *Wisconsin: An experiment in democracy.* New York: C. Scribner's Sons.

Huberman, M. (1987). Steps toward an integrated model of research utilization. *Knowledge: Creation, Diffusion, Utilization, 8*(4), 586–611.

Huston, A. C. (2002). From research to policy: Choosing questions and interpreting the answers. In A. Higgins-D'Alessandro & K. R. B. Jankowski (Eds.), *New directions for child and adolescent development, No. 98* (pp. 29–42). San Francisco: Jossey-Bass.

Huston, A. C. (2008). From research to policy and back. *Child Development, 79*(1), 1–12.

Innvaer, S., Vist, G., Trommald, M., & Oxman, A. (2002). Health policy-makers' perceptions of their use of evidence: A systematic review. *Journal of Health Services Research and Policy, 7*(4), 239–244.

Jacobs, F. H., & Davies, M. W. (1994). Introduction. In F. H. Jacobs & M. W. Davies (Eds.), *More than kissing babies? Current child and family policy in the United States* (pp. 1–8). Westport, CT: Auburn House.

Jacobson, N., Butterill, D., & Goering, P. (2003). Development of a framework for knowledge translation: Understanding user context. *Journal of Health Services Research and Policy, 8*(2), 94–99.

Jefferys, M., Troy, K., Slawik, N., & Lightfoot, E. (2007). *Issues in bridging the divide between policymakers and researchers.* Minneapolis: University of Minnesota Press.

Jonas, R. K. (1999). Against the whim: State legislatures' use of program evaluation. In R. K. Jonas (Ed.), *New directions for evaluation, No. 81* (pp. 3–10). San Francisco: Jossey-Bass.

Kaufman, I. (1993). Family research in state and local policy making. In G. E. Hendershot & F. B. LeClere (Eds.), *Family health: From data to policy* (pp. 113–115). Minneapolis, MN: National Council on Family Relations.

Kellogg Commission. (1999). *Returning to our roots: The engaged institution.* Washington, DC: National Association of State Universities and Land-Grant Colleges.

Kerschner, S. W., & Cohen, J. A. (2002). Legislative decision making and health policy: A phenomenological study of state legislators and individual decision making. *Policy, Politics, and Nursing Practice, 3*(2), 118–128.

Kersting, K. (2003). A life's work in developmental psychology. *Monitor on Psychology, 34*(6), 38. Retrieved May 13, 2008, from http://www.apa.org/monitor/jun03/lifeswork.html

Kingdon, J. W. (2003). *Agendas, alternatives, and public policies* (2nd ed.). New York: Longman.

Kreider, H., & Bouffard, S. (2005). A conversation with Thomas R. Guskey. *Evaluation Exchange, 11*(4), 12–14.

Kumpfer, K. L. (1999, April). *Strengthening America's families: Exemplary parenting and family strategies for delinquency prevention. A user's guide.* Paper prepared for the U.S. Department of Justice under Grant No. 87-JS-CX-K495. Retrieved July 2, 2007, from http://www.strengtheningfamilies.org/html/lit_review_1999_toc.html

Lamb, T. (2005). The retrospective pretest: An imperfect but useful tool. *Evaluation Exchange, 11*(2), 18.

Langworth, R. (Ed.). (2008). *Churchill by himself: The definitive collection of quotations.* UK: Ebury Press.

Lester Frank Ward. (2008, May 27). Wikipedia. Retrieved May 27, 2008, from http://en.wikipedia.org/wiki/Lester_Frank_Ward

Levin, B. R. (2003, November 8). *Improving research–policy relationships: Lessons from the case of literacy.* Paper prepared for the OISE/UT International Literacy Conference: Literacy Policies for the Schools We Need, Toronto, Canada.

Levin, B. R. (2005). *Governing education.* Toronto: University of Toronto Press. (Original work published 1952.)

Lindblom, C. E. (1968). *The policymaking process.* Englewood Cliffs, NJ: Prentice Hall.

Lindblom, C. E. (2005). The science of muddling through. In R. J. Stillman, II (Ed.), *Public administration: Concepts and cases.* Boston: Houghton Mifflin.

Lindblom, C. E., & Cohen, D. K. (1979). *Usable knowledge: Social science and social problem solving.* New Haven, CT: Yale University Press.

Linquist, E. A. (1990). The third community, policy inquiry, and social scientists. In S. Brooks & A. G. Gagnon (Eds.), *Social scientists, policy, and the state* (pp. 21–51). New York: Praeger.

Lipsky, M. (1980). *Street-level bureaucracy: Dilemmas of the individual in public services.* New York: Russell Sage Foundation.

Loewenberg, G. (2007). Paradoxes of legislatures. *Daedalus: Journal of the American Academy of Arts and Sciences, 136*(3), 56–66.

Loftus, T. (1994). *The art of legislative politics.* Washington, DC: Congressional Policy Press.

Lynn, L. E., Jr. (Ed.). (1978). *Knowledge and policy: The uncertain connection.* Washington, DC: National Academy of Sciences.

Lynton, E. A., & Elman, S. E. (1987). *New priorities for the university.* San Francisco: Jossey-Bass.

Mark, M. M., & Shotland, R. L. (1985). Toward more useful social science. In R. L. Shotland & M. M. Mark (Eds.), *Social science and social policy* (pp. 335–370). Beverly Hills, CA: Sage.

Matthews, D. R., & Stimson, J. A. (1975). *Yeas and nays: Normal decision-making in the U.S. House of Representatives*. New York: John Wiley & Sons.

Mayer, R., & Hutchins, V. (1998). District of Columbia Family Impact Seminar: A tool for devolution. *Maternal and Child Health Journal, 2*(1), 59–62.

Maynard, R. A. (2006). Evidence-based decision making: What will it take for the decision makers to care? *Journal of Policy Analysis and Management, 25*(2), 249–265.

McCall, R. B. (1996). The concept and practice of education, research, and public service in university psychology departments. *American Psychologist, 51,* 379–388.

McCall, R. B., & Green, B. L. (2004). Beyond the methodological gold standards of behavioral research: Considerations for practice and policy. *Social Policy Report, 18,* 3–19.

McCall, R. B., Groark, C. J., & Nelkin, R. P. (2004). Integrating developmental scholarship and society: From dissemination and accountability to evidence-based programming and policies. *Merrill-Palmer Quarterly, 50*(3), 326–340.

McClintock, C. (1999). Policy seminars for state and community leaders. In T. R. Chibucos & R. M. Lerner (Eds.), *Serving children and families through community–university partnerships: Success stories* (pp. 269–274). Norwell, MA: Kluwer Academic.

McLuhan, M., & Watson, W. (1970). *From cliché to archetype.* New York: Viking Press.

Mead, L. M. (2004). *Government matters.* Princeton, NJ: Princeton University Press.

Melton, G. B. (1995, September). Bringing psychology to Capitol Hill: Briefings on child and family policy. *American Psychologist, 50,* 766–770.

Meyers, M. K., Gornick, J. C., & Peck, L. R. (2001). Packaging support for low-income families: Policy variation across the United States. *Journal of Policy Analysis and Management, 20,* 457–483.

Miles, M. B., & Huberman, A. M. (1994). *Qualitative data analysis: An expanded sourcebook* (2nd ed.). Thousand Oaks, CA: Sage.

Miller, G. (1996). Children and the Congress: A time to speak out. In R. P. Lorion, I. Iscoe, P. H. DeLeon, & G. R. VandenBos (Eds.), *Psychology and public policy: Balancing public service and professional need* (pp. 331–342). Washington, DC: American Psychological Association.

Milligan, G. W., & Cooper, M. C. (1987). Methodology review: Clustering methods. *Applied Psychological Measurement, 11,* 329–354.

Minuchin, S. (1974). *Families and family therapy.* Cambridge, MA: Harvard University Press.

Mooney, C. Z. (1992). Putting it on paper: The content of written information used in state lawmaking. *American Politics Quarterly, 20,* 345–365.

Murray, C. (1984). *Losing ground: American social policy, 1950–1980.* New York: Basic Books.

Myers-Walls, J. A. (2000). An odd couple with promise: Researchers and practitioners in evaluation settings. *Family Relations, 49,* 341–347.

Nagel, T. (1986). *The view from nowhere.* New York: Oxford University Press.

Nathan, R. (2000). *Social science in government: The role of policy researchers.* Albany, NY: Rockefeller Institute Press.

National Conference of State Legislatures. (2003). *Size of state legislative staff: 1979, 1988, 1996, 2003.* Denver, CO: Author. Retrieved March 20, 2007, from http://www.ncsl. org/programs/legismgt/about/staffcount2003.htm

National Conference of State Legislatures. (2004). *Full- and part-time legislatures* (NCSL Backgrounder). Denver, CO: Author. Retrieved March 20, 2007, from http://www. ncsl.org/programs/press/2004/backgrounder_fullandpart.htm

National Research Council. (1979). *Evaluating federal support for poverty research.* Washington, DC: National Academy of Sciences.

Nelson, C. E., Roberts, J., Maederer, C. M., Wertheimer, B., & Johnson, B. (1987). The utilization of social science information by policymakers. *American Behavioral Scientist, 30*(6), 569–577.

Newall, B. (1990). Helping at the margins. *Focus, 12*(3), 37–38.

Newspaper. (2008, May 26). Wikipedia. Retrieved May 27, 2008, from http://en.wikipedia.org/wiki/Newspaper#Circulation_and_readership

Nielsen Media Research. (2007, December 19). *Nielsen study shows DVD players surpass VCRs: Most media technology trending up, according to Nielsen's quarterly home tech study* [Press release]. Retrieved May 27, 2008, from http://www.nielsenmedia.com/nc/portal/site/Public/menuitem.55dc65b4a7d5adff3f65936147a062a0/?vgnextoid=4673a1bcb279f010VgnVCM100000ac0a260aRCRD

Noyes, J. L. (2007). *Project on family economic success: A public policy partnership of the National Conference of State Legislatures and the Annie E. Casey Foundation* (Evaluation report prepared for the National Conference of State Legislatures). Madison: Institute for Research on Poverty, University of Wisconsin–Madison.

Nutley, S. M., Walter, I., & Davies, H. T. O. (2007). *Using evidence: How research can inform public services.* Bristol, UK: Policy Press.

Nye, F. I., & McDonald, G. W. (1979). Family policy research: Emergent models and some theoretical issues. *Journal of Marriage and the Family, 41,* 473–485.

Obama, B. (2006). *The audacity of hope: Thoughts on reclaiming the American dream.* New York: Crown.

O'Connor, A. (2002). *Poverty knowledge: Social science, social policy, and the poor in twentieth-century U.S. history.* Princeton, NJ: Princeton University Press.

Oh, C. H. (1997). Explaining the impact of policy information on policy-making. *Knowledge and Policy: The International Journal of Knowledge Transfer and Utilization, 10*(3), 25–55.

Olds, D. (2009, April). *Evidence matters: Examining the case of the Nurse-Family Partnership.* Paper presented at the biennial meeting of the Society for Research in Child Development, Denver, CO.

Overall, J. E., Gibson, J. M., & Novy, D. M. (1993). Population recovery capabilities of 35 cluster analysis methods. *Journal of Clinical Psychology, 49,* 459–470.

Patton, M. Q. (1997). *Utilization-focused evaluation* (3rd ed.). Thousand Oaks, CA: Sage.

Patton, M. Q. (2001). *Qualitative research and evaluation methods* (3rd ed.). Beverly Hills: Sage.

Pettigrew, T. E. (1985). Can social scientists be effective actors in the policy arena? In R. L. Shotland & M. M. Mark (Eds.), *Social science and social policy* (pp. 121–134). Beverly Hills, CA: Sage.

Philliber, S. (1998). The virtue of specificity in theory of change evaluation: Practitioner reflections. In K. Fullbright-Anderson, A. C. Kubisch, & J. P. Connell (Eds.), *New approaches to evaluating community initiatives: Vol. 2. Theory, measurement, and analysis* (pp. 87–99). Washington, DC: Aspen Institute.

Pittman, K. (2008, May). Precision engineering. *Youth Today,* 19.

Pratt, C., McGuigan, W., & Katzev, A. (2000). Measuring program outcomes: Using retrospective pretest methodology. *American Journal of Evaluation, 21,* 341–349.

Putnam, R. D. (1995). Bowling alone: America's declining social capital. *Journal of Democracy, 6*(1), 65–78.

Putnam, R. D. (2002). Bowling together: The United States of America. *American Prospect, 13*(3), 20–22.

Rabb, J., & Winstead, D. (2003). Perspectives of the ultimate consumers: Policymakers and program managers. In M. C. Lennon & T. Corbett (Eds.), *Policy into action: Implementation research and welfare reform* (pp. 21–38). Washington, DC: Urban Institute.

Reagan, R. (1983). Address to the nation on national security. Retrieved June 25, 2009, from http://www.fas.org/spp/starwars/offdocs/rrspch.htm

Rice, R. M. (1977). *American family policy: Content and context.* Milwaukee, WI: Family Service America.

Rich, A. (2001). The politics of expertise in Congress and the news media. *Social Science Quarterly, 82*(3), 583–601.

Riley, D. (1997). Using local research to change 100 communities for children and families. *American Psychologist, 52*(4), 424–433.

Riley, D. (2008, June). *Are your seminars effective? How do you know?* Paper presented at the Policy Institute for Family Impact Seminars Summer Conference, Madison, WI.

Riley, D., Meinhardt, G., Nelson, C., Salisbury, M. J., & Winnett, T. (1991). How effective are age-paced newsletters for new parents? A replication and extension of earlier studies. *Family Relations, 40,* 247–253.

Ringwalt, C., Ennett, S. T., & Holt, K. D. (1990, October). *An outcome evaluation of Project DARE: Drug abuse resistance education; What do we know about school-based prevention strategies?* Paper presented at University of San Diego Extension Conference, San Diego, CA.

Rist, R. C. (1994). Influencing the policy process with qualitative research. In N. Denzin & Y. Lincoln (Eds.), *Handbook of qualitative research* (pp. 545–558). Thousand Oaks, CA: Sage.

Rittel, H., & Webber, M. (1973). Dilemmas in a general theory of planning. *Policy Sciences, 4*(2), 155–169.

Rivlin, A. (1973). Forensic social science. *Harvard Educational Review, 43,* 61–75.

Rivlin, A., & Krugman, P. (2006, November). *Is America too polarized to make public policy?* Plenary session presented at the 28th annual Association for Public Policy Analysis and Management research conference, Madison, WI.

Roosevelt, T. (1912). Address given before the Convention of the National Progressive Party in Chicago. Retrieved June 17, 2009, from http://www.ssa.gov/history/trspeech.html

Ross, R., & Staines, G. L. (1972). The politics of analyzing social problems. *Social Problems, 20,* 18–40.

SAL Consulting. (2001). *Review of the Welfare Peer Assistance Network* (Report prepared for the Joyce Foundation). Chicago: Author.

Sandfort, J. (2004). Why is human services integration so difficult to achieve? *Focus, 23*(2), 35–38.

Scholz, J. K., Moffitt, R., & Cowan, B. (2008, May). *Trends in income support.* Paper presented at the Changing Poverty conference, Institute for Research on Poverty, University of Wisconsin–Madison.

Scott, K. G., Mason, C. A., & Chapman, D. A. (1999). The use of epidemiological methodology as a means of influencing public policy. *Child Development, 70,* 1263–1272.

Seeley, D. (1985). *Education through partnership.* Washington, DC: American Enterprise Institute.

Segal, J. (1983). Utilization of stress and coping research: Issues of public education and public policy. In N. Garmezy & M. Rutter (Eds.), *Stress, coping, and development in children* (pp. 239–252). New York: McGraw-Hill.

Shonkoff, J. P. (2000). Science, policy, and practice: Three cultures in search of a shared mission. *Child Development, 71*(1), 181–187.

Shonkoff, J. P. (2004). Evaluating early childhood services: What's really behind the curtain. *Evaluation Exchange, 10*(2), 3–4.

Shonkoff, J. P. (2007, March). *Teaching, not preaching, as a strategy for social change.* Paper presented at the biennial meeting of the Society for Research on Child Development, Boston.

Shulock, N. (1999). The paradox of policy analysis: If it is not used, why do we produce so much of it? *Journal of Policy Analysis and Management, 18,* 226–244.

Small, S. A. (2005). Bridging research and practice in the family and human sciences. *Family Relations, 54*(2), 320–334.

Smith, J. A. (1991). *The idea brokers: Think tanks and the rise of the new policy elite*. New York: Free Press.

Snow, C. P. (1961). *Science and government*. Cambridge, MA: Harvard University Press.

Spoth, R. L., Kavanagh, K. A., & Dishion, T. (2002). Family-centered preventive intervention science: Toward benefits to larger populations of children, youth, and families. *Prevention Science, 3*(3), 145–152.

Stark, J. (1995). The Wisconsin Idea: The university's service to the state. In *State of Wisconsin 1995–1996 Blue Book* (pp. 101–179). Madison: Wisconsin Legislative Reference Bureau.

State Legislative Leaders Foundation. (1995). *State legislative leaders: Keys to effective legislation for children and families*. Centerville, MA: Author.

Sternberg, R. J., & Grigorenko, E. L. (2002). E pluribus unum. *American Psychologist, 57*(12), 1129–1130.

Strickland, T. (1996). Moving psychology toward (self) recognition as a public resource: The views of a congressman psychologist. In R. P. Lorion, I. Iscoe, P. H. DeLeon, & G. R. VandenBos (Eds.), *Psychology and public policy: Balancing public service and professional need* (pp. 369–389). Washington, DC: American Psychological Association.

Stromsdorfer, E. (1985). Social science research and the formulation of public policy. In J. Hausman & D. Wise (Eds.), *Social experimentation*. Chicago: University of Chicago Press.

Takanishi, R. (2002). Where are you from? Child advocacy and the benefits of marginality. In A. Higgins-D'Alessandro & K. R. B. Jankowski (Eds.), *Science for society: Informing policy and practice through research in developmental psychology* (pp. 17–28). San Francisco: Jossey-Bass.

Television Set Ownership. (n.d.). Retrieved May 27, 2008, from http://www.tvhistory.tv/TV-VCR-Remote-Cable_Ownership.JPG

Thompson, J. (1967). *Organizations in action: Social science bases of administrative theory*. New York: McGraw-Hill.

Thompson, T., & Bennett, W. J. (1997, March 6). The good news about welfare reform: Wisconsin's success story [Transcript]. *Heritage Lecture No. 593*. Washington, DC: Heritage Foundation.

Tough, A. M. (1971). *The adult's learning projects* (Research in Education Series No. 1). Toronto: Ontario Institute for Studies in Education.

Trattner, W. I. (1974). *From poor law to welfare state: A history of social welfare in America*. New York: Free Press.

Tseng, V. (2008, March). *Studying the use of research evidence in policy and practice* (W. T. Grant Foundation annual report essay). New York: William T. Grant Foundation.

U.S. Census Bureau. (2006). Information and communications. In *Statistical abstract of the United States: 2007* (126th ed., Sect. 24). Retrieved May 24, 2008, from http://www.census.gov/prod/2006pubs/07statab/infocomm.pdf

U.S. House of Representatives. (1977). *Final report of the Commission on Administrative Review, Vol. 2* (95th Congress, 1st session). Washington, DC: Government Printing Office.

Van der Kloot, W. A., Spaans, A. M. J., & Heiser, W. J. (2005). Instability of hierarchical cluster analysis due to input order of the data: The PermuCLUSTER solution. *Psychological Methods, 10*, 468–476.

Van Langenhove, L. (2001). Can the social sciences act as an agent of change in society? In Organization for Economic Cooperation and Development (Ed.), *Social sciences for knowledge and decision making* (pp. 15–21). Paris: Organization for Economic Cooperation and Development.

Walter, I., Nutley, S., & Davies, H. (2005). What works to promote evidence-based practice? A cross-sector review. *Evidence and Policy, 1*(3), 335–363.

Wandersman, A., Snell-Johns, J., Lentz, B. E., Fetterman, D. M., Keener, D. C., Livet, M., et al. (2005). The principles of empowerment evaluation. In D. M. Fetterman & A. Wandersman (Eds.), *Empowerment evaluation principles in practice* (pp. 27–41). New York: Guilford.

Webber, D. J. (1986). Explaining policymakers' use of policy information: The relative importance of the two-community theory versus decision-maker orientation. *Science Communication, 7*, 249–290.

Webber, D. J. (1992). The distribution and use of policy knowledge in the policy process. *Knowledge and Policy: The International Journal of Knowledge Transfer and Utilization, 4*(4), 6–35.

Weiss, C. H. (1972). *Evaluation research: Methods of assessing program effectiveness.* Englewood Cliffs, NJ: Prentice Hall.

Weiss, C. H. (1978). Improving the linkage between social research and public policy. In L. E. Lynn, Jr. (Ed.), *Knowledge and policy: The uncertain connection* (pp. 23–81). Washington, DC: National Academy of Sciences.

Weiss, C. H. (1979). The many meanings of research utilization. *Public Administration Review, 39*, 426–431.

Weiss, C. H. (1983). Ideology, interests, and information: The basis of policy positions. In D. Callahan & B. Jennings (Eds.), *Ethics, the social sciences, and policy analysis* (pp. 213–245). New York: Plenum.

Weiss, C. H. (1987a). The circuitry of enlightenment: Diffusion of social science research to policymakers. *Knowledge: Creation, Diffusion, Utilization, 8*(2), 274–281.

Weiss, C. H. (1987b). Congressional committee staffs (do, do not) use analysis. In M. Bulmer (Ed.), *Social science research and government: Comparative essays on Britain and the United States* (pp. 94–112). New York: Cambridge University Press.

Weiss, C. H. (1989). Congressional committees as users of analysis. *Journal of Policy Analysis and Management, 8*(3), 411–431.

Weiss, C. H. (1990). The uneasy partnership endures: Social science and government. In S. Brooks & A. G. Gagnon (Eds.), *Social scientists, policy, and the state* (pp. 97–112). New York: Praeger.

Weiss, C. H. (1995). Nothing as practical as good theory: Exploring theory-based evaluation for comprehensive community initiatives for children and families. In J. P. Connell, A. C. Kubisch, L. B. Schorr, & C. H. Weiss (Eds.), *New approaches to evaluating community initiatives: Vol. 1. Concepts, methods, and contexts* (pp. 65–92). Washington, DC: Aspen Institute.

Weiss, C. H. (1997). How can theory-based evaluation make greater headway? *Evaluation Review, 21*(4), 501–524.

Weiss, C. H. (1999). Research–policy linkages: How much influence does social science research have? In *UNESCO, World Social Science report 1999* (pp. 194–205). Paris: UNESCO.

Weiss, C. H., & Bucuvalas, M. J. (1980). *Social science research and decision making.* New York: Columbia University Press.

Weiss, C. H., Murphy-Graham, E., Petrosino, A., & Gandhi, A. G. (2008). The fairy godmother—and her warts: Making the dream of evidence-based policy come true. *American Journal of Evaluation, 29*(1), 29–47.

Whitehead, B. D. (1993). Dan Quayle was right. *Atlantic Monthly, 271*(4), 47–84. Retrieved August 25, 2008, from http://www.theatlantic.com/politics/family/danquayl.htm

Wilcox, B. L., Weisz, V. P., & Miller, M. K. (2005). Practical guidelines for educating policymakers: The Family Impact Seminar as an approach to advancing the interests of children and families in the policy arena. *Journal of Clinical Child and Adolescent Psychology, 34*(4), 638–645.

Wilensky, H. L. (1997). Social science and the public agenda: Reflections on the relation to knowledge to policy in the United States and abroad. *Journal of Health Politics, 22,* 1241–1256.

Williams, C. (2006, June). *How policy-makers view evidence: Lessons from the Robert Wood Johnson Foundation Synthesis Project.* Retrieved June 26, 2009, from http://www.academyhealth.org/files/2006/tuesday/612/williams.ppt

Wisconsin Department of Health and Social Services. (1979). *Report and recommendations of the Welfare Reform Study Advisory Committee.* Madison, WI: Author.

Wisconsin Work Projects Administration. (1941). *Wisconsin: A guide to the Badger State.* New York: Duell, Sloan, and Pearce.

Wiseman, M. (1993). Welfare reform in the states: The Bush legacy. *Focus, 15*(1), 19.

Wishart, D. (2006). *ClustanGraphics primer: A guide to cluster analysis* (4th ed.). Edinburgh, Scotland: Clustan Limited.

Wong, K. (2007, May 21). *Considering the politics in the research-policymaking nexus.* Presentation at the American Enterprise Institute Conference, Washington, DC [Transcript]. Retrieved May 29, 2008, from http://www.aei.org/events/filter.,eventID.1455/transcript.asp

Yankelovich, D. (1995, Fall). Three destructive trends. *The Kettering Review,* 6–15.

Yarmolinsky, A. (1969). The beginnings of OEO. In J. Sundquist (Ed.), *On fighting poverty: Perspectives from experience.* New York: Basic Books.

Zigler, E. (1998). A place of value for applied and policy studies. *Child Development, 69*(2), 532–542.

Zigler, E., Phillips, D., Moorehouse, M., & Watson, S. (2009, April). *Child development science and policy: Where have we been? Where are we going?* Presentation and discussion session held at the biennial meeting of the Society for Research in Child Development, Denver, CO.

Zigler, E., & Styfco, S. J. (2002). A life lived at the crossroads of knowledge and children's policy. In A. Higgins-D'Alessandro & K. R. B. Jankowski (Eds.), *Science for society: Informing policy and practice through research in developmental psychology* (pp. 5–15). San Francisco: Jossey-Bass.

Author Index

A

Aaron, H. J., 9, 15, 90, 327
Aldenderfer, M. S., 324, 327
Anderson, A., 268, 289, 327
Aos, S., 9, 106, 327

B

Bane, M. J., 94, 151, 153, 327
Banfield, E. C., 309, 327
Barrows, R., xiv, 169, 227, 228, 229, 240, 246,
    247, 248, 327
Bartholomew, D. J., 324, 327
Bennett, R. F., 244–245, 327
Bennett, W. J., 245, 259, 327
Berger, S., 1, 327
Bergman, M., 243, 327
Betz, D. L., 278, 327
Beyer, J. M., 26, 33, 43, 194, 195, 327
Bimber, B., 5, 21, 53, 64, 84, 117, 195, 238, 239,
    248, 255, 256, 261, 327
Blasé, K. A., 288, 330
Blashfield, R. K., 324, 327
Boehnen, E., 68, 327
Bogenschneider, K., xii, xiv, xv, 3, 76, 77, 79,
    108, 111, 112, 113, 144, 176, 192,
    194, 226, 228, 253, 261, 273, 280,
    284, 286, 315, 316, 317, 318, 323, 325,
    326, 327, 328, 330
Booth, T. A., 77, 78, 328
Bouffard, S., 259, 332
Boyer, E. L., 78, 328
Breckler, S. J., 227, 251, 252, 328
Brooks-Gunn, J., 280, 328
Brown, B., 96, 331
Brown, P., 254, 288, 290, 328
Browne, W. P., 320, 328
Bucuvalas, M. J., 32, 33, 34, 78, 135, 144, 145,
    195, 238, 275, 321, 322, 323, 324,
    337
Bulmer, M., 104, 108, 263, 265, 328
Butterill, D., 32, 194, 332

C

Cabinet Office, 2, 328
Cabrer, B., 324, 328
California Research Bureau, 270, 287, 328
Caplan, N., 6, 42, 75, 77, 78, 79, 110, 125, 142,
    144, 151, 280, 292, 321, 322, 323,
    324, 328
Carlson, A., 5, 328
Cartwright, N., 12, 328

Center on the Developing Child, 306, 328
Chamberlin, T., 55, 328
Chandler, S. M., 159, 222, 328
Chapman, D. A., 78, 210, 301, 335
Coffman, J., 254, 261, 329
Cohen, D. K., 6, 99, 309, 332
Cohen, J. A., 162, 239, 332
Cohen, L., 295, 329
Collins, A. A., 255, 329
Commager, H. S., 229, 329
Commons, J. R., 58, 59, 60, 62, 229, 230, 329
Congressional Budget Office, 6, 229, 238, 306,
    329
Contreras, D., 324, 328
Cook, T., 296, 329
Cooper, M. C., 324, 333
Corbett, T., xii, xiv, xv, 11, 13, 68, 72, 164, 165,
    215, 232, 259, 264, 327, 329, 335
Cowan, B., 20, 335

D

Danziger, S., 4, 59, 61, 175, 178, 179, 259, 264,
    329
Davidson, R. H., 163, 329
Davies, H. T. O., 4, 26, 27, 33, 42, 44, 52, 54,
    99, 104, 105, 108, 125, 154, 194, 195,
    252, 253, 254, 260, 269, 276, 287,
    293, 298, 329, 334, 337
Davies, M. W., 3, 331
Deichtman, S. J., 6, 329
DeLeon, P. H., 78, 329, 333, 336
Dimas, J., 82, 329
Dishion, T., 280, 336
Doherty, W. J., 76, 251, 330
Drake, E., 9, 106, 327
Dror, Y., 158, 330
Duncan, G. J., 257, 280, 328
Dunn, W. N., 33, 43, 111, 195, 242, 330
Dunworth, T., 2, 330

E

Elazar, D. J., 142, 320, 330
Einstein, A., 253, 330
Elman, S. E., 78, 333
Ennett, S. T., 261, 335

F

Farley, F., 26, 330
Featherman, D. L., 5, 329, 330
Feldman, P. H., 26, 33, 195, 330

Fenno, R. F., Jr., 45, 137, 138, 139, 140, 141, 161–162, 330
Fetterman, D. M., 288, 337
Fiorina, M. P., 9, 330
Fixsen, D. L., 288, 330
Friedman, R. M., 288, 330
Flinchbaugh, B., 169, 210, 215, 216, 246, 278, 330
Fong, J., 82, 329
FrameWorks Institute, 306, 330
Friese, B., xiv, 176, 192, 194, 226, 315, 316, 318, 326, 330

G

Gailbraith, J. I., 324, 327
Gallup Organization, 172, 330
Gandhi, A. G., 26, 104, 195, 261, 337
Gibson, J. M., 324, 334
Glenn, N. D., 248, 330
Goering, P., 32, 194, 332
Gornick, J. C., 319, 333
Green, B. L., 254, 263, 333
Greenberg, D. H., 26, 33, 34, 195, 330
Grigorenko, E. L., 247, 263, 336
Groark, C. J., 45, 219, 333
Gueron, J. M., 264, 330
Gursen, M., 26, 33, 195, 330

H

Hannaway, J., 2, 330
Harvard Family Research Project, 255, 331
Haskins, R., 1, 4, 260, 331
Hauser, R., 96, 331
Haveman, R. H., 6, 58, 59, 61, 62, 101, 331
Hayek, F., 6, 331
Heckman, J., 3, 30, 210, 278, 331
Heiser, W. J., 324, 336
Helprin, M., 310, 331
Henig, J. R., 32, 331
Herfurth, T., 243, 331
Hill, J. H., 264, 290, 331
Hill, L. G., 278, 331
Hird, J. A., 36, 42, 43, 78, 195, 237, 275, 309, 310, 331
Holahan, J., 2, 330
Hollister, R. G., 264, 290, 331
Holt, K. D., 261, 335
Holzer, H., 22, 84, 331
Hotz, V. J., 286, 331
Howard, M., 86, 87, 331
Howe, F. C., 230, 331
Huberman, A. M., 318, 333
Huberman, M., 195, 331
Huston, A. C., 195, 253, 257, 275, 276, 331
Hutchins, V., 270, 287, 333

I

Innvaer, S., 26, 33, 195, 331

J

Jacobs, F. H., 3, 331
Jacobson, N., 32, 194, 332
Jefferys, M., 45, 47, 332
Johnson, B., 26, 33, 43, 78, 195, 260, 334
Johnson, K., xiv, 144, 280, 316, 319, 326, 327
Jonas, R. K., 45, 171, 332

K

Kaplan, T., 261, 327
Katzev, A., 278, 334
Kaufman, I., 161, 166, 332
Kavanagh, K. A., 280, 336
Keener, D. C., 288, 337
Kellogg Commission, 223, 308, 332
Kerschner, S. W., 162, 239, 332
Kersting, K., 235, 332
Kingdon, J. W., 8, 144, 321, 322, 323, 332
Klebanov, P. K., 280, 328
Kraut, A. G., 78, 329
Kreider, H., 259, 332
Krugman, P., 9
Kumpfer, K. L., 280, 332

L

Lamb, T., 278, 332
Langworth, R., 172, 332
Lentz, B. E., 288, 337
Levin, B. R., 29, 47, 52, 135, 136, 150, 151, 154, 156, 158, 159, 160, 161, 162, 163, 164, 167, 172, 332
Liaw, F., 280, 328
Lightfoot, E., 45, 47, 332
Lindblom, C. E., 6, 44, 99, 150, 151, 154, 157, 164, 167, 309, 332
Linksz, D., 26, 33, 34, 195, 330
Linney, K. D., 77, 79, 108, 111, 112, 113, 228, 317, 323, 326
Linquist, E. A., 77, 332
Lipsky, M., 18, 97, 332
Livet, M., 288, 337
Loewenberg, G., 157, 160, 332
Loftus, T., 180, 231, 232, 233, 310, 332
Lynn, L. E., Jr., 170, 215, 332, 333, 337
Lynton, E. A., 78, 333

M

Maederer, C. M., 26, 33, 43, 78, 195, 260, 334
Mandell, M. B., 26, 33, 34, 195, 330
Manion, L., 295, 329

Mark, M. M., 16, 333, 334
Mason, C. A., 78, 210, 301, 335
Matthews, D. R., 30, 263, 333
Mayer, R., 270, 287, 333
Maynard, R. A., 67, 108, 333
McCall, R. B., 45, 77, 78, 219, 254, 263, 333
McClintock, C., 270, 287, 333
McDonald, G. W., 228, 334
McGuigan, W., 278, 334
McLuhan, M., 243, 333
Mead, L. M., 63, 79, 199, 232, 257, 333
Meinhardt, G., 280, 284, 335
Melton, G. B., 270, 287, 333
Meyers, M. K., 319, 333
Miles, M. B., 318, 333
Miller, G., 16, 50, 333
Miller, M., 9, 106, 327
Miller, M. K., 270, 287, 338
Milligan, G. W., 324, 333
Mills, J., 77, 79, 108, 111, 112, 113, 228, 317,
        323, 326
Minuchin, S., 280, 333
Miravete, E. J., 324, 328
Moffit, R., 20, 335
Mooney, C. Z., 78, 151, 275, 333
Moorehouse, M., 176, 185, 186, 187, 190, 191,
        213, 221–222, 338
Morgan, K., 261, 327
Morrison, A., 78, 142, 144, 151, 321, 322, 323,
        324, 328
Morrison, K., 295, 329
Moustaki, I., 324, 327
Murray, C., 6, 232, 333
Murphy-Graham, E., 26, 104, 195, 261, 337
Myers-Walls, J. A., 108, 110, 111, 333

N

Nadash, P., 26, 33, 195, 330
Nagel, T., 247, 333
Naoom, S. F., 288, 330
Nathan, R., 5, 13, 72, 333
National Conference of State Legislatures, 22,
        319, 333
National Research Council, 6, 309, 328, 334
Nelkin, R. P., 45, 219, 333
Nelson, C., 280, 284, 335
Nelson, C. E., 26, 33, 43, 78, 195, 260, 334
Newall, B., 61, 334
Nielsen Media Research, 243, 334
Normandin, H., xiv, 144, 253, 280, 316, 319,
        325, 326, 327, 328
Novy, D. M., 324, 334
Noyes, J. L., 22, 72, 82, 329, 334
Nutley, S. M., 4, 26, 27, 33, 42, 44, 52, 54, 99,
        104, 105, 108, 125, 154, 194, 195,
        252, 253, 254, 260, 269, 276, 287,
        293, 298, 329, 334, 337

Nye, F. I., 228, 334

O

Obama, B., 158, 170, 243, 244, 245, 246, 247,
        334
O'Connor, A., 4, 334
Oh, C. H., 195, 334
O'Keefe, A. M., 78, 329
Olds, D., 120–121, 268, 334
Olson, J. R., 77, 79, 108, 111, 112, 113, 228, 317,
        323, 326
Ooms, T., 68, 327
Overall, J. E., 324, 334
Overton, W. F., 255, 329
Oxman, A., 26, 33, 195, 331

P

Patton, M. Q., 78, 260, 268, 334
Peck, L. R., 319, 333
Petrosino, A., 26, 104, 195, 261, 337
Pettigrew, T. E., 8, 104, 263, 334
Philliber, S., 289, 334
Phillips, D., 176, 185, 186, 187, 190, 191, 213,
        221–222, 338
Pittman, K., 288, 290, 334
Pratt, C., 278, 334
Prosser, W., 96, 331
Putnam, R. D., 172

R

Rabb, J., 1, 157, 205, 207, 251, 335
Reagan, R., 5, 155, 245, 335
Rice, R. M., 247, 335
Rich, A., 236, 243, 335
Riley, D., 132, 136, 166, 171, 201, 203, 205, 207,
        208, 220, 221, 225, 226, 240, 246,
        262, 280, 284, 335
Ringwalt, C., 261, 335
Rist, R. C., 175, 335
Rittel, H., 164, 335
Rivlin, A., 9, 15, 31, 335
Roberts, J., 26, 33, 43, 78, 195, 260, 334
Roosevelt, T., 5, 55, 230, 335
Ross, R., 151, 169, 335

S

SAL Consulting, 21, 313, 326, 335
Salisbury, M. J., 280, 284, 335
Sandfort, J., 82, 335
Scholz, J. K., 20, 258, 286, 331, 335
Scott, K. G., 78, 210, 301, 335
Seeley, D., 167, 335
Segal, J., 254, 335
Shadish, W. R., Jr., 296, 329

Shonkoff, J. P., 75, 77, 79, 108, 111, 112, 165, 168, 254, 259, 263, 292, 306, 323, 335, 336
Shotland, R. L., 16, 333, 334
Shulock, N., 2, 29, 30, 104, 144, 321, 322, 336
Slawik, N., 45, 47, 332
Small, S. A., 78, 108, 111, 336
Smith, J. A., 2, 23, 51, 150, 193, 223, 228, 229, 233, 241, 277, 281, 336,
Snell-Johns, J., 288, 337
Snow, C. P., 76, 149, 171, 225, 292, 336
Spaans, A. M. J., 324, 336
Spoth, R. L., 280, 336
Staines, G. L., 151, 169, 335
Stambaugh, R. J., 78, 142, 144, 151, 321, 322, 323, 324, 328
Stark, J., 55, 56–57, 230, 336
State Legislative Leaders Foundation, 25, 280, 336
Steele, S., 324, 327
Sternberg, R. J., 247, 263, 336
Stimson, J. A., 30, 263, 333
Strickland, T., 237, 336
Stromsdorfer, E., 15, 336
Styfco, S. J., 132, 159, 222, 234, 251, 338

T

Takanishi, R., 197, 222, 238, 240, 336
Thompson, J., 83, 336
Thompson, T., 62, 63, 72, 101, 199, 232, 233, 259, 336
Tough, A. M., 48, 135, 336
Trattner, W. I., 5, 336
Trice, H. M., 26, 33, 43, 194, 195, 327
Trommald, M., 26, 33, 195, 331
Troy, K., 45, 47, 332
Tseng, V., xiii, 26, 31, 105, 257, 269, 287, 291, 336
Turner, M. A., 2, 330

U

U.S. Census Bureau, 243, 336
U.S. House of Representatives, 163, 336

V

VandenBos, G. R., 78, 329, 333, 336
Van der Kloot, W. A., 324, 336
Van Langenhove, L., 213, 337

Vinovskis, M. A., 5, 329, 330
Vist, G., 26, 33, 195, 331

W

Wallace, F., 288, 330
Walter, I., 26, 27, 33, 42, 44, 52, 54, 99, 104, 105, 108, 125, 154, 194, 195, 252, 253, 254, 260, 269, 276, 287, 293, 298, 334, 337
Wandersman, A., 288, 337
Watson, S., 176, 185, 186, 187, 190, 191, 213, 221–222, 338
Watson, W., 243, 333
Webber, D. J., 42, 78, 151, 276, 280, 337
Webber, M., 164, 335
Weiss, C. H., 6, 11, 26, 27, 31, 32, 33, 34, 37, 45, 78, 104, 105, 135, 144, 145, 155, 158, 161, 162, 173, 195, 215, 219, 222, 223, 238, 247, 254, 260, 261, 262, 265, 266, 268, 270, 275, 281, 283, 287, 288, 289, 290, 293, 321, 322, 323, 324, 328, 331, 337
Weisz, V. P., 270, 287, 338
Werner, A., 259, 264, 329
Wertheimer, B., 26, 33, 43, 78, 195, 260, 334
Whitehead, B. D., 86, 337
Wilcox, B. L., 270, 287, 338
Wilensky, H. L., 10, 338
Williams, C., 193, 338
Winnett, T., 280, 284, 335
Winstead, D., 1, 157, 205, 207, 251, 335
Wisconsin Department of Health and Social Services, 62, 338
Wisconsin Work Projects Administration, 2, 338
Wiseman, M., 79, 257, 262, 338
Wishart, D., 324, 338
Wong, K., 217, 338
Wong, V., 296, 329

Y

Yankelovich, D., 172, 338
Yarmolinsky, A., 6, 338

Z

Zigler, E., 83, 132, 159, 176, 185, 186, 187, 190, 191, 195, 213, 221–222, 233, 234, 235, 251, 266, 338

Subject Index

A

Action agenda, 298–309
    changing the culture of knowledge
        consumers, 305–307
    changing the culture of knowledge
        producers, 302–305
    attracting promising new scholars,
        301–302
    developing policy internships, 304
    developing policy curricula, 304
    encouraging policy-relevant research,
        302–304
    exploring systemic strategies, 307–309
    studying research utilization 300–302
Adams, John, 75, 155
Advocacy
    approach, 218, 227, 229, 276
    definitions, 228, 235, 240
    effectiveness of, 42–44, 53, 236–237, 241,
        248, 249
    examples of, 176, 178–181, 235, 240–242
    historical perspective, 229, 242
Aid to Families with Dependent Children, or
    AFDC, 62, 79, 101, 151, 232
Anderson Moore, Kristin, 131, 202, 203–204,
    206, 209, 265
Annie E. Casey Foundation, 22, 96, 257
Antaramian, John, 102, 197
Attribution questions, 107, 271, 280

B

Barriers
    cultural, 82, 165, 181–188, 191–192, 296
    lack of rewards, 186–188
    language, 185–186
    misunderstanding of policymakers, 182–183
    overcoming, 130, 147, 191, 223–225
    time frames, 184–185
    unfamiliarity with the policy process,
        183–184, 211–212
Brevity, 73, 185, 204, 205, 207, 208, 275
Brief communication, see Brevity
Briefing reports
    accessibility of, 34–35, 37, 39, 52, 53, 113
    Family Impact Seminars, 66, 67, 146, 261
    WELPAN, 69, 70, 250
Bush, George W., 199, 235, 243

C

Child support, 14, 62, 63, 204, 230–233
Child Trends, 95, 131, 202, 203, 206, 265, 313

Churchill, Sir Winston, 172
Cinderella Complex, 52
Clinton, Bill, 23, 91, 94, 124, 220, 245, 266
Communicating evidence to policymakers
    approach
        assume educator role, 216–218
        build relationships, see Relationships
            with policymakers
        gain access, 198–203, 224
    attitudes
        be patient and self-rewarding, 220–222,
            225
        show respect for policymakers, 218–220,
            224
    knowledge
        learn about policymakers, 147, 203–204
        learn about policymaking process, 171,
            211–212
    skills
        communicate to meet policymakers'
            information needs, 205–209
        provide timely response to policymakers'
            questions, 212–216, 225
        use clear, careful language, 206–207,
            209–210
Community
    definition of, 76, 78, 79, 110, 111, 112, 115
    disconnect, 15–16, 76–77, 129–130
    dissonance, examples of 100–103
Community dissonance theory
    conceptualization of, 108–127
    definition of, 15–16, 77, 79
    implications for evidence use, 127, 130, 196
Compromise
    limitations of, 9, 157
    role in a democracy, 158, 241, 246
    value of, 156, 171, 277
Constitution, U.S., 155, 158, 247
Core technology, 77, 83, 108–110, 142
Cue-giver, 30, 263
Culture
    clash of, 38, 84, 134, 168, 171, 223
    components of, 83, 108
    definitions of, 79, 111
    dimensions, 77, 114–117, 223
    domains, 111–112, 114, 115, 116, 117, 118,
        196
        cognitive frameworks, 115, 116, 118,
            120–122, 196, 223
        contextual preferences, 115, 117, 118,
            124–125, 196, 223
        feedback loops, 115, 117, 118, 122–124,
            196, 224, 293

focal interests, 115, 116, 117, 118–119, 196, 223
interactional preferences, 115, 116, 118, 122, 196, 223
targets of interest, 115, 116, 118, 119–120, 122, 196, 223
implications for evidence use, 38, 127
importance of, 22, 79, 126, 181, 223
institutional
conceptualization of, 82–84
definition of, 79
examples of 79–82, 110
implications for evidence use, 127
intersection of institutional and professional culture, 87–92
professional
conceptualization of, 84–87, 89
definition of, 84
implications for evidence use, 127, 181, 184
work, 112, 113

D

Debate, 123, 157, 158, 196, 212–216, 266, 297
Democracy
commitment to, 246–247
consistency with education approach, 218, 251, 310
features of, 154, 158, 172, 184, 220, 229
implications for evidence use in policymaking, 7, 9–10, 23, 76, 104
influence on policymakers and policymaking, 136, 160, 162
Disconnect between research and policy, 1–3, 8–9, 11–12, 75, 81–82, 126–127, 291–292, 293
Discussion opportunities, 51–52, 73

E

Earned Income Tax Credit, or EITC, 62, 63, 101, 106, 153, 258, 286
Education approach, see Public policy education
Eisenhower, Dwight D., 150
Enlightenment model of research use, 104, 265, 266
Evaluation of research use in policymaking
difficulties of, 254, 256–257, 263, 287, 309
methodological complexity, 262–265
outcome complexity, 260–262
stakeholder complexity, 259–260
time complexity, 265–266
how to detect small differences, 266
indicators, 256, 266
lack of, 254
limitations in measurement, 295
value of, 255

what to look for, 256
when to look, 256, 266
where to look, 256, 266
Evidence-based policy, 2, 4, 253, 308, 309, 311

F

Fairchild, Mary, 26, 131, 133, 157, 160, 162, 163, 181, 196–197, 204, 222, 277
Families, 209–210, 234–235, 239, 247, 262, 267, 278, 280–281, 301, 306
Family Impact Seminars, or FIS
description of, 63–67, 267, 313–314
evaluation methods, protocols, and strategies, 266–268, 271
evaluation of, 49, 65, 66–67, 106–107, 248, 266–286, 316–319
examples of, 66–67, 80–81, 258
features of, 72–73, 216, 237, 249, 315
Family policy, 13, 22, 287–288, 301, 304
Family policy education theory of change
definition of, 254, 268–270, 287–288
elements of
attracts the policy community to dialogue, 271, 276–277
builds relationships, 271, 281–283
changes attitudes, 271, 280–281
engages policymakers and experts to identify family issues, 271, 273–275
gains knowledge, 271, 278–279
policymakers use research in their jobs, 271, 283–286
provide research, 271, 275–276
evaluation protocols and procedures, 267–268, 271–272
iterative nature of, 270, 287
limitations, 289–290
value of, 268, 270, 287–290
Federal Interagency Forum, 23
Functional category, 108–110

G

Go-to person, 30, 263, 300; see also Cue-giver
Government settings, 92, 96–97
Grigsby, Tamara, 274, 276

H

Head Start, 159, 171, 176, 200, 221, 233, 234, 266
Hilgenberg, Steve, 169
Home styles in their district, see Policymakers
Hypodermic model of research use, 8, 104

I

Information for policymakers

formats, 44–53, 48–49, 171, 173, 298
needs, 40–41, 77, 80–81, 113, 196, 205–209
sources, 41–44, 53, 113, 147, 197, 284, 285
types, 41, 323
Institute for Research on Poverty, or IRP, 6, 19, 61–62, 199
Institutional culture, *see* Culture
Institutional settings, 19, 91–97
Intermediaries, 44, 91, 92, 115, 121, 122, 123–124, 198–203, 295
Intermediary organizations, 44, 92, 94–96, 299, 305

J

Jefferson, Thomas, 155
Johnson, Lyndon, 60, 159, 266
Joyce Foundation, 68, 69, 70, 96

K

Kennedy, John F., 5–6, 10, 59, 60, 61, 94, 221
Knowledge consumers, 2, 8, 13–15, 17–18, 20–21, 75, 77, 79, 92–93, 168, 299–300, 305–307; *see* also Policymakers
Knowledge producers, 2, 8, 13–15, 18–19, 20–21, 75, 77–79, 91–93, 168, 299, 302–304; *see also* Researchers

L

La Follette, Robert, 57, 58, 59, 60
Legislative service agencies, 9, 42, 43, 53, 96, 143, 237, 255, 272, 279
Lincoln, Abraham, 12–13
Lobbyists
growth in, 14
influence of, 44, 83, 251, 284, 285
pervasiveness, 50, 238
purpose of, 228
Lynde and Harry Bradley Foundation, 96

M

Madison, James, 193
Massinga, Ruth, 200–201, 214, 215
Masters, Mark, 45, 157, 211
McCarthy, Charles, 2, 57, 58, 59
Methodology, 313–326
Meyer, Daniel, 205, 216, 217
Miller, Mark, 28, 48, 277, 279, 282–283
Moynihan, Daniel Patrick, 101, 245
Myth, 196, 209–210

N

New Hope, 257–258, 261
Nixon, Richard M., 233, 234

Nonpartisan
reputation, 195, 235, 241, 249–250, 319
setting, 50, 53, 66, 73, 250, 267, 269, 271, 272, 276–277

O

Obama, Barack, 158, 170, 243–244, 247
Objectivity, 33, 40, 71, 73, 227, 241, 247–248, 294
Office of Technology Assessment, or OTA, 255–257, 261
Olsen, Luther, 43, 155, 275
Open policy windows, 216, 269, 273, 287
Oregon Family Impact Seminars, 258

P

Packard Foundation, 72, 96
Philanthropy, 72, 92, 96, 112, 291, 297, 299–300, 302, 308–309
Policy briefs, see Briefing reports
Policy, definition of, 3
Policy Institute for Family Impact Seminars, 64, 65, 290, 304, 305, 313, 315
Policymakers, 26, 112, 115, 118, 121, 122, 123, 124, 125, 131, 132, 133
constraints, 133–134, 162–165, 211
differences, 18, 135–147
home style in their district, 137–142
articulating the issues, 137, 140
issues independence plus one-on-one, 137, 139–140
person to person, 137, 138, 141
popular local boy, 137, 138–139
service to the district, 137
skills, 13
types of research users, 142–146
enthusiastic nonusers, 143–144, 265
enthusiastic users, 40, 143–144, 265, 301, 306
skeptical nonusers, 143–144
skeptical users, 143–144
Policy process
complexity, 166–168
consequences, 150–151, 172
definitions, 150
force of the status quo, 170–171
influence of, 151
oppositional nature, 160–162
pace, 159–160, 163, 211–212, 222
politics of, 155–156, 216
rationality of, 154–155
role of values, 168–170
short-term perspective, 211
unpredictability, 158–159
views of, 150, 151

Policy questions, 8, 16–17, 212–216, 302–303, 307, 308
Politics, 158, 217
  partisan nature, 21–22, 31, 157, 249
  polarization, 9, 22, 23
Professional culture, 84–87, 89, 114, 117; *see also* Culture
Program drift, 288–289
Public policy education, 216–218
  attaining credibility, 249–250
  definitions, 228–229, 235
  effectiveness, 235–237
  evidence in support of, 233–237
  historical perspective, 230
  operationalization, 251
  rationale for, 237–247

R

Randomized control trials, 12, 121, 257, 260, 263
Reagan, Ronald, 5, 155, 245
Relationships with policymakers, 194–198, 223, 224–225, 281–283, 307, 311
Research
  characteristics policymakers prefer, 33, 34, 144, 145, 146
  criterion for use
    accessibility test, 34, 37, 39, 53, 195, 275
    credibility test, 34, 35–37, 39, 45, 153, 195
    timeliness test, 33, 34, 38–39, 53, 195, 275
  definition, 321
  goals, 77
  growth of, 242
  history of, 2–3, 4–7
  limitations of, *see* Disconnect between research and policy
  type of use, traditional conceptualization
    conceptual, 104, 105, 125
    imposed, 104, 105
    instrumental, 104, 105, 125
    process, 104, 105
    tactical, also called forensic use, 31, 104, 105, 125
  types of use, updated conceptualization
    allocation shifting, 105, 106, 107, 119, 125, 288
    awareness shifting, 105, 106, 107, 125
    framework shifting, 105, 106, 107, 119, 125, 288
    salience shifting, 105, 106, 107, 119, 125
    solutions shifting, 105, 106, 107, 119, 125, 288
    tactics shifting, 105, 106, 107, 119
  types of users, *see* Policymakers
  use by policymakers, 255–258, 283–284

  value to policymakers, 26–31
Relevance of research, 33, 38–39, 72, 122, 187, 190, 212–214, 275
Researchers, 112, 115, 118, 120, 121, 122, 123, 124, 296
Responsiveness, 72, 212–216, 219, 237–238
Retrospective pre- and posttest methodology, 278–279
Rewards, 191
  expertise is respected, 190
  making the world better, 189
  seeing research applied, 189–190
Riley, Dave, 132, 136–137, 171, 201, 203, 205, 207, 208, 220, 221, 225, 226, 240, 246, 284
Roessler, Carol, 43, 44, 45, 253, 274, 279, 286
Roosevelt
  Franklin Delano, 5
  Theodore, 5

S

Sandefur, Gary, 102, 160, 201, 203, 219, 220
Scrooge Complex, 52
Smith, Peyton, 286
Social desirability bias, 280, 283, 284
Social policy, 3
Social research, 4, 321
Special Milk Amendment, 180, 183, 184, 185, 189
State agency officials, 34, 35, 39, 40, 41, 67, 325
Statistical significance, 11, 13, 119, 121, 208, 305; see also Substantive significance
Stereotypes, 129, 130, 131, 134, 147, 182, 197, 282
Substantive significance, 11, 208; *see also* Statistical significance

T

Theories, 76, 100, 124, 125
  character of the policymaking process, 7, 8–9
  community dissonance, *see* Community dissonance theory
  constructive theories of learning, 269
  elaborated multi-cultural theory, 77, 78, 112, 113
  institutional environments in which knowledge producers operate, 8, 13–15
  Kingdon's theory of open windows, 269, 273
  limitations and complexities of scientific inquiry, 8, 10–11
  social learning, 282
  structure of democratic institutions, 7, 9–10
  thorny nature of social problems, 8, 12–13
  three cultures, 77, 78

two communities, 77, 78, 318
   value of, ix, x, 222–223
Theory of change, 263, 268, 288–289
Think tanks, 42–43, 51, 92, 95, 235–237
Thompson, Tommy, 62–63, 72, 101–102, 199, 232–233, 259
Timeliness, 33, 34, 38–39, 53, 72, 122, 195, 212–216
Truman, Harry, 150, 266
Trust, 40, 102, 122, 123, 124, 125, 195, 196, 208

U

Underutilization of research
   conceptualization of, 97–98, 126–127, 130
   elements of, 15, 268–270
   explanations of, 76–79, 222–223
Unemployment compensation, 60, 63, 230

V

Vrakas, Dan, 50, 241, 283
Vulnerable populations, 196, 209–210, 299, 301

W

Welfare Peer Assistance Network, or WELPAN, 18, 56, 63–64, 67–74, 229, 313
Welfare reform, 62–63, 67–68, 71–72, 151–153
Wicked problems, or wicked social problems, 12, 13, 20, 107, 108, 164–166, 167, 171, 311
Wilson, Woodrow, 229
Wisconsin Idea, 55–64, 73, 74, 101, 199
Wisconsin Taxpayers Alliance, or WISTAX, 235
W. K. Kellogg Foundation, or Kellogg Foundation, 96
Work culture, *see* Culture
Workers' compensation, 59, 63, 230
Writing for policymakers, 112–113, 206, 208, 210
W. T. Grant Foundation, 291

Y

Young, Rebecca, 158